Power with People

How to Handle Just About Anyone to Accomplish Just About Anything

Power with People

How to Handle Just About Anyone to Accomplish Just About Anything

by

Gregory W. Lester, Ph.D.

Ashcroft Press

Although the author and publisher have made every effort to ensure the accuracy and completeness of information contained in this book, we assume no responsibility for errors, inaccuracies, omissions, or any inconsistency herein. Any slights of people, places, or organizations are unintentional. The purpose of this book is to provide information that can be useful for improving relations with and dealings with people. However, as is the case with any book, it is general information and is in no way designed to serve as or to take the place of professional advice or consultation with psychological or medical professionals regarding relationships, personal behavior, or the behavior or mental condition of any person.

Readers are urged to use the information in this book responsibly and appropriately. Because the actual implementation of the information is, of course, out of the author's and publisher's hands and is entirely up to the reader, the author and publisher can in no way take responsibility for any specific application of the information or for the results of its application. The reader is completely responsible for the application, risks, and results produced by using the information. The author and publisher specifically disclaim responsibility for those risks and results.

If readers have any questions about their ability to be responsible and appropriate with the information presented in this book, consult an appropriate mental health professional before attempting to apply any of the information. If readers determine they are not able to use the information responsibly, do not use it. The book may be returned to the publisher for a refund.

While all examples used in this book are taken from, and are faithful to, actual occurrences, great care has been taken to protect the identity of any individuals who have not given permission to have their identity disclosed. To this end, all identifying data have been substantially altered and many examples are mixtures of several different incidents and individuals.

First printing 1995   Fourth printing 2001
Second printing 2000   Fifth printing 2002
Third printing 2000   Sixth printing 2004

ISBN 0-9641458-0-4
LCCN 94-72057

Design, typesetting, and printing services provided by About Books, Inc., 425 Cedar Street, Buena Vista, CO 81211, 800-548-1876.

ATTENTION CORPORATIONS, COLLEGES, AND PROFESSIONAL ORGANIZATIONS: Quantity discounts are available on bulk purchases of this book for educational purposes or fund raising. Special books or book excerpts can also be created to fit specific needs. For information, please contact Bookworks Distributing, 15110 Benfer Road, Houston, TX 77069.

Table of Contents

Acknowledgments

When strung together into a single cohesive sentence, the four most misleading words in the English language are, "I wrote a book." Books may be read, but they are not "written." They are conceived, gestated, birthed, and reared. They are the result of many generations, an entire family tree of knowledge.

This book is no exception. Its ancestry is graced with a distinguished group of theorists, academicians, and clinicians. These people—including such luminaries as Gregory Bateson, Carl Rogers, Fritz Perls, Eric Berne, B.F. Skinner, and Milton Erikson—started it all by innovatively studying relationships and interpersonal behavior. This book is fortunate to have as one parent those individuals who personally taught me about human beings and their behavior. These teachers, too numerous to mention, include my professors, colleagues, consulting clients, clinical patients, and students. As its other parent, the book has me. I am the one responsible for its upbringing.

Power With People has also been cared for by several other generous, intelligent, and insightful individuals outside of its direct bloodline. These people came from a variety of fields: Susan Smith (soon to be Dr. Smith) from clinical psychology, Peter Stempien from social work, Daryl Shepherd from industrial psychology, Dave Corey from sales and marketing, and Marilyn Ross from editing and publishing. They all did a great job. The book could not exist without them.

As always, in any group of people involved in doing anything, there are some individuals who are special, who require their own category, and whose contribution cannot be adequately articulated by even the best writers. This category belongs to my wife, Pam. She not only reviewed the manuscript and allowed me to include her in examples in the book, she managed to create the enormous space needed in our lives for me to write this book while maintaining a full-time consulting, speaking, and clinical psychology practice. Her support and faith in me is such a constant in my life, so fundamental, reliable, and natural, that sunrise seems like a lucky accident by comparison. The world is made better by her existence. She keeps my life warm.

Finally, one other individual helped by keeping me warm in a different way. It seems silly to have been assisted in writing a book by what is essentially a thick lump of striped fur with big green eyes, but it was always of great comfort to me that Kaboodle so frequently wanted to sit in my lap during many difficult hours in front of the word processor. I not only appreciate it, I wish I could purr that loudly.

Part I

Foundations

Chapter 1

Learning to Handle People Effectively

The ability to handle people effectively is a requirement for achieving anything in life. In over two decades of personal and business consulting I have seen no factor more important for success nor more responsible for failure than people-handling abilities. I have seen more companies fail, more careers stall, more families suffer, more marriages end, and more people fail to accomplish their goals because of bad people-handling than any other single factor. While self-help books promote "working on yourself" as the road to happiness, surveys consistently show that most individuals consider the quality of their relationships with others to be the single most important element affecting them. The ability to deal effectively with other people, more than anything else, leads to success and happiness.

The notion of the "self-made" man or woman is an illusion. Success always requires other people. If you want to achieve in business, you have to get customers to buy from you. If you want to win in politics, you have to get voters to elect you. If you want to be successful as a parent, you have to be able to help your children grow and develop. When a consulting client of mine complained about his retail business being especially difficult because it was a "people business," I challenged him to name a business that was not a people business. Every enterprise ultimately comes down to humans dealing with each other. Even manufacturing depends entirely on workers cooperating to produce products and to get customers to buy them. No matter how much technology is involved, the basis of all business is still people dealing with each other; if they can't work with each other, the company will fail.

Sometimes the importance of people-handling is a difficult lesson to learn. David Kearns, the president of Xerox, learned it the hard way. The most successful company in American history, his company was bludgeoned nearly out of existence by Japanese competition. The reason? The Japanese did the one thing Xerox had forgotten to do: deal effectively with the customer. Only after instigating a lengthy corporate cultural revolution requiring all in the company to learn to treat everyone differently was Kearns able to see Xerox recover and become the first U.S. company to regain lost market share from the Japanese.

Divorce statistics reveal that Xerox is not alone in struggling to learn the importance of people-handling. Many people do not even begin to examine the manner in which they interact with a spouse until their second or third marriage starts to fall apart. Only then do they begin to take seriously the idea that how they treat their mate is part of the problem.

I, too, learned the importance of people-handling the hard way. As a college undergraduate majoring in media communications, I initiated an independent study project where I taught a fourth-grade class to make an animated movie. I thought it would be a positive experience, the kids would enjoy learning, and I would get the experience of directing a movie.

At first, it went very well. I taught the kids how to operate a camera, set up the lighting, do a story board, and plan the film. They came up with a story about an animated dragon. They practiced with the camera and lights and became proficient at the technical aspects of making a movie. We had a great time. But then, after the kids finished learning the filming techniques and we set out to actually shoot the movie, my happy little class turned into The Independent Study Project from Hell.

The kids, the ones who did such a beautiful job of learning sophisticated cinematic techniques, could not work with each other! Instead of teamwork, they engaged in fights, squabbles, miscues, errors, and screaming matches. Camera shots were taken at the wrong time. People were in the way when the camera was running. The camera operator and the animator accused each other of doing things wrong. Filming stopped repeatedly due to upsets and hurt

4

feelings. The kids' inability to deal with each other far outweighed their technical skills. They produced a disastrous movie that looked like some kind of nightmarish Fellini horror film where an animated dragon flails around the screen while disembodied human hands, faces, and torsos flash wildly in and out of the picture.

In retrospect, I realized that I would have been much better off if I'd spent a relatively small amount of time showing the kids the technical aspects of film-making and a whole lot of time teaching them how to deal with each other. I had a great deal of time to reflect on this during the nights I spent in the editing room desperately trying to cut out the disembodied human body parts so I could pass the class. It was then I realized the kids were not the only ones whose people-handling abilities had failed. I had done a poor job of managing them. Shortly thereafter I decided to study psychology.

It might be tempting to dismiss my experience with the class as simply the typical problems encountered when teaching fourth-graders. It's no surprise kids are not good at dealing with each other; they are young and immature. It might be tempting to assume that adults, older and supposedly wiser, would not interact so badly with each other.

It might be tempting, but it would be wrong. Graphic displays of poor people-handling seem to be everywhere: brutality, discrimination, harassment, wars, accusations, recriminations, denials, and arrogance bombard us on the nightly news. Those are just the public examples. Personal life often reveals a similar landscape: arguments, fights, conflicts, and divorces. In the business world there are firings, lost customers, lost sales, and failed firms. The list goes on and on. At the bottom of nearly all this trouble lies the failure of people to deal effectively with each other.

Take this excerpt from a marriage counseling session in my office. The husband turned to the wife and said:

"I'm sick and tired of you being so rude all the time."

The wife started to reply, but before she could speak I interrupted. "How do you think she's going to respond to your statement?"

"Oh," he huffed. "I know exactly what she'll do. She'll deny that she's rude, and then she'll start to complain about how I never talk to her. That's what she always does."

"So you already know what she's going to say in response to your comment. Is that what you want to have happen, to have her complain about you not talking to her?"

"God, no." he replied. "I hate it! That's what drives me crazy about her. She nags at me constantly!"

"Then let me ask you something else," I continued. "Does saying something to her like what you just said get her to quit being rude to you? Does it get her to change her behavior or give you a response you want?"

"No," he said slowly.

"After you say something like that does she ever do something you want, such as agree with you and say she'll try harder, or that she understands your feelings, or anything like that?" I asked.

"No," he again replied.

"Then don't you find it interesting that you continue to say things like, 'I'm sick and tired of you being so rude all the time' when you know very well your statement is not only not going to get her to change her responses, it is going to trigger the very behavior you can't stand?"

He looked away and was quiet. I turned to the wife. "Is he right?" I asked. "Is that what you would do in response? Complain about him never talking to you?"

"He never does talk to me," she said, shooting an angry glance his way. "He completely ignores me most of the time. Drives me absolutely crazy."

I turned back to the husband. "You were right, weren't you? You knew the response your statement would get, and now you're getting it. In fact, you're getting it even though she's talking to me, even though I interrupted your conversation, even though I talked to you for a minute and even though you're not involved in talking to her right now."

I turned back to the wife. "Predict for me how he is going to react to what you just said."

"Like he usually does," she said. "By clamming up. Like I said, he never talks to me. When I talk like that he just turns off. He sulks. Like a child."

"Is that what you want him to do?" I asked.

"Of course not!" she blurted out. "That's the whole point. I want him to talk to me! He never talks to me!"

"Do you usually clam up when she complains about how you don't talk?"

The husband was silent. He had a sour, disgusted look on his face. He let out a heavy, wordless sigh.

"He sure does clam up in response to you, doesn't he? It's happening right now. So don't you think it's interesting that you continue to talk to him like you just did when you already know the way you're talking is going to result in his doing exactly what you don't want?"

The wife was silent.

It didn't take a genius to see that these partners were behaving in ways that were guaranteed to get exactly what they didn't want from each other. They performed the same behaviors over and over again; hammering away at each other with the same old words, the same old tones, and the same old style in an attempt to get the responses they wanted. They kept hoping, somehow, this time it would be different, this time there would be a miracle and the other person would respond like they wanted.

Only it never happened. Nothing ever changed. They got the same old responses time and time again. This didn't occur for mysterious reasons or because of deep dark secrets in their personal histories. It happened because they used unsuccessful methods of dealing with each other over and over again. But they could not see it. They couldn't understand what was right under their nose. If they changed how they handled each other, the responses they would get would change.

That's typical of how people deal with each other. They do things over and over again that don't produce the desired results. But they keep on doing them. Then they blame the other person for not responding like they want them to respond.

As a species, humans have advanced very little in our ability to interact with each other. Even with all of the problems we face in the physical world, such as pollution and dwindling natural resources, we have still done a much better job of learning to master the physical world than we have of learning to deal with each other. We have produced technological advances such as global travel, personal computers, wireless telephones, lasers and holograms. But we still use inefficient, haphazard, and destructive methods in associating with each other. They are the same techniques used in the Middle Ages and before. They often produce the same undesirable results. We engage in unproductive arguments, conflicts, and fights. We hurt the very people we most love.

Sometimes, when we do manage to accomplish our goals with people, the manipulative and underhanded methods we use to achieve them are what cause trouble for us. If the mistakes we made dealing with the physical world were as bad as the mistakes we make in dealing with each other, very few of us would be alive today. Those of us who were would be busy hunting mastodons with spears. When it comes to interacting with other people, most of us don't use the equivalent of a laser or a computer, we use the equivalent of a stick on a cave wall.

Why Handling People Is Difficult

Dealing with people can be difficult. It can seem as though it requires someone who is nursemaid, parent, professor, confidant, pal, and lion-tamer. There are several elements that go into people-handling that make it difficult:

1. People Don't Operate Like We Want Them to or Think They Should

We want others to be rational, decent, and sensible. We want them to be able to see the obvious, to know their impact on and to understand us. We expect them to see the world as we see it. But people often don't. They surprise us. They do things that don't make sense to us. They do things that are so opposed to the way we think things should be done we end up wondering how anyone could do them. We wonder how they could say some of the things they say. We end up confused about why people seem so difficult.

It's very hard to be effective in dealing with anything you don't understand. It's like trying to speak an unfamiliar language or to assemble a kit without instructions. There is little chance we can do a good job at it. By not understanding people, we easily get lost in trying to deal with them.

2. No Approach is Always Effective

If you are a mechanic, taking off a bolt is pretty much the same every time. You use a wrench to turn the bolt. Being effective with people is not like that at all. It's highly complex and variable. The specific methods, techniques, and approaches used in being competent with others change enormously depending on many factors. At one point it may involve the use of assertive behaviors while at others it involves the use of passive behaviors. Sometimes you may need to be nice, and sometimes tough.

Such variability of approach is often difficult because individuals like to stick with familiar ways. Those who already know how to argue want arguing to accomplish their goals. People who already know how to be empathic and conciliatory don't want to argue. But it isn't that simple because, there is too much variability in human responses. As a result, being skillful in dealing with people means being able to do different things in different ways at different times with different people.

3. Most Interpersonal Behavior
Comes from Old Behavior Patterns

The way people deal with each other is frequently generated by old behavior patterns they learned in the past. This means their present behavior is controlled by past experience, not by the requirements of the current situation. As a result, responses often don't produce good results. This is so common that much success in dealing with others is purely accidental. It only occurs when the effects of old patterns and the needs of a current situation happen to coincide. This is the same principle that governs a stopped clock; it may not work but it's still accurate twice a day. Because of this, individuals end up with a hodge-podge of hits and misses when dealing with others. They can't improve because they don't understand what's going wrong.

Nevertheless, people keep on doing the same thing over and over because they think their behaviors are designed to produce the desired results. Their internal assessment of their behavior tells them these are the "right" behaviors to use in accomplishing their goal. But this internal assessment is a relic of the past. It, like the behavior patterns themselves, was created long ago in a different place and time, and was based on situations that aren't around anymore.

So the sense that particular behaviors are right is based on an obsolete standard. It actually might have been right to handle your raging mother by withdrawal and blind obedience, but it may not work at all when responding to your angry spouse. It may have been right to argue within your family in order to keep from being run over by authoritarian parents, but it might not work at all with your boss.

The dominance of old patterns makes learning to be effective at handling people a difficult process. Old patterns rarely give up without a fight. Because your internal assessment considers those old behaviors to be the correct thing to do, learning to do something different often feels wrong, uncomfortable, and confusing. Your internal assessment will not readily consider new ways of doing things to be a good thing, even if they produce better results.

This was the case for a man who came to see me because of family problems. His response, when faced with nearly any kind of conflict, was an expression of anger. His reaction to problems with his children was to launch into intense criticism, lecturing, and yelling. While none of these behaviors is inherently wrong, this man could not see that they weren't working. They never produced the results he wanted. His children's grades did not improve, their behavior did not improve, and their response to him did not improve. In fact, the only thing that did improve was the man's standing as the family scapegoat. Everyone in the family had an easy excuse for any problem: "Dad's a jerk." But he kept on performing the behaviors because they felt right to him.

It took several months for me to get through to this man that his behaviors were not going to produce the effects he wanted. Despite all of the evidence that his yelling and screaming were ineffective, he insisted what he was doing was the right thing, that it should work. The man didn't want to give up his behavior, he wanted it to work. If he stopped, he would have to hear his internal assessment tell him he was doing something bad, that he was "letting them get away with it" or "failing to teach them responsibility." I had to remind him over and over again that his yelling and screaming may have felt right, but it had yet to successfully prevent his kids from getting away with anything, or teach them any responsibility.

Finally, after several months, the man began to relent. It was difficult for him at first, but as he came to see better results doing things differently, he became more comfortable using new behaviors.

4. It's Very Difficult to Judge Your Own People-Handling Abilities

In everyday life there is almost no reliable method for assessing your own people-handling skills. Most people in your life are much too afraid of your reaction to tell you how adept you are at interacting with them. You don't get truthful feedback. Even if they did tell you, who's to say you'd believe them, or that they would be accurate? There isn't any standard scoring system for quality of people-handling as there is for, say, Olympic ice skating.

Your own assessment of your abilities doesn't help much. It's totally unreliable, and almost certainly overestimates your abilities. People typically think they are much better at dealing with others than they really are. Most figure if they haven't been divorced eight times or had their picture hanging on the post office wall, they're pretty decent people-handlers. A 1989 Gallup poll showed 80% of people think they rank in the top 10% in their ability to get along with and relate to others.

Such overly positive self-assessments are what I call the "Good Driver Syndrome." I live in a big city where there are lots of streets, cars, and large, heavily travelled freeways. Every single day people do crazy things on the roads. But under almost no circumstance will you hear anyone admit to being a bad driver. I suspect a poll of the entire city would uncover only a handful of admittedly bad drivers. Nearly everyone figures the trouble on the roads is caused by someone else.

Perhaps you've had the kind of experience I had when I was riding in a car going about fifty-five miles an hour when I observed we were coming very close to making contact with the back bumper of the car in front of us. We were three or four feet away when I started getting nervous.

"Um," I said to the driver. "Are we a little close to that car?"

You would have thought I had insulted his newborn baby. "I'm a good six feet behind!" the driver snapped back, clearly miffed that I would have the gall to suggest his driving was anything but flawless.

Self-assessment is generally a giant study in self-delusion. This is true for people-handling skills as well as driving skills. There are many people who are bad at dealing with others, but few of them think they are. They think problems occur in their interactions because of the other people, not because of their own behavior. Most people who regularly do irrational things when dealing with other people—things that cause themselves and others all kinds of trouble that prevent them from getting what they want—really don't think that they are doing anything wrong. They have no idea their actions worsen and create problems. Even the most obnoxious, abrasive persons, whose behavior makes everyone hate them, will hotly deny their way of treating people has anything to do with trouble they are having.

What this means is you, like most other people, have no credible idea how good your skills are. In all likelihood you think they are better than they really are. The only thing you can be certain of is that your life will work better if you improve them.

5. People Resist Learning How to Deal With Each Other

Not only are people reluctant to try new behaviors because the behaviors feel wrong, they are often reluctant because they think anything that is not natural in their responses is automatically artificial and phony. So the idea of learning new ways can be frightening.

People also resist learning to deal with others because they don't want to think of themselves as "handling" people. They think it's bad, conniving, or manipulative. They don't want to try to influence anyone, to try to do anything "to" anyone.

The truth is, it's impossible *not* to handle people. You do it all the time. Whether or not you realize it, much of your behavior is already designed to affect people. It's not always natural behavior, it's unconsciously altered and is designed to influence people—to change them. Studies consistently show that while many behaviors seem like they are designed to communicate information, they are actually designed to influence others' thoughts, feelings, and behavior.

If you watch a videotape of two people talking, you can literally track the second-to-second influence one person's behavior has on the other. A raised tone of voice serves to quiet someone; a smile gets someone talking more; a frown makes someone slow down. To anyone watching the tape, it's obvious the subject's behavior is designed to affect each other. The only ones who usually don't know it are those on the tape. They are focused on the content of the conversation, unaware the behaviors they are using to communicate are also intended to control each other's thoughts, feelings, and behavior.

You don't get a choice about whether or not you influence people. You always handle people and you always will. However, you do get the choice of whether you handle people consciously and intentionally, or unconsciously and accidentally. It's not being phony, it's being skillful. By learning to consciously deal with people, you're not really doing anything new, just learning to become aware of what you are already doing.

People also shy away from learning to handle people because it can sound like "manipulating people." Most have had the experience of being manipulated, and they don't want to take advantage of others. They also don't want those who are manipulative to be better trained at it.

But handling people and manipulating people are not the same thing. "Handling people" is a general term that includes any number of ways of dealing with others, while "manipulating people" is a term that refers to one specific method of handling people. The element that distinguishes manipulation from other people-handling methods is the use of deceit.

Manipulation always involves the conscious and intentional use of subterfuge in dealing with people. You manipulate when you tell someone something that isn't true in order to get them to respond in some way they would not have responded if they knew the truth. For example, it is manipulative to tell someone you love them when you really don't, in order to get them to go to bed with you.

There's no question manipulation can get you what you want over the short-term if you don't mind lying and misleading people. But manipulation carries with it several serious problems. It requires you to violate your own integrity. You know you're lying, you know you're not trustworthy, you know you are being underhanded. Knowing that about yourself doesn't make for good feelings, a positive self-image, or success in life.

Manipulative methods also set up trouble for you later on. Manipulation works by sacrificing the future to service the immediate. Sooner or later other people always discover they have been deceived. They resent it. They begin to resist and retaliate. As a result, people who use manipulation ultimately find themselves spending increasing portions of their lives running from the effects of their actions.

Manipulation also abuses the one thing that helps you achieve happiness and success—other people. It alienates people, and people are the primary resource you have in life. To mistreat others is to disable yourself as well as them. That's why this book is titled *Power **with** People*, not Power **Over** People, and why it is not a training manual for manipulation. Deceit doesn't work; I have never met one single person who achieved genuine, enduring happiness and satisfaction through manipulation. If you want to achieve enduring success, you have to learn to be effective in dealing with people without abusing, mistreating, or deceiving them.

I had a teenage patient who beautifully demonstrated this principle. He relied exclusively on manipulation to make his way through life. He got great immediate, short-term results: he got people off his back, he conned them into letting him do what he wanted most of the time, and he successfully avoided doing a lot of things he was supposed to do. But his manipulation always backfired. One day I confronted him about it.

"So," I asked. "What would you call the way you deal with people? Would you call it 'sneaky?' Do you consider yourself to be a con artist?"

"No," he replied. "Not sneaky. I'm not a con artist. I am what I call 'crafty.' I like to think of myself as a crafty person. A smart person."

"Crafty," I repeated. "That's a nice term. It does make your way of doing things sound smart. But I've been wondering what effects your craftiness produces in your life. We already know it gets you out of a lot of stuff, and you like that. But I wonder what else it does. Tell me about your freedom."

"I don't have any," he groused. "I'm always grounded. My parents say they can't trust me. I never get to do anything."

"OK," I said. "I guess that's the result of being crafty with your parents. How about your driver's license?"

"I don't have it, either," he huffed. "I have to be passing in school to be able to get it, and I'm not."

"OK, I suppose that comes from your craftiness in handling your teachers," I replied. "Well, how about your finances. How's your spending money?"

"Don't have any," he mumbled.

"Why not?"

"I got fired from my sacker job at the grocery store."

"A result of your craftiness with your boss, I'd say. So let's see, no freedom, no drivers' license, no money. That's being crafty. Well, crafty doesn't sound so smart to me anymore. It sounds stupid."

My young friend was really good at manipulating. If manipulation were effective in creating a successful life, this kid would have one of the greatest lives in the world. But it didn't. It did just the opposite. His skill produced absolutely terrible results.

Manipulation always backfires. It's a poor substitute for good people-handling. To produce positive short and long-term results, you can't afford to manipulate. You must clearly understand that lying, misleading, and duplicity don't work—and that they undermine your long-term efforts.

Appropriate people-handling produces good long and short-term results, happy families, successful businesses, and productive careers. It takes intelligence, thought, and work, but it's the farthest thing imaginable from being cold and calculating. Good people skills involve dealing with people in ways that are appropriate to the circumstances, and the nature of your relationship with them.

6. The Usual Approaches Don't Work

Unfortunately, while there are many things written about handling people, most of them contain serious flaws. Most are based on wishful thinking rather than on how things really work.

Many approaches focus on one particular method or technique, such as being "assertive." This view states: "In order to be successful in dealing with people, you just need to do one thing called being assertive." This is of limited value, because just one technique isn't always going to work. What do you do if you're being assertive and it isn't working? Or when it's actually making things worse?

I once asked a friend of mine who is a flight attendant if she had received any special training on handling hijackers. She said she had. It was called, "Do Whatever They Tell You To Do"—not exactly a manual on assertiveness, but certainly appropriate to the situation. Specific techniques, such as being empathic, using "I" messages, or asking open-ended questions, don't fit all situations.

Other approaches present a formula that tells you what to do. Such approaches categorize people according to their behavior, then apply a particular technique to each category. For example, with someone whose behavior might classify them as a Bulldozer, you're supposed to be assertive. With a Waffler, you're advised to be noncommittal. A Resister would require you to be straightforward, and so on.

This method carries with it the same problem as the single technique approach. Does it make sense to you that one particular type of person will always be handled by one particular technique? Do you really think people are that simple and predictable? If they are, then why do we have such trouble between people? And if they aren't, what are you supposed to do on the frequent occasions when a particular technique doesn't work?

What if you are being quiet and nondirect with the Waffler, just like you're supposed to be, and he continues to waffle? What happens when your assertiveness with a Bulldozer results in his getting worse? If you're not very good at performing the particular behaviors that are supposedly required to handle one of the types, does that mean you can never be effective?

I remember teaching a parenting class in graduate school based on a particular formula of parenting behavior. Not far into the class one of the parents said, "Last night I tried out something I learned in here, but I ran into a problem. I did what the book said I was supposed to do, but my kid didn't do what the book said he was supposed to do. What was I supposed to do then?"

An additional problem with such categorization approaches is the requirement that you remember the different categories and which technique is applied to each. A patient of mine took a course based on a system of people-handling that used categories. She joked that, "Now she needed to flip through a card file to find out what she was supposed to do with anyone."

Unfortunately, dealing with people is just not simple enough to be reduced to a formula. There is too much variability and complexity in behavior. If an approach doesn't allow for the unexpected in people's responses, it will result more in confusion than clarity.

A related problem with most approaches is that they apply techniques to people and situations in ways based on obvious logic. It's sensible that one would stand up to a Bulldozer, or refuse to take over for a Waffler, but the logic is itself a problem. Behavior is not always logical or rational. To deal effectively with people, sometimes you have to do things that are not so logical.

When I was first in practice many years ago, I had a patient who ran up a bill of several hundred dollars. I sent him bills every month without fail; he never paid me a cent. After this went on for many months I skipped a month. Soon a check for a portion of what he owed appeared in my mail. Intrigued, I decided to try it again. I sent him bills for a few more months, during which time no additional payments appeared. Then I skipped another month. This time his secretary called me on the phone, apologized for his "terrible lateness" in paying the bill, and sent me a check for the remaining balance!

Nowhere in business, finance, or psychology have I ever been taught that it made sense to skip sending a bill in order to get someone to pay it. It's illogical. Who would guess it would work? People are not as rational as we like to think. If you limit yourself to only logical methods, you're going to be severely limited.

No place in the universe is more filled with paradox, irony, and irrationality than the human psyche. There are several different, distinct, and at times conflicting, levels of functioning involved in generating human behavior. This results in the self-contradictions and paradoxes that characterize human beings. It's important to understand this and take it into account.

Therapists run into the illogical nature of human behavior all the time. Sometimes upset people feel better when therapists are tough and hard with them rather than when they are nice. Occasionally refusing to help someone helps them the most. I once produced a therapeutic effect in a particularly resistant college kid when I unceremoniously threw him out of my office and refused to ever see him again. It was the only thing that ever got him to be honest with himself about the mess he was making of his life.

The point is, every specific technique, every people-handling formula, and every logical method will break down at some point. You need information and techniques that will allow you to adjust, adapt, try new things, break old patterns, and think creatively.

The final problem with most approaches to people-handling is so many focus only on those who are currently being a concern or on "difficult" people. Certainly no one is going to dispute that there are some people who are more trying to deal with than others, but to automatically label someone as inherently difficult often creates more problems than it solves. The truth is, people's behavior, even their difficult behavior, varies from time to time and circumstance to circumstance. Nearly everyone is more difficult at some times and less at others. Someone may also be hard for one person to handle, but easy for someone else. Others can also be trying only in particular circumstances. I once screamed at a rental-car clerk in order to interrupt his pattern of behavior, and while I don't scream often, I'm quite sure that to him I now fit into the difficult category.

Labeling someone as difficult is often inaccurate and misleading. It can lock you into a needlessly defensive stance that restricts rather than improves your ability to deal with them. You can feel anxious and tense around them, reducing your ability to think clearly and to try new things. Labeling them is also frequently part of a pattern of abdicating responsibility for behavior with other people. Spouses do this a lot.

In marriage therapy they will look at me with earnest, soulful, exasperated expressions that say "I'm married to Cro-Magnon man (or woman), who, by their very innate, inborn nature, is a totally impossible creature. This person is unreasonable and irrational in every way, completely unable to be reasonably dealt with by any normal human being such as myself. As a result, I can't be faulted for my own behavior with this person. No matter how nasty, cruel, or unkind I am, it's not my fault. It means nothing about me as a person, only about them, because it's the only way I can possibly deal with them." Then that spouse proceeds to act like a jerk, and to feel fully justified in doing so.

Married couples are certainly not the only people who do this. It happens everywhere. A colleague of mine had terrible service at a restaurant, and left a substantially diminished tip. The waiter followed her into the parking lot to complain! He had absolutely no understanding that the reduced tip was related to his behavior. He abdicated any responsibility for his behavior in the situation by labeling her as a difficult patron. He did exactly what people do when they are confronted with a difficult interpersonal situation while abdicating responsibility for their own behavior; he made things worse.

Managers do the same thing with their employees. By the time they are furious about the behavior or performance of an employee, they have usually mishandled the situation so badly they have made it significantly worse. The crisis might never have occurred had they handled it appropriately along the way. But because they did not do so they can only see that the problem is the difficult employee.

Limiting one's focus to difficult people also creates a crisis mentality. People often don't start to think about effective people-handling until something major goes wrong. The little problems that build up to the big problems are not addressed. Any good sports coach will tell you you're most vulnerable when things are going well, because you're less alert at those times and thus more vulnerable to making mistakes. But most people pay little or no attention to people-handling when things are going well.

Focusing only on those who are being onerous is like a football coach limiting his coaching to when the team is down by thirty-five points and the other team is poised on the one yard line. While methods for dealing with crises are important, the best thing to do is handle things in such a way that the mess never occurs in the first place.

Becoming Effective

I'm not writing about developing some kind of supernatural power that guarantees you can get people to do what you want and walk away smiling. It rarely works like that. What I am talking about in becoming effective is becoming skillful. Being skillful means one is adept with certain principles and methods and can apply them in a manner that maximizes the chance for success. Skillfulness is the result of study, understanding, and practice. It never results in a guarantee of success, but it does increase the probability. If you become skillful in handling people, you still won't get every outcome you want, but you will get more of them.

Skillfulness in handling people requires three things: awareness, understanding fundamental information, and knowing what to do.

1. Awareness

It's no accident we use the phrase, "they don't know what they're doing" for those who are unskilled. Being awake to what you're doing is a fundamental element of being skillful. When it comes to dealing with others, knowing what you're doing isn't very easy.

One Sunday morning I walked in on a huge, heated argument at a bagel shop. When I entered, the manager and a patron were screaming at each other. The angry patron slammed out the door after hurling one final insult and the manager screamed something back before stalking off into the storeroom. The shop was packed with customers. As I looked around at the stunned faces, I wondered whether the manager and the patron knew what they were doing, because what they did was:

1. Upset themselves and each other
2. Bought no bagels
3. Sold no bagels
4. Diminished the store's market share by at least one customer
5. Traumatized all of the customers in the store, decreasing the likelihood of their returning

Clearly, the manager and the patron didn't know what they were doing, because the result was certainly not what they desired. When reading about the incident it may seem obvious the situation was mishandled, but in all probability neither the manager nor the patron could see that while the incident was occurring.

Being aware of what you're doing when you are a participant in an incident is much more difficult to do than when reading about it. When you find yourself yelling ineffectively at your child, brooding with silent, self-righteous anger during an altercation with your boss, or unable to reach an agreement in a conflict with your spouse, it will be difficult for you to see your behavior is part of the problem. When you find yourself responding out of automatic guilt—when you watch your sales diminish, your customers leave, and your employees complain—you're unlikely to be aware you're mishandling people. When actually involved in the situation, it's much easier to see how other people are mishandling things than how you are doing so. It's the ability to stay conscious of your own behavior that is an essential element of skillfulness.

2. Fundamental Information

Fundamental information is what tells you why you need to use the skills necessary to be effective. It explains the principles in a particular area. This is the information that helps what you are doing make sense, that fits all the pieces together in your mind. Without possessing fundamental information people are not truly skillful, but simply technicians following a recipe. They can't make informed judgments, necessary alterations in approach, or figure out what to do when something doesn't work.

In any endeavor in life—be it nuclear physics, chemistry, oceanography, or people-handling, fundamental information is an absolute necessity. That's why physicians study anatomy and physiology in addition to learning how to give a shot, and chemists study atomic theory besides learning laboratory technique. You have to know why you're doing what you're doing in addition to knowing what to do.

In people-handling, fundamental information explains why people are the way they are and why they do the things they do. Many times people think they already possess fundamental information. But just being a person dealing with people doesn't give you knowledge about how human beings function any more than driving a car gives you the basic facts about how cars work. What generally masquerades as fundamental information about people are short, informal theories that most people come up with when they're upset with someone. These theories are usually something like, "He's a fool" or, "She's insecure." These are what I call "non-explanation explanations" because they seem to explain someone's behavior, but they really don't. Their logic is circular. If you try to use them to help you figure out what to do with someone, they take you nowhere.

I demonstrated this point to a college-age participant at one of my presentations on interpersonal effectiveness. He was having trouble with a teacher, and his explanation for the teacher's behavior was that she was an idiot. I drew a circle on the blackboard with one side of the circle labeled "idiot" and the other side identifying the behavior of the teacher the student didn't like. I pointed out how his explanation worked: the teacher was an idiot because of the behavior he didn't like, and the teacher behaved in the way he didn't like because the teacher was an idiot. What good did the explanation do? Nothing had been done but label the teacher's behavior with an insulting term. Behavior the student didn't like, and the explanation called "idiot," referenced only each other, not to any new understanding or any new options for dealing with the teacher.

Even if you learn many people-handling techniques, without understanding fundamental information you will get baffled every time you run into something unexpected. Then you're severely handicapped and will get stuck frequently. Until you understand what drives people's behavior—including the unreasonable, strange, and difficult—just learning techniques will help you very little.

3. Knowing What To Do

An old Chinese proverb says, "Knowing and not doing is the same thing as not knowing." In dealing with people, you need to know what to do in addition to understanding the fundamental information. This means that you need to learn the effective techniques that constitute effective people-handling. Often, people don't know there are many techniques available because they aren't able to use more than one or two. But there are dozens, and the more of them you're skilled in, the better off you'll be.

How This Book Is Different

This book differs from the usual approaches to people-handling in several important ways:

1. The Presentation of Fundamental Information

It doesn't start out talking about techniques, rather it presents fundamental information about how and why people function the way they do. Don't skip these sections! Without understanding them, you will not be able to use the techniques with any degree of sophistication. They enable you to be flexible and adaptive to the people and circumstances you deal with.

2. No Formula

There is no intent to present one "correct" way of dealing with people. That approach limits you. My purpose is to open up many new options. The point is for you to think for yourself, to pick and choose what will work for you. If you're not good at a particular kind of behavior, that's fine. Search through the techniques for other methods that you can substitute.

Specific behaviors that you can use are presented, applying particular behaviors in particular situations. The book even talks about those who are being difficult and some who are difficult due to special factors. These guidelines are suggestions, ways to start you thinking and being creative. In general, there are no categories or formulas that you're supposed to follow or memorize.

3. Organized By Purpose, Not By Personality Type

In *Power with People* you learn to deal with different people in your life for different reasons and purposes. It's these purposes that are the driving force in your behavior. As a result, the most natural organization for information about handling people is by the purpose you are trying to accomplish. After all, you probably want to produce very different results with your spouse or your children than with your boss.

4. Presentation of Methods to Prevent Problems

The first thing emphasized in almost every field of endeavor other than people-handling is prevention. Think of the security business. Any security expert will tell you the primary purpose of any security measure, from bodyguards to alarm systems to attack dogs, is not to stop a crime after it starts. It's to prevent a crime from ever happening. Bodyguards, alarm stickers, and dogs are designed to be obvious and intimidating to potential troublemakers.

I once asked a friend of mine who was a martial-arts expert looking for a job why he didn't work as a bouncer in a night club. I knew he could overcome almost anyone. He replied that he would make a lousy bouncer because he was small in stature. That meant he would actually have to fight people. For a bouncer, preventive power comes with being large and physically intimidating.

When it comes to handling people, very little attention is typically paid to the principle of prevention. Instead, people do what comes naturally until there's trouble. The best way is to focus on making things work well even when there's not a problem, and do what prevents problems in the first place. If you find yourself in a position where you do have to deal with a difficult person, it's a good bet that your best people-handling strategy—prevention—has failed, and you're left with the second-best strategy. So in addition to discussing methods for handling people who are being a problem, this book also focuses on how to handle people to prevent problems.

The lack of preventive thinking in people-handling makes mental health professionals tear their hair. It's not uncommon that the first call from a married couple seeking counseling comes when one of the spouses packs their bags and announces they're leaving. The other spouse frantically calls a therapist begging to be seen immediately. When asked how long the problems have been going on, they reply, "About ten years." Therapists know that things would have been much easier to fix if the phone call had come ten years earlier.

Learning to handle people effectively is a complex area, one where knowledge and skillfulness don't happen overnight. Understanding, practice, and awareness are required.

The whole point of this book is to lay out the essential information for you to use to if you want to improve your people-handling skills. It contains the fundamental information, principles, techniques, and specific applications you can use to improve your abilities in dealing with other people. The information is here. Everything else—studying it, learning it, practicing it, and using it responsibly—is up to you.

Chapter 2

Why People Are the Way They Are

While there are many psychological theories that attempt to explain why people behave the way they do, few of them are useful in building a foundation for learning to handle them effectively. Not only are most of the theories complex, difficult to learn, and inapplicable to many people-handling situations; nearly all overlook the most fundamental, powerful force in human functioning—biology. Without understanding certain principles and mechanisms of biology, it's impossible to understand why people do the things they do.

The term biology which explains human behavior is different from what is taught in school. Basic biology focuses on the physical characteristics of living substances. Knowing the names of different types of cells, or the substances present in blood doesn't help explain why people are the way they are. That which explains human functioning I call "functional" biology.

Fortunately, functional biology is much more simple and easy to learn than is the classical subject. It involves learning only a few basic principles. Once you understand them you will know all you need to know about the basic workings of human beings.

Functional Biology

The processes of all living creatures are based in biology. It ultimately determines what operational capacities are available to any living thing. If you have the biological capacity to do something, you can do it. A dog can hear high-pitched sounds that you can't hear because it has the ability. You can learn algebra and a cat can't because you have the capacity and the cat doesn't.

Although there is a tendency to talk about certain functions such as "psychology" or the "mind" as if they were independent of biological processes, they're not. The brain's physiology determines what kind of thinking and feeling can occur. The only mental and psychological abilities that are available are those that are possible given a particular neurology and structure.

Biology's Purpose

Although the state of being called "life" is unique and differs from the states called "dead" or "inanimate," from a biological perspective life differs from other states of being in one important way: Life is the only state of being that will end if it doesn't receive proper maintenance.

Life doesn't continue automatically. Rocks continue in their inanimate state all by themselves. A dead tree doesn't need anything to stay dead. Only living things require specific tasks be performed to maintain their state of being. Only living things face the possibility of losing that state. Computers may break down and rocks may shatter into pieces, but none of these changes alter their state of being.

Because life requires maintenance to continue, and because biology is the producer of life, biology is charged with the task of maintaining it. Biology is designed to see to it that the tasks required are performed. Survival is what matters most and is always its first interest.

If there is such a thing as a human soul that lives beyond biological death, that's all fine and dandy for the soul, but biology could care less. It doesn't share in any eternal life the soul might enjoy, life is all there is. There is no consolation prize, no second chance, no safety net. As a result, biology's interests lie only in survival.

If you ever wondered how people can believe in life after death, but still fear dying, this is the reason. A fear of death is generated as part of accomplishing the primary task—staying alive. The brain and the body generate the fear because it's useful in avoiding danger. Biology itself doesn't care about life after death, so despite a human belief in it, biology is still going to try to preserve life by producing the fear of death.

Biology's Priorities

Because biology has survival as its basic task, its priorities are very simple. The importance of any function or any action is determined by its ability to assist in survival. Activities most likely to ensure living are the activities it will favor. If there is a choice between several possible actions, the one most effectively serving the purpose of staying alive is the one it will generate.

This prioritizing can be seen in the way biology arranges bodily functions. Those processes most immediately required for survival are the ones most valued—and are automatic. This makes them the most reliable and dependable and they're not subordinate to other functions less immediately essential for life. Because you can last only a few minutes without a heartbeat, biology makes it automatic so you can't die because you forget to do it. You also can last only a few minutes without breathing, so the same principle applies.

Other bodily functions not as immediately necessary for survival, but still important for survival, are not automatic. Instead, they are drives, needs, or cravings. Eating, for example, is not automatic, it requires an act of will and can be subordinated to other activities. That makes good survival sense, because you can survive if you put off eating until later, while you can't survive if you put off a heartbeat and breathing until later.

Because there's only so much energy available at any time, biology diverts whatever energy is available to whatever functions are most immediately required for life support. It responds to any threat by removing energy from less urgent functions, and diverting it to those that address the immediate problem. If an action isn't important for immediate survival, biology is willing to sacrifice it. A coma, for example, occurs when biology has to choose between putting energy into maintaining consciousness and putting energy into maintaining essential operations. Consciousness is less important than is a heartbeat or breathing.

This is also why you're tired when you have the flu. Your body diverts energy to your immune system to fight off the virus. As a result, you have little strength available for other activities.

This diversion of energy occurs on every level, from the cellular to the behavioral. If you're sitting at a bus stop, hungrily gobbling a sandwich, and you see an out-of-control bus careening toward you at ninety miles an hour, it will no longer matter how hungry you are. Your biology will instantly re-evaluate priorities and determine you can last without lunch, but you can't last if that bus reaches you. It will take energy out of your eating behavior and put it into your senses and muscles in preparation to jump out of the way. Your pupils will dilate, your heart rate will speed up, your breathing will quicken, and your muscles will tense. It's of little consequence that lunch will be strewn across the sidewalk or that you don't get to eat dessert.

Biology stays constantly alert for any possible threat to survival, and uses a monitoring system that helps it at all times. If it picks up signs of possible dangers, it's prepared to divert energy and attention to wherever it's needed.

Biology's Monitoring System

Biology's monitoring system tells it if things are going well. The system uses a set of perceptions which indicate the current state of conditions. These perceptions are usually referred to by a name which doesn't sound like it's related to survival—the "pleasure principle."

It has been known for many years living things seek pleasure and avoid pain. Why is pleasure pleasurable, and pain painful? Why is it designed that way? What's the point?

The reason is biological, pleasure is not simply a pleasant sensation and pain an unpleasant one. Pleasure and pain are readings on a gauge that indicates how well biology is accomplishing its task. Pleasure is an indication that all is well and should continue. Pain is an indication danger is present, and something needs to be changed.

That's why it's difficult to get out of bed in the morning when your alarm clock rings. It's not that you're lazy; biology reads the comfort you feel as a sign that lying in bed is helpful for survival. Biology tries to get it to continue, and resists your attempts to get up. If you do something painful, such as trying to squeeze your foot into a shoe that is too small, biology reads the pain generated as an indication of a possible threat to survival, and it tries to get you to stop.

This means conditions that interfere with the ability to sense pleasure and pain aren't just a nuisance, they can be life-threatening. There are people born with a rare neurological disease that prevents them from experiencing pain. As a result, they don't know when they've been injured. Such people have to be very careful and most don't live very long. Similarly, there's a condition called "anhedonia," an inability to experience pleasure. This condition also often leads to an early death, because not only do people suffer the physical effects of serious depression, they commit suicide.

The pleasure principle has enormous, fundamental power in directing the behavior of all living things. Even a one-celled organism moves away from an electric shock. At its core, the behavior of biological entities isn't all that complex. Their basic function is to survive, and they do things designed to enhance that possibility. Biology monitors the range of sensations from pleasure to pain, and seeks pleasure and avoids pain. Consciousness is not even required; you do these things in your sleep.

Human Functional Biology

So far I've been talking about general functional biology. Its principles are common to all creatures. But they only partially explain human behavior. Like all living things humans tend to seek pleasure and avoid pain, but they also do things that seem to contradict the principle of survival. They harm themselves physically and emotionally, and they do pleasurable things that are self-destructive such as taking drugs and drinking excessively. Such apparent contradictions to the principle of survival aren't adequately explained by general functional biology. In order to fully understand human behavior, more specific information about human biology is required.

The Biology Unique to Humans

Every species has certain biological characteristics that make it unique. Giraffes have long necks for eating leaves off the top of trees, bats squeal in a way that allows navigation in the dark, and birds have wings to flee from predators. Humans have specific biological characteristics that are unique. However, humans' special biology isn't in obvious areas such as body shape or physical strength. In most of these areas we are remarkably ordinary. Our biological uniqueness lies in an area more difficult to see.

What's unique to humans is in the brain. While notably middle-of-the-road in overall physical prowess, humans have special brain wiring that allows us to do something other creatures can't do. No one is certain exactly where in the brain the special wiring is, but there is no doubt it exists. It may have to do with the neo-cortex, or with the temporal lobes. It may not be one specific "section" of the brain so much as how the sections are wired to communicate with each other.

In any case, whatever it is that is special about human brain wiring results in humans possessing a very special capacity. Humans have the ability to not only perceive and process information received from our senses, but also to perceive and process information about things that don't originate externally. They are things no other creature, as far as we know, can perceive. The name we give these is "concepts."

Concepts

Concepts are unique because they are entities. They are "things," but they're not sensory. You can't project a picture of a concept onto a screen, or photograph a "reasonable" the same way you can photograph a chair or a rhinoceros or a cabbage. "Reasonable" is a concept that exists strictly in human brain wiring. It can be referred to through language, and can be used in conjunction with entities and information in the external world, and sensory objects can be used as examples of it.

We could project a picture of someone talking in a calm tone of voice, and call that being reasonable. But there's no sensory entity on the screen we see with our eyes or hear with our ears that is, literally, a "reasonable," just a human being talking in a calm tone. Reasonable is a concept that comes from the human brain and is applied to the action. If a creature other than a human, one without the brain wiring to be able to perceive concepts, saw that same screen, they would only see the moving images of the action that was occurring. No such thing as reasonable would exist for them.

Concepts are real, but only in human brain wiring. We refer to them by such names as meanings, principles, values, beliefs, standards, and interpretations. We can do to concepts all of the things we do to any "things." We can identify them, share them, exchange them, keep them, change them, and lose them. They exist in the brains of human beings, referred to through the use of language, and applied to sensory events and objects.

The importance of the ability to perceive concepts for the functioning of human beings can hardly be overestimated. The ability to create, process, and manipulate conceptual entities such as principles, values and beliefs, is a unique and profound biological capability, a genuine breakthrough in functioning. Concepts, along with conceptual language, represent a qualitative shift in biological ability from all other creatures. It's not just "better" hearing, as a dog has better hearing than a human. It's a whole new world of functioning. No other creatures base their actions on beliefs, values, principles, or any other conceptual or abstract entity. They don't take stands on moral issues or react to such concepts as justice, fairness, or rudeness. Animals have never had a war over theological or ideological issues, they don't feel upset over someone being rude, and they don't get mad about anything being unfair. Your dog may act like he understands the concept "bad" when you scold him, but he doesn't. That is simply the way you understand his behavior. In reality, he is only reacting to your scolding tone of voice.

Because humans use language, some words refer to sensory entities and some refer to conceptual entities. Words that are examples of the distinction between the conceptual and the sensory are presented in Figure 1. Notice how different the two lists are. Sensory words refer to things or actions that, without interpretation or explanation, can be seen or heard. The meaning of the words is obvious and specific because the entities to which they are referring is perceived similarly by different people. Conceptual words, on the other hand, refer to abstractions which do not reference specific sensory data. Instead, they refer to an idea or a quality. As a result, they don't have a standard meaning, action or physical entity they

FIGURE 1

Sensory World	Conceptual World
table	truth
chair	kindness
walk	justice
sit	cruelty
touch	appropriate
blue	responsible
foot	reasonable
wood	caring
hit	messy
push	interesting
hold	applicable
shake	doubt
book	adequate
pencil	honor
car	cherish
cat	represent
door	good
throw	acceptable
cut	bad
point	ridiculous
rise	nonsense
clap	expect
dark	hope

refer to. How they are applied in the sensory world is open to interpretation.

The Conceptual World

Concepts come from a world of their own, a world that coexists with, but is separate from, the physical world. People live in this world every bit as much as they live in the physical one. You can "stand on" a concept, "live with" an idea, or "resist" because of a principle, as in the saying, "it's the principle of the thing." You base actions on them and use them as tools.

Benefits

There are some distinct advantages to possessing the capacity to live in a world of concepts as well as a sensory world. The conceptual enriches, deepens, and expands the experience of life. It makes available reality that doesn't exist in the sensory world. There are powerful things available in the conceptual world, such as dreams, ideas, visions, and possibilities. None of these are sensory. Animals, without the brain wiring for conceptual thought, don't have them and can't react to or use them.

The presence of concepts also makes communication efficient and powerful. Words that refer to them frequently convey a category of information. They can quickly communicate a large amount of data. Assessing a lecture by using the conceptual term "fascinating" says a lot more about it than could any one-word description using sensory language.

Concepts can also communicate emotional experience more readily than sensory language. It's much easier to relate your experience of having been at a party by calling the party "fun" than reporting every physical aspect and action from the event in an effort to get someone else to understand what the party was like for you.

Most of the time people don't consciously separate the sensory from the conceptual. People use words without ever noticing that they're accessing two entirely different worlds of existence. It's like being bilingual, unintentionally mixing words from two languages in the same sentence.

It's important that people be able to easily shuttle between the two worlds because the power of language comes from the ability to go back and forth smoothly and seamlessly. It's the reason "the pen is mightier than the sword." Patrick Henry's famous statement, "Give me liberty or give me death" is a good example. "Liberty" is a concept, a category into which a variety of possible sensory or physical occurrences, actions, and behaviors can fit. It's strictly a conceptual world entity that doesn't exist in the world outside of human brain wiring. "Death," however, is not a concept. It's a sensory entity. You can see it, touch it, or project it on a screen like you can project "falling."

The reason Mr. Henry's statement has such power is he's stating he's willing to undergo something undesirable in the sensory world in service of something desirable in the conceptual world. This places a conceptual entity higher in importance than a sensory entity. Because the conceptual is what distinguishes humans from the rest of the world, Mr. Henry rises above being one of any number of creatures, and shows himself to be fully human. We consider people who do this to be the most honorable, the most noble, of humans.

You can test the significance of shuttling between the conceptual and sensory worlds by substituting any sensory object for the conceptual in Mr. Henry's sentence. It completely loses its power. No matter what you insert, the phrase becomes meaningless, almost comical. "Give me a cheeseburger or give me death. Give me a Rolls Royce or give me death." Not quite the same impact. However, insert any other conceptual entity into the sentence, and it will change its meaning, but it will not become nonsensical or lose power. "Give me truth or give me death. Give me kindness or give me death." They all work.

Costs

The richness of experiences and the efficiency of communications brought about by having access to a conceptual world are wonderful, but they carry with them a very high price indeed. By living in both worlds, human beings have to struggle for survival in two worlds.

It's important to remember the conceptual world is a function of biology. It's not the world of the spirit or the "soul." It's brain wiring, pure and simple. In fact, people who have certain kinds of brain diseases or injuries can lose their conceptual abilities. Oliver Saks reports several such cases in his book *The Man Who Mistook His Wife for a Hat.* He presents a case where a man with a brain malfunction could see the literal physical characteristics of a glove, the shape and material, but was unable to think beyond physical characteristics in order to apply the concept "glove" to his perceptions.

Because the conceptual world is biological, biology's primary goal of survival is every bit as fundamental, inherent, and inescapable there as it is in the sensory world. Imagine what this means. Most creatures have a hard enough time trying to survive in the physical world. It takes all of their time and energy. But human beings, because of their special brain wiring, are forced to struggle to survive in two different worlds simultaneously. There is the risk of death in both.

If you've ever wondered why life seems so difficult, why there seems to be so much struggle and suffering in being human, or why the Buddha is said to have made his First Noble Truth "Life is Suffering," this is the reason. Humans are at twice the risk of any other creature. Human biology must cope with risks from two different directions at the same time. Humans are like warriors fighting on two fronts at once, and in both worlds the stakes are always the same—life and death.

Lest you think when I talk about survival in the conceptual world I am talking about something abstract or academic, let me introduce some recollections from Dr. Viktor Frankl. He was an Austrian psychiatrist who survived German concentration camps in World War II. His observations about those who did and those who did not survive the camps are instructive as regards the importance of the conceptual world.

Frankl noted a prevalent syndrome existed in the concentration camp. A prisoner would lose his ability to believe in the future. At that point, the prisoner would suddenly stop functioning. Nothing anyone did would help get the person active. He would simply give up, refuse to get out of bed, refuse to take care of himself in any way. Usually, even if nothing had been physically wrong with him, he would be dead within forty-eight hours.

Frankl writes of a particularly chilling case. A prisoner strongly believed in a dream he had that the camp would be liberated on March twenty-ninth, and the war would end March thirtieth. The news reaching the camp indicated these events were not going to occur. On March twenty-ninth the man started running a high fever. On March thirtieth he was delirious. On March thirty-first he died.

In a similar occurrence, Frankl wrote that at the end of 1944, in the week between Christmas and New Year's, the death rate in the camp suddenly rose significantly and unexpectedly. The reason appeared to be that many prisoners had suffered dashed hopes they would be home for the new year. The loss of conceptual entities such as "belief," "hope," and "faith," can result in physical death. So make no mistake. When I talk about survival in the conceptual world, I am talking about physical life and death. In fact, while separating the two worlds is necessary to understand the fundamental functioning of human beings, biology can't tell them apart. For biology, survival is survival, and a threat is a threat. It doesn't differentiate between being stabbed in the chest or shot through the belief.

The way we use language reveals we already know the conceptual place is a world of life and death. We call the origin of an idea its "birth." We say a dream has "died." These wordings are not accidental or meaningless.

Human Existence in the Conceptual World

The reason trouble in the conceptual world can result in physical death is that humans have a conceptual body. This must be kept alive and functioning. If it's destroyed you die just as surely as if your physical body were destroyed.

The structure of the conceptual body is similar to the physical. The material body is made up of different parts, such as the heart, lungs, kidneys, liver, and brain. The conceptual is also made up of different parts—the concepts you identify with. In the physical body, organs work together as one system to maintain life—interconnected and interdependent. The same is true in the conceptual body. The concepts, values, principles, and meanings that you hold as "yours" interlock, working together as one system. As you identify with your physical self you also identify with your inner self—your self-concept.

We refer to a collection of interrelated concepts—thoughts, principles, and ideas—as a "body" of work. This phrasing is not a semantic accident or a coincidence. It's an acknowledgment that we intuitively know concepts combine and form a body.

Survival in the Conceptual World

Because the physical world is perceived by the senses, it's easy to see what maintains life and what kills it. In contrast, the conceptual world is not perceived by the senses and is only accessed through language references. As a result, the factors involved in life and death are not easy to see. There is no blood to keep flowing in order to stay alive. Concepts don't eat food. So if conceptual entities need to stay alive, how is that accomplished?

Life in the Conceptual World

Metaphorically speaking, there is a form of blood that must flow through conceptual entities. This blood is the one thing required if a principle, belief, or idea is to continue on, passed from one generation to another, and avoid being killed off. The lifeblood of concepts is that they be "right." Just as all the parts of your physical body must continue to be supplied with blood, all of your conceptual body must be endowed with "rightness" in order to live. Certainly you can have passing thoughts you know are not right, but unless an idea seems right to you, you can't hold it as a viable belief, value, or principle. It can't become yours, a part of your self-concept.

Being right enables concepts to exist as viable entities. The belief the world is flat was a conviction on which people based actions. It's no longer a viable concept because it's not true.

Your conceptual body consists of those thoughts you consider to be right. Nothing else belongs there. In fact, you can't believe anything you don't think is right. This does not necessarily mean you "like" these concepts or they feel good. If you find this difficult to accept, try it for yourself. Try to believe that your name is George Washington. Try to believe it. It's impossible. You can't do it anymore than you can pick up someone else's arm and make it part of your own body.

Death in the Conceptual World

If the equivalent of life in the conceptual world is being right, then the equivalent of death is being "wrong." Whatever becomes wrong can no longer exist. It dies off. Being wrong hurts, is painful, and if it's bad enough, can be fatal.

This explains how, as happened with Frankl's fellow prisoners, someone can die from having their beliefs, hopes, or expectations become wrong. If a belief that is part of your self-concept is made wrong, that part of your body is injured. It would be like injuring your arm. If the injured belief is one that is fundamental to your self-concept, its wrongness could be the equivalent of an injury to your heart—then you could die from it. Why do you think depressed people kill themselves? Because they consider themselves so deeply and profoundly wrong. It's not just metaphorical when we say that at times people "lose heart." They do—conceptual heart.

Being Right

Because being right is what conceptual world survival is all about, human beings are driven to be right every bit as much as they are driven to survive. People will run out of a burning building to preserve their physical body; they will run into a burning building to preserve their rightness. The need to be right is no less serious and fundamental than biology's demand that your heart beat, your lungs breathe, and you get out of the way of an oncoming bus.

This special aspect of human biology explains the behaviors which seem to contradict the principle of survival. No human behavior is contradictory to the principle of survival. The issue is what is required for survival in the conceptual world can contradict what is required for survival in the physical. When that happens you get behavior we call "self-destructive." Someone who kills himself does so because he believes he is wrong. It appears his action is self-destructive. That's inaccurate. His action actually saves him in the conceptual world. Killing someone who is as wrong as he is, is the right thing to do.

In fact, if you think about any self-destructive behavior, you will find it's driven by survival in the conceptual world. Biology can't tell the difference between the physical and conceptual, so being right is equivalent to physical survival. Behaviors may have nothing to do with what is good for the physical body.

It may sound strange that you have to be right. The confusion usually occurs because trying to be right, a universal human motivator, is often confused with an arrogant, pompous interpersonal style. Those with more pleasant interpersonal styles are not seen in this manner. As a result, it can be difficult to see how everyone, including people with pleasant interpersonal styles, are always driven to be right. The key is there are many possible ways in which one can maintain one's rightness.

When in seminars on handling people, I talk about the inherent, unavoidable, absolute human drive to be right, participants invariably thrust their hands into the air and declare they don't have to be right. After I ask them if they consider that statement to be "right," they usually reconsider. In one seminar, a man carried the issue further, declaring the proper way to deal with people was to "completely throw out right and wrong, just make it irrelevant. It doesn't matter."

I asked him if he had been able to do so. He said he had. I told him I didn't think it was possible for anyone to throw out right and wrong, because it's so fundamental to human functioning. He replied it was possible, and he had done it. We continued with me calling him wrong and him saying he was right until the rest of the participants were howling with laughter. They had witnessed the innate human drive to be right demonstrated by someone saying that he didn't have to be right.

Methods of Maintaining Rightness

The mechanisms used for staying right in the conceptual world operate in a manner very similar to the processes for staying alive in the physical world. Physical survival systems operate by manipulating and arranging things in a way that keeps the body alive. Food is digested, air is pulled into and out of our lungs, and we grab a handrail when we stumble on a flight of stairs. Conceptual mechanisms work in the same way. Meanings are altered, beliefs adjusted, and interpretations designed to maintain a state of rightness.

Freud was the first to define conceptual operations that intentionally rearrange objects in the abstract. He named these "defense mechanisms" because he believed they were designed to defend against anxiety and unacceptable impulses. I have often wondered if Freud really knew just how accurate he was. These psychic systems not only defend against anxiety, they protect against actual threats to living.

The inner environment's defense mechanisms are no less powerful, ingrained, and necessary than those of the real world. You can, as Frankl showed, die if they fail. And while "defensiveness" is often thought of as an unpleasant social interaction, it serves a necessary purpose. If someone were being attacked by an alligator you would hardly be critical of them for being defensive. It's more difficult to understand defensiveness in the conceptual realm, because the "threat" isn't obvious. As a result, when someone gets defensive with us, we often feel they are being ridiculous rather than being appropriately protective.

A response to a conceptual threat has many of the same manifestations as a response to a physical one: dilated pupils, tense muscles rapid heart rate, and rapid breathing. Think of yourself during an argument, you have many of the same physical reactions you have if you're in a fight. There is, however, one important difference. The usefulness of tensed muscles, rapid breathing, and dilated pupils is of limited value in concepts. You can't punch-out or wrestle a principle to the ground. As a result, an abstract survival threat energizes not only physical responses, but also conceptual defenses called "upset."

Upset

Upset usually manifests as increases in emotions such as anger, fury, fear, and guilt. These are the mind's version of dilated pupils, rapid heart rate, and tensed muscles. They are the increased energy that prepares the inner self for defensive action. When you're mad, for example, you're more likely to be able to use the tools of maintaining rightness such as emotional words or quickened speech. Similarly, if you're afraid you're less likely to say anything that might further inflame the attack on your rightness. And just as heightened physical reactions take a while to fade after a threat, heightened emotional reactions take time to go away. After you've been mad, frightened, or guilty, it takes a while for your feelings to calm down to normal levels. There is "leftover" energy from the energy fed to your defenses, and it is just like the breathlessness and palpitations you feel after a near-wreck in your car.

Defense Mechanisms

The purpose of upset is to energize defenses against threats. There are a variety of defensive methods that can be activated for use in being right. Each method rearranges perceptions in order to maintain rightness. Each one rearranges them in a slightly different way.

One defense procedure is to simply refuse conceptual identity to sensory data. When done, there can be no threat in one's conceptual world because there's no idea present that's related to the sensory data. Someone using this technique agrees the action exists, but denies that it means anything. Yes, they say, their spouse complains about their drinking, they may be late for work at times, and they tend to feel bad in the mornings but, that doesn't mean they have a drinking problem or are an "alcoholic." All of that data, they insist, doesn't connect to any concept called "alcoholic" or "drinking problem." This denies the sensory data any conceptual existence (alcoholism), hence the term "denial." Denial allows the person to escape a threat to their self-concept. If being an alcoholic is wrong to the person's way of thinking, then it's a dangerous concept, and denial allows an escape. The events in the sensory world are seen simply as events and occurrences, not a pattern that represents a particular meaning.

A man consulted me after his wife left him because of his hitting her. The man would admit that he hit her, but he became incensed if I ever referred to it as "spouse abuse," an "abusive relationship," or to him as a "wife beater." He would angrily tell me those terms were not true of him, that he hit her, but he was not "like that." Even though he admitted he hit her, he denied his behavior meant anything. This kept any threat to his self-concept at bay.

Given that this is the way denial works, it's easy to see why programs such as Alcoholics Anonymous insist people state verbally they are an alcoholic. If a conceptual identity is not consistently connected to the drinking behaviors, the problem will literally cease to exist for the person. Then there is no reason to stop drinking, because the threatening problem no longer exists.

Instead of denying sensory data conceptual identity, another defense mechanism gives conceptual identity to information, but in a way carefully screened according to what will leave rightness intact. Thus, someone who cheats on their taxes may admit they cheated, but cite "good reasons" for it, such as "they pay too much already," and "everybody cheats on them anyway." This enables them to do something generally considered to be wrong, but to maintain their legitimacy.

This is called rationalization. The reasons selected for acknowledgment may be quite accurate, so it's difficult to tell there is anything amiss. The problem isn't that the particular reasons cited are invalid, only that they don't tell the whole story. It's not the use of reasons that makes a rationalization, but rather the presence of an ulterior motive when selecting reasons to consider credible.

Rationalization is similar to the technique used by a trial lawyer to build a case: all evidence that confirms his side is presented and emphasized, while all evidence that contradicts it is ignored, discounted, or discredited. The difference between rationalization as a mechanism for maintaining rightness and the technique for building a court case is the courtroom technique is used intentionally and consciously, while rationalization is used automatically and unconsciously. In fact, as is the case with all defense mechanisms, it's not even experienced as a "mechanism," it's just experienced as "the truth."

Rationalization is largely misunderstood and the term is often used incorrectly. Simply citing reasons for something is not necessarily rationalizing. If you're late for a meeting and you explain why you were late, you may not be rationalizing, simply explaining. Explanations are often useful and necessary. It might be quite helpful for people to know why you were late; maybe they need to know it was not because you didn't care, or because you didn't want to be there. If the reasons you acknowledge for your tardiness are chosen without regard for keeping you right, but instead for their truth value, then you are simply explaining. But if you select only the reasons that keep you right, leaving out others that are also valid but do not make you right, you are rationalizing. You are presenting a partial story, and your secret purpose is to maintain your rightness rather than to tell the truth.

A married, middle-aged man consulted me after his wife found out he was having an affair. He said he believed that he and the woman with whom he was having the affair had "been together in a previous life," and were "supposed" to be together through eternity in their different incarnations. Because of this, he felt there was a "cosmic importance" to the relationship that took precedence over any marital agreements he made in this lifetime. As a result, he felt the affair was justified, felt no guilt, and had no intention to stop it. He explained all of this to me in great detail.

What makes this interpretation a rationalization rather than an explanation is not that it's untrue. Who knows whether it's true? What makes it a rationalization is that there are other aspects of the situation, aspects that challenge his rightness, but that he completely discounts. First, he and his wife were not getting along well. He was angry with her and had already committed several upsetting acts. Hostility was driving his behavior. Second, he was drinking too much and as a result had done several things which involved poor judgment. So chemical abuse was another factor. Third, the woman with whom he was having the affair was also married. His actions were involving other people beyond himself and the woman. Fourth, his behavior involved lying, sneaking around, and covering up, which are hardly behaviors typically representative of someone who feels what they are doing is "fine." Fifth, his actions were causing trouble for his entire family. It was hardly fair for his kids to pay the price for his sneaky behavior.

So even if this were a "cosmically" ordained relationship, it does not invalidate the other factors involved, elements that strongly suggest he mishandled the whole matter. If he felt this was a cosmic relationship, he could still have managed things appropriately, and behaved with integrity and compassion. He could have obtained a separation or divorce before undertaking this affair, and avoided being a liar and sneak about it. His wife was no less deserving of care, compassion and honesty than she was before he found his new cosmic soul mate. That he left out all reasons except the one that kept him right made his explanation a rationalization. He was more interested in maintaining his rightness than in the truth.

Another defense mechanism uses a particular type of comparison known as "projection." In this, one's own rightness is maintained by focusing on other people's wrongness. It is called projection because the wrongness attached to one's behavior is "projected" out into the world rather than being acknowledged in one's own internal world. By doing this, no matter what you do, you don't seem so bad.

In prison, for example, there is a very strict code of morality, of who is good and who is bad, with murderers at the top and child molesters at the bottom. To the murderer, the child molester is wrong. He is bad, he is not the "right" kind of criminal.

Similarly, the alcoholic father of a teenaged patient of mine read a newspaper article about someone who killed some people while driving drunk. He raged to his family, "See, I'm not that bad, I've never done that." This, even though he had been arrested for driving while drunk, got into a serious fight with the arresting officer, regularly passed out on his front lawn, and nearly burned the house down on occasion.

All defense mechanisms, including denial, rationalization, and projection reorganize truth so as to maintain rightness. It may sound like it shouldn't be that way, that truth should be what matters most, but as far as biology is concerned, loyalty to survival comes before loyalty to truth. If someone rushed into your house armed with a machete and threatened to stab and kill you, you would probably be willing to lie to him in order to protect yourself. Similarly, if someone rushed into your conversation armed with a value, principle, or belief that could mortally wound one of your values, principles, or beliefs, is it surprising that you would lie to protect that too?

Have you had the experience of a belief or value that you hold dear, on which you base your actions, shown to be wrong? It's no less traumatic, terrifying, and damaging than a physical injury. It hurts. It can be equivalent to anything from stubbing your toe to getting shot through the heart. Why do you think the Catholic Church threatened Galileo unless he recanted his claim that the earth orbited around the sun? His concept threatened their concepts.

We all defend our rightness naturally and readily, just like we defend our physical bodies. We don't walk alone through dangerous places in the middle of the night, we don't get too close to ledges on high places, and we don't knowingly step into quicksand. We do the same thing in the conceptual world. We don't expose ourselves to situations that are dangerous to our concepts by hanging around with people who think our ideas are wrong. We readily interpret new data as consistent with what we already believe, and we hang around with people who agree with us. When we watch the news, politicians who agree with the concepts we already have are right and those who disagree with them are wrong. We read things that we agree with, and dismiss those that we don't. It's all very natural, very ordinary, just like swatting mosquitoes or staying out of the rain. When a serious threat to our rightness appears, biology diverts energy into escalated defensive reactions. We deny, rationalize, and project.

Personality

In discussing why people are the way they are, this chapter has not focused on the very thing most books about people emphasize: personality characteristics. This is because they are only the patterns of thought, feeling, and behavior our biology uses to maintain our rightness. Although we tend to equate individuals with their personality traits, for the people-handler it is important to realize personality is not what drives human behavior. Personality is just a tool biology uses for survival. It's an effect, not a cause. The cause is survival, the need to be right.

If you deal with people only on the basis of personality traits, you will not have much effectiveness with them. Power lies beyond the traits, in the factors that cause them—survival and being right. Trying to handle people by dealing only with personality traits is like trying to bargain with a company by talking to an assistant rather than the boss. You can't get as much accomplished. Attending to survival and being right, gives you access to "the boss" in human functioning. That's why the name of this book is *Power with People*; power comes from being aware of and able to deal with the issues that drive human behavior, "Being right."

Conclusion

The point of this chapter is to teach you five particulars about human beings you need to know in dealing with them:

1. What drives human beings, like all life forms, is staying alive, seeking pleasure, and avoiding pain. But for human

beings, staying alive includes staying right; it is an essential component of human functioning. As a result, the right/wrong aspect of situations, conversations, words, meanings, and implications, is always present and has a huge impact on what happens between yourself and other people.

2. People react to concepts as strongly as they react to physical occurrences. Someone can have as strong a defensive reaction to a statement or an idea as they would to a mugger or a murderer. The world of the conceptual is as dangerous as the physical world. "Sticks and stones may break my bones but words will never hurt me" is the most precisely inaccurate saying of all time. Words can hurt. Words can kill.

3. People automatically rewrite the world to maintain their rightness. They are driven to do this. It doesn't mean they are happy with how they are or with what they do. It means being right is more important than happiness. Indeed, many people feel being happy is wrong. So in order to understand someone, the primary thing you need to know is how they keep themselves right.

   If you think someone with a poor self-image, low self-esteem, or who is depressed and "down on themselves" is not "being right," you don't understand them. If you don't believe me, try to talk them out of their depression or low self-esteem. They will fight you all the way. They will tell you they are right that they are wrong.

4. You must take people's defensiveness very seriously. To attack the methods by which someone stays right is a very tricky business, and it is important to think long and hard about doing such a thing. Their defense of their rightness is no less intense than their defense of their physical body. People are defensive for good reason; they will not relinquish it or their rightness easily.

5. You can't alter beliefs, values, principles, or interpretations in other people easily, or simply, any more than you can alter their physical body easily. In fact, you can't do it in yourself, either. This is the reason self-help books that state you can be successful by changing your beliefs sound so good and work so badly. They are quite right; changing beliefs does

have powerful results. But so would transplanting Einstein's brain into your head. The process of intentionally achieving a change in beliefs is extremely difficult. It can't be accomplished through repetition of nice words or good thoughts. It involves altering what is right and what is true. Someone else's concepts are not going to dissolve just because you have a reasonable argument against them.

Chapter 3

How People Can Be Such Jerks

How many times have you felt, thought or said, "How can people be such jerks?" How often have you wondered why people seem so capable of being inappropriate, resistive, obstinate, oppositional, demanding, rude, cruel, mean, uncaring, rebellious, insulting, lying, self-centered, obnoxious, arrogant, self-righteous, nasty, hurtful, and hypocritical? How many times have you wondered why you can be entirely appropriate and other people can still be awful to you?

Everyone behaves badly at times, and some people behave badly a great deal of the time. Understanding the reasons behind such behavior is an essential part of learning to handle people effectively. If you're going to deal with them you're going to have to deal with their jerky, difficult behaviors in addition to their pleasant and appropriate ones. You need to understand where jerky behaviors come from.

The usual method used for understanding people who are acting like jerks is to categorize them into different types based on the particular way they act. As I noted in Chapter Two, this approach lacks power because it doesn't access the factors that drive jerky behavior. It also fails to take into account there are many more ways for people to act like jerks than there are possible categories.

Take, for example, a telephone conversation I had with the manager of a repair service with whom I was unhappy. During the conversation I noted the following behaviors from him: distortion of the facts; accusing, demeaning, and patronizing tones of voice; a constantly shifting story; misleading analogies; glossing over discrepancies in his behavior; saying I was wrong for questioning him. How do you fit all of those behaviors into a single category?

Understanding unpleasant, difficult behavior requires knowledge that goes beyond categories of personality traits, and into the underlying forces that create the behavior. For people who are being difficult—for jerks—this means understanding the cause and the purpose of their actions.

Jerks

There are several underlying factors involved in turning people into what we call jerks.

1. Troublesome Behavior

People who are being jerks behave in ways that are a problem for us. They upset or interfere with us. They irritate us. They annoy us. We wonder why they are being so difficult.

There is, essentially, one reason why people generate these kinds of behaviors—defensive reactions. These responses do not produce troublesome and unpleasant behavior by accident. Rather they are designed to make people act badly. They are supposed to turn people into a problem. In addition, the degree to which someone's behavior is a problem is directly proportional to the strength of their defensive reaction. The more intense the defensive reaction, the more problematic the behaviors. The more frequent the defensive reactions, the more frequently the difficult behaviors will occur.

Why are defensive reactions designed this way? Because the whole purpose is to make trouble, to be destructive, disabling, dangerous and fearsome. Defense is biology's weapon against threats to survival. Whether the danger occurs in the sensory world or the conceptual, it is the job of defenses to make enough trouble for the threat that it is prevented from causing harm. Defenses are designed to stop threats, just like barbed wire is designed to stop trespassers.

The world of defensive reactions is a place where logic is turned upside-down. Bad behavior is good, good behavior is bad, and worse behavior is better. The more difficult and destructive a behavior is, the more likely it is to accomplish its purpose of interfering with a threat and thereby preventing it from accomplishing its purpose. If you are being attacked by an alligator you want the sharpest, longest, most dangerous knife you can find to help defend yourself. Similarly, if you are unhappy with the way a relationship is going, you want the most effective behaviors you can get to stop or alter the relationship.

It can be difficult to tell the purpose of jerky behavior is defense, because people who are being a problem often aren't behaving as if they're defending anything. They may not seem scared or threatened. To the contrary, they may seem attacking and assaultive. Their behavior may be rude, aggressive, hostile, demeaning, demanding, or arrogant. They look and sound nasty. So how is such behavior defensive?

The behavior is called defensive because it is designed to ward off a threat. But purpose does not dictate method. Just because something is defensive does not mean it is passive. In fact, passive methods do biology little good, since most threats are active. Active defenses always rely on some kind of attack as their primary method. Biology takes seriously the old saying "the best defense is a good offense."

This principle of attack-as-defense is a common one. The defensive squad on a football team uses attack. The players chase, hit, grab, and knock down the opposing players. Barbed wire cuts, snags, and slices anyone who tries to climb it. The immune system seeks out, engulfs, and kills invading germs. Human behavior also uses attack. If there's a threat in either the sensory or the conceptual world, behavior becomes upsetting in an attempt to interfere with it.

The principle that defense underlies jerky behavior is very important to keep in mind, because effectively dealing with it can require dealing with its protective purpose in addition to or instead of its attacking method. Understanding there are two options for dealing with this behavior can result in a vastly improved ability to manage it.

2. Inappropriate Behavior

If defensive behavior is appropriate to a situation, the person involved does not look like a jerk, but instead looks justified in their behavior. If you were to spray mace into the face of someone who tried to mug you, you have attacked them, but your behavior is proportional to the threat presented. No one, except possibly the mugger, is going to consider you a jerk. But if you were to spray mace into the face of a little old lady who says good morning to you, you would be. Your defensive behavior is out of proportion to the threat present in the situation.

The idea that jerky behavior is defensive while at the same time being out of proportion to the threat present in the situation creates an apparent contradiction. How can defense be the purpose of a behavior when there is no threat? If you are pleasant to someone and they are jerky in response, how can we call their response to you defensive, since you didn't do anything to threaten them?

This apparent contradiction is the result of some peculiarities in the way biology operates. First, remember biology has all of its eggs in the one basket—survival. When it comes to defensive reactions, it takes no chances. As far as biology is concerned, fewer potential problems are created by excessive, as opposed to insufficient, defending. Too much defense can cause trouble, but is less likely to endanger survival. Even though there may be only the most minor provocations in a situation, out-of-proportion defensive behaviors may occur simply because that's the way biology tends to err.

Second, nearly all defenses operate on the principle of one-upmanship. Because a defensive reaction is designed to neutralize a threat, the reaction must not only match the intensity of the threat, it must go one step beyond it. A defense is not designed to produce a stalemate. It automatically ratchets the magnitude up one notch further than the threat in an attempt to overcome it.

This is one reason why the nasty behavior you get back from someone else often seems worse than your own behavior. It isn't necessarily a trick played on you by your perceptions; the other person's response to you may actually be worse. Shoving matches don't stay shoving matches because after I shove you, you shove me a little bit harder than I shoved you. Then I shove you a little bit harder than you shoved me. Pretty soon that's as hard as we can push, so one of us escalates to the next level and takes a swing at the other one. It builds from there into a full-fledged fight.

Another peculiarity of defensive reactions is they are not a finely-honed, pinpoint technology like a laser beam. Defensive behaviors are much more crude. They are like cluster bombs that demolish a large area in order to be certain of effectively hitting the target. The reason for this is biology doesn't just produce defensive behaviors, it shifts the whole organism into a defensive mode. This produces the effect of "generalizing." The behaviors become more general than is warranted by the circumstances. They leak into situations where they don't belong. These are the times when people look like jerks.

Generalization occurs in all animals, not just in humans. My cat, for instance, is normally a docile, playful, affectionate feline. He has a wonderful personality, and wouldn't harm a hair on your head. But one day his territory, the inside of our house, was "violated" by a neighbor cat who snuck in and made a mark. This was a major survival threat to our cat, and he managed to slip out the door and take off after the intruder. While my wife Pam chased him, he cornered the offending cat and produced a variety of threatening "vicious kitty" sounds and gestures. Pam called him to prevent the fight from escalating. He nearly always comes to her call and he did this time, too. Then he promptly bit her—really hard—drawing blood through a ski parka, a sweater, and a turtleneck. Then he turned around to have another go at the neighbor's cat.

Although our cat attacked Pam, he hadn't suddenly decided that he hated her, that she was bad, or that she was a threat to him. He came to her when she called, like he always does, looking calm and pleasant. But he was not in a calm and pleasant state. He was in "attack mode," and that cannot be turned off in the time it took him to walk from the other cat to Pam. Instead, his defensive state continued and the behaviors were directed toward Pam. A neighbor got involved in the situation, too, and was the next target of his attack. It was all because they happened to be there, at the wrong place at the wrong time, when our cat was acting like a jerk.

This means defensive behaviors are not "threat-specific." If you are in the middle of a fight with your spouse and someone calls on the phone, your behavior with them is unlikely to be pleasant even though they have nothing to do with the fight. If you are having a bad day at the office, you may not be a very pleasant lunch companion for a colleague. In both cases your defensive state will cause jerky behavior because it is inappropriate. Your behaviors may have been appropriate to the particular circumstance that triggered them, but they don't automatically turn off just because the situation changes.

Survival reactions not only generalize across circumstances, they also generalize across time. Biology keeps records of threats it has experienced and the responses it used against them. Because biology figures that it successfully dealt with that threat the last time, it stores recognizable aspects of it and the maneuvers used. This template enables it to be efficient and quick in any future defense against that same threat.

This process is standard biological procedure, and is a basic principle of many operations, including the immune system. The immune system is better at fighting off bugs it has encountered previously because it has a record and has stored antibodies against it. In contrast, when a new bug appears, one not seen before, its defense is less efficient because it first has to investigate what kind of defense is needed before it can be efficient in fighting it off.

Because biology stores templates of past threats and the defenses used against them, defensive behavior in the here-and-now does not have to be caused by a present threat. All that needs to happen is for some aspect of a current situation to resemble some aspect of an old threat. But because the present circumstances are different, the defensive behaviors are not appropriate, and the person acts like a jerk.

This type of response is often referred to as "transference" in psychotherapy. In transference a patient uses defensive behaviors he or she learned in the past, against the therapist. The behaviors are out of place because the therapist is not the threat a person in the past was. But some aspect of the situation is reminiscent of the old one, so the patient launches a defensive attack. It's often through understanding these attacks the patient is able to take stock of their defensive maneuvers and to begin to change so they deal with current realities in a way that's more appropriate and effective.

I can almost always identify old, traumatic or difficult situations in people's lives from the defensive behaviors they display during therapy. When a reaction is out of place in the present, there's always a past situation where it was appropriate. They're not difficult to find once you understand this principle.

A father and his teenage son came to see me because they were locked in combat over the cleanliness of the son's room. The teenager kept a messy room, there was no doubt about that, but it drove the father so crazy the situation had erupted into all-out war. Ultimately the wife demanded the father and son work out the conflict, and they ended up in my office.

As we investigated the issue I asked the father what the son's messy room meant to him. This was a question designed to illuminate the threat the father was experiencing in the conceptual world. It didn't take long to find it. The father grew up with a younger brother who had long been favored by their parents. As a child the father had been ordered to pick up after the little brother, and a variety of excuses for the little brother's untidiness were given. The younger brother delighted in his parent-sanctioned power, and he used it to taunt and torment his older brother. This left the older brother powerless and enraged.

As a result of this past experience, when the father saw that his son's room was messy, it snapped into his old template of "mess = manipulation," he had a strong feeling this situation was wrong, and it set off his old defensive reactions. Instead of being a father dealing with a teenage son, the father became an enraged, powerless older brother fighting for recognition, validation, and control with a powerful and malicious little brother. This meant the father took the son's messy room "personally," its messiness was a personal attack on the father, and resulted in the father ranting, raving, sulking, and in general acting like a jerk. The son, being the teenager that he was, delighted in pointing out the jerkiness of the father's behavior. This served to further validate that the current situation fit the old template, and inflamed the father's defensive attacks.

In order to resolve the issue between them, the father had to learn to handle a teenage son and his messy room in ways appropriate to that situation rather than to a situation involving a parent-enabled, manipulative younger brother of thirty years earlier. This required him to learn new behaviors and techniques for dealing with the son.

Because nearly all of us have old traumas and upsets we have defended against in the past, nearly everyone carries with them historical templates and ready-made defenses. If anything in present life resembles one of those templates, we defend, which usually means we attack, even though it may be completely unwarranted by the realities of the present circumstance. This is what I was referring to in Chapter One when I noted that most people-handling behavior comes from old behavior patterns. And people who have had very threatening, difficult, or nasty histories often display the most frequent difficult behavior. A greater portion of their behavior is generated by their old defensive patterns, and the defenses are intense and extreme.

This is why people seem so ready and willing to get upset or nasty with little or no provocation. If something in the present circumstance resembles an old threat, perhaps a tone of voice, the content of a conversation, a smell, or a bodily sensation, a response that is out of proportion may occur. This is when we scratch our heads about someone's behavior and say "What was that all about?" or "What in the world brought that on?"

Even innocent actions can trigger these old defensive reactions. If you tell a group of people to do something, even if you are the boss and your job is to tell them what to do, someone in the group is likely to have had controlling, demanding, unreasonable parents, against whom they developed defensive reactions. As a result, they hear your instructions as a threat instead of an appropriate instruction. Instead of cooperation in accomplishing the task, you get defensive behavior, and they begin to cause trouble.

Maybe they're late getting their part of the task done, or they complain and stir up bad feelings in themselves and others. Maybe they drive you crazy with questions about their part, even "forget" or "misunderstand" some aspect of it and so ruin it. In any case, because their behavior is defensive, it will be upsetting, resistive, or destructive.

However, there are also circumstances where seemingly "innocent" behaviors that should not provoke a defensive response are not so innocent after all, and the defensive reaction actually fits the situation. This frequently happens with married couples. Often one of the partners repeatedly does small things that drives the other one crazy, and despite the best efforts of the other partner the behaviors continue. One day the other partner "snaps" and has a tirade, a full-blown defensive attack.

This behavior looks out of proportion to the immediate circumstance, because the other partner has done something quite small at that moment. But what is difficult to see is the "survival threat" was in the conceptual realm and accumulated over time. So there was a proportional threat that triggered the response, it was just very difficult to see because it was spread out over time.

It's not just with married couples this happens. Many times threats really are present in a situation but are difficult to see. A family consulted me for counseling, and their young teenage son was clearly unhappy to be in the session. As the session progressed he began to generate increasingly problematic behaviors. First, he refused to talk or to answer questions. Then he began to spin around wildly in one of my swivel chairs. After that he started whispering to his mother that he wanted to leave. Next, he increased the volume and speed of his request to leave until it was one long, loud, continuous shout over which the adults had to talk. Finally, he grabbed his mother's purse and began flinging its contents around my office; credit cards went flying, combs and brushes scattered here and there, and money floated through the air.

To his humiliated and helpless family, the kid's obnoxious behavior was making him a total jerk. They were embarrassed, exasperated, and angry. They could see no reason for his disruptive behavior. Nobody was being mean to him, he wasn't going to get a shot, he wasn't going to get locked up, he wasn't going to be injured. There was no obvious danger to him. His behavior seemed inappropriate and out of place.

But he wasn't being a jerk in my eyes. After only a few minutes I knew he was responding to a real, present, very dangerous threat: me. He was terrified I was going to be able to return to his parents some of the power they had abdicated to him. If that happened, he would no longer be able to get his way so easily, and his control in the family would become limited. He had grown up in an extremely chaotic household, had come to feel the need to control everything, and as a result was extremely reluctant to give up any control. Having his family meet with me was a terrible threat to him. His disruptive behavior was a defense against my being able to hurt him. So his behavior was proportional to the very real threat no one else could perceive. Because I could see this, I was not upset by his behavior at all. The family couldn't understand why I could smile at his behavior and even make light of it.

3. Self-Righteousness

Because defensive escalations almost always involve an escalation in "being right," defensive reactions generally involve steadily increasing attempts to be right. It doesn't take long for such escalations to become self-righteousness. You've probably noticed one of the prominent characteristics of people who are being jerks is they're extremely self-righteous. That's one of the very behaviors that makes them difficult. This comes from a high level of energy being put into defending themselves, which involves intensely defending their rightness.

This is another reason people who act like jerks seem attacking rather than "threatened." Self-righteousness is designed to create invulnerability especially to threats in the conceptual world-threats of "being wrong." People having a defensive reaction that makes them act like a jerk typically don't experience a situation as threatening. Instead, they sense it as one in which something is wrong and needs to be corrected. They are doing the "right" thing by crusading to amend it.

Anything perceived as being wrong is a threat in the conceptual world, even if it's not something done directly to you. It's like a killer on the loose; he's a danger that needs to be stopped even if he isn't currently on your doorstep. Because biology goes all-out for survival, anything that is wrong triggers defensive reactions. So people have defensive reactions even though they aren't the ones involved in the issue. In fact, many people experience defensive reactions watching the news, or when reading the editorial page of the newspaper. Letters to the editor are almost always highly charged conceptual-world defensive attacks, and self-righteous terms such as "appalled," "outraged," and "shocked" are standard.

In fact, the ability of concepts to provoke defensive reactions is what makes daytime television talk-shows popular and their hosts celebrities. They effectively stir up defensive reactions in people. Notice that the people appearing on the show aren't directly threatening the audience at all. They're just discussing some topic. And yet, audience members become extremely angry, self-righteous, and attacking. Why? Why should they care? They care because they still experience a threat when a person is propagating some concept in opposition to a concept they hold. As a result, they feel this is a wrong, a danger in the conceptual world that must be fought against. It is fought against with self-righteousness.

This means the guy who honks and yells at you at the stoplight doesn't see you as a threat, he sees you as wrong. But that *is* the threat. If you were to say to him, "What's threatening you about my not immediately starting to move after the light turned green?" He would respond, "I'm not threatened by anything, you moron. You're just an idiot for not moving!"

4. Unproductive Behavior

As survival reactions escalate, they require increasing amounts of energy. Because the human body and psyche only have so much energy available, energy has to be removed from other tasks to support the defensive behaviors. This means someone who is busy being defensive can't engage in other activities. They start to lose their ability to cooperate, think, reason, and work. If you're working with someone on a project and their survival reactions get stirred up, they're not going to be an effective partner. They will get distracted from the task at hand in order to attend to the threat, maintain their rightness, and defend.

Diversion of energy is often an indication something is wrong in any situation. If the energy present is low, it's likely getting drained off, probably in a defensive reaction of some sort. For example, if you are in a meeting where for no apparent reason there is boredom or emotional "flatness," there is probably a defensive reaction going on that is draining energy. I consulted with an organization where the staff was terrifically defensive with the administration. In my meetings with them, the energy was so low that sometimes I had to struggle to stay awake.

This is also why there is generally such a marked increase in the energy level of people and organizations who resolve old issues. Energy is no longer being diverted to defenses. But until that happens, defensive reactions can result in diminishing cooperation, communications breaking down, projects getting stalled, and people not being able to work together or focus on the task at hand.

5. Unreasonable Behavior

"Jerks" are people who are being unreasonable. They aren't interested in logic, they are interested in being right. As a result, they also can't reason about their own behavior. They can't see what they are doing is defending instead of being rational. They don't see that their behavior is inappropriate and problematic. They only see that their behavior is "right."

One of the primary signs of emotional health is the ability to productively self-examine. This means the ability to examine one's own behavior in such a way as to see how to alter it to produce better outcomes. This talent always requires a willingness to see where one is wrong, where one is not doing as well as one could, and how one can improve. As you already know, that by itself is not a particularly easy thing for humans to do, and when someone is in the midst of a defensive reaction it becomes virtually impossible. A survival reaction inherently involves escalating one's own rightness; becoming self-righteous. The ability to see one's possible wrongness at those times diminishes in direct proportion.

If you confront someone who is acting like a jerk about their behavior or question their motives, logic, or intentions, you are not likely to get a response where they acknowledge that you might be right, that they might be behaving inappropriately. Instead, you will probably get an escalation of their defensive behavior, a further escalation of their rightness. They may change tactics, like going from arguing to sarcasm ("Gee, I guess you are right. How did I get to be so lucky as to know someone as smart as you are. Lucky me!") or retreat into angry, stony silence, but what they probably will not do is begin to examine themselves. During their defensive reaction, disagreement or contradictory information isn't up for consideration or for reasoning. They see you as just being wrong.

The escalated rightness involved in defending also produces the irony that people who do the worst things are often the most self-righteous and haughty. Earlier I discussed the system of morality in prison, with murderers being on the top and child molesters on the bottom of the hierarchy. It goes further, though. Prisons have an incredibly rigid system of morality among the prisoners. There are specific and intense rules about what is right and what is wrong. The reason for this is criminals' psyches are always on defensive alert, always in danger of being wrong because of the crimes they committed. They have a perpetual survival reaction going on. If some new threat appears, they escalate quickly and strongly, with little provocation.

This is also the process behind the political candidate who appears at the press conference to self-righteously, "categorically deny the scurrilous, scandalous, slanderous, politically motivated, totally false lies and allegations" the day before he agrees to a plea-bargain, accepting a deal without having to admit wrongdoing. What happens is the stuff he did wrong is in the background of his mind, keeping his defensive reactions in high gear. He comes on with great self-righteousness while behind the scenes he cuts a deal to save himself from the effects of his own wrongdoing. So you can see the logic behind the idea of people who are most guilty often proclaim their innocence the loudest. Or, as Shakespeare said, "She doth protest too much, methinks."

I was consulting with an insurance company about people who called to complain or inquire about a claim or some other issue. We determined that the ones who were the most nasty when they called were almost always the ones who had done something wrong themselves; they had tried to cheat the company, had not paid their part of the bill or had been late in a payment. It's the same principle—when someone's defensive behaviors are already operating at a high level, anything else produces high escalation, resulting in haughty self-righteousness.

I knew a man who said he wanted to learn how to "better communicate" with people. When that vague conceptual request was further defined, he said his wife "misunderstood" him and he wanted to know how to correct her misperceptions. Her misunderstanding was that she perceived him to be a difficult person to get along with, and he wanted to be able to communicate to her that he was not. He was extremely self-righteous in his denials that he was difficult to get along with. He went on and on about how he wasn't difficult to get along with at all, how he couldn't imagine how she could think that, how it wasn't true and it hurt his feelings. He was upset by it. She was being crazy. He wasn't difficult at all, and so on. Finally, he was asked if anyone else in his life thought he was difficult to get along with. The man paused for a minute and said, "Well, yes, my boss does." Anyone else? "Well, yes, my kids do, too."

In fact, everyone in his life did! He was difficult to get along with for nearly everyone. A perfect example of how someone who is doing things wrong often gets self-righteous and defensive; he makes others wrong, because of the escalation in defensive reactions caused by his own wrongdoing.

6. Limited Behaviors

People often behave badly because they're unable to generate alternate behaviors that might be more appropriate to a situation. This occurs because many people have a limited number of behaviors available to them to deal with people. Defensive reactions also diminish behavioral options because they tend to produce only the same behaviors used in situations in the past. There's often little real "thinking" that occurs in conjunction with them, and little chance for behavioral flexibility. During defensive reactions people can lose their ability to alter their behavior, and they get stuck in behavior patterns that don't work and are inappropriate.

In addition, if people have only a few behaviors available, biology is going to see to it the ones they do have are highly effective as a means of defense. That means they're probably going to be some of the more difficult and unpleasant behaviors, those that can be used as effective defenses; which means they will be on the more troublesome end of the spectrum. It would be like sending an army into a war and having to decide between sending them in with nuclear weapons or no weapons at all. If existence itself were at stake, as it always is for biology, you go for the big guns.

Randolph came to see me because he was nearly forty years old and he could not, in his words, "get his life in gear." He had never married, had no relationship, was in an uncomfortable situation with a roommate he did not get along with, and in an unpleasant, high-pressure, but dead-end job. He didn't like much about his life, other than watching movies on his VCR.

But Randolph did know how to do one thing very, very well. He knew how to complain. He came to me complaining about his roommate, his aging parents, his job, his life, his finances, and even his own behavior. He complained and complained. Predictably, it didn't take him long before he also started griping about therapy and about me, too. Week after week he would come in whining about his life, that therapy was disappointing him, or that it wasn't helping him. He complained I wasn't doing my job, that the whole thing was stupid, and he didn't know if he should come back.

It may seem as though Randolph didn't want to get better, but that wasn't the case at all. He didn't know how to get better because the only behavior he had for dealing with anything was complaining. He complained so much he drove everyone crazy. He whined, he bitched, and he griped constantly. He was an expert. When I challenged him, it set off more defenses, he complained harder and harder. It was the only behavior he seemed able to generate. As a result, he was widely considered by his colleagues and acquaintances to be an absolute jerk.

Everyone, of course, is defensive from time to time and fits these categories that result in their acting like a jerk. In fact, it's often this very thing that makes for difficulties in relationships. When I do workshops or courses, there's an entire section called "What Kind of Jerk Am I" so people can start to see how they behave when their survival wiring is set off. Pam occasionally does this course with me, and we sing "What Kind of Jerk Am I" to the tune of "What Kind of Fool Am I" to introduce that section of the course.

Why Jerks Are Difficult for You

Just because someone is acting like a jerk doesn't mean they're going to be difficult for you to handle. If you perceive someone's defensive behavior to be appropriate to the level of threat they're experiencing, you will not consider them to be a jerk at all. This was the case for me with the young teenage boy who was being disruptive during my session with his family. I knew I was a threat to his power, so to me his behavior made sense. It still wasn't very pleasant, but it didn't upset me or get in my way of dealing with him.

If you don't think someone's response is proportional to a present threat, you're going to think they are a jerk. But that still doesn't mean you're going to have trouble dealing with them or find them upsetting. Some types of jerky behavior are not going to bother you and others are going to drive you up the wall. Why? Because jerks are only a problem for you when they set off your defensive reactions, when they involve something that you consider to be wrong.

There are some behaviors that are almost universally threatening to survival, such as someone pointing a gun at your head, and in these cases, unless staying alive is not important, they are likely to set off just about anyone's survival wiring, including yours. But in less dramatic examples, and especially in the world of concepts, people will only seem bad or wrong to you to the degree they threaten something important in your conceptual world. If you don't value kindness or sociability, rudeness will probably not push your survival buttons, and you won't have much difficulty with rude people. But if you value honesty, you will have a survival reaction to lying, and will find liars to be jerks. If you value logic, you will find irrationality jerky. And so on. Those jerks who push your survival buttons are going to be the jerks who you have trouble with.

I had a patient who spent a good six months trying to upset me. He had a good deal to hide, so he lived his life manipulating people to protect himself. His technique was usually to flatter to get someone absorbed in their own rightness, or to attack and get someone into their own wrongness. This made the other person the issue, and he was off the hook. He had been able to do this with many therapists, and as a result no therapist had been effective with him. His problems continued to worsen.

To this man's horror, however, he discovered I was not vulnerable to his manipulations. He could hardly believe it, but no matter what he tried to do he couldn't find a way to get me involved in the issue of my own rightness or wrongness. He couldn't get me focused on myself rather than on him. This threatened him terribly because it kept him as the focus of the sessions, and threatened to expose him. He didn't know what to do about it.

Of course, he escalated. He tried everything he could think of to upset me. He stared at me, used sarcastic and harsh tones of voice, implied I was not doing my job, refused to talk, accused me of withholding from him, demanded I do things his way, threatened to quit, complained that I was manipulative, and became highly indignant and self-righteous. I sat impassively through it all, being as direct and straight as possible, interpreting to him what he was trying to do, and refusing to focus on myself. Finally, in desperation, he had a full-blown temper tantrum and insulted me every way he could think of. He called me names, he accused me of being haughty, and told me he frequently reminded himself of my faults and imperfections. He called me stupid. He called me little. He called me ugly. He called me socially inept.

Then he paused, just for an instant, to see if it had worked. For the briefest of moments I could see a desperate, inquiring look pass across his eyes to see if this time he was able to throw me off, to get me defensive.

If his concepts (stupid, little, ugly, and socially inept) had made me doubt my rightness, or if his rude behavior had seemed wrong to me, I would have found myself dealing with him out of my defenses rather than out of what was good treatment for him. If I had a defensive reaction take over, if I had been offended, hurt, angered or outraged, I would have found myself being the issue, not him. I would have lost my power, and I would have been unable to deal effectively with him. That was, of course, exactly what he wanted.

As it was, I knew what was going on. I knew the defensive purpose of his behavior, I knew why he was threatened, and I didn't have a survival reaction at all. What he said didn't bother me in the least. In fact, the hardest thing for me was to keep from laughing. I waited a moment and then asked him if saying those things helped him to feel better. That left him speechless.

Make no mistake. Like everyone else, I have beliefs, values, principles, and concepts that make me vulnerable. I have my own tendencies to defensive reactions. But this particular man was never able to find any of them, and that's what allowed me to continue to be effective. In fact, this is what all helping professions are based on. Good professionals earn their living by keeping their own defenses from contaminating situations. This keeps their vision clear and that's what they're paid for. Therapists and consultants are outsiders because it is easier to diminish the likelihood of defensive behaviors. That's also why people tend to be more pleasant with strangers than with the important people in their lives. There is less need for defensive reactions with people we don't know well, because we are at less risk with them.

While defensive reactions are not, in reality, 100% eliminated from any situation, the person who has the fewest has the most effectiveness. I call it, "keeping your life out of the room." When a professional's defenses do get stirred up, as they will from time to time, a responsible therapist or consultant gets a consult on the case, takes a trip to their own therapist, or refers the case to someone else.

What can you do about your defensive reactions with people in order to help you be more effective? Treatment or training are required in order to diminish the occurrence of defensive reactions. You can't get that from a book. But there is a short-cut.

As far as people-handling goes, the disabling element of defensive reactions is the constriction in behavioral options for handling people it produces. By learning a wider set of people-handling behaviors, this constriction is diminished.

The problem in handling people is behavioral constriction. Increased options is the solution. That is what this book is designed to present.

Part II

Principles

Chapter 4

The Basic Principles of People-handling

This chapter begins the shift from discussing fundamental information to the practical aspects of people-handling. This and the next chapter present the principles that underlie the techniques for effective people-handling.

1. You Are Always Handling People

As was mentioned in Chapter One, you do not have the option of not handling people. Your behavior automatically alters to influence and affect others. This happens whether or not you know it, or like it. Whether or not you think you should, or you are successful at it. The only choice you have is whether or not you want to be conscious and intentional about the way you handle people.

There are benefits to being conscious and intentional about the way you handle people. It gives you more options, possibilities, and methods. This means that you won't get as stuck when dealing with people you're having trouble with. You'll be more effective in a wider variety of situations with a wider variety of people, have a better chance of creating and maintaining good relationships, and see potential trouble with people, and stop it before it starts.

Nevertheless, being conscious about people-handling has some drawbacks. It requires increased thought, effort, and work on your part. It means you have to do some things or talk in ways you are unaccustomed to, that at times don't feel "natural," or might be somewhat uncomfortable for you.

You'll have to decide for yourself whether you want to be conscious about your people-handling. If you do, the principles and techniques in the rest of the book are designed to be helpful to you.

2. Purpose Drives All People-handling

Whatever it is you're trying to accomplish is the most basic, essential, powerful force in determining how you handle someone. Purpose determines what behaviors are appropriate and creates the standard against which you evaluate your dealings with someone.

A common mistake about people-handling is that it is, or should be, driven by other people's personality characteristics. While personality characteristics always have to be taken into account in dealing with people, they're not the fundamental driving force. Purpose is.

If other people's personality style, rather than your purpose, were the driving force behind people-handling you would treat the same person the same way under all circumstances. You'd deal with your child the same way if they were about to knock over your Ming vase as you would if they had just fallen and skinned their knee. You'd deal with your spouse the same way if you were feeling amorous as you would if you were furious with them. You'd deal with a customer the same way if they were buying something from you or if they were stealing something from you.

You can see how silly that would be. So the single most important factor in being effective is knowing what it is that you're trying to accomplish. You need to know why you're dealing with this person. What is the point? What is it you want to have happen? What is your short-term, long-term, and overall purpose? The answers to questions like these are the first and most basic steps in successfully handling people.

Determining your purpose with people is often more difficult than it might seem. It's easy to get what you're doing mixed up with why you're doing it. For example, someone might say their purpose is to "share their feelings." That's not a purpose. It's a method, the way they are trying to accomplish their purpose. Their purpose is whatever it is they hope to accomplish by "sharing their feelings." What is that designed to produce? Do they want to feel better, give information, change someone? The purpose is the point and determines the method. In fact, in my talks I often use the formula of Purpose + Personality = Power. Purpose always comes first in the equation.

Unfortunately, many people have the notion that there are inherently "right" and "wrong" ways to deal with people no matter what your purpose is. People often think you should always be "honest," or "sharing," or "assertive," or "tactful," or something of the sort. The problem is that the "goodness" or "badness" of any particular method of handling people can only be judged in relation to the purpose it's designed to accomplish. Something that sounds good, like expressing your feelings, is not always good. Even if you were furious with a customer you might not express your feelings with him, because to do so could be to lose his business. In that instance "expressing your feelings" could be bad. In addition, something that seems bad, like yelling, is not always bad. You may very well yell at your child if they are about to run into the street in front of a car.

This principle is true even for "extreme" people-handling behaviors such as violence. In general, we consider violence to be bad. Often it is. As a parent, for example, your goal is to raise happy, healthy, and well-functioning kids. Physical violence is considered inappropriate to that purpose. It's wrong, and could be called child abuse. But if you're a police officer and you catch someone in the act of assaulting an innocent person, physical violence is not inappropriate to your purpose. In fact, not being violent, if violence is required to stop the assault, would be wrong. It could be called dereliction of duty. So even violence, something that most of the time most of us consider to be wrong, can only be judged as good or bad on the basis of its purpose.

Practically speaking, the only thing that's really unhealthy in dealing with people is intending to accomplish one purpose while doing things that cause something else, often something undesirable, to happen. If you're a parent who physically abuses your child, it's unhealthy because it's inconsistent with the purpose of a parent to nurture and assist children. If you're a police officer and you stand idly by during an assault, it's unhealthy because it's inconsistent with your purpose as a police officer. Behaving in a manner inconsistent with your purpose is what mental health professionals call things like "neurotic" and "self-defeating."

In this discussion I am talking exclusively about positive, good, or "constructive" purposes. Certainly there are bad purposes, where people intend to cause destruction and harm. I don't consider such purposes to be included in the category of effective people-handling. People-handling is only about accomplishing purposes that are constructive, and have to do with success and happiness. It is certainly effective people-handling to be able to prevent someone else from accomplishing destructive purposes, but learning to accomplish destructive purposes is absolutely excluded from the topic called "people-handling."

For people-handling, the most important point about the quality of purpose is that human beings often have mixed motives in the things they do. One of the most challenging things about learning new ways to be effective in dealing with people is you can discover you have mixed motives, you want to accomplish both constructive and destructive things. You may be surprised to learn you're reluctant to use new, effective methods, because part of you doesn't want to stop making trouble. This can be shocking to see in oneself because most of the time we keep such motives hidden.

I attended a tennis match where a half-drunk man sitting in front of me had shouted out a couple of nasty, sexist comments during breaks in the action. It upset everyone around him, myself included. His wife got up and left. I finally decided to do something that would shut down his behavior, which I successfully did, and he quit. A little while later I heard him whisper to a companion that he wanted to say just one more thing before the match ended, "Just to show the guy behind him." He was well aware his purpose was to upset me.

But usually people are not so honest with themselves about their destructive motives. I've seen spouses stay married, employees stay in jobs, and kids continue to live with their parents, all to make the other people miserable. They aren't aware of the destructive part of their purpose. They don't think they're out to make trouble. Instead, they blame the results on a failure to know what to do. They complain they are "trying" to make things work out well and they "just can't seem to be able to do it."

By learning how to be effective in people-handling, you lose your ability to excuse your own troublemaking behavior by complaining you don't know what to do. You will have to honestly examine why you might find yourself reluctant to do the things that have a higher probability of working than what you were doing before. This will require you to acknowledge and deal with any mixed or destructive motives you might find in yourself.

3. People-handling Is Judged by its Results

Although this principle may sound obvious, when it comes to dealing with people it's rarely applied. People are frequently ineffective in their dealings with others because they don't judge their people-handling by the results that are produced. Instead, they judge it by whether they're doing what they think they should be doing or what they want to be doing. If these methods do not achieve the results they desire, they blame the other people and maintain their rightness by rationalizing and projecting.

There's nothing wrong with handling people by using behaviors you think you should use or you want to use. All you have to do is be willing to accept the results those behaviors produce. You're free to yell and scream at your spouse or your boss or your children whenever you feel like it, as long as you are prepared to deal with the results that your yelling and screaming will produce. A problem only occurs if you want to produce a particular result, but the way that you want to do it won't work. That means the way you want to act and the result you want to produce are incompatible. This is what often happens when parents want to produce a "close" relationship with their children, but they also want to be harsh and critical whenever they like. Or when salespeople don't want to cater to their customers but still want to keep their business.

I have had countless people say to me, "Why shouldn't I be able to 'express my feelings'?" The implication is that "expressing your feelings" is good and therefore should not produce bad results. But it doesn't work like that. You can express your feelings any time and place you want, but you will get whatever results expressing your feelings produces in that situation. In some situations it will probably not produce the results you want. Then you have to decide whether you want your results or you want to be able to express your feelings. Doing it either way is fine, but many times you can't have both.

If you pay attention to results, you find a feedback loop exists between people-handling methods and the results they produce. This is a very powerful aid in handling people effectively. It gives you ongoing feedback about how your efforts are going. This allows you to alter the things you are doing that are not working, and continue the things that are working. In this respect, handling people is no different from anything else in life. Every system uses feedback loops in order to function. When you type, the letter that appears on the paper is feedback for your hands. When you ride a bicycle, feedback from your balance communicates how you should lean. Not using results to monitor your people-handling is like riding a bicycle while ignoring the information your balance is registering.

Amazingly, when it comes to people-handling, people often ignore the feedback in favor of their preconceived notions about how people should be handled or how they want to handle other people. While shopping for a new car I stopped into a dealership to look at a particular car I thought I might be interested in. Although the salesman told me they didn't have the specific version I wanted, I agreed to drive a different model so that I could try out that particular make of car. After our drive, the salesman took me into his office and, without further conversation, completed a sales contract, pushed it across the desk at me, and said cheerfully, "Just sign here, and you'll be all set."

While he didn't define the concept "all set," I had no doubt it involved buying the car. Surprised at his apparent presumptuousness, I reminded him I had already told him I was in the "looking" stage, that the car he showed me was not the one I was looking for, that I never expressed any interest in buying that car, that I didn't want to buy it, and that I was not about to sign anything.

At that point the salesman excused himself and returned with his sales manager, who asked me to come into the hall to speak to me "confidentially."

"This guy," he said, pointing toward the salesman's office, "is new. I'd really like to see him get a good sale under his belt. I know this car doesn't have the equipment you want, but whether you want it or not, it's the best equipment. It's a great car and I know you'd really like it."

What was happening was I was being tag-teamed by a salesman and his manager, working in the way that they thought they were "supposed" to work with reluctant prospects. But had either of them paid any attention at all to the results they were producing they would have seen that instead of an increased chance of making a sale, they were producing steadily increasing resistance, resentment, and anger. Their method may have worked with some prospects, but not with me. They weren't paying any attention to the signs. And the signs were not subtle.

Irritated and annoyed, I interrupted the manager. I reminded him of my original statements regarding the particular car I wanted and my agreement to drive the other car simply to see how the model line drove. I told him I didn't appreciate his guilt-induction approach in the least, that he was apparently paying no attention to me or to what I had been saying, that our conversation was over, and I would never be his customer. I left, and ultimately bought a car at another dealership.

The salesman and manager were paying more attention to what was going on in their heads than the results they were producing with me. Initially, there was a very good chance that, handled properly, I would have been willing to return to the dealership and that salesman to buy the car I was interested in when they obtained one. In fact, they could have handled it so I would have gladly come back. But by not paying attention to their results, to how I was reacting and what I was saying, they lost a customer for life.

Ignoring results is not the only problem people have with judging their people-handling based on the results it produces. Another difficulty is people resist the whole idea of focusing on results because they confuse it with the idea that "the ends justify the means." People think that by focusing on results rather than on "shoulds" or "wants," they are likely to become a Machiavellian manipulator, intent on doing anything necessary to produce the results they want. They are afraid this principle is a license to lie, cheat, steal, coerce, and mistreat people.

But nothing could be further from the truth. In fact, this logic is exactly backwards. In order to become Machiavellian manipulators, where the ends justify the means and any technique for handling people is justified no matter how destructive, people must actually disregard results. The only reason the car salesman and his manager could treat me with their heavy-handed, guilt-inducing approach was they ignored their results. Had they been paying attention to the behaviors being produced, they would have had to alter what they were doing. The only reason spouses can mistreat each other, people in business can mistreat customers, or virtually anyone can mistreat anyone else is they don't pay attention to the results they produce.

The reason for this is, in dealing with people, no result is achieved in isolation. Many other outcomes, some just as powerful, are produced in addition to the result that you desire. If you don't attend to these, you can completely invalidate the accomplishment of your primary purpose. You can certainly get a lot of money by robbing a bank. But if you do, you also get to spend the rest of your life as a fugitive. If you want to get someone to marry you, you are free to get them by lying and pretension, but you also get the result of either spending your life maintaining the show, or suffering the bad consequences when you give up the disguise. You're free to get productivity-at-all-cost in your business, but you'll also "get" the result of low morale, high turnover, high rates of error, and frequent sick days.

Perhaps the most dramatic example of this principle is demonstrated by criminals spending their life in prison. They present highly persuasive reasons why it's wrong that they're in prison: they did not get a fair trial, they had been misunderstood, what they did wasn't their fault. By the time you finish a conversation with them, you start to believe they shouldn't be in prison. But all of this overlooks one thing; they are in prison. Whatever it is they did, whether it was right or wrong, it got them sent to prison. That was the result. Do they really need any more facts than that to get the point?

Focusing on results means paying attention to what you are producing. It means paying attention to everything. Open your ears and hear, open your eyes and see. Are the results productive and good? Or are other effects occurring? Forget about the "should's" and "should not's." Look and listen to what's happening.

The truth is you are free to handle people any way you like. You are free, like the car salesman and his manager, to try to coerce someone into doing what you want. You are free to get money by robbing a bank. You are free to handle your spouse with hostile and demeaning behavior. But you will have to live with the results you produce. All the results. And when you start judging your people-handling by the results it produces instead of some notion in your head, you're likely to find your results with people, as well as in your life, improve dramatically.

4. Effective People-handling Obeys "Human Nature"

Francis Bacon is credited with having said, "Nature, to be commanded, must be obeyed." This paradoxical saying reveals an important truth. In order to produce results in any area you have to do things in accordance with the underlying principles that govern that area. You can't get good results by trying to violate the basic laws of reality. In people-handling we say something similar, "Human nature, to be commanded, must be obeyed."

In order to produce good results with people, one has to follow the rules that govern how people are wired. Most people don't do that. They resist human nature. If you repeatedly tried to violate physical laws, you'd look pretty stupid. If, over and over, you held out dinner plates, let them go, watched them smash on the floor, and said, "Damn that gravity, it shouldn't operate like that. I shouldn't have to hold onto these plates to keep them from falling if I don't want to! It's not right!" there would be plenty of evidence to commit you.

But it's easy to avoid looking stupid while repeatedly violating the laws governing human nature. All you have to do is to keep doing things that won't work and then blame the other person for your failure to achieve results. If you do this, you can yell at your kids over and over without ever producing a desirable result, and never look stupid as long as you declare your kids to be wrong. You can say, "They should change! They shouldn't keep doing what they're doing after they hear what I have to say!" Do you see how this sounds much more logical and rational than declaring that gravity is wrong?

After all, people can change, while gravity can't, so it doesn't sound as stupid to declare them wrong as it does to declare gravity wrong. In fact, if you're really good at it, you can probably get lots of other people to solemnly shake their heads in agreement with you and to pity you for your plight at having such wrong children.

Of course, just like the prisoners you're overlooking one fact; the kids are not changing as a result of your yelling. Maybe they should change, but they're not. Your yelling is failing to produce the results you want. It's no different from wanting gravity not to be gravity.

The manager of a company I was working with to increase their productivity by improving their interpersonal effectiveness, confided in me he felt "left out" in his company. Some of his associates had begun to achieve some status and recognition. This man didn't achieve the acclaim they did, even though he, too, was bright, competitive, and fully capable and competent in his work. In order to get recognition in his company, he complained, you had to "toot your own horn" to others, and "display your achievements." He was not, he assured me, going to "play that game."

That's absolutely fine, but if he didn't play that game, he wouldn't get the results he wanted. Period. What he derisively called playing the game was the way his company worked regarding recognition. He either did that and got recognition, or he didn't and got no recognition. He didn't want the company to work according to that principle. He didn't want to have to use those rules to get what he wanted. He wanted the company to work according to the principles he liked.

That's how it is in dealing with people, too. You can go along with the principles that govern their functioning and get the results or not go along with the principles and not get the results. But you can't have it both ways, because the way it works was not determined by you. The way human beings operate is governed by principles that are every bit as solid as those governing the physical world. People can change, just like the physical world can change. But they change only according to the things that change them, and those might or might not be the things that you think "should" change them.

I talked about some of the rules governing human beings back in Chapter Two. I talked about how they are governed by survival wiring and behaviors that are wired into that system. In truth, people's survival wiring is consistent with their history and past experience. So despite our often not liking how people work, they work right. They work the way that is appropriate to their history, and is accurate to what they needed to do in order to survive. For you to get good results with people you are going to have to work with the way they work, not try to violate it or act as if it doesn't exist.

Let me personally acknowledge that people work the way they work and not the way we think they should work. I'm sorry if you think good sense and reason should drive people, not idiosyncratically formed survival wiring and an endless drive to be right. I'm sorry if you feel people should be more caring, altruistic, reasonable, or more understanding than they are. I'm sorry if you feel they should understand you rather than you having to understand them. I'm sorry if your spouse is touchy, your boss is demanding, your kids push limits, and you have to deal with them the way they are. I'm sorry if it is difficult and a hassle to figure out how to deal with people in such a manner as to make things work for both you and for them because people are so imperfect, damaged, and difficult. I'm sorry if, in order to achieve your goals with people, you have to do things that you don't think you should have to do because of the way people are. I'm sorry you are the one who has to accept others the way they already work if you want to produce good results with them in your life.

I'm also sorry if you think gravity should pull up, that there should be eight days in the week, that you should be able to walk in the rain without getting wet, and clouds should be clear. It doesn't matter what you think about people or about the physical world, they both still work the way they work, and if you are going to get good results with either one you are going to have to work with them according to the way they are right now.

Does that mean you should never try to change anyone or anything they do? Of course not. It just means the ways you go about changing them, and the pitfalls present in trying to change someone, are the way they are and work the way they work. Your alternative to dealing with people as they are is to fail to get your results. You can do that if you like, but the self-righteousness you produce is a poor consolation prize. If you do something and someone reacts badly, it doesn't matter whether or not their reaction is crazy, touchy, or silly. That is their reaction, and you have to deal with it. Period.

5. Method Is Different from Purpose

I have mentioned this principle several times already, but because it is so important I want to highlight it. Of all of the reasons for ineffectiveness in dealing with people, failure to understand this principle is perhaps the most common one. How you go about trying to accomplish something with someone is different from what you are trying to accomplish. Because most of the time people make no distinction between the "what" and the "how," they come to think one purpose has only one way it can be accomplished. As a result, they quickly get stuck and frustrated.

Not only are there different methods for achieving different purposes, there are many different methods that can be applied to achieve one purpose. This is fortunate, because people's behavior is too unpredictable and changeable for there to be one method that always accomplishes one purpose. While your purpose may remain the same, your method may vary a great deal.

Think of dealing with people as being similar to going on a trip. You might expect to get to your destination by driving down a particular street, but you might unexpectedly discover a tree has fallen across the street, blocking your path. As a result, the method you planned to use is blocked. But because many methods can apply to any one purpose, there are other ways you can go about reaching your destination; you can back up and find another route, drive off the road and go around the tree, get a chain saw and cut up the tree, call for a helicopter, or walk to the other side of the tree and hitch a ride.

6. Nothing Always Works

There are some things in life that you can count on to work all of the time—gravity, sunrise. But that's not the case when dealing with people. With people, you can be certain of only one thing: nothing will always work. What works with one person may not work with another person, and what works with one person at one time may not work with that same person at another time.

There is no particularly good way to predict what will and what will not work with someone, because why and when something will or won't work isn't always logical. Remember my example of the man who paid his bill only when I skipped a month of sending it to him? He seemed a logical enough fellow, and I would never have suspected he would have a paradoxical response to receiving bills. The last time I checked, I counted about 150 different psychological theories that teach psychotherapists how to deal with patients, and each theory teaches a different approach. If even people who make their living "dealing with people" need that many options, handling humans in daily life is certainly not going to fit one particular formula or set of rules. So forget about what is "supposed to work."

Nevertheless, to avoid feeling lost, and have some place to start, some guidelines for dealing with people are important to have. Part four of this book is entirely devoted to such guidelines, and as long as you remember they are not hard-and-fast rules, they can be useful. In addition to the specific guidelines presented in that section of the book, there are two general guidelines that can give you a place to start when you are dealing with someone.

First, try an approach based on common sense. Human behavior does not always react according to common sense, but sometimes it does. Often people don't start out trying the most obvious and sensible approach. If you don't, you can make your task more difficult than it needs to be. So try the most simple, sensible things first. If you want someone to do something, ask them to do it. If you want someone to calm down, tell them to calm down. If you want to resolve something with someone, tell them. If someone is behaving in a way that is frightening you or upsetting you, tell them. If you want someone to change, tell them the change you want them to make.

Whenever I consult with people about handling someone, I always ask whether they have done the thing that, in their particular circumstance, would be the most sensible or logical thing to do. Frequently they haven't, but just assumed it wouldn't work. I once stopped a patient's twenty-year-old compulsive behavior by simply telling her to stop. Despite years of therapy, no one had ever tried it with her before. No one had ever said, simply, "stop." This approach doesn't work with all compulsive behaviors, but it happened to be what she needed to hear. So until someone tries the most common-sense approach first, more involved and sophisticated techniques should probably wait.

Second, try what has worked in the past. Past experience is certainly no guaranteed predictor of the future, but it does tend to have more reliability than most other methods. In fact, even though there are many different psychological tests designed to assess people's behavioral style, the most reliable method of predicting future behavior continues to be past behavior. Just be aware that even though this is the best method it is still not close to being a guarantee. So ask yourself some questions about this person, and situation. How have they reacted before? What was effective in dealing with them before? What seemed to make things worse? How have they behaved in other, similar situations? By answering these questions, you can come up with an initial strategy that may make your dealings with them easier.

7. There Are Probabilities but There Are No Certainties

Because human behavior is so variable and unpredictable, effectiveness in handling people means you increase your probability of success. The point of becoming skilled with people is not to attempt to achieve a 100% success rate, because that's not going to happen. The point is to improve your percentages. You don't need perfection, because the difference between success and failure always occurs in the margins: Olympic runners win the gold medal by running only a fraction of a second faster than the other runners, and it only takes 2%—the difference between 49% and 51%—to win the election.

8. If Something Doesn't Work, Try Something Else

This principle may also sound obvious, but it's one of the most difficult things for people to do when dealing with other people. The problem is, whatever you are already doing with someone is the thing that makes sense to you to do. So doing something else often means doing something that seems less sensible to you. Most people are understandably resistive.

Instead of trying something different, people frequently switch to a slightly different version of what they are already doing. It's like putting a new coat of paint on the same car. It isn't really trying something different, but it can seem as though it is.

The parents of a teenager approached me after one of my talks, and said it had made them realize they frequently began conversations with their son by telling him he was wrong about something. They could see this approach energized his defenses against them and made their parenting more difficult than it needed to be. The father wanted to know what I thought of his idea that instead of saying to their son he was wrong about what he was doing, they would say to him his way was fine, but they wanted to show him a better way.

Words and phrasings are important when dealing with people because they can change what they refer to in the conceptual world. They can alter meanings. But changing words without changing meanings is usually not helpful. Do you think this man's son is going to think his parents now believe what he is doing is really fine simply because they use a different word? Do you think he will feel less "wrong" because of this phrasing? Do you think he's not going to notice that telling him their way is better, automatically implies that his way is worse?

Being effective with people is not about being tricky with words. It may involve altering words when that alteration makes a difference in meaning, but simple word changes do not necessarily accomplish that. Unfortunately, though, this is the kind of change that frequently passes for doing something different. The parents' new words were a variation of the same thing they had already been doing. There was no particular harm in trying it to see what happened, but it is important to realize it is not substantially different from what they were already doing.

Doing something that doesn't make as much logical sense to you as what you are already doing is what I call "counter-intuitive." It's difficult for people to be counter-intuitive, but it's also the only way people can have options. Later chapters will describe counter-intuitive methods, and the explanations will help to ease your discomfort in doing things not immediately logical.

Failing to do something different happens to everyone. It happened to me when I was consulting with a manager who felt anxious when dealing with people. When he talked to others he felt inadequate and unsure of himself. He wanted to talk to people more comfortably and naturally. So we worked on that issue and developed some ways for him to talk to himself to keep himself from experiencing so much anxiety when he talked with his employees and colleagues. As a result, he felt better and his work improved. I thought he could do even better, though, and I decided he was ready to tackle a more serious issue, the issue that was at the core of his anxiety. When this man talked with people he often came across badly to them, and people experienced him as controlling, demeaning, and condescending. People reacted negatively to these qualities in him, and even though he didn't consciously know he was perceived in these ways, he reacted to their negative reaction with anxiety. I suggested that by dealing with this, he could achieve even better results.

The only problem was he couldn't see this was the way others perceived him, and that's when I got into trouble because I mistakenly thought I was trying different methods when I wasn't. The conversation went something like this: I pointed out how he behaved badly or how others perceived him badly, and he denied it. I pointed out the evidence, and he invalidated it. I gave examples, and he justified himself. I confronted his denials, and he made me wrong.

My impression of my own behavior during this conversation was that I was trying different things with him. I referred to many examples, from both the consulting session and with people in his outside life. I talked about his relationships with different people, including his employees, in his personal life, and me. I used many styles of talking to him. Still, he was having none of it.

Finally I realized that I was doing things that were all slightly different versions of the same thing. No matter what I did I was doing the same thing; I was telling him he was wrong. The man was no fool, no matter how I phrased it or guised it, he had a survival reaction to my message he was wrong. As a result, he couldn't hear a thing I was saying and all I had succeeded in doing was finding lots of ways to energize his defenses.

At that point I realized I needed a real change, so I relaxed, was quiet for a minute, and said, "Listen, I just realized something. I'm making you defend yourself and justify yourself to me. I'm accusing you of doing things wrong in an area that you really don't see as a problem for you. I do see it as one, but that doesn't guarantee I'm right about it, and even if I am right about it there's no law that says you have to care about it. I feel like I'm badgering you, and that's not my intention and it's not what you're here for. You're here to work on your anxiety, and I am failing to work with you on what you want changed. Instead, I'm trying to push my opinions down your throat. I'm sorry I got us off track. Let's get back to talking about your anxiety, and please forgive me for getting us off the subject."

The technical name for what I did was to use a paradoxical statement combined with a process comment and sharing. All of those techniques are presented in later chapters. In any case, I meant every word of what I said, and I prepared to return to talking about his anxiety and the self-talk we had been discussing previously. At that point I also noticed I had been feeling very tense, and the tension had suddenly disappeared. I felt better, more clear, more aware, and more effective. I could again concentrate on results. Although the change I made in some ways felt like I was giving up, I realized I wasn't doing something that was working—I needed to change.

Then the strangest thing happened. He refused to let me change the subject.

"Wait a minute," he said. "Not so fast. I mean, I heard what you were saying, and if you think this is an area that is a problem for me, maybe it is. I mean, I'm here because I'm having trouble dealing with people, and you're the person who knows about that stuff."

He hesitated, then continued. "Really, I do think you're right, you know, that I do offend people. Other people have already told me exactly the same thing as what you're saying. I've heard it before. In almost those exact same words. So I don't really think you're so wrong. Can we talk about it some more? Why do you think I do that?"

We then proceeded to work on the issue again, but this time it was different. This time the conversation took us somewhere, made things happen, and produced better results.

It's important to recognize that the ability to do something different is very important, and it's very tricky. It's easy to think you are doing something different when you're really doing the same thing with a slight variation. So don't take for granted that just because this principle sounds obvious, you already do it.

9. Try a Method Sufficiently Before Discarding it

One trap people fall into when trying something new is they try it a couple of times and if they don't get immediate results, they decide it doesn't work and discard it. They try something else, and when they get no immediate results they discard that method, too. After doing this several times, pretty soon they've run through lots of methods, and they adopt the stance that nothing works, and write off the person or the situation as hopeless.

But it may not be hopeless at all. It may only seem hopeless because they think they have tried everything, but it often takes more than a couple of times for something to work. Sometimes much more. Very few things work on the first try, or even on the second. This is especially true if you're dealing with a pattern in someone's life. If you respond in a new way that violates old patterns, there's going to be a lot of history trying to maintain the old responses. So other people may not respond in a new way until your new behaviors have become established as a new pattern as well.

This happens even with rats. If you put a rat in a box and train it that every time it presses a lever it gets fed, do you know what happens when you suddenly stop giving it food when it presses the lever? It doesn't stop pressing the lever. Instead, it begins to push the lever even harder and faster. It's as if the rat is thinking, "Wait a minute, this used to work, I obviously just need to do it more."

But just because the rat presses the bar more doesn't mean that stopping the food when it presses the bar is ineffective in getting it to stop pressing the bar. It will work. But it takes some time to work. If you didn't know that, though, you would think that by stopping its food you were being ineffective or even making things worse. You might abandon your approach prematurely.

Patterns of behavior take time and repetition to establish, and they take time and repetition to break. So most of the time it will be important to expect you will have to persist for some time in order to see if it will work. Don't write off any particular method just because you don't get results the first time.

An additional factor that can make something seem like it doesn't work is you have not done it well enough. It takes a lot of effort to be good at something. Could anyone walk in off the street, without any skills or training, and immediately do as good a job at your work as you do? Probably not, if your job requires any skill at all. But if someone didn't think your job took practice and they were to try to do it and things didn't turn out right the first time, they might very well figure your job was impossible, and give up on it.

The same thing is true in handling people effectively. It's like any other skill, and if you're just beginning to be conscious of your methods of handling people, don't be certain what you think you are doing is what you are actually doing. You may need refinement to be sure your methods are working the way you think.

10. Don't Persist at a Method That Is Clearly Failing

This principle is the opposite of the previous principle. While you don't want to give up on a method without giving it a fair try, neither do you want to persist at it beyond a reasonable expectation of producing results. People often continue to try something for a very long time even though it clearly isn't working.

A woman who was unhappy in her marriage consulted me. One of the first things I discovered was she had never shared with her husband the things that were making her unhappy. Instead, she held back, assuming he would not understand. Her method of trying to get him to meet her needs was to do things for him, and as a result, she felt resentful she didn't get what she wanted. It made sense to her to use this approach, but I pointed out she had been trying the same thing over and over for years, and it had yet to work. She had done things this way well beyond the point where it would have worked if it were going to work. It was time for her to try a new way.

Resolving the issue of how long to try something before you stop and try a new technique is the "art" portion of the art and science of dealing with people. You have to try long enough to effectively see if it will work, but you don't want to keep beating your head against a wall. How do you know when something has been given a fair try? Unfortunately, there's no particular time limit or rule. You have to work with it, test it out. As I said, this is the art of working with people.

Nevertheless, some guidelines for how long to try a method before giving up is helpful. As I discussed in the guidelines about what approach to try, these are merely general guidelines to get you started. There is no certainty or final authority.

There is an old saying, "One time tells you nothing, two times tells you maybe, and three times tells you for sure." I don't agree three times is "for sure," but I think the rule is generally valid three times is the minimum to know whether something is worth continuing.

Whatever you try should start to show some effect, in a reasonable amount of time. Remember the rat who stopped getting food—he pushed the bar harder and faster. Even if your method seems to have a worsening effect, it shows it's having an influence. You'll have to judge whether the worsening effect is ultimately a good sign.

When you're dealing with a pattern of behavior, the time frame is the important factor. There's a saying in psychology that it takes at least a month to establish a new habit. You may want to think of trying a procedure out for a month to see if it produces results.

You can also monitor your own frustration level to evaluate the effectiveness of a technique. If you're starting to feel frustrated, it might be a sign the approach has been tried long enough. Track your own frustration level.

I also sometimes suggest what I call the "once more" principle. When you reach the point where you think the way you're handling someone is not working, try it once more. By trying once more you give the method one final test with your awareness raised just a little bit higher. The only caution to remember is there is no such thing as more than one "once more."

11. Handling People Always Has a Price Attached to it

I always find it amusing when people, often parents or spouses, ask me for advice and then complain about my suggestions because, even though they are easier than their current approach, they still require effort or adaptation on their part. This often happens during a talk or presentation when I answer a question about a specific situation and recommend some options. "But that means I still have to pay a price!" people sometimes grouse.

A thorough articulation of the meaning behind their complaint would sound something like this, "Why can't you tell me a way to deal effectively with this person while avoiding all problems, upsets, costs, or difficulties to me? I want to be able to continue being exactly the way I am, doing exactly what I am doing, and not having to put out any more effort, time, or energy. I do not want it to be a hassle for me, and I don't want to have to change, be uncomfortable, take any risks, or relinquish any portion of my rightness. And I want immediate results."

I can often assist people in coming up with better and more effective ways of dealing with a person or an issue, even ways to solve the problem. Sometimes those methods are much less troublesome than those they are currently using, sometimes they even produce immediate results. But sometimes it isn't that way at all. When I was a new therapist I asked my supervisor why the work we did was so hard. She smiled kindly and said, "Because the things we want to accomplish are hard." When dealing with people you may have to accomplish hard things. Those will not be easy no matter how sophisticated your methods.

For people-handling, as well as everything else in life, there is always a cost—a "downside." You may have to give up something, tolerate a situation, be uncomfortable or counter-intuitive, try methods you've never done before, give up being right, or give up a point of view. You may even have to face the possibility you can't do what you are wanting to do, and make new decisions based on that fact.

It is inaccurate to think there is a way to deal with people without something being required of you. To borrow a saying by the well-known psychologist Albert Ellis, "Much of the time, handling people is spelled H-A-S-S-L-E."

For some reason people tend to get it in their heads that it should be possible to make things happen with people without having to think about it, work at it, or experience discomfort. Especially if the other person is the one causing the problem. But in virtually any endeavor in life, the more you want something, the more important that something is, the more it is going to cost you. Want to be president? The price is devoting your whole life to the task. It's fine if you're not willing to pay that price, but don't expect to get a chance to be the president. It's a package deal.

For several years I studied the martial art called Tae Kwon Do, and I had an instructor who was exceptionally blunt. He used to say that while the various practice exercises we did on the floor of the gym were precise and pretty, real fighting was anything but that. Real fighting, he used to say, was messy and ugly, and we needed to know what we were getting into if we were to really use our skills.

"You must be prepared to sacrifice to produce your result," he would say. "If you want to hurt someone, you must be willing to sacrifice your comfort and feel pain. If you want to break someone's bones you must be willing to sacrifice your flesh. If you want to take someone's life, you must be willing to sacrifice your bones."

His point was, the television programs showing people fighting and walking away smiling, rubbing their jaws, are just television shows. The cost of really fighting someone, and really winning, is a willingness to suffer damage to yourself that was only one step below the damage you would cause to the other. His caution was humbling and made us all think twice about being anxious to actually get into a fight.

Translating that principle into people-handling, means those fantasies that it should be easy, effortless, and painless to deal effectively with people are just fantasies. If you want to accomplish something with someone, there's going to be a cost to you. If you want intimacy, you may have to sacrifice your comfort, pride, or righteousness. If you want to change someone, you may have to sacrifice your current behavior, what you consider to be your "rights," even the quality of your relationship with that person. If you want to produce teamwork, you may have to sacrifice efficiency, control, or certainty. In all cases there's going to be some cost, even if the nature of the price is not immediately apparent.

It's interesting that so often it's upsetting to people that handling others can be such a bother, that it can be so difficult. What's new about it being a bother? It's also interesting that, while we may not jump for joy about them, we seem to feel far less morally outraged by the difficulties involved in handling the physical world than those involved in handling people. But the physical world is often not easy, either. We know when it's hot we'll perspire, and when it rains we'll get wet. The difference is that we rarely feel personally affronted by it. We may get frustrated and angry when it rains on days we had a picnic planned, but we don't go around screaming that the world is evil, or turning the matter into a self-righteous issue of morality.

But we do get this way when people don't operate according to the principles by which we think they should. We react this way when they're messy to deal with, when we consider them to be bad or wrong, when we suffer an outrage we feel we shouldn't have to suffer, because, "they don't have to be that way."

But people do have to be that way. They have to be whatever way is consistent with their history and experience. It doesn't mean we have to passively accept bad behavior or that no one ever changes, but it does mean handling people is, and probably always will be, a bother. You're walking into someone's history. Dealing with them can be messy, inexact, surprising, often troublesome, uncomfortable, and, at times, upsetting. But it's not personal, it's no different from handling any other aspect of life, and there are great rewards to those who are skilled.

Chapter 5

Diversity in Thinking, Diversity in Behavior

Although the principles for handling people presented in Chapter Four are fundamental to effective people-handling, two additional principles are so important they merit a chapter to themselves. These principles are, Diversity in Thinking, and Diversity in Behavior.

Diversity

Diversity in thinking and behavior are specific versions of the general principle called "Diversity." It means variations or differences exist within one larger entity. Biological diversity occurs when there are different types of cells or tissues performing different functions within one creature. Cultural diversity occurs when there are several different sub-cultures within one larger culture. Investment diversity occurs when a variety of investment instruments are used in one investment portfolio.

This is an important principle. In biology, diversity enhances the ability to survive. While a herd of wild animals is made up of members of the same species, their skills and tasks within the herd vary. Some animals are fighters, others are nurturers, and some are leaders. This diversity of skills creates a group with an enhanced ability to survive.

The survival of individual animals also benefits because animals with a diverse heritage tend to have a more adaptable temperament, a more healthy and disease-resistant constitution than do pure-bred animals. Pure-bred animals tend to have more frequent, severe physical problems and impairments than do animals with diverse backgrounds.

In technological fields, diversity is a sign of sophisticated knowledge. There was very little variability in medicine when it was a primitive science that understood little about biology. No matter what symptoms you presented to a physician during the Middle Ages you would receive the same treatment. It was only with increased knowledge and sophistication that medicine began to diversify, identifying different diseases and different treatments.

In fields involving skill, diversity creates power and effectiveness. Someone who can build not only bookcases but also chairs, tables, and wooden staircases, is called a master carpenter. Someone who can play not only Bach, but also Joplin rags and Billy Joel songs, is called a talented pianist. And someone who can handle a wide range of people, in a wide range of circumstances, for a wide range of purposes, is called an expert people-handler.

Diversity in Thinking

An important characteristic of skilled people is a thorough understanding of their craft. I've talked previously about how understanding people involves understanding survival issues, defenses, and the sensory and conceptual worlds. In practical people-handling, understanding someone's conceptual world means understanding their point of view. A point of view is the conceptual-world interpretation, or conclusion, someone applies to the world. Points of view are, "Warm climates are more comfortable," or "Everyone should have equal rights."

Understanding people's points of view is difficult when theirs differs from yours. Most people only understand their own, the point of view they consider to be right. This leads to an inability to understand people well enough to be effective in dealing with them because understanding only one's own point of view traps you inside your own survival wiring.

You're stuck defending your own rightness and you can only see other people as being right or wrong depending on whether or not they agree with you. To understand people thoroughly, in a manner that goes beyond this limitation, you need to be able to understand their point of view. The ability to do this is called Diversity in Thinking.

Diversity in Thinking is the ability to see the validity of points of view that disagree with yours. There is an important difference between something being "right" and something being "valid." "Right" is about survival. "Right" seeks agreement. Validity, on the other hand, has nothing to do with rightness, survival, or agreement. It involves the logical connection between a conclusion and the data and premises that lead to it. A point of view is valid when the conclusion fits the data and the primary assumptions. For example, it's valid for you to conclude it's nighttime outside if you look out your windows and it's dark. Your point of view may be wrong, because there may be an eclipse, or there may be a severe storm setting in, but it's valid if the only data you have to go on is that it's dark outside your window.

A valid point of view is any conclusion or interpretation that's a logical outgrowth of the data and the basic assumptions. The data and the basic assumptions may be wrong, but a conclusion consistent with them is valid. Validity is a sign of internal consistency, a sign the conclusions logically result from the given premises. In practical terms, Diversity in Thinking is the ability and the willingness to do what's necessary to understand the data and assumptions that underlie someone else's actions, even if you find their actions to be objectionable or wrong.

A woman who was very upset with a relative consulted me. Something this relative had said had been very upsetting to her. As she related the story she became very upset, sobbing deeply about how much hurt she felt over this relative's statement. She was barely able to tell me what happened. Given her reaction, I expected the statement to be some grossly obscene and insulting personal slander. But when the woman finished telling me the story I thought she hadn't told me the offending statement. The conversation, as reported to me, was quite benign. I had to have the woman go over the conversation several times so I was sure what she was upset about and what had hurt her so badly.

From my point of view, the woman's reaction was out of proportion to the relative's comments. Based on the data I had, her reaction did not fit. It looked "wrong," and as though she "shouldn't" be reacting in this way. Had I only been able to deal with the woman from my own viewpoint, I couldn't have helped with her upset. Instead, I would have made her feel worse by making her feel wrong. In order to help her to feel better, I needed to be able to validate her reaction, which I couldn't do based on my own point of view.

Diversity in Thinking allowed me to understand her point of view. I had to understand the assumptions and premises that led to her reaction. Once I did I could understand her reaction. I explored the data, discovering she had very little contact with this relative and thought a great deal of him. In addition, she always assumed that he was kind and thought well of her. Finally, the comment was in an area of special importance to her. The result was a combination of factors that resulted in a strong reaction on her part. So even though I personally found her upset to be excessive, I could deal effectively with her reaction because I understood the validity of her point of view.

Diversity in Thinking is the principle underlying empathy, the ability to resonate with someone else's experience even though it varies from your own. Diversity in Thinking is also the basis for respect, tolerance, and compassion. It allows people to understand each other even if they disagree. Empathy, understanding, and compassion are essential for effective people-handling because they're signs of genuine understanding.

One area where it's easy to see Diversity in Thinking is in dealing with children. When a child wails as though the world is ending because he dropped his ice cream cone, we adults know this reaction is excessive. However, at the same time we also understand the validity of the view. When you're a child, the loss of an ice cream cone is a big deal. So we can make room for this view, and we have options for dealing with the reaction other than telling the child he's wrong.

The power Diversity in Thinking provides for handling people is the ability to get "unstuck" from your own survival wiring and your own point of view. This provides flexibility. Without being able to understand multiple, valid points of view, you'll be severely limited. If you're going to deal successfully with people, you're going to need creativity and options. Diversity in Thinking allows you to say, "Maybe I'm missing something here, maybe I don't completely understand, maybe there's another way to look at this that will serve me better." Diversity in Thinking provides an antidote for becoming stuck in your own survival wiring and your own self-righteousness.

Diversity in Behavior

Simply having diverse behaviors is insufficient to be effective in handling people. In all likelihood you already have diversity in your behavior. You can probably deal with people in a variety of ways; you can cry or not cry, yell or talk nicely, assert or be passive, talk or listen. This principle is not just about being able to perform these diverse behaviors, but about being able to generate them consciously, intentionally, and willfully, even in the face of external forces attempting to trigger other behavior. It's about having freedom of choice in your interpersonal behavior.

Most of the time people don't have much freedom in their interpersonal behavior, and their perception that they do is largely an illusion. In fact, most behaviors are under the control of factors outside conscious intention and decision. They're generated by external or internal forces about which people have little awareness and thus little control. This is often the case even when people think they're "choosing" their behaviors.

Penfield, and other brain researchers, have clearly demonstrated that behaviors can be experienced as intentional when they are induced by outside factors. During brain surgery, when patients are under local anesthetic, a mild electrical stimulation of the motor area of the brain can produce a reaction, such as the patient lifting his arm. When asked by the surgeon why the patient lifted his arm, his usual response is that he "wanted" to. He experienced the behavior as volitional, even though it was actually generated externally.

Researchers have demonstrated the same phenomenon using reinforcement and other behavioral techniques. Changing someone's behavior through the use of altered reinforcements doesn't require conscious awareness on the part of the subject. When he is asked why he changed his behavior, the person reports he "decided" to change, or "wanted" to change. However, the change was actually generated by an alteration in the reinforcement schedule acting on him.

This phenomenon is frequently seen in addictions. While actively addicted to chemicals people experience their chemical use as an act of free will, a "wanting to," something under the control of their intentions. When an addict indignantly declares he can stop "any time he wants," he means it. But it isn't true. The chemical use is compulsive, a behavior outside of volitional control. It just isn't experienced as out of control.

Diversity in Behavior involves the ability to choose and alter people-handling behaviors based on the results they produce rather than some old internal pattern or automatic response to external cues or demands. The point is to be able to produce diverse behaviors by an act of will, based on goals and purposes. If, when angry, you don't have the freedom to choose whether or not to act on your anger and how to act on it, you don't have Diversity in Behavior.

The principle of Diversity in Behavior conflicts with the idea that there is a cosmically determined "right" set of behaviors in dealing with people. Instead, it makes the individual performing the behaving responsible for it. With Diversity in Behavior, there is no one to blame. You generate the behavior, and you generate the results. You can't say, "My mother told me to do it that way so it's not my fault," or "My therapist told me to do it that way so it's not my fault." All you can say is "I did it that way and here is the result."

Diversity in Behavior is a direct outgrowth of Diversity in Thinking. The only way you can, in good conscience, generate diverse behaviors is to have the ability to perceive valid points of view that make those behaviors consistent with the data at hand. In essence, Diversity in Thinking provides the data, principles, and rationale. And Diversity in Behavior provides the direct people-handling tools.

An example of how these principles operate and provide options occurred in one of my therapist consultation groups. A therapist in my group was seeing a married couple experiencing a variety of problems and upsets. The therapist felt stuck on the case, and needed help. I asked the therapist for her formulation of the case. She said the problem seemed to be the husband, who was willing to attend the marriage counseling sessions, but denied his behavior was part of the problem. He felt it was "all his wife." The wife disagreed strongly. In fact for years she had been badgering the husband about the problems in the marriage and his need to change. He finally agreed to accompany the wife to therapy, but he continued to refute the idea he was the problem in the relationship.

The therapist's viewpoint was that the husband was the "sick" one in the relationship. It was a valid viewpoint because it fit the data that the husband was denying any part in the problems which was a highly unlikely state of affairs. As a result, a logical conclusion was that the husband needed to get over his denial and to begin taking responsibility for his behavior.

The therapist's confusion about what to do was not the result of this being an invalid viewpoint, but rather that this was the only point of view she understood. After she exhausted her attempts to work with the couple based on this point of view, she became stuck and ineffective. She didn't know what to do. I introduced Diversity in Thinking by suggesting several possible alternative viewpoints on the case.

One alternate view was that the overt appearance of the husband as the sicker of the partners, was mistaken; it was the wife who was actually sicker. The husband, while denying his role in the problems, was at least behaving in a manner that was consistent with his beliefs, however erroneous his beliefs may have been. The wife, however, during years of unsuccessful badgering of the husband, was persisting in behaviors which ran counter to what she said she wanted to achieve in the marriage. She said she wanted the relationship to work, but her behavior consistently caused trouble between them. Her behavior could be defined as "sadistic" because it not only didn't help, it actively induced upset and bad feelings. In fact, it was quite possible that the husband's denial was actually a defense against the wife's sadistic behavior rather than the cause of it.

A second alternate view was that the husband and the wife were actually not sick at all, but were getting important psychological needs met by being married to each other. The wife may have been someone who was quite insecure and felt better about herself when she had someone else around to whom she felt superior. A good way to do this was to stay with a man whom she considered to be wrong, giving her the benefit of being the "better" of the two—and achieving a moral high ground. The husband may also have been quite insecure, and could have been unwilling to take the risk of leading or making decisions. Perhaps he preferred to feel safe by having a partner who would lead, push, and take responsibility.

Yet another possibility was this was a couple fearful of intimacy and the vulnerability it involves. But because they didn't want to be alone they had to find a way to be together without risking intimacy. An effective solution would be to keep problems and upsets stirred so there would be a justifiable reason to not get close.

Understanding the validity of these diverse points of view, that they fit the data presented, and that any of them could be true, is Diversity in Thinking. Each of the viewpoints leads naturally to a different approach and set of behaviors for the therapist. If the husband is sicker, as the original viewpoint held, then methods to break through his denial are appropriate. If the wife is sicker, then methods to alter her sadistic behavior or to enlighten her to its presence are appropriate. Even if one of the alternate viewpoints doesn't seem right to the therapist she can still, in good conscience, try out methods based on the possibility the viewpoint may be right. This freedom to try out different behaviors is Diversity in Behavior.

Diversity in Thinking and Diversity in Behavior are strong antidotes to getting stuck or lost when dealing with people. They also allow for greater understanding, connection, and effectiveness in relating to people. You may feel right in your point of view, but there are other points of view as valid as yours, and may, in fact, be more right than yours.

Part III

Techniques

Chapter 6

Communication Behaviors

This chapter begins the section on specific, practical techniques useful in dealing effectively with people. Some of the techniques may sound familiar to you. If they do, don't assume your familiarity with them means you've mastered them. People are often the least skilled at what is most familiar. Other techniques may be new to you. They may be confusing at first and you may have to read them several times before you understand them completely.

I describe techniques, give examples of their use, and offer some opinions about their effectiveness. I don't talk extensively about the application of the techniques to particular situations or purposes because the following section is devoted entirely to these subjects. If, as you read the technique chapters, you find you want more information about the use of a particular technique, you can look ahead to find more information.

While my purpose is to present each technique in a manner that makes it understandable and usable, limitations prevent me from exploring every detail and use of every technique. In reality, whole books could be written about many of them. In fact whole books have been written about some of them. As a result, additional literature is available and if you'd like to learn more about them, I have included a bibliography.

Talking

Of all people-handling techniques, talking is the most frequent and fundamental. As a result, understanding the aspects of talking that give it power and effectiveness is necessary to handle people effectively.

For most people, most of the time, talking is not a powerful people-handling technique. It doesn't help them accomplish their purposes, or does so only when easy, or under optimal circumstances. It frequently doesn't help people produce closeness, intimacy, resolve problems, or change what they don't like. Talk is, as the old saying goes, cheap, and a lot of it is done without producing any results.

But talk is not inherently cheap. It can have enormous power. Talking has started and ended wars, built great civilizations, and produced great technological breakthroughs. It has produced spiritual conversions and changed lives. But people often don't know the aspects of talking that make it powerful, and make several common mistakes.

1. People Avoid Talking

Most people have the impression they talk a great deal, or at least a sufficient amount with the people in their lives. However, studies have shown this is a mistaken perception. People don't talk to each other nearly as much as they think they do. The members of many families talk to each other for less than ten minutes a day. But it can seem like more, and because they think they do so, they attribute their difficulties with people to a failure of talking rather than to a failure to talk.

During workshops, presentations, or consultations, I'll frequently ask people who are upset about an issue with someone whether they have talked with the person involved. It's more common they haven't than have. If someone is unwilling to talk with someone about issues they have with them, they are seriously handicapped in dealing with them. If a manager can't open a dialogue with an employee about issues, problems, or plans; if a parent can't engage in a conversation with their child about important matters; or if a business owner can't talk freely to a partner, difficulties will be created and problems magnified.

The reason people often avoid talking with others is they fear talking won't do any good, or the other person will have a bad reaction, or both. These fears are usually the result of people not knowing how to talk with someone in a manner designed to maximize success and minimize bad reactions. You can't do much about someone's psychological makeup and their tendency to react badly, but there is a great deal you can do about conducting a conversation with them in a manner that increases your probability of success. You need to know what kind of talking is useful for producing specific outcomes, and apply the appropriate method to the circumstances.

2. People Use the Wrong Kind of Talking for Their Purpose

Different kinds of talking are appropriate to different purposes and produce different results. Using the wrong kind to accomplish a particular purpose is one of the most common reasons people feel talking is not powerful as a method of dealing with others. However, this conclusion would be no more warranted than a mechanic deciding that tools don't help to fix a car after he has repeatedly tried to unscrew a bolt with a hammer. Talking is only powerful when the right kind is applied to the right purpose.

3. People Fail to see Talking as a Process

Effective talking rarely occurs as a single event. While some things can be dealt with in one session, one conversation is often insufficient to produce the desired results. Talking often has to be an ongoing dialogue—a process.

A process goes through various stages, and is designed to produce certain results. The process involved in talking with someone can be compared to the process you go through when looking for misplaced car keys.

You have to take time to look in several different places, and feel as if you're getting nowhere. You have to think and work at it.

Talking, as a process, is often referred to as a conversation. It can take place over minutes, hours, days, or even years. Sales is often an ongoing conversation. A salesperson may talk with a prospect many times and the conversation may go through various stages of interest, resistance, and exploration before a sale is closed. Before we were married, Pam and I had a conversation about marriage that lasted many months. It went through various stages and ultimately took us to our marriage.

Staying engaged in that conversation made our process of marrying much smoother, pleasant, and rewarding. It solved a lot of problems and prevented a lot of difficulties. But it didn't happen in one sitting. It happened at different times, ways, and places.

In learning to be effective in handling people, it's important to consider not only how much you talk to people, but also how well your talking matches your purpose. If you're someone who gives up when you don't achieve the results you want after you talk with someone once you're likely to be ineffective. If you're someone who considers situations hopeless when a conversation gets frustrating or bogs down, you're going to have trouble.

4. Talking Isn't Communicating

The term communication is often a block to learning to deal effectively with other people. While this may surprise you, the problem is communication is a word people often use, but it doesn't have a consistent meaning. As a result, people are not necessarily communicating when they talk. Because of this, it's much more useful to change your focus from whether you're communicating with someone to *how* you're communicating with them.

Communication Behaviors

In specific terms, the how of communicating consists of the behaviors you use to talk. I call these "communication behaviors." They're the observable, external actions others see and hear as you speak with them. Communication behaviors are both nonverbal, such as body position, facial expressions, eye movement, tone of voice, and breathing patterns, and verbal—words.

Communication behaviors are very powerful and have a strong impact on others. Human senses are uniquely sensitive to communication behaviors. Even small variations can make big differences in the effect your talking has on people. Minute changes in facial expressions, eye movements, body position, and skin coloring, voice rhythm, and tone of voice are registered.

As a result, huge amounts of data can be communicated between people with very small, almost imperceptible actions. A change in tone of voice that may be much less than one note on a musical scale can alter the meaning in an entire conversation.

A common cause of troubled relationships is a lack of awareness of the impact of communication behaviors. While many distressed married couples complain they have communication problems, they often have nothing of the sort. If, by communication, is meant their ability to transmit and receive information from each other, their communication is excellent. The behaviors they use to communicate transmit whole paragraphs of meaning. A momentary pause, an eye movement, or creases in a forehead, can tell the other partner volumes. The problem is they communicate hurtful things to each other. In fact, they could improve their relationship by communicating less effectively.

Most of the time people pay very little attention to their communication behaviors. The actions seem like small, inconsequential things that are trivial compared with the content of the conversation. People tend to think other people should pay attention to the content, and not to what seems irrelevant.

This belief results in people failing to realize no matter how it seems it should be, the behaviors used to communicate are every bit as important as the content. In fact, communication behaviors frequently have a much greater impact than does the content. The wrong behaviors destroy the ability to communicate content. The right communication behaviors, on the other hand, make the content irresistible.

Because your communication behaviors have a great deal of effect on other people, understanding their impact is vitally important.

It's important to keep several principles in mind:

1. People React *Only* to Behavior

As wrong or as unfair as it may seem, the impact you have on other people, and the nature of other people's reactions to you, has little or nothing to do with what you are really feeling, thinking, or what you intend to be saying to them. Your thoughts and feelings are not directly accessible by others. The only way to perceive your thoughts or feelings is to interpret your communication behaviors—your actions and words. If your communication behaviors do not accurately represent your thoughts, feelings, or intentions, the other person is not going to receive the message you think they should be receiving.

Because it's difficult to know when your behavior is sending strange signals, you may automatically assume that other people misunderstand you. But if you tend to get strange reactions from other people, or if they consistently seem to misunderstand you, it may not be the result of their misinterpretation at all. It may be your behavior isn't effectively displaying your thoughts and feelings, or is doing so in a manner that makes it impossible for other people to understand you.

In order to truly be effective in handling people, you need to know what your communication behaviors are transmitting. This doesn't mean you have to be painfully self-conscious of the smallest twitch of your eyelashes. But you do need to be aware of the impact of your communication behaviors at least as much as you are aware of the impact of the content of your speech.

2. Communication Behaviors Communicate Rightness and Wrongness

Virtually all behavior involved in talking with people not only communicates content, but also communicates a message as to whether the other person is considered to be right or wrong. Because right and wrong are such important survival issues, people react to this implication. In fact, in many cases they react more strongly to this than to the content of the conversation.

One of the most important and powerful aspects of talking is the difference between categories of communication behaviors that convey rightness and wrongness. Other people's responses will be very different depending on which category is being used, even if the behavior is extremely subtle.

The name for communication behaviors that imply rightness is "positive communication behaviors." The name for communication behaviors that imply wrongness is "negative communication behaviors." Positive communication behaviors are those behaviors that communicate to you that I think you are being right. If I smile at you and nod my head, I am communicating a positive, "you're being right" message to you. Positive communication behaviors include such actions as pleasant tones of voice, smiles, head nods, and eye contact. Positive communication behaviors are not always good. They are called positive because they communicate rightness. But they can be bad when used in the wrong way or for the wrong purpose.

Negative communication behaviors are those behaviors that inform you I think you are being wrong. If I give you a dirty look, I'm communicating a "you're being wrong" message. Negative communication behaviors include such things as harsh tones of voice, scowls, frowns, sarcastic tones, and tense finger pointing.

Figure 2 summarizes typical positive and negative communication behaviors. Notice that behaviors are defined as positive or negative based on the typical interpretation given to them by other people, not by the feelings or intentions of the person engaging in the behavior.

FIGURE 2

Comunication Behavior	Positive	Negative
Voice Tone	Even, pleasant, cheerful, thoughtful, moderate volume, smooth	Loud, harsh, clipped, terse, sarcastic, soft, mumbled, gruff, hesitant
Facial Expression	Smile, open-eyed, neutral	Frown, grimace, scowl, confused, sneering, blank
Response Time	Natural, regular rhythm	Interrupting, extra pause
Verbal and Nonverbal Behaviors	Matching	Discrepant
Eye Movement	Eye contact with breaks	Lack of eye contact, glares, eye-rolls, upward movement
Body Position	Oriented toward person	Oriented away from person
Breathing	Normal, paced	Heavy sighs

Even if you're scowling because you're thinking rather than because you are displeased, the behavior is likely to be interpreted by others as a negative communication behavior because the typical meaning of a scowl is displeasure, disagreement, or disapproval. Remember, people can't read your mind, they can't know what you are thinking or feeling. They can only attempt to read your behavior. And there are typical culturally established interpretations for many communication behaviors.

The functioning and effects of positive and negative communication behaviors have been studied extensively. Research has identified two basic principles that govern their functioning. These principles are called Reciprocity and Relative Power.

Reciprocity

Researchers discovered when a person uses positive or negative communication behaviors, other people tend to respond with the same type of communication behaviors. This principle is called "reciprocity." It means, in essence, your mother was right; to get other people to be nice to you, you should be nice to them first.

Reciprocity of communication behavior works according to the category of behavior that is sent out, not according to any specific behavior. If you smile at someone you increase the likelihood you will get some kind of positive communication behavior in response. But not necessarily a smile. It may be increased eye contact, a pleasant tone of voice, or a nod of the head. Similarly, any specific negative communication behavior, such as a scowl, increases the likelihood of producing a frown, a harsh tone of voice, or a hesitation.

Because reciprocity operates by category rather than individual behavior, it can sometimes seem only one person in an argument is behaving badly when, in fact, the seemingly pleasant one is just as responsible for the negative interaction as the obvious one. Some people's negative communication behaviors may be loud, obvious and dramatic, other people's may be subtle, and low-key, and difficult to see.

During a people-handling workshop a woman asked me to help her figure out what to do about her husband, who "watched TV all the time and never talked to her." I asked how she handled the situation and she said that she talked to him about it. When I pursued further and asked what, specifically, she said to him, she replied she often remarked that his behavior was "awfully rude." When she said this she had her hands on her hips, disgust in her voice, and a sneer on her face.

Clearly, this woman was involved in a reciprocity of negative communication behaviors. Her husband's negative communication behaviors were those involving lack of attention: no eye contact, few words, and slow response time. Her negative communication behaviors involved harsh words, sarcastic tones of voice, and unpleasant facial expressions. His were more subtle, in that he was not behaving in a way that would typically be called "mean" or "harsh." Nevertheless, this was a couple locked in a negative communication reciprocity.

The wife couldn't see why her attempts to change her husband's behaviors didn't succeed. She felt she was trying to change the situation. Her behaviors didn't feel inappropriate to her so she couldn't understand why his behavior didn't change. In truth, her behaviors were part of the reason that her husband's undesirable behaviors continued.

The reason people fail to see their own part in negative reciprocity is that it feels right to be reciprocal in your communication behavior. To the woman in the workshop, generating negative communication behaviors in response to her husband felt completely appropriate, so she couldn't imagine her behavior could be part of the problem.

When I challenged the manner in which she was approaching her husband about the problem, she began applying negative communication behaviors to me, sarcastically asking, "Should I just be all sweetness and light no matter how much of a jerk he's being? Is that what you're telling me to do?" To her, using positive behaviors felt as though she were surrendering. Why should she be nice to a man who was ignoring her? She did what felt right, to return negative communication behaviors with negative communication behaviors. And although it felt right, it actually helped propagate the problem.

Reciprocity is powerful not only because it feels like the right thing to do, but also because it feeds on itself and can become a perpetual pattern until something actively interrupts the cycle. Couples often engage in negative reciprocity for months or years.

It doesn't produce the results desired, but because it feels like the right thing to do, and humans are powerfully drawn to the right thing, it's very difficult to give up.

A therapist in one of my consultation groups was dealing with a man who didn't have a well-developed sense of right and wrong. He was a con artist who caused himself and other people a good deal of trouble. However, the man had a very pleasant interpersonal style. He was gentle, polite, and always presented himself with an endearing, understandable rationale that explained away his blame in the difficulties he created. When I suggested to the therapist that he confront the man, strongly and vigorously challenge the man's behavior and rationalizations even to the point of being critical and harsh, the therapist expressed confusion and discomfort. "But I don't want to hurt him," he complained. "He's such a nice guy."

The truth was that the man was not a nice guy. He caused lots of trouble for lots of people and abdicated his responsibility for it. However, he had adopted an interpersonal style of positive communication behaviors which resulted in discomfort for anyone who ever tried to confront him about his misbehavior and rationalizations. Other people felt wrong when they set out to be hard on him. By being critical of him or confrontive with him, people were forced to violate the positive reciprocity his behaviors set up. People were reluctant to do this. They felt mean or unfair using confrontive behaviors. As a result, his misbehavior and rationalizations usually went unchallenged.

The feeling that being reciprocal in one's communication behaviors is right is one of the reasons Behavioral Diversity can be a struggle to achieve. Behavioral Diversity requires you be willing to violate a positive or a negative reciprocity, and unless you are aware of the principle of reciprocity, doing so feels wrong. To be nice to someone who is being mean to you, or to be tough with someone who is being nice to you, can feel very strange. To judge your behavior independently of the reciprocity set up by the other person's behavior is something most people are unaccustomed to doing.

Because of the reluctance of most people to violating communication behavior reciprocity, it's easy to become part of a problem rather than part of a solution when difficulties arise in dealing with people. A person's first impulse is to return mean with mean, and to be nice to someone who is being nice. This means people unwittingly solidify negative communication behaviors with their own negative communication behaviors, and they can overlook important issues with people who generate positive communication behaviors.

Relative Power

Researchers discovered positive and negative communication behavior do not have equal power. They aren't equal in their ability to affect people's behavior. So while, in general, your mother was right that you should be nice to other people in order to get them to be nice to you, she didn't tell you the whole story. It's not that simple.

Negative communication behaviors are more powerful than positive communication behaviors. While this may seem unfortunate, it's logical given what we have already discussed about how human beings function. Biology's first concern is to attend to any potential threat to survival. It will react immediately and strongly to anything that's perceived to be a threat. Negative communication behaviors threaten rightness. Positive communication behaviors don't threaten rightness. As a result, biology considers negative communication behaviors to be more important than positive ones, and reacts more strongly to the negative. This means if a negative communication behavior and a positive communication behavior of equal intensity occur, the negative communication behavior is likely to have the greater impact and be the one that generates the response- controls the reciprocity. This is the reason if you get three compliments and one criticism, you react more strongly to the criticism.

In a conversation having a balance of positive and negative communication behaviors, the negative have the most impact and tend to take over. This is the reason human interactions have a greater tendency to go from pleasant to unpleasant than from unpleasant to pleasant. It's more difficult to change an argument into a discussion than to change a discussion into an argument. This is also the reason it takes less energy to teach people how to fight and squabble than it does to teach people how to get along well. When there are problems, fighting and squabbling is much more natural.

I was consulting in a managers' meeting where the boss would occasionally stop participating in the conversation for perhaps thirty seconds. During this time he would sometimes let out a heavy sigh. It was clear to me he didn't do this on purpose, he didn't feel upset or unhappy; he was probably just catching his breath. He wasn't even aware of these behaviors. But during a meeting, silence and heavy sighing are negative communication behaviors.

This meeting was no exception. His behaviors didn't pass unnoticed by the participants. Their behavior was strongly affected by his behaviors. The person talking when these behaviors occurred began to show negative communication behaviors in themselves. They began to pause, use a hesitant tone of voice, stop making eye contact, frown, and have an edge to their voice. Remember, negative communication behaviors are not just those that are usually interpreted as hostile, but also those usually interpreted as confused, uncertain, hesitant, or resistive.

When the boss looked up from his short break, he had no idea the other participants' behavior had been affected by his own. However, he immediately sensed the conversation was different, and something was wrong. As a result, his behavior began to react to the negative communication behaviors coming his way. In turn, the participants reacted to his negative communication behavior. Negative reciprocity took hold of the meeting, and although it was not dramatic and no one was yelling or screaming, it was not going very well.

The biggest problem was although the boss and the participants were reacting negatively to each other's behaviors, they were completely ignorant of the fact that they were reacting to them. Instead, everyone involved thought the negative behavior and the bad feelings were caused by the content of their discussion. They figured what was being said must be wrong in some way. In response, they began to alter what they were saying in an attempt to make others' responses better. They scrapped ideas, changed their plans, modified agreements, and decided to rethink decisions. But because the content was not the problem in the first place, the meeting didn't produce good results. The participants ended up wondering why they weren't meeting their goals. They didn't feel like they got anywhere.

This same mistake frequently occurs in families as well. When an issue is being discussed, one person in the conversation uses a behavior or word that implies wrongness on the part of the other. Then, instead of the conversation continuing to focus on the topic, the conversation changes course. It begins to focus around that one negative communication behavior. The original topic is lost and the conversation becomes an argument about the validity of that implication.

It's a well established psychological principle that the more immediate a reaction is to a stimulus, the more powerfully that behavior is ingrained in response to the stimulus. This means negative reciprocity happens more quickly, and takes hold more strongly, than does positive reciprocity. I witnessed the speed of negative communication behavior reciprocity at a resort when vacationing. I watched two staff members get into a heated argument, and it took no more than several seconds for the negative communication behaviors to be quickly flying back and forth. A harsh tone triggered exasperated upturned palms, which triggered a quick, jerk-away motion of the eyes, which provoked a louder volume, then an angry shrug of the shoulders, a scowl, and a sarcastic tone.

For me, the intriguing part of watching this conversation was that the two staff members were speaking French, which I don't understand, so I was able to observe their communication behavior reciprocity completely dissociated from the content of the argument. I could see the behaviors rapidly trigger each other, even without knowing what they were talking about.

The power of negative communication behaviors and the immediacy of reaction they create are the reason people tend to use negative communication behaviors when they want to get someone's attention or to get something done or changed. Negative communication behaviors are designed to tweak someone's survival wiring, to get them to react strongly and immediately. This is the reason people tend to treat each other so badly when they are unhappy with each other. Their behavior is an attempt to get a reaction. The result is spouses treat each other badly when they are unhappy, dissatisfied customers get nasty, and children scream, cry, and pout when they want something.

In contrast to negative communication behaviors, positive communication behaviors are not a survival threat. They don't prompt an immediate response because biology is not as concerned with them. When a positive communication behavior is sent out, there can be a delay, perhaps a significant delay, in a positive communication behavior being returned.

The result of this slowed response time in positive communication behavior reciprocity is that it is more difficult to turn a negative conversation into a positive one than it is to turn a positive conversation into a negative one. Although it can be done, it often takes time. This slowness is often the reason people don't get conflicts resolved. People give up trying to change the conversation to a positive one long before a positive reciprocity has a chance to take hold. The other person's negative communication behavior may not alter in response to positive communication behaviors for seconds, minutes, or even longer. In addition, a few positive communication behaviors might not do it, even though a few negative communication behaviors might very well be enough to set up a negative reciprocity.

Words

Verbal behavior is also a communication behavior that carries an implication of right and wrong. However, the impact of words on people is a bit more complex, because in addition to carrying implications of right and wrong, words also convey content and fall into both the conceptual and sensory categories.

Conceptual Words

As was discussed in Chapter Two, conceptual words reference the conceptual world, the world of human experience where survival is a matter of being right. As a result, conceptual worlds almost always have an implication of right or wrong automatically built into them. "Responsible," for example, generally has a positive implication, as in, "He is very responsible." "Ridiculous" tends to carry a negative implication, as in, "Having to wait this long is ridiculous." Examples of the positive and negative loadings of various conceptual words are presented in Figure 3.

Because conceptual words carry a positive or negative implication, they fall into being positive and negative communication behaviors. Words with negative implications stir up survival reactions and immediate responses, which set up a negative communication behavior reciprocity. Similarly, words with positive implications operate the same way as do other positive communication behaviors producing a delayed effect and tending to create a positive communication behavior reciprocity.

Sensory Words

Sensory words reference the sensory world, the world that can be seen, heard, smelled or touched. These words directly describe events or objects. Survival in the sensory world involves physical soundness rather than right and wrong, and as a result, sensory words tend to have much less positive and negative implication than do conceptual words. Examples of sensory words are presented in Figure 4. Notice how they have a much less inherent right and wrong implication as compared to the conceptual words in the previous table.

As a result, sensory words do not function as either positive or negative communication behaviors in the same way as conceptual words or nonverbal behaviors. Sensory words are the closest thing to neutral communication behaviors that exist. You can sense this difference when you hear something like a police report, where the emphasis is on sensory words. Much of the right and wrong tone is removed, and neither a negative nor a positive reciprocity is automatically triggered. "The individual observed at the house was seen to run past the front door, through the yard, and into the street. At that time the officer at the scene pursued the individual to the other side of the street." Such a sensory description of the event is much different from a conceptual version such as "He tried to get away, so I tried to catch him."

Talking

In order to effectively deal with people, you have to be aware not only of the content of your conversations with them, but also of your communication behaviors as well. Communication behaviors can have more effect on people than the content of your conversation, so attention to your communication behaviors and your word choice can have a great deal of effect on your effectiveness with people.

There are a variety of different possible combinations of positive and negative communication behaviors, positive and negative word choice, and neutral (sensory) word choice. These combinations provide the ability to greatly alter your impact on people. If you know the mix of messages you're sending out, you can have a great deal of increased effectiveness.

For example, if you want to get someone's attention, negative communication behaviors can be effective. If you want to calm someone down or stop an argument, positive communication behaviors can be powerful. If you want to get your point across in the clearest fashion with the least emotional implication, or with the least possibility of inflaming someone, neutral, sensory words can be effective.

If you pair sensory words with positive communication behaviors, you can be even more effective. Many more examples of the uses of the different kinds of communication behaviors and different mixes of communication behaviors are included in the chapters on different purposes in Section Four of the book.

Of course, conversations are not static, so you can also shift and change the different communication behaviors you use throughout a conversation. I once had a doorman give me a hard time about what I was doing. I decided to try to keep him from bothering me by using multiple and shifting communication behaviors. I started with positive words combined with a set of negative communication behaviors. Halfway though my sentences I switched them. The doorman couldn't tell if I was being nice, mean, polite, or uppity. As a result, he had no consistent category of communication behavior to respond to in reciprocity. No particular style of response felt right to him, so he had a very difficult time responding. I continued on my way, doing what I was doing, as he began to stare at me—confused and suspicious, but unable to respond. The conversation is summarized in Figure 5.

In the whole area of learning to be effective with people, perhaps the single, most valuable thing you can do is become aware

FIGURE 3

Right/Wrong Loadings of Conceptual Words

Right/Good	Wrong/Bad
Responsible	Irresponsible
Sensitive	Insensitive
Aware	Unaware
Free	Stuck
Kind	Mean
True	Lie
Neat	Messy
Organized	Disorganized
Effective	Ineffective
Agreeable	Disagreeable
Helpful	Hurtful
Efficient	Inefficient

FIGURE 4

Neutral Sensory Words

swing
car
truck
lift
hold
walk
talk
blink
speak
fly
stop
touch
green
toe

FIGURE 5

The Doorman and Me

Example of Shifting and Changing
Words and Communication Behaviors

Doorman: negative words—"You can't come through here!"
        combined with
        negative behaviors—glaring, harsh tone of voice, pointing.

Me: positive words—"I understand completely."
        combined with
        negative behaviors—sighing, hands on hips, glaring.

Doorman: (weakened) negative words—"What are you . . . "
        combined with
        (weakened) negative behaviors—hesitant tone, puzzled expression.

Me: negative words—"Doesn't matter, this is a real problem."
        combined with
        positive behaviors—smiling, nodding, pleasant tone of voice.

Doorman: delay in response, confused expression, just about to speak.

Me: positive words—"You! Have a nice day!"
        combined with both
        negative behaviors—interrupting, harsh tone, pointing, *and*
        positive behaviors—smiling, pleasant eye-contact, nodding.

Doorman: silence, blinking, confused expression.

Me: looking away, continuing on my way.

of and in control of your communication behaviors. It's not easy to know your own communication behaviors because you're not likely to be aware of the nuances you don't feel but others see in your behavior. Once you know what different communication behaviors feel like to you, and once you know what those behaviors communicate, you can improve your effectiveness. Then, once you achieve Behavioral Diversity and alter your behaviors independently of reciprocity, your effectiveness with people will be far greater than you have ever experienced previously.

Chapter 7

Techniques of Alliance

This chapter discusses several people-handling techniques that tend to have as a common characteristic the effect of calming people's survival reactions. These techniques often deplete or prevent defensiveness in other people. They are used in situations where you want to ally with people, to be in partnership with them, or create a workable relationship with them.

Just Listening

Listening has, over the years, taken on a variety of names. It has been called reflective listening or empathic listening or active listening. But no matter what the label, it's all the same thing—just listening.

The reason "just listening" to people has taken on so many different names is it's a very powerful people-handling technique, but the name "listening" doesn't make it sound like it is. It sounds ordinary, passive, and as though you aren't really doing anything. It sounds like something everyone already knows how to do. This belies the fact that true listening is actually a very skillful and sometimes difficult thing to do.

If you were to ask people whether they were good listeners, nearly everyone would say they were. After all, what is there to listening but to just sit, and be quiet, hearing the words the other person says? Actually, there is a lot more to it. Listening has a very specific meaning. It means that your sole focus is on what someone is saying. Doing that is a whole lot harder than it sounds because the words the other person is saying are not the only thing going on you can pay attention to.

Everyone has editorial comments going on in their heads all the time. There is a committee in our heads that provides running commentary on everything. Richard Bach, in his book *The Bridge Across Forever*, calls it The Observer. Most of the time, when people are listening, what they are actually doing is attending to the editorial voices, not to what is being said by the other person.

When you're actually listening to someone, you don't editorialize. You don't add to what they're saying, make them right or wrong, spend your time waiting until it's your turn to talk. Instead, you absorb what they're saying, you take it in, you consider it, you examine it, you look at it. You take it in like you'd drink a glass of water.

There are a variety of reasons why just listening to others is difficult to do. Sometimes it can feel strange because it feels like you aren't doing anything. Other times your internal editorializing can be so loud and strong that to ignore it in favor of listening to the other person can be uncomfortable. If you have "That's wrong!" or "What, why that's absurd!" running through your head, it can be very distracting.

But listening is very powerful. It can have strong effects even though it may not seem like you're doing anything. Sometimes people need to say something and have someone hear it before they can get on with what they are doing. They need to put their thoughts or feelings into words. Sometimes we call this "getting something off their chest" or "venting." Sometimes people just need the attention, to feel important. One of the powerful things about listening is it makes the other person and their comments the most important thing present.

When you're listening to someone, it doesn't mean you're doing anything special or intense. You can do many of the things you normally do in conversation, as ask questions, inquire for clarification, or explanation. Listening doesn't mean you never say anything. It means what you're doing is paying attention to what they say as the focus of the conversation.

People often come to feel close to those who are able to listen to them. It can be a major force for building trust, closeness, and understanding between people. It can also be uncomfortable for the listener, because we are so accustomed to reacting from our internal editorials rather than what the other person is saying.

Empathic Responding

Empathy is a fancy word for saying you share another person's experience, that you can feel it, understand it, or identify with it. In essence, it tells them you know what they are talking about. Empathic responses make people feel safe with you, it lets them know you aren't feeling antagonistic, or uncaring.

Empathic responses are the simplest of things. They are statements that put your words to what the other person is experiencing. Generally, empathic responses convey feelings, such as "It sounds like you're feeling sad." Using feeling words makes for good empathic responses, but empathic responses don't have to include feeling words. They can be any phrasing that conveys an understanding or acceptance of someone's experience. Even a simple, "I understand," or "I see," or saying back to them what they have already said are effective empathic responses.

Empathic responses tend to diminish survival reactions because they remove the sign of any threat to survival. They demonstrate there's not going to be any competition for the precious resource of attention, and no one is going to fight them over their statements, feelings, or concepts. They show the speaker is not going to be made wrong. The only thing present in the conversation is that person's experience, and it's going to be understood rather than challenged. As a result, empathic responses can be very helpful when you want to diminish someone's survival reactions and ally with them. This is why they are often used by therapists. In fact, a man named Carl Rogers started a whole school of psychotherapy based entirely on empathic responses. Some examples of empathic responses include:

"Sounds like you're upset."
"I think you really liked that."
"You seem like you're having a really good time."
"You had some trouble with that."
"You seem angry about that."
"I can understand that."
"I see."

"I understand completely."

"What you're saying makes sense."

"I don't blame you for that."

"I would feel that way, too."

"I know what you mean."

"I hear what you're saying."

"I can connect with that."

Empathic responding is very flexible and can be used at any time when you're listening to someone. It tells them you're listening, you understand, and you're not going to make them wrong for their experience. It's exactly the opposite of saying to someone, "You shouldn't feel like that," or "That's wrong," or "Listen to me," all of which can set off survival wiring.

Sharing

Sharing is a term that gained wide popularity during the days of the Human Potential Movement of the 1970s. Over the years the term has come to be overused and misunderstood. Sharing now means you're telling someone something. But that's not what sharing is. Sharing is giving someone a piece of what you have. If I have pot roast for dinner and I share my dinner with you, it means you're going to get some pot roast. When sharing occurs in a conversation, it means that when I share with you, you're able to feel or take on a bit of my experience. Just like with dinner, you get some of what I have.

People can literally share feelings. They can transmit to someone some of what they're feeling. Have you ever been talking to someone who's angry, and you start to feel angry, too? You might feel angry about what they're feeling angry about, or you might feel angry about how they're behaving, or about something totally unrelated. In any case, the operative mechanism is they are sharing their anger, and you are taking some of it on. You're "getting" some of their anger.

Sharing is one reason psychotherapists have such a high suicide rate. Therapists spend all day with people who are sharing their pain. This is an appropriate and healthy activity in psychotherapy. But it's also hazardous to the therapist because unless a therapist is very careful he or she can absorb that pain and begin to carry it around.

I was giving a presentation on handling people effectively to a sales staff when one salesman noted his work was not going well. He couldn't figure out why, but he seemed to be having a great deal of trouble keeping accounts. Many people were quitting him shortly after signing on with his company. Going into the session I felt fine. I was calm, alert, prepared, and in no specific emotional distress. Nothing was "wrong." In fact, it had been a good day for me, so if anything I was in a good mood. But after talking to this man for about ten minutes I found myself consumed with fury. The content of my angry thoughts and feelings had little or nothing to do with the man who was consulting me. I didn't feel mad at him or about the things he was saying. Instead, what was going through my mind were past wrongs, slights, and upsets I had experienced. Things I hadn't thought about in a long time.

What was happening was the salesman carried with him a tremendous reservoir of rage, and everywhere he went, in almost every behavior he performed, anger seeped out. However, the anger was very difficult to see, because he wasn't dramatic or overt in his expressions. The countless little ways his anger oozed out resulted in others absorbing and feeling it. He was, essentially, "sharing" his anger with others. This was useful for him because he felt less anger when others took some of it, just like you would have less trash if someone took some of it.

So the others around this man, without knowing that they were doing it, absorbed his rage and began to feel it, too. But, like me, when they took it on they couldn't tell that it was from him, so they didn't blame him for their feeling bad. Nevertheless, because they felt bad when he was around, they began to avoid being around him. They didn't know why they were avoiding him, so they found rational-sounding reasons for not doing business with him, reasons they thought were true and accounted for their need to stop using his services.

I became aware the anger I was experiencing was coming from him. I began to do maneuvers designed to prevent me from taking on his anger (this is called "blocking feelings transfers" which I'll talk about in a later chapter). When I did that, what do you suppose happened? Well, what happens if I come over to your house for dinner and I refuse your pot roast?

First, I'm being rude by not taking what you have to share with me. That's upsetting all by itself. In addition, because I don't eat my share, you end up with more pot roast than you were expecting to have. As I began to turn down the invitations to experience this man's anger, he began to consciously experience more anger himself. He began to show obvious signs of being angry. He could no longer have his anger diluted by my taking some of it; he had to experience it all himself. As a result, he got increasingly agitated and upset. By the end of the talk he was being downright hostile, and his deep reservoir of anger was apparent, giving him the opportunity to deal with and resolve it.

In dealing with people, sharing means you tell them about yourself or a part of yourself in such a way that they get to experience what you experience. If your sharing is successful, they get to internally recreate what you have been through. This is a major part of being emotionally close with people and developing intimacy. But just telling someone something is insufficient. That's why watching someone else's slides of their vacation is boring. It doesn't allow you to experience their vacation. It doesn't share. It's that transmission of experience that is powerful, that makes things interesting, not the data provided.

Many times sharing means someone actually feels what you feel. If someone shares with you how much they love someone, you can feel it. It touches you. If they share with you an outrage they have experienced, your blood can boil. When I am consulting with therapists on a case and all of the people in the presentation group begin to feel angry at the patient being presented, it's clear the therapist presenting the case is angry at the patient, others are picking up and taking on that anger as well.

The primary reason sharing is powerful is that it opposes survival wiring. For you to share with someone, you have to open up, you have to lower your defensive fields enough to open a channel through which you can deliver your experience. This requires that you be vulnerable. The other person has to do the same. So sharing actually creates vulnerability, and survival wiring is designed to prevent vulnerability. Sharing involves throwing down your weapons, unlocking your fortress doors, and letting others into the private and protected parts of your conceptual world.

Because of the vulnerability created by sharing, it can be difficult for people to do. It can be frightening to do consciously and intentionally. But because sharing transcends survival wiring, it's one of the only things that can connect human beings at a level deeper and closer than the cordial distance allowed by survival wiring. It's the only thing that really, genuinely, creates deep connection between people.

One of the important characteristics of sharing is it doesn't make others wrong. People sometimes mislabel giving criticism as sharing their feelings. There's nothing wrong with criticism, but it's different from sharing. Sharing opens a channel to other people, while criticism tends to shut it down.

Many years ago, when I was just starting out in psychology, a therapist I was seeing shared a story with me. I still remember the story, even though it has been well over a decade since that session. I can't remember what I was talking about that the story was designed to address, but I had been talking about something I was afraid to do. The therapist listened for a while and told me not long ago she had been on a hike in the Grand Canyon with a tour group. They were descending from a high place, which required navigating down the side of a cliff on a very narrow, steep path. She was terrified she said, so terrified she just wanted to sit down, and cry. "But no helicopter was going to come pluck me off the side of that mountain so there was no other choice than to just keep going."

The point, of course, was that sometimes one just has to keep going in the face of fear. But the way I got that message, that has lasted with me for over a decade, was through her sharing an incident of fear that she had experienced.

The major problem with sharing is people tend to do it unconsciously and unintentionally, not as part of their focus or purpose. As a result its power becomes diluted. We give others our angers, upsets and troubles and mess things up rather than achieve our purposes. Often, in fact, people end up sharing the upset, the bad feelings, rather than the good feelings, and then wonder why people around them are so unpleasant or angry.

When I am teaching people-handling I often use sharing as an aid, because it can produce such powerful imprinting. Sometimes I'll share with people my reaction to them and how they're behaving. I'll share how I feel and what my thoughts are when I'm role-playing with them. This makes me vulnerable, of course, because people can (and have) said, "Well, that's just you, just your reaction, it isn't necessarily true about me."

I was in an executive meeting at a company where plans for a major expansion were being discussed. Everyone was excited about the plans except one executive who was quiet for a long time. Finally he said he felt like he was a minority of one, but that he had some grave concerns and some powerful fears about the whole project. He said he felt like a wet blanket, but he was concerned about the risks the company was taking on in the new project. He talked about his concerns and worries.

His sharing was very powerful. You could have heard a pin drop in the room. It took courage to be the person sharing a contrary opinion in the face of one's colleagues who wanted to proceed full steam ahead. He risked looking foolish, being thought of as a pessimist, and engendering dissention in the ranks. So for him to share his feelings that the downside needed to be further examined was a true act of courage. It was also very helpful to the process, because many of his concerns and fears turned out to be grounded in a hard reality that nobody else was willing to look at.

Sharing always involves transcending or overcoming fear. In fact, it's one of the few times in life where the anxiety of existence is overcome rather than defended against, or denied. Sharing actually pierces through the anxiety of individual existence and for a moment allows us an emotional connection with others that is difficult for us to experience otherwise.

Sharing involves statements such as:

"What happens to me when that occurs, is . . . "

"My feelings about it are . . . "

"I'll tell you how I make sense out of it . . . "

"My experience in the situation was that . . . "

"I can't see it that way. My view is . . . "

"I'm not sure this is exactly what you mean, but . . . "

In all of these cases, the statements that make up sharing are statements that are about you, about your experience, feelings, or ideas. They are not about the other person. There is no attempt to pass them off as eternal truth, something others have to agree with in order to stay right, or as general laws of the universe. They don't blame anyone else, or if they do, they are acknowledged as doing that.

Meshing

Meshing is behavior that merges with someone else's behavior; you're doing the behavior that is complementary to theirs. It's called "meshing" because your behavior meshes with someone else's like one jigsaw puzzle piece meshes with its matching piece. An audience meshes with a speaker by being quiet while the speaker talks. A child meshes with a parent when they are quiet when the parent is talking to them. One person meshes with another when the other person is sad and crying and the other puts their arms around them.

Meshing comes naturally to humans. Babies tend to mesh automatically. When they receive a bottle, they suck. When they are held, they snuggle in. As a result, later in life meshing is frequently a first, or instinctive reaction. If someone yells at us, we fall silent. Someone comes at us, we recoil. Someone is quiet, we find ourselves talking. When someone new gets on an elevator, we move aside slightly.

Meshing is a very important ability to have, and failure to mesh can have unpleasant consequences. During my internship I experienced one of the consequences of failure to mesh. I was administering a chronic pain clinic. It required close work with the staff of the rehab unit, and I had certain job responsibilities including checking regularly with the ward staff about the progress of patients.

I discovered, to my dismay, every time I went to the unit to check on things, my supervisor had already been there and handled things. As a result, there was nothing for me to do. My supervisor was unable to mesh, to back off so I could be more active. He kept operating as though I didn't exist.

I see this same thing happen with many managers, both in the health fields and in business. They get in the way of their employees by not becoming more passive in the areas in which the employees are supposed to be more active. This undercuts the effectiveness of the employees who often begin to mesh with the manager's activity level, becoming even more passive themselves.

Then the managers wonder why their employees seem so unproductive while the managers are working so hard.

However, during my time at the pain clinic, even though my supervisor was unable to mesh with me, I unconsciously began to mesh with him. Without being aware of it, I started becoming more passive in response to his high activity level. Slowly I devoted less time to my work in the clinic and more on other tasks. This behavior didn't go unnoticed by my supervisor, though. He couldn't see his own failure to mesh, he could only see that I wasn't following through. His upset initiated a confrontation that ultimately illuminated the problem and straightened it out.

Meshing is not complicated and is natural for most of us. The problem with it tends to be the same problem that occurs for all these techniques, especially ones that tend to come naturally: people do it without awareness, which results in overuse and using it when another method is more appropriate.

Representational Matching

This technique is based on the theory that human beings generate an internal representation of the world that serves as their guide in dealing with it. It's an internal map which contains information, experience, and other references accessed in order to make decisions and utilize information. With an internal representation of the world, a person doesn't have to be in the actual presence of something to deal with it. You can know what a newspaper is like without having one in front of you because you have an internal representation of "newspaper" you can rely on when you're not in front of one.

The theory holds that in order to successfully store information into an internal representation of the world, you need some sensory medium in which to code the information. Because humans primarily use three of our five basic sensory channels for information: sight, sound, and touch, the information is stored in these forms. However, most people don't have equal talent or equal ability with all three sensory channels. As a result, every person has certain preferred channels in which they represent the world. So someone primarily uses the verbal channel, the visual channel, or the tactile channel for their internal representation of the world.

Using representational matching in dealing with people means you use words that match someone's favored sensory channel so they can more easily relate to, understand, and deal with you and your information. The way you do this is to listen for people's favored representational channel and match that channel to the words you use.

For example, if someone talks about being "stuck" in an uncomfortable position in a business deal they're speaking in tactile, feeling words. To match representational channels you would respond in the same terms. You would say something like, "Do you have a feeling about what we should do?" You don't use visual terms like, "Can you see what we ought to do" or auditory terms such as, "What sounds best to you?"

On the other hand, if someone says "I see no clear way for us to come out ahead in this business deal because the whole thing has gotten pretty foggy," they are using visual representations. In that case, respond in visual terms like, "I see what you're saying. I think it's important to get this cleared up. What do you think we need to focus on?"

I've always been skeptical of this theory because it seems oversimplified. I have also frequently noted that people often don't use one consistent channel of sensory representations when speaking. When someone doesn't use one preferred channel of sensory words, it's difficult to do representational matching in any way that's particularly helpful. However, on the occasions when I've heard a clear and consistent use of particular sensory language from someone and I've responded in that same sensory channel, it does seem to enhance their ability to understand what I'm saying.

When I was giving a people-handling program for teachers, an elementary school teacher didn't seem to understand the points I was making. I listened closely and realized she talked strictly in tactile and spatial terms. ("I can't get over this, it's so big.") Her representational system made sense—she worked with kids who were young, not very verbal and her work with them was primarily in physical activities. She was the perfect person to work with that group.

I began to use spatial and tactile terms, and talked about "making room" for things and "getting problems cut down to size." When I began to use those terms I noticed a substantial improvement in her ability to listen, consider what I said and accomplish the tasks I was helping her to complete.

There are many words which emphasize a particular sensory channel and can be used when you're talking about just about anything. Some examples are:

Visual: See, focus, foggy, clear, bright, dim, dark, black-and-white, pretty, look, vision, cloudy.

Auditory: Hear, ring, resonate, "clunk," sound, click, buzz.

Tactile: Feel, fit, over, inflate, deflate, touch, handle, jolt, smooth.

My suggestion about representational matching is similar to my feelings on all the techniques. Try it out if it seems as though it could be useful, but don't get stuck in it if it doesn't seem to be helpful. Don't spend all of your time listening for someone's representational mode rather than paying attention to other important elements in the conversation.

Chapter 8

Techniques of Confrontation

The techniques covered here are those which tend to be confrontational in nature. By "confrontive" I don't necessarily mean aggressive or hostile. I mean it in the sense of "facing up to." People often find confrontation unpleasant, and it can trigger survival reactions. It can also create emotional distance. But there are times in dealing with people when the use of confrontive techniques is appropriate or necessary to what you are trying to accomplish. In therapy, for example, people often have to confront their dysfunctional patterns. It's the therapist's job to help the person come face-to-face with them.

Matching

Matching is the opposite of "meshing." It means one of two things: First, it can mean you "match" the other person's behavior by doing the same thing they're doing. You can "Mirror" their behavior, such as sitting in the same position they're in, or apply to them some version of what they're applying to you. If they're yelling, you can yell back. If they're talking nicely, you can talk back nicely. Second, it's competing. Doing what they're doing, but in an attempt to outdo them. If we're playing tennis and I hit a hard serve at you, you can try to hit a harder return back at me.

Matching, like meshing, is natural for most people. Even very small children match. For example, pull on someone and see if they don't pull back. Push on them and see if they don't push back.

This kind of activity happened to me during a session at my office. I was seeing a twelve-year-old girl along with her mother, and I sent the mother back into the reception room so I could talk with the girl alone. The girl was a tyrant at home and had learned if she made just enough trouble she could have her own way. As a result, when her mother left the room she decided she was not sitting still for me, and she bolted for the door. I scrambled up out of my chair in time to push myself against the door so she couldn't open it. In response, she matched me, by pulling harder on the door. She was very strong, and I'm not sure how I was able to do it, but I matched her effectively, and kept the door shut. She eventually gave up, sat back down and talked to me. It turned out to be an important, even decisive step. I was the first person to successfully match her behavior.

In a later session, I discovered the secret to my strength in being able to hold the door shut. The girl's mother confided to me that she had heard the commotion in my office, come to the outside of the door, realized the girl was trying to escape, and helped me by holding the door shut from her side! It turned out it took a team effort to match the girl's behavior.

Matching someone's behavior is useful in breaking up someone's behavioral patterns. When I was dealing with a woman who not only talked a great deal, but talked louder when I tried to interrupt, I simply began to talk even more loudly as she increased her volume. This resulted in her becoming more quiet.

Escalating

Escalating is perhaps the most natural of all methods of people-handling and it's the natural extension of matching. It means you increase the intensity of your behavior. Whatever you're doing you do more of or harder. If you ask for something and don't get it, you demand it. If you speak firmly about something, you start shouting about it. If you are being nice, you become nicer, perhaps solicitous.

You can escalate in either the sensory world or the conceptual. Sensory escalations are like the example where I spoke louder. In such cases you actually "do" more of, or a more intense version of, what you are already doing. Escalation in the conceptual world means you increase the right and wrong implication of the words you're using. If you're a little upset with someone you say you don't like what they did. If you get more upset, you tell them what they did was stupid. More upset, you call it irresponsible. Still more upset you call it unbelievable. If you like something, you call it good; like it more and you call it great; like it a whole bunch and you call it terrific.

Whether done in the sensory or conceptual world, escalation raises the survival stakes. There's more of a survival threat present if I'm yelling than if I'm talking in a normal tone. There is also more of a survival threat if I call your actions awful than if I call them OK.

Many kids use escalation in attempting to handle their parents. When the parent says no, the kid escalates. They ask more, and louder. They whine, stomp, plead, and cry.

Parents commonly use escalation with their children. The parent asks the kid to do something, the kid doesn't do it. They ask again, a little more pointedly, the kid still doesn't do it. They then yell their request at the kid, face-to-face, hands-on-hips. This is so common many kids have an internal measuring guide to their parents' seriousness, judging the degree of escalation in their behavior. Then they learn to only respond to the highest level of escalation. Their parents then wonder why they have to yell to get the child to do anything.

Escalations include such progressions as:

Speaking, to firm speaking, to yelling, to screaming.

Speaking, to soft speaking, to whispering, to silence.

Gazing, to looking, to staring, to intense glaring.

"OK," to "good," to "very good," to "excellent," to "fantastic."

Asking, to pleading, to begging.

Transferring Feelings

Feelings can be transferred from one person to another. I've already discussed how this occurs in the section on sharing. However, there are other ways to transfer feelings in addition to sharing.

Behaviors that transfer feelings are generally the positive or negative communication behaviors listed in Chapter 6. Positive communication behaviors tend to transfer positive feelings, and negative communication behaviors tend to transfer negative feelings. If I want to get rid of my upset feelings, I can deal with you by yelling, being sarcastic, snide, snippy, withdrawing, or expressing disgust. If I want to share my positive feelings, I can smile, use positively loaded conceptual terms, nod, and use neutral terminology.

Negative feeling transfers have clear survival value. They're a way to get rid of those toxic feelings. If you have upset feelings, you'll feel better, your survival wiring will calm down, if you give those feelings to someone else. It's like the game of hot potato where the goal is to be the one who does not end up holding the hot potato. Most arguments are a competition of feelings-transfer methods. The rule is the one who ends up with the bad feelings loses, so the argument is a contest to see who can transfer the bad feelings to the other person.

Feelings transfers can also be blocked, as I did with my salesman patient in the previous chapter. Have you ever been upset with someone about something they did, but you were unable to get them to feel bad about it? It can make you more angry and more upset. This is what happened in the session with the angry salesman.

There are two primary ways to block feelings transfers. One method is to refuse to participate in the style of communication behaviors that the other person is engaged in. It involves violating reciprocity. By engaging in the opposite form of communication behaviors, much of the ability to transfer feelings can be prevented. If you're using angry communication behaviors with me, and I stay calm, use neutral tones, sensory terms, and neutral communication behaviors, your ability to transfer feelings to me is going to be limited.

The second method of blocking is to out-escalate the other person. This, in essence, is winning an argument. If you're successful in your escalation, and you win you may avoid taking on the other person's feelings. However, arguments produce upset feelings all their own, so this method is a bit more tricky and hazardous than the previous technique.

Adolescents are experts at blocking feelings transfers. This is one of the things that drives us crazy about them. You chew them out for their latest antisocial and previously unimaginable behavioral transgression, and they look at you with a detached, mocking smirk, and in a derisive tone of voice say, "Gosh, this is really exciting. Are you done yet?"

If you weren't already ready to kill them and bury their body, you feel like doing it after they do that to you. For most parents, if they saw even a little upset in the teen, if they took on a little remorse the parent would feel better.

But that's not what's really going on. In reality we feel better mostly because we've been able to effect a feelings transfer, and we're not stuck with all the feelings—they get some, too. So what happens when they turn down the feelings transfer is we escalate to try to accomplish it. So parents yell louder, ground longer, or use higher-level make-wrong words. They may not want to admit it, but they're doing it to try to upset the kid, to see some of their upset in them.

We don't talk much about feelings transfers because thinking that we transfer upset feelings to other people isn't very nice. Few of us like to think of ourselves as doing things that aren't very nice. But the fact of the matter is feelings transfers, especially of bad feelings, is very common. It's what revenge, and even (in the social and legal sense) punishment is all about.

Many times you will take on feelings transfers without knowing that's what you're doing. Have you ever been talking to someone and start to feel some way you hadn't felt previously? It may be a feeling that comes over you pretty quickly. You may get it just walking into a room with them. Many times this is a feelings transfer. You are taking on whatever they're feeling.

Upset customers usually want to accomplish a feelings transfer. The patron feels the upset feelings do not belong to her, they belong to the people responsible for them—the company. The complaint is an attempt to get them to take back the bad feelings, so they escalate and behave in upsetting ways. Think of how hard it is to complain without upsetting someone. It's possible, but it's not easy or natural.

As with all of these techniques, consciousness about feelings transfers is essential in learning to handle people. You need to understand what behaviors of yours transfer feelings, and how to block feelings transfers from others.

Making the Covert Overt

In nearly all human relations and communications, only a few of the messages sent, received, or perceived, are ever actually acknowledged by being put into words. The rest pass by unnamed, unlabeled, and, as a result, unnoticed. But unnoticed doesn't mean inconsequential. They still have an effect. In fact, implied messages often have more power than openly stated messages because they can't be addressed or defended against.

Making the covert overt means stating directly, in words, a message that is only implied in a conversation. This removes the message's power because many times such messages are only influential when they're left undefined.

An executive board I was a consultant to was discussing financial projections and a loan they needed to undertake a project, and what they would need to accomplish to show a profit. They only talked in vague terms about what would happen if they didn't make their projected earnings. But no one said what would happen.

And that's why people hire consultants. To say the difficult things.

"So," I commented, "If this doesn't go pretty much how you plan for it to go, you're going to go broke. Is that right?" The board members looked at me in horror. There was a long silence.

"Yes," one of them replied tentatively.

"Does that mean bankruptcy?" I asked. They began to shift in their chairs.

"Probably," came the reply.

"Then I suggest you start working on worst-case scenarios, and what you'll do if that happens, because certainly there's a chance it will happen."

Quite understandably, the executives didn't want to entertain the possibility they would have to declare bankruptcy. But as long as they just hinted at it, talked around it, it remained an undefined fear, a discomfort that controlled them in the background.

Messages are often left on the implied level because bringing them up is uncomfortable and requires unpleasant things be talked about. Often to openly state something implied is considered rude, and people often avoid being rude. This may be appropriate at a cocktail party, but when dealing with millions of dollars and the chance of bankruptcy, politeness can take a back seat to results.

The nice thing about making the covert overt is while it can be uncomfortable to say what is implied, once it's said, that particular implication loses much of its power. It works even if the other person denies that what you said is accurate. It's not necessarily important they admit what you say is right so much as the whole issue is given words. You're showing a willingness to acknowledge it, to face it up-front.

A married couple consulted me and the husband complained the wife would say, "If that happens, then you can forget it, buster."

I asked her what she meant by "forget it." She hesitated, and simply repeated that he could just "Forget it, forget the whole thing."

"Does that mean 'forget' the marriage, that you'll leave him?" I asked.

"I don't know," she said.

"Well, that's what it sounds like it means, and I think you should be clear about it if that's what you mean, so that he knows what you're talking about."

Another example where making the covert overt is important is in suicide. People can get so afraid of talking openly about concerns over someone's possible suicidal intentions, they'll actually encourage those ideas. So many people leave the issue unspoken. Unfortunately, that gives the issue power. To take away its power, it must be spoken, and something like, "Are you thinking of killing yourself?" must be stated.

Process Comments

Process comments are similar to the technique of making the covert overt. However, they don't reflect on the topic of the conversation, but on its style. While making the covert overt defines another aspect of the subject, process comments change the subject. They're about the manner of the conversation. They put into words some aspect of the conversation style or the nature of the relationship between the people speaking, that has not been stated.

Process comments are very powerful, and as a result you have to be careful with them. They can completely alter a conversation or even your relationship with someone. In fact, there are strict, unwritten social rules about them, and in many settings all process comments are considered rude. This is because they suddenly raise the level of intimacy and vulnerability. They speak directly about someone's behavior, right here and now. As a result, they set off survival wiring.

Process comments are much of what therapists and consultants are paid to do, because they're too dangerous for someone in the family or business to do themselves. It's safer if an outsider, someone neutral, does them. I've pointed out in families where someone seems to be trying to hurt someone. I've pointed out in managers' meetings that a manager seems to be alienating the others through something in his or her speaking style. I've noted when people's style brings a conversation to a halt, or when they jolt the conversation off-topic. I once confronted a manager for simply the amount that he talked, and challenged him to keep his mouth shut. I've called people's sarcasm to their attention, confronted their changing the subject, making other people wrong, and defending themselves instead of facing the issue at hand. By using process comments, the "noise" interfering with a conversation can be reduced, making for a much more effective interaction.

Process comments are statements such as, "I notice you are being quiet. What is that about?" Or, "When I say one idea, you seem to counter with another. Are you trying to thwart me?" Or even, "The way you are saying that is hurting my feelings and offending me, so I'm having a hard time listening to you."

I used process comments with a manager who was complaining about a new boss. I was doing some interpreting of the boss's behavior to the manager, at which point the manager said something particularly harsh about the boss, but with a glare at me, and a harsh tone of voice seemingly directed toward me. I agreed with the content of what the manager said, saying, "I think you may have a good point there," while in the same sentence adding a process comment, "You said that with a lot of hostility directed toward me."

I said this without rancor in my voice (the quality was more puzzlement and concern). The reason I did it was I didn't want a pattern (the manager speaking to me harshly) to be covertly set up so by naming the behaviors, even without asking for validation, I removed its power, and a pattern of harshness toward me never materialized.

Process comments can be questions. "You're looking puzzled. Am I not being clear?" Or, a comment I actually made to a client, "Every time I say anything that is the least bit unflattering to you, you crinkle your forehead, turn your head to the side, and make a face that looks like you think what I'm saying is crazy. Is that accurate to what's going on inside you?"

These examples show how pointed and raw process comments can be. Their power often occurs when there is something strange going on between people, when unacknowledged or unpleasant behaviors are running the show in some way you don't want. Process comments can disempower those behaviors.

Chapter 9

Techniques of Meaning

This chapter presents techniques that function by addressing the conceptual world—dealing with meanings.

Glossing and Deglossing

Words can be used to increase understanding, or make things clear. Words can also be used to hide and obscure. The technique of using words to conceal is called "glossing" as in "glossing over" something. This method hides meaning in the generality of words or idiosyncratic meaning. The technique of using words to illuminate, to specify, is called "deglossing" because getting specific takes off the shine that hides things from sight.

In general, conceptual words are used to gloss, and sensory words are used to degloss. This is because conceptual words tend to be categories and idiosyncratic in meaning. Sensory words are specific and have standard interpretations. Notice the use of conceptual words to gloss and the attempted use of sensory words to degloss in the following dialogue which took place in my office in response to my question about the nature of someone's background.

"Oh, you know, everybody was fine. Just the few normal skeletons in the closet. Nothing notable."

Notice the conceptual terms that do not convey a precise meaning. The family was fine, but according to what definition of fine? The skeletons were normal according to what definition of normal? In addition, what was meant by skeletons, and what was the definition of notable? The statement means virtually nothing

147

specific, outside of "My family was OK, leave it at that." So I pressed further.

"I don't understand what you mean by the 'normal skeletons'. Tell me what you mean."

"Oh, you know, everybody has their idiosyncrasies," was the reply.

This time the gloss was idiosyncrasies, a word designed to sound not too bad. However, it continued to cover things up. There was no way to know if by idiosyncrasies people liked to put ketchup on their peas, or they liked to run naked through the streets in winter.

"What did they do that was idiosyncratic?" I asked. Notice that I was now asking directly for sensory words—what did they do—in an attempt to degloss.

"Oh, I don't know, just silly stuff," came the reply.

Yet another gloss, this time silly stuff, which is still not sensory. It has no specific consensual meaning, and therefore continued to leave me without the pertinent information.

This is an example of glossing and the process of deglossing. Glosses are accomplished by communicating the positive/negative slant without giving off specifics. This is what we do when someone asks how we are and we say fine even though there may be lots of problems in our lives. It's your saying your day was pretty good. Glosses are designed to look like they are being complete, without being complete. They are saying, "Look, I'm giving you the general tone as to whether things are good or bad, and that's enough. Don't press further. I'm staying hidden here."

Deglossing means getting the language into terms that mean the same thing to you as they do to the other person. This can take effort, and you have to push. You have to ask questions like, "What happened?" and, "What did they say.?" I'll have people complain to me they have brought up some topic with the person they want to handle, and it went nowhere.

When I ask what the other person did when they brought up the issue they say, "Nothing." So I say something like, "So you said 'I want to talk to you about this' and they just stared at you blankly and silently," never saying anything?"

Of course this isn't what happened. Something went wrong in the conversation, and that's the issue, not that the other person said, "nothing."

When glossing occurs, unless you degloss, unless you are absolutely certain what someone means by their conceptual terms, then you're not going to understand and you potentially set yourself up for future problems by making agreements which are not clear agreements.

Distinguishing Purpose from Methodology

One difficulty people often have with each other is how to be confrontive and still ally with them. Criticism tends to set off survival wiring, so people are hesitant to criticize, even when it's their job. They don't want to be offensive or hurt someone's feelings.

There is a way to give even critical feedback and minimize the triggering of survival wiring. The key is to understand there's a distinction between purpose and methodology. As I discussed previously, intention is the side most closely connected with people's sense of self and a criticism of this is going to feel personal. They may not think a criticism of behavior is great, but it's one step removed from self so is easier to take.

By understanding the distinction between intention and methodology, you can either inflame someone's survival wiring and get them to feel offended and defensive (as a trial attorney might want to do in cross examination), or you can minimize the potential personal reaction of someone (as a negotiator might want to do to try to bring two parties closer together on a deal). By selectively criticizing either someone's intentions or their methodology, you can get them to agree or disagree more easily, or even find the basis for negotiations. You can even selectively compliment the intention or the methodology and criticize the other, and get a variety of interesting, powerful responses as a result.

For example, a simple comment which makes this distinction is to say, "I know you didn't intend for this to happen, but what you said hurt my feelings." This statement offers a reassurance about your thoughts on the person's intention. You're saying, in effect, "I'm not calling you a bad or malevolent person who did this maliciously. I know you meant well, so you're still, at core, OK to me. I like you and want to stay friends with you." The person is more able to listen because they're not afraid of their core value being threatened.

Other statements that distinguish intention from methodology are statements like:

"I think you were trying to be helpful, but I ended up angry about it."

"The way you did that made me think what you intended was to . . ."

"I'm not sure what you meant to do, but what you did was a problem."

"You upset me. Did you mean to do that?"

The basic technique is always the same—to address intention and methodology as distinct, and not necessarily uniform, elements in someone's functioning.

Metaphors

Metaphors communicate a point, concept, or an idea. Their power is that the topic used can be adjusted and changed in many ways while still communicating the same point. As a result, the topic can be altered to make it as easy as possible for someone to understand.

For example, if I want to talk about the concept "freedom" with someone who didn't understand, I could use any number of metaphors to try to get the idea across. I could talk about a baby bird learning to fly, about concentration camp prisoners being set free, or climbing a mountain and seeing for many miles around. Because the actual content is not what is important in a metaphor, it can be shifted as needed in order to "talk the person's language." Metaphors offer a very flexible and powerful way of making points to people who listen in a variety of ways.

Some writers have thought so much of metaphors they've theorized they're at the very heart of human communication and understanding. Symbols are forms of metaphors, which Carl Jung studied extensively. So are myths, which Joseph Campbell examined. Jesus talked in extended metaphors called parables. They're powerful because they convey a universal point, and can be tailored to any culture or individual.

Techniques of Meaning

Metaphors operate on the principle of generalization. Specific examples or events can be very different on the surface, but when looked at in the world of the conceptual, similarities can be seen that don't exist in the sensory world. In this way a point can be communicated about life, or an experience can be more clearly conveyed than if it were simply told to someone else.

The Sufis, the mystics of Islam, primarily use metaphorical stories in their teachings. For example, there's a story about a Sufi master seeing a man in a field who had dug a hundred two-foot holes. When the master asked what he was doing the man said, "Looking for water." The master then asked if it wouldn't be better to dig one two-hundred foot hole.

This is not a story about holes or water, rather about commitment, staying on course, and persistence. The topic is water because the Middle East is a desert, and water is a precious commodity. A story about water matters, and is easy for people to think about and to realize the meaning of.

For a time I had a perfect metaphorical entree into people's lives at my office. Over the course of a year the city dug up the streets, sewers, and sidewalks all around my office. It was a terrible mess, and for a while it seemed I was surrounded by a moat, as the streets in front and down the side of my building were nothing but mud when it rained.

Because of the construction my consulting and clinical clients often had to park a block or two away and carefully make their way through the mud, dust, dirt, workers, and bulldozers. Since most were unaccustomed to the experience and found it to be unpleasant, or at least strange, they often commented on it as they arrived at my office. I began to notice their comments about the streets were often metaphors for where they were in their lives, work or themselves.

For example, I had several clients trying to dig themselves out of substantial personal or professional messes. They were just getting into the process and didn't yet see the end. Their comments were, "Boy, it sure is a mess out there. It's awful. It looks like it's never going to get done."

They were expressing the same feelings about my streets as they had about their lives. Other clients were seeing distinct progress in

151

their lives. Their comments were "I bet you'll be glad when they're done." Or, "I see they're coming along."

When I discovered people talked about the roadwork from the same perspective they were seeing their lives, I found I could talk to them in the same metaphorical language, and communicate new perspectives they needed to have. To people feeling mired and hopeless, I said, "It sure is a mess, isn't it? It's easy to forget that if they just keep at it the roads are going to be a lot nicer. It takes faith on my part to remember that it will get better when I'm in the middle of the mess."

To those who could see progress in their lives I would use validating, metaphorical comments like, "Yeah, it's really nice to see progress and to know the streets are going to be nicer when it's all done." It seemed we were talking about the streets, when we were really talking about their lives.

It's this ability to alter the content of a metaphor so it uses whatever content is most readily understood that makes metaphors a powerful people-handling tool. If you use a content familiar to someone or consistent with how someone sees the world, you'll be able to communicate about virtually anything.

For example, if you wanted to show someone a particular situation is completely unworkable when they aren't so sure that's the case, you could use a wide variety of metaphors, from the hokey to the profound.

1. Travel or trip metaphor: "It's a dead-end."
2. Game or puzzle metaphor: "The pieces just aren't going to fit."
3. Academic metaphor: "It's history."
4. Driving metaphor: "You can't get there from here."
5. Meteorological or baseball: "It's a washout."
6. Aerospace or airline metaphor: "It's a no-go."

One of my first introductions to the power of metaphors occurred during a medical conference. The staff would interview a person being treated for cancer, in order to explore their experience with the disease and the treatment personnel, and to learn about how best to deal with people in their situation. During one session an interviewee had a tumor that caused blindness in one eye. When he was asked about the effects of his cancer, he reported various effects including his one eye "blowing out." This was hardly a literal description, physically it was intact and had a normal appearance.

I was surprised by his metaphorical reference to a blowout and I recall turning to a colleague and whispering, "I wonder where he got that." A little while later the interviewer asked what the man did for a living—he was an electrician! So of course he thought of his eye as having "blown out." That's what electrical things do, blow out and go dark. He saw the world through electrician's logic.

If I were dealing with this man I would work electrician's logic into the way I talked to him. If I were inquiring into his emotional state, I would not ask him about stress, which is a term from physics and psychology. Instead, I would ask him about feeling overloaded or burned out. If I wanted to set up a time to talk with him I wouldn't talk about a session, I would talk about arranging a time where we could connect.

A specific, distinct, content-based, logical structure for seeing the world is not unique to electricians. Everyone thinks about life in the logic appropriate to their history, or their profession. There's almost always a particular reasoning that can be used to talk with people metaphorically.

In another instance a professional football player consulted me because he had been injured, which threw him into a tremendously uncertain position about his future. He was upset, hadn't been sleeping well, and feared his career was about to be cut short. Given the nature of his injury, that wasn't an altogether irrational fear.

He talked about this injury "really knocking him for a loop" and that he was "down and having trouble getting up again." It made him feel "weak" and "low" to be "sidelined." If I started talking to this man in medicalogical, humanistic, psychology terms, about "healing" or "being easy on himself" or "being accepting and understanding" of himself, he would have listened to me as if I were some bleeding-heart goofball who didn't understand him at all.

I had to talk to him in "football logic." I talked about how he took a "real hard hit" where it was like "several things coming at him at once." I talked about how it's no fun to get knocked like that, especially when it was a "blindside." I also talked about his emotions, that he was having to "push through that (emotional) pain." I talked about "resilience," getting "knocked down and getting back up," "huddling" with his medical people, and taking "time out" to get better.

As regards his feelings of hopelessness about his future, I spoke of "getting a new position" in his life if he could not return to football, and needing some training. I pointed out other professions and activities were not "second string" but required new training, new drills, and new skills.

My speaking to him in this way helped him listen and understand what I was saying. He could "tune in" because he didn't have to translate my logic into his logic. I didn't sound "shrinky," I sounded "normal." I just, in his words, "made sense." He could hear me easily.

Many of the metaphorical phrases may have sounded too obvious and even silly, but when they resonate in the world as you hear the world, they don't sound hokey. They sound sensible. Not once did the football player feel my talking sounded strange or I was being pretentious.

The failure to use appropriate metaphorical language can result in someone feeling you don't understand them or you're not realistic about their situation. For example, many people hear psychological language as airy-fairy or "psychobabble" and so can't take value from it. That's because their world operates with different terms and a different logical base. Although it takes some thought and energy, it's often much, much easier to talk in other people's language to get your point across rather than to try to get them to listen in yours.

A colleague of mine and I used metaphors almost constantly when we ran groups for adolescents. Dealing effectively with them requires a translation from "adultese" into "teenagerese" It's a translation most people don't make. But if you don't, teenagers write you off. We found metaphors worked very well in making the transition easier for us. We used metaphors from whatever area the kids cared about—music, clothes, friends, computers, movies. Whatever we could get our hands on.

One of the things that's especially difficult to do with adolescents is to "humanize" their parents for them, to get them to view their parents more realistically than they tend to do. We also used metaphors to repeatedly talk about how their parents weren't perfect, weren't going to be perfect, and how they had to learn to handle them.

One of their favorite metaphors was about how people get "stuck" psychologically. Psychological development can be like walking forward, but sometimes people get their psychological growth stopped, like getting your foot caught in bubblegum. (Teenagers are very familiar with chewing gum.) We even had them walk across the room and act like their foot was "stuck" when they were talking about their parents' imperfections.

Metaphors are also powerful in their ability to convey experience. You can't communicate experience well if someone else has never experienced anything similar to yours. Metaphorical language can solve the problem by using a content which shares comparable experience. Bill Cosby is a master of this technique. He has a great routine about how his wife shows him what it's like to go through childbirth by grabbing his lower lip and pulling it up and over his head.

In later chapters that talk about purpose, where metaphors are used for specific reasons, their use will become obvious. Metaphors can be used to communicate or induce experience, get principles and points across, and give information either overtly or subtly.

Reframing

When I was repainting the interior of my house, I chose a paint for the living room, took a sample home, and put a splotch of it on the wall to see how it looked. To my horror, I saw it was nowhere near the color I had picked in the store. It looked terrible. I examined the label which said it was the color I had chosen. It looked good in the store, but looked terrible in my living room.

The walls I was painting were a pale blue, and I wondered if they could be producing an optical illusion about the new color. But the paint color was so far off I couldn't imagine it was just the result of the background color. But I decided that it wouldn't hurt to go into another room with white walls and put up another splotch of paint and see how it looked. Amazingly, that splotch was exactly the right color. The wrongness of the color had, in fact, been an illusion created by its contrast with the pale blue walls. When it was surrounded by white it looked fine. I went ahead and painted the living room with the paint, even though the optical illusion remained almost to the very end.

This is the principle behind a technique called reframing. The nature, or quality, of anything changes depending on what it's surrounded by. Meaning is always the result of a contrast between the particular issue in question and what surrounds it. Reframing is the technical name for altering the background or the comparison against which something is placed. This surrounding area is called the "frame."

The term originated in the art world. The look of paintings (much like the look of my new living room paint) is largely determined by the frame they're surrounded by. The frame can make a painting look good or bad. Similarly, by altering the conceptual territory "around" an issue, a new perspective or new meaning can be generated without ever having to touch the issue itself. This can be a very important ability to have, because some issues can't be changed.

I was asked to consult on a case in which a therapist was working with a woman in a dilemma. She and her husband had an awful relationship. They argued frequently. Periodically one would pack the other's things and threaten to throw them out. Ultimately they would relent, and everything would be OK for a while. Then accusations would start again and the whole cycle would recur.

The woman was quite young and from a family where her parents had virtually an identical relationship. For years her father threatened to leave her mother, and her mother threatened to throw her father out. But every time someone would relent, and at the last minute they would reconcile.

The issue for which I was sought was the woman had finally moved out after their last fight and was staying with a friend. But she couldn't afford to stay on her own for long. She was having trouble choosing between moving in with her parents, or moving back with her husband, where the cycle of upsets would start up again.

In fact, neither choice was very good. There was nothing that could be done about it. There was no changing the "facts" that the woman had to live somewhere, and both of her options weren't great. So to be able to get her out of her dilemma, the situation had to be reframed. I offered a new frame around the issue of moving in with her parents or her husband. I suggested it didn't really matter which choice she made.

The frame I offered was that the choice of place to live was a minor issue they should pay fairly little attention to. I suggested that wherever the woman chose to live now was strictly temporary, a place of transition. The real issue was her life and how she was going to build it into a successful one. She needed to concentrate on that issue, the long-term issue of her goals and aspirations, and what she was doing to accomplish them. In fact, she could decide where to live based on which place would be the least hindrance to her progressing with her life. Her living arrangement would be an unfortunate interim part of reaching her goals, but all goals require struggle and compromises in the process.

What I did in this example was to "enlarge" the frame in which the issue was seen. No longer was it a "here and now" question, instead, it became simply one small aspect of how she was going to work on herself to make her life work.

That enlarged frame took the pressure off her decision, removed the anxiety from it and got her unstuck. This broadened frame didn't change the reality she was going to have to deal with, but it changed the meaning of her decision. It took it from being the most important problem in the world to an issue of least-intrusive temporary lodging while focusing her energy on her overall life.

Another time I was working with a CEO of a company that was doing fine but was not growing, only keeping pace by constantly improving controls and costs. The CEO was upset about why nothing he was doing was working. He began to feel incompetent and inadequate. He considered quitting or retiring, but then he attended a national conference of his particular industry and discovered, much to his surprise, that virtually everyone in his business was experiencing exactly the same problem. He returned from the conference a much different man, feeling better, more confident, and more able to work.

Why? The information didn't change. He was still having trouble expanding his business. In fact, in some ways he received worse news, the whole industry was suffering. What the meeting did was change the frame inside of which he was reacting. He had been reacting as if everyone else was OK, and some personal inadequacy was resulting in his failure.

That frame was replaced by a new one. The new outlook "business is just difficult right now," took the pressure off him personally. He felt less distressed about himself because it was no longer an issue of him or his competence. As a result he could find ways to respond to the changing marketplace, stop berating himself, and get on with trying to increase his business.

A manager I consulted with was bemoaning his progress. His group was not doing particularly well, while those of several of his colleagues were very successful. He wasn't producing the numbers the other groups were producing. He was irritable with his employees, was having trouble sleeping, and had other signs of distress. I reviewed in great detail the history of his particular group. As it turned out, when he took over the division it was deep in the hole. He didn't know it at that time, but none of the other groups were in the same kind of trouble as his. When seen from that view, it was clear that he had made substantial progress; as much as the others, and in fact, in some ways, quite a bit more. He had performed as well—or better—than the others had. When viewed through this frame, his performance was at least on a par with the other managers.

This kind of reframing is one reason psychotherapy patients are often asked to recount their history and examine their childhood. Not only does this review often provide useful information, but it expands the frame in which their current issue is seen. People tend to think they shouldn't have the problems they're having. But when their current struggles are seen against their history, they see that their problems make sense. It alters the meaning of their distress, makes it not so personal, not so much about their quality as a person.

Expanding a frame is often used when working with families as well. I was working with a family in which the teenage son was generally a good kid, but he also had quite a stubborn streak. It was clearly acquired from the father, who was often extremely unyielding. The father complained about the mulishness of the son and about his difficulty getting the son to do what he wanted him to do. Chores were a problem, as were curfews.

I asked the father if the son took drugs or if his son belonged to gangs. To both he said no. So I asked the father how he thought his son had the ability to say no to drugs and gangs, given the pressures present in his school. The father said he didn't know, and had never really thought about it. I asked him to think some about it. I pointed out it might have to do with his stubbornness. I noted that in the context of the father wanting the son to do things, the stubbornness was certainly a problem, but in the context of his son not being a patsy for others who did not have his best interests at heart, his stubbornness was a great asset.

The father agreed this made sense. I went further, to frame his son's stubbornness as a gift the father had given him that could stand the son in good stead when there were pressures on him to misbehave in life. The father had never thought about it. He had only seen the son's obstinance as a personal attack, a challenge to his authority. Once he didn't take the son's stubbornness so personally, we could move on to talking about realistic methods of negotiation and consequence regarding the chores and other issues.

In this example I again expanded the frame from the chores to the broad view of the son's life. I offered a broader perspective, that showed the son as an independent person, and the importance of "stubborn" behavior in order to get through life successfully.

Reframing is based in the principle that nearly every human behavior is valuable and useful—in the right circumstances. By altering the circumstances through which a behavior is viewed, it takes on new meanings. This change in meanings can powerfully affect people and your dealings with them.

Instead of expanding the frame, it is also possible to "shift" a frame. This means taking the behavior and putting a whole new group of elements around it.

There's a scene that demonstrates a shift in frame in the movie *The Right Stuff* about the early days of the space program. In it, some of the original astronauts are getting into an argument because of some sexual exploits they have been involved with. At that point another astronaut stops the argument by saying that sex isn't the issue, but "monkeys" are. Russia has been sending monkeys into space, and is liable to beat the Americans in the space race. That, he says, is the real issue. This silences the others, completely changes their feelings, conversation, and behavior. They realize what they are focused on is the wrong thing, that they're viewing themselves and each other from the wrong perspective.

This type of reframing can be very effective with teenagers. In fact, it can be used to drive teenagers absolutely crazy. Adolescents have, as a major goal in life, proving they aren't like their parents. They are "independent—their own person." Of course, nothing could be farther from the truth, since they are slaves to the opinions of each other. Their definition of independence is that they acted differently from how their parents wanted them to act. What I frequently do with teenagers is describe how their behavior, especially their most troublesome behavior, is not only not different from what their parents want them to do, it's exactly what their parents want them to do.

For example, I saw one kid whose father was a trial lawyer. He and his father were constantly arguing over the son's habits; he liked to play his guitar and not study. The kid complained about all the arguing and told me what a creep his dad was.

I said to the kid, "A creep? If I were you I wouldn't be so unkind, because you're going to turn out to be just like him. You're already in training. I can already tell that you're not going to be a musician. You're going to be a lawyer like your dad."

"No way!" he shrieked. "Like, I'm going to be a musician, man. A good one."

I chuckled. "I don't think so. You're already farther along the road to being a lawyer than a musician. I know you practice your guitar, but you don't practice it nearly as much as you practice something else. You know what you're most practiced at? Arguing. And arguing is what lawyers do. Musicians don't spend their time arguing. They avoid arguments because they interfere with their practice. But that's not you, you'd rather argue than practice. You pick up on any chance to argue. No, you're not training to be a musician, you're training to be a lawyer, just like your dad. Suits, ties, briefcases, and BMWs."

This shift in frame gave a whole new meaning to his arguing. He had thought that his arguing meant he was independent, that he was "standing up" to his father. But now it meant he was behaving just like his father, just like a budding lawyer. That wasn't what he wanted at all. After this conversation, for the first time he actually started refusing to argue. Once his arguing did not serve his intended purpose, he didn't want to do it anymore. The arguing diminished substantially.

This is the power of reframing, and this kind of outcome is not uncommon. When you give a new frame or new perspective to the circumstances surrounding an event or data, a new meaning appears. And because meanings are so important in our conceptual worlds, a change in them often makes changes elsewhere including behavior.

A man consulted me who was hated by nearly everyone. He was angry, irritable, controlling, and unpleasant to be with. His greatest talent seemed to be to alienate people. I listened to his angry stories and complaints about everyone. He even complained about previous therapists who had told him he was angry.

Instead of telling him how angry he was, I reframed the issue. I told him I knew what underlies anger is hurt, and he was a hurt person much more than an angry person. I pointed out how, for human beings, feelings of hurt and fear are the basis for anger, and he must have been mistreated quite badly at some point in his life. He had never heard anyone frame his behavior in this way, and he was immediately touched by it. It almost immediately changed his view of himself, and he began to soften up. He felt touched and understood like "he had never been before." And where he had never been able to tolerate working on himself for more than a few sessions at a time he proceeded to work for over five years and completely change how he dealt with people.

The third type of reframing is to "contract" the frame through which the issue is seen. In contracting the frame, you make fewer elements surrounding the issue relevant. You get it more focused. For example, "exception" is a contracted frame. It means "forget the big picture just this once, and focus on this time as being special."

I used to do a lot of mountain biking, and I learned that long distance mountain bicyclists use a form of sensory frame contracting when they do endurance bicycle rides. Going up a steep grade on a bike, despite the low gear is no fun. It's hard work, and your body says it can't do it, that you'll never make it. If you look up ahead at the road, at the peak you are trying to climb, your mind sees what you have to do, and you begin to feel tired and overwhelmed. But if you keep your eyes focused about a foot in front of your front tire, and just watch that spot, you'll not feel so fatigued. This contracted view helps you forget about the grade, forget about the big picture and concentrate on riding, on this one pedal push.

Contracting the frame is what Alcoholics Anonymous helps people do when they talk about living "one day at a time." Forget tomorrow, the day after, next year, or how you're going to be able to tolerate living your life without alcohol. That may very well be impossible to tolerate and create upset that then becomes a reason to drink. So just look at it for today, that's all. You can tolerate it for just twenty-four hours.

Contracting a frame of reference can often be a tool to "bring someone back down to reality," to get them to face something "right here and right now." A contraction of the frame, for example, is the appropriate response to that irritating criticism "What if everyone did what you're doing?" You contract the frame with, "If that were the case it would be a real mess. But it isn't the case, not everyone is doing what I'm doing, so it's not the issue. And by the way, why don't you like what I'm doing?"

Frame contracting is also what people working on an intense project have to do to keep themselves at the energy level required to accomplish the project. They say to themselves, "This is one month out of my life, that's all. Just one month. I can give up one month to this project. It will not go on forever. I can survive it."

Myself and many of my fellow students used this technique regarding graduate school. As anyone who has been through any sort of professional school can attest, graduate education is an endurance contest as much as anything. It's essentially a rite of passage where you jump through as many flaming hoops as the faculty can gleefully set up for you. While it's not something someone who is thoroughly sane would put themselves through, it's required if one desires to join certain professional clubs. What helped us get through it was to remind ourselves it was only a specified period of time. We wouldn't be in graduate school forever. So we could tolerate it for some time. We mentally set aside the few years it would take, and devoted ourselves to getting through in that time.

Many activities in life that have to do with meanings and agreements are entirely based on frames and reframing. Political positions are good or bad depending on the background against which you view them. In seeing the world through the frame of individual liberties, property rights, personal freedom, individual choice and responsibility, typical Republican platforms make sense. But viewing the world through the frame of caring for people, desires to alleviate human suffering, and needed social service, typical Democratic platforms make sense. They're both right depending on the frame you put them in. That's also why arguing politics almost never works; they are based on different frames, which makes for two valid but irreconcilable conversations. I'm arguing about how the lake looks on sunny days, and you're arguing about how the lake looks on snowy days.

Making Reframing Work

In order for reframing to be effective, several elements have to be present. It works because there are different valid levels of logic that control how the world works. In order to reframe, you have to redraft the issue from a different point of view. Reframing is not the same as offering some sort of palatable lie you think someone will swallow. As I've commented before, that kind of deception may work over the short term, but over the long haul it'll backfire. The lack of genuineness will come back to haunt you. Real reframing relies on Cognitive Diversity, because you have to see a different way of looking at the issue that is as least as valid or perhaps even more valid than the current one. In all the examples I used at times I reframed, I really believed the new frame I was offering. You should never, ever, offer a frame that you don't see as valid.

In order to be an effective reframer, you have to see many aspects of the world, the truth about how the world works on many levels. If you have a very narrow, constricted world-view, only one way of seeing the world or one way of viewing human beings, reframing may be difficult or impossible for you to do. If this is true of you, you might not want to use reframing.

It's best, though, to see the many truths that run the world. Remember how I said masterful people-handling often requires personal growth? This is what I'm talking about. In order to be an effective people-handler, you have to have more freedom of movement in the conceptual world than does whoever you are handling. That means you had best develop some abilities to see the world in different ways. The best people handlers see the truths in many different places and people.

In addition to a new frame being valid for you, the frame you present must be valid to the receiver as well. It does no good to present a frame that's going to be so outlandish to the person you're dealing with they write it off immediately. It's important reframing be done carefully and thoughtfully, not impulsively or rashly.

It's also important to understand it can be wrenching, even reality-shaking, to have one's frame altered. The interaction between the frame and the event or the issue is what makes up reality in the conceptual world. It can cause a feeling of being unbalanced, of being "shaken up." So you have to understand and not indiscriminately blow people out of the water with new frames.

Paradox

A paradox looks like it should produce one outcome, and produces its opposite. It's paradoxical if the louder you yell, the softer your voice becomes.

There's a technique for dealing with people called a "paradox" which is designed to produce the opposite of what it seems it should produce. Its mechanism of operation is very different from most techniques in dealing with people because it addresses two different levels of human functioning at the same time.

As I've noted before, the human psyche and human functioning is filled with irony and paradox. What this means is people often don't do what they do for the reasons they say. Even if they think those reasons are valid, there may be another level of cause that is often driving their behavior. For human beings, this deeper level of cause is usually resistance. It's the direction and purpose of this resistance that is addressed by paradox.

When we try to change people, get people to do something, or intervene with them in some way, we often end up unwittingly resisting their resistance. This produces the classic "unstoppable force meeting an immovable object" phenomenon, and instead of getting results, we get stuck. When this occurs, it's often necessary to give up our resistance to their resistance, which can produce results. We can also encourage what they're doing already, which, if based on resistance, will change because they must continue to resist us. Those effects are called paradox.

I was seeing a family in therapy, and this group had been having some pretty rowdy fights. They spent the first session complaining about the fights, demonstrating to me how they fought, and all the while talking about how much they wanted to stop the fights. But they continued.

I thought it was likely the fights were fueled by resistance to each other's resistance to fighting. To not fight would be to "give in" so instead of trying to stop the fights, I told the family we needed to understand how the fights worked in great detail (which was absolutely true). So I instructed them to have a full-blown fight before the next session. I carefully and individually got agreement from every family member to have, and participate in, a fight before the next session.

When the family returned for the next session they admitted, with great embarrassment and shame, they had not been able to fight as they were instructed. They had failed their assignment. For the first week in memory, they didn't fight.

The family members were no longer able to resist each other's desire to stop fighting by fighting. They had all agreed to fight, so to fight would be to give in to each other. They couldn't resist in the same way they always had. But they could still resist—they could resist me. Instead of a conflict with each other, they set up a conflict with me. I instructed them to fight, and they resisted "giving in," which produced the paradoxical result of preventing fights.

In another case I was giving a workshop to a large association. During one part of the talk the group was to break into small groups to practice some people-handling exercises. I was told before the talk this group was famous for being slow to get into small groups, and we were in danger of losing up to fifteen minutes of time as they milled around, got coffee, water, went to the bathroom, and talked. We were on a tight time schedule. That kind of delay would throw our whole schedule off. So I needed to do something to get them to the rooms on time.

Now, the most logical approach would be to escalate and to tell them how important it was to get to the rooms quickly. But this group had been to many workshops before, and were accustomed to speakers saying that kind of thing. I figured that kind of approach would never work. Instead, I chose a paradox.

When I had completed the first part of my talk, I told them now was the time to break into small groups, but that I wanted to say something. I told them we were on a tight time schedule, and they had to get to their rooms quickly, but I knew most of them would not do so. I told them I knew some of them had been told to "go to their rooms" when they were a child, so they were resistive to anyone telling them to go to their room and they would take their time in complying. I also told them I knew some of them simply didn't like being told what to do, and would be slow for that reason. I told them that it was understandable if they were late and sent them off to their rooms for the small groups.

The rest of the workshop went very well, and at the end, when I was meeting with my assistants who had run the small groups, they could not stop laughing because they had never seen that group of people run so fast in their lives. They said the participants were falling all over each other to be on time, and the very few who were late came running in profusely apologetic.

My intervention of being "understanding" about lateness and their resistance to being on time didn't sound like it should have produced the outcome of speedier attendance. Instead, I was giving license for them to be late, but it got them to hurry. I set up an internal conflict for them, between their own resistance and the realization their resistance was foolish and would cost them in their learning. They had to decide whether to go with their foolish resistance behavior, or to be on time.

There are several elements to a paradoxical intervention, all of which must be followed, or it won't work. First, you must agree with someone's resistance. You must stop making them wrong, and make them right for their resistance. With the workshop group I told them their resistance was understandable. Second, you must give reasons for their resistance that make it right, but in addition set up an internal conflict for them. With the workshop group I defined the reason for their resistance as being childhood rebellion. Not one of those people wanted to be seen as a childish, rebellious person, so they were caught between resisting hurrying and resisting being childish.

Third, you must make the reasons that they don't like OK with you. You have to tell them that it's not a problem for you they have these reasons. I was clear with the workshop participants that I understood their reasons for being resistive, and it was OK with me. You can't make their reasons wrong. Otherwise, you set up resistance to you, or what you want, and that's the very thing you are trying to avoid. (Unless you are specifically getting them to resist something as I did with the family.) Finally, you must maintain your position no matter what happens.

I did the paradox differently with the family that fought in one respect. I actually gave them something to resist, namely my instruction to fight. The difference between this and the usual form of paradox, was that I was working on their relationship with each other, not with me, so I was free to trigger their resistance to me. What I was doing was removing their resistance to each other. That followed all three steps of paradox. They were told to go with their resistance (that is, to fight with each other), that there was good reason to go with their resistance (so that we could see how a fight works in great detail), and that it was OK with each of them to go with their resistance (they each individually agreed to do so). So the intervention was inserted between them rather than between a group and myself, as was done in the workshop.

But the most important aspects of paradox are two other elements. These are basic to all paradox, and if they're missing paradox won't work.

First, you cannot say anything you don't believe. Just like with reframing, this isn't a manipulation where you give an acceptable lie in order to manipulate an outcome. That doesn't work because people can feel the lack of genuineness. Instead, whatever reasons you give them, and whatever you encourage, you have to see as valid. This is where Cognitive Diversity is again required. With the family, I really would like to have had them conscious and aware during a fight so I could hear what starts it and how it progresses. If they really had done what I asked instead of resisting me, it would have been just as good. With the workshop participants, I really did believe childhood resistance ran their resistance to getting to rooms on time. I've worked with thousands of people, and I think that was the most prevalent reason for them being late. So in neither case was I saying anything I didn't absolutely believe. They were mechanisms operating on different levels that I had enough Cognitive Diversity to be able to see.

Second, you have to be OK with not getting your outcome. A paradox is only true if it is a paradox for you as well as them. This means in order to use a paradox, you have to let go of your own desire for the outcome you want. You must be willing for their response not to be the one you want. As I noted before, it was really OK with me if the family did fight. And while I preferred that the workshop participants be on time, I had long before resigned myself to the probability that no matter what I did they would not be, and I had made peace with myself about it. I could have comfortably attributed it to survival wiring, and not been upset about it at all.

I can't emphasize enough that paradox is not manipulation. It's not "reverse psychology." Paradox has to be truly paradoxical in order to be effective. And to be truly paradoxical, it has to include your intention as well as theirs. It requires that you give up your attachment to your outcome. In the previous chapter, when I told my patient I was sorry I was nagging him and that we needed to get back to what he was talking about, I meant it. I wouldn't have been upset if he had done what I asked. It wasn't a trick! But it produced a paradoxical effect. When the man paid his bill when I skipped a month of sending him statements, I was resigned to the possibility of his not paying his bill.

What this means is you must have a high level of Cognitive Diversity in order to do good paradox, and you have to be willing to let go of your desired outcomes. These are not easy things, and you should only use paradox to the extent that you have these abilities. Otherwise, you're being manipulative, and that doesn't work.

Let me give you a couple more examples of paradox. It's difficult to give examples out of context, so I'm not going to list them as I have some other techniques. We'll talk more about paradox in the chapters on purpose.

I had a consulting agreement with an agency that hired a new director. When I met him I told him my goal was to be helpful to the agency, and in order to do that I needed to support him and the way he wanted to work. He had my explicit permission to tear up the present agreement and make a new one where he used me anywhere from not at all to much more. The outcome was he doubled both my fee and the time he contracted for. If he had said goodbye, I would have been sad, but unresistive, because I had already made peace with the possibility I would lose the contract.

When I have someone new consult with me about therapy, I nearly always encourage them to shop around for therapists if they so desire, or to think overnight about their decision to start therapy with me. I want my clients to have freedom and what's best for them, and I mean it. If that means I have no clients, I'll do something else. But in over 90% of the cases, they return. Its effect is paradoxical. Permission to leave produces a desire to stay.

Paradox is extremely powerful, and can be easily corrupted into manipulation. You have to know what you're doing and be sure of your own integrity to use it well. If you can do those things, you have at your disposal one of the most powerful techniques there is for relating to people. If you can't, you need to avoid paradox like the plague. Becoming manipulative will not help you to be more effective with people.

Chapter 10

Techniques of Behavior

This chapter discusses methods that deal with people by addressing behavior. Of all the means presented in this book, these rely the least on talking.

About Behavior

It's easy to think you, and other people, choose your behavior through conscious processes, knowing and understanding the reasons for what you do. It isn't true. The things that control your behavior may be very different from what you think they are. We already talked about two examples of this; communication behavior, when you think the content of a conversation is affecting you, and resistance when you don't feel you're resisting. Behavior is often controlled by, and can be affected through, causes we aren't readily aware of. This chapter talks about many of the forces that affect behavior, but are often not readily apparent.

Reinforcement

Reinforcement is not, as is commonly thought, something that feels good. It's not the same as "reward." Sometimes reinforcements do feel good, but that's not the quality that makes them so. A reinforcement is what causes a behavior to repeat. Despite how it may seem to you, it's not always things that feel good which cause behaviors to repeat.

Because we tend to think of reinforcements as things that feel good, it's very easy to inadvertently train someone to act in the very ways that you don't want. Because we tend to think that doing things that feel bad to someone will not make their behavior repeat, we can overlook the reinforcers that are occurring. An example of this is the pattern of negative reciprocity discussed in Chapter 6. In negative reciprocity, my use of negative communication behaviors reinforces your use of them. And your use of them reinforces my use of them. We may be operating on the notion that if I do things that feel bad to you you'll change, but in negative reciprocity the opposite is true. Negative communication behaviors reinforce negative communication behaviors. So don't confuse feeling good with reinforcement, because by only looking for things that feel good you won't see the actual reinforcements generating or maintaining behavior.

Parents fall into a trap related to this. They think if they do something to a kid that she doesn't like (such as being grounded or taking away privileges), it will inherently stop the behavior, or at least diminish it. And in some kids it will. But in other kids punishment actually reinforces misbehavior. Why? Perhaps because kids experience themselves as powerful when they can upset parents, and parents punishing them is a sign that they've been successful. But for whatever reason, parents have been known to say, "I keep taking away stuff they like, and they keep doing what I don't want them to do."

You see, it all depends on what happens to be reinforcing to any particular person and behavior. And what reinforces you, or some behavior in you, may not be the same which is reinforcing to my behavior or to me. So what you must do is find what is reinforcing to any particular behavior you want. How do you do that? Through observation and trial and error.

A woman who consulted me was very intolerant of feeling good. Every time I complemented her, she got upset and immediately stopped what she was doing. I discovered that the best way to reinforce any behavior in her was to challenge it, question, or doubt it. If I criticized what she was doing, she would often increase it. If she were smiling and I wanted to reinforce her smiling, I would challenge what she was talking about. But if I were to ever say, "it's nice to see you happy," in about two minutes she would have been in tears. So I learned to reinforce behavior by being confronting rather than nice. In essence, I trained her to be happy by challenging her happiness.

I could list common reinforcements, but it would rapidly become nonsensical, because virtually anything is reinforcing to some behaviors and people at some times. It may be unpleasant to think about, but even other people being upset can reinforce behavior in us. I'll give more specific examples of using reinforcements in the chapter on changing people, but for now just be aware reinforcements are not necessarily what you think they should be. Reinforcements are things—whatever—that cause behavior to repeat. They are often discovered by trial and error.

Punishment

Where reinforcement is not necessarily something that feels good, punishment is not necessarily something that feels bad. In behavioral terms, punishment is simply something that diminishes the likelihood of a behavior repeating.

Punishment is a lot trickier technique than reinforcement because researchers noticed early on that while effective punishment can indeed diminish behaviors, it often causes significant side-effects. In addition to the punished behavior diminishing, other behavior, often unpredictable in nature, can appear.

The reason is that punishment is designed to diminish behaviors. Since most behaviors are in some way tapped into survival wiring, by punishing behavior you're in essence diminishing the ability of the person to generate survival behaviors. This raises the level of threat present, and the person generates alternative defensive behaviors to take the place of the diminished ones. You can get a rat to stop doing something by shocking the floor under its feet, but the rat will also turn and attack any other rat in the cage.

Punishment is just like reinforcement; what is punishing to any particular person or any particular behavior varies greatly. One person may diminish behavior in response to being yelled at, but it may have no effect on someone else. Or, like my therapy patient, being nice to someone may be punishing. So, again, I am not going to list possible punishing responses, because they vary so much. I'll talk about applications for punishment in the chapter on changing people.

Extinction

Extinction is a technique that "extinguishes" behavior. This differs from punishment where something is done in order to actively diminish behavior. Extinction simply removes whatever is causing the behavior to continue. You might punish a rat's food-seeking behavior by shocking the floor every time it tries to push a lever. You would extinguish its food-seeking behavior by simply not giving it food when it pushes the lever.

You can extinguish people's job-related behaviors by not paying them. You can often extinguish most people's request behavior by ignoring their request. You can see the principle of extinction operating when people are waiting for an elevator that never comes. Someone pushes the button, and if the car doesn't come for a while, they push it a couple more times. Then they walk around and get agitated (a typical behavior during the process of extinction) and push the button a couple more times. Then they quit pushing the button at all, and stop their waiting behavior. They leave or take the stairs. Their "elevator-seeking" behavior has been extinguished because it was not reinforced—no elevator showed up.

I notice a lot of parents complain about their children's TV watching behavior, but they don't extinguish it by removing the TV. I've seen college classes extinguish the lecturing behavior of a professor by no one ever showing up for class. I once extinguished a colleague's behavior of talking about inappropriate subjects with me by removing my attention whenever he began talking about one of those topics. Every time he started I excused myself and left for a few minutes. I removed the reinforcer—my attention.

Most of the time people use extinction naturally, and most of the time it doesn't work. The reason is extinction runs a predictable course, and at one point in the course it doesn't appear it's working. In fact, it can look like it's making things worse. At that point most people figure they're not doing any good and stop. But they have just failed to complete the course of extinction.

The first thing that happens when you remove a reinforcement from a behavior is the behavior increases. Because that isn't what you want, at that point it looks like you're making things worse. The rat, who got food by pressing a bar but no longer gets food for pressing it, doesn't immediately give up pressing the bar. Instead, it starts pushing the bar harder and faster. The people waiting for the elevator don't immediately head for the stairs when the elevator doesn't come. Instead, they push the button harder and faster. It's as if biology thinks, "This used to work, and it still should. I just need to do it a little more."

The second thing that happens is the person gets agitated. Again, this can look like you're making things worse. The people waiting for the elevator have now pushed the button harder and faster, and still no elevator, so they begin to pace and complain. This agitation is biology's reaction to a threat by energizing defensive energies.

At this point the person is likely to be able to generate new behaviors so agitation is often a very good sign. But it can look like trouble because it's, in a manner of speaking, "withdrawal" symptoms like withdrawal from a drug addiction. If people didn't give up when the behavior increased initially, they often do now.

Finally, in the third stage the extinguished behavior diminishes. It responds to the lack of reinforcement and occurs less and less often.

What is required for extinction to succeed is the process to be completed, because only at the end does the behavior finally diminish. It takes stamina to sit through these phases, and it can be trying. This, for example, is when people trying to get out of a relationship often fail. They aren't prepared for the increased relationship-seeking behavior generated by their former partner as a result of removing the reinforcement of their presence. When the partner comes on stronger, they are unprepared and thrown off, and have trouble sticking to the course of extinction.

An example of the use of extinction was my consultation with a family where the children would not go to bed on time. After the kids were put to bed there was an endless parade of appearances in the living room, requests for water, complaints of fears, "needs" to tell the parents something, sibling arguments, anything that would keep the children out of bed and engaged with the parents.

Prior to consulting with me, the parents had responded with escalations. They had been yelling, screaming, threatening, and punishing. They were at a loss to explain why this did nothing to diminish the behavior.

The reason the unpleasant behaviors didn't diminish the kids' behavior was the kids were being reinforced by involvement with and reactions from the parents. Remember, it doesn't have to feel good to be reinforcing. The kids were just as reinforced getting yelled at as getting talked to nicely. There was no amount of threat or punishment that was going to work. Even so, my suggestions about how to deal with this behavior sounded strange, and they were only willing to try it after they had become convinced that their way was not going to work.

I taught the parents to extinguish the behavior of the kids. Stop escalating and remove the reinforcement. In this case, the reinforcement was the parents' involvement with the kids. The plan sounded a bit bizarre, and it went like this: When the parents put the children to bed, they told them they would see them in the morning, they were not going to talk to them until then because it was after their bedtime and they were supposed to be asleep. They kissed them good night, tucked them into bed, and went back into the living room.

The first night the kid parade started right on time, as usual. But the parents did something different. They completely ignored the kids. They didn't talk to them, scold them, do things for them, or even act like they existed. The parents let the kids roam doing whatever they wanted. Can you see how the counter-intuitive nature of this could set off the parents' survival wiring called "letting them get away with this?" A child would appear with a request for a drink of water. No response from either parent. A child would appear with some kind of complaint. No response from either parent. No matter what the kids did, the parents would just talk to each other and watch TV.

At one point, one child climbed into the lap of a parent. The parent quickly asked the other if they would like some water then stood up, unceremoniously dumping the child onto the floor and went into the kitchen.

For the first couple of nights the house was an absolute circus as the kids' behavior increased in response to the extinction. They were running around, watching TV with the parents, getting water, doing all kinds of stuff. This was the "increase in behavior" stage. The next few nights found them not so active, but displaying more milling around, looking uncomfortable. They were less verbal, and stayed in one place for less time. This was the "agitation" stage.

Then, after a few more nights the attention-seeking behavior of the kids began to diminish. The parades became shorter, quieter, and less frequent. By a week from the date of starting the extinction, all of the kids were going to bed on time and, with very few exceptions, were not coming downstairs.

The mother even reported this event: One night one of the kids called out for "Mom" several times. While on previous occasions this would have been the start of all kids getting in on the act and ending up downstairs, this time the mother was silent. She heard another child call from their room, "You might as well give up, she's not going to answer you." The child was quiet.

The reason this extinction worked was the reinforcement for the children's behavior was parental attention. Had it been something else, a different strategy would have been called for. It's important to remember extinction only works when you have the reinforcer identified and it can be removed. If this can occur, extinction is a powerful tool.

Association

There are two general categories of behavioral principles. One category is called "operant conditioning," where a particular behavior is reinforced or extinguished. Those are the techniques I just discussed. The second is called "classical conditioning" where behaviors are connected to new triggers. This is the technique used by Pavlov to train his dogs to salivate. He associated food with a bell, so the typical response to food also became the response to a bell. This is called association.

Association works by a response "paired" with a trigger (called a stimulus) so that the response begins to occur in reaction to the trigger. Let me give you an example.

When I was in graduate school I lived in a duplex, and for some insane reason the people next door got a dog. They left it on the front porch when they were gone, leashed to its doghouse. The dog never seemed to much mind but it liked to bark if it was still on the porch after dark. It barked at cars, the moon, me, anything. It barked, it barked, and it barked. Eventually I got annoyed and decided that I wanted to diminish or eliminate its barking behavior.

I didn't want to hurt the dog. I didn't have control over the reinforcers, so I couldn't do extinction, so I decided to begin by punishing the barking. One night, when it began to bark, I opened my front door, shoved my head out, and squirted the dog with water from a spray bottle. The dog didn't like it, and retreated into its doghouse, where it was quiet for a while. After a few minutes, when the coast looked clear, it came out and started barking again. I repeated the squirting and it stopped barking for a few minutes.

I had punished the barking successfully. The only problem was I had to open my door and squirt it every time it started to bark. I didn't want to have to do that, so I decided that I would use association to make my task easier. Each time, immediately before I opened my door and squirted the dog, I loudly flipped the lever on the deadbolt. The sound was distinct and could be heard by the dog. I would immediately jerk the door open and squirt the dog. I did this several times. Soon when I threw back the lever the dog immediately retreated into its doghouse and was silent. The response of retreating into the doghouse was now triggered by the sound of the lock on my door. It had become associated with that sound.

This pretty much solved my problem. Any time the dog started barking, all I had to do was to go to my front door and flick the lever. At that sound the dog would slink into his doghouse and be quiet. It was very little trouble for me, and worked well for weeks, after which the family removed the dog.

There are three steps involved in association. First, you have to get the behavior or response you want to occur in some way at some time. Second, you have to identify the event that elicits the response. Third, you have to pair a new trigger with the event that elicits the response. In that way, the new trigger becomes associated with the current trigger, and begins to elicit the response.

For example, your child has been inadvertently trained by you to only respond to your third request that they do something, like take out the trash. You notice what finally triggers their complying with your request is that you yell and turn off the TV. So your yelling and turning off the TV is the stimulus which produces their taking out the trash. You want them to do it with a gentle reminder instead of yelling and turning off the TV. So you give a gentle reminder, and then immediately yell and turn off the TV. Do this repeatedly. Then begin to phase-out your yelling and turning off the TV. If association has been successful, your new "gentle reminder" trigger should be paired with your previous yelling and turning off the TV, to produce the behavior of taking out the trash.

Shaping

The techniques so far are all based on the person you're dealing with already having a particular behavioral response in their repertoire. Your intervention into that response is designed to increase their behavior, decrease the response, or associate it to a new trigger. A problem occurs, though, when someone never does what you want them to do at all. There is nothing to reinforce, nothing to try to repeat or increase. In this case you have to elicit new behaviors rather than increase or decrease or associate current behaviors.

A powerful tool for eliciting new behaviors is called "shaping." It's a technique based on the principle that most behavior doesn't spring forth full-grown, but appears in bits and pieces and gradually becomes more complete and complex. Think of a toddler learning to walk. They don't do it very well at first. They do it in small increments. It takes practice and learning.

This is the major problem when people want other people to do things they are not doing now. They assume the behavior is "in there somewhere" and that they just have to unlock it. The bad news is even behaviors that seem quite ordinary to you may be ones someone else hasn't been able to generate. That means they will be new behaviors, and like the toddler learning to walk, they're not going to be able to generate them full-blown.

Here's where the technique of shaping comes in. Shaping means you use reinforcement to get small pieces of the behavior to repeat and increase until the full-blown response is present. This is called reinforcing "successive approximations" of the behavior you want. Each successive approximation is a step in the right direction. It's a building block for the final desired behavior or behaviors.

A failure to shape behavior is common when people fail in their dealings with other people. A spouse who wants more affection from her partner, for instance, is likely to be punishing unless the behavior she wants springs full-grown from their partner. Shaping never takes place if incomplete approximations are punished.

A partner who is a good people-handler will reinforce each successive approximation of affectionate behavior. First, reinforce the partner for sitting closer. Then reinforce any physical contact. Then reinforce increased physical contact. In this way, the final behavior is "built" out of the successive approximations.

Unfortunately, people don't realize, as is in the case with extinction, shaping is a process that takes time. If you think about it, most forms of training involve shaping. For example, in training salespeople, the activities involved are learned little by little. First, someone learns to walk into a potential customer's office and talk to them. Then they learn to ask for an appointment, or give a short sales pitch. From there they further refine their behaviors so they tailor them to the situation and potential customer. The same kind of shaping occurs when learning to type, drive, write, and do other life-skills.

The problem occurs when we feel someone already "should" be able to generate these behaviors, we read their lack of generating them as wrong. And whenever they're wrong we automatically punish their response. However, if you reinforce closer and closer versions of responses to what you want, you're much more likely to get it than you're punishing incomplete responses.

I use a lot of shaping when I am consulting with managers. Let's say there's a manager who has a tendency to interrupt others when they're talking. What I'll do is praise the manager (usually in private) for being able to wait longer "this time" before interrupting, even if the "longer" is only a second or two. So I reinforce (assuming that praise is reinforcing to this particular manager) even a slight movement toward the desired behavior. I might even nod and smile at him during the meeting any time he doesn't interrupt. The goal is to continue to increase the desired behavior.

Shaping is counter-intuitive, because you're consciously reinforcing behavior that isn't what you want. It can be uncomfortable to do. But the point is you're reinforcing more and more of what you want.

I did shaping with a group of therapists I consulted with. I met them as a group to consult on cases they were seeing, and they deferred to me almost completely, which made for very little interaction. I started complimenting what they said anytime anyone spoke about anything. I didn't care if they said they had to go to the bathroom, or if they made a joke. Maybe they just coughed or made some other sound. What was important was it was a piece of participating behavior, of verbal behavior. That was a step in the right direction. My goal was to have this behavior increase so that the group was fully participating each session. To get them there I had to reinforce behavior that was not, ultimately, desirable, because it was off-topic, or irrelevant, but I gradually shaped their behavior until it was both verbal and relevant.

The problem with shaping is that it's gradual. You don't get the full behavior until the end of the process. For most of us it's frustrating not to get the full behavior right away, so it's uncomfortable to stay with the process. This is only natural, because it's how our survival wiring reacts; it searches out and defends against a deficiency. But the unfortunate truth is in order to improve someone's functioning or performance, there has to be a gradual increasing and refining of the behavior rather than a sudden occurrence of the behavior.

Using shaping is actually very simple. You simply find out what is reinforcing to someone (find something that makes their behavior tend to repeat) and use it each time you get a little bit more of what you're wanting. It's like the M & M's the kid put in front of E.T. to guide him up the stairs and down the hall. You "lead their behavior" where you want it to go.

Pattern Interrupts

Human behavior can be thought of as occurring in two categories: events and patterns. An event is something someone does as a one-time thing, a special case. Sneezing is often an event. A pattern, on the other hand, is a repetitive set of behaviors; there is a consistent order and pattern to your actions. Habits are patterns, and because human beings tend to be creatures of habit, most human behavior is controlled by and is part of patterns. It can be difficult to see this, because patterns can occur over time and may not look like a pattern at any one time.

A man consulted me regarding his dissatisfaction with his career. He felt bored, restless, and wanted to try something new. This is not altogether unusual, people change jobs and careers, so you don't necessarily need to see a psychologist for it. It doesn't inherently mean anything's "wrong." Sometimes people are just ready for a change. This would be an "event."

But the reason this man came to see me was he had finally realized this was not just an event but a pattern in his life. After graduating from college he had a job or two that he got bored with and left. He chalked that up to being young and not knowing what he wanted. He went back to school to get an advanced degree and began working at what was then a higher paying, more prestigious job. Again, though, he fairly quickly found himself dissatisfied and changed jobs again. He marked that as being new in the field. But in his new job the same thing happened—he switched once more. In his present job, the same feelings surfaced, and he realized for him job dissatisfaction and switching was a pattern rather than an event.

The same happens in marriages. I once heard Bob Eubanks, host of *The Newlywed Game*, interviewed on a talk show. He said the most striking thing to him after his many years as host was to see the people who had been on the show as a newlywed return to be on the show with a new spouse. He noted that the second spouse was almost always a carbon-copy of the first in behaviors and responses. He could clearly see people were following a pattern in choice of spouse.

What is important to know about a pattern of behavior is, each element of a pattern is dependent on another element before the behavior occurs. If you leave out some of the letters in a sentence it loses its meaning. For example: "H do t e mans fis" doesn't mean much if you can't fill in the missing elements so you can read, "How do they make sense of this.?" By interrupting the configuration the meaning is taken from the words. The same thing is true if you scramble the elements of a pattern instead of removing them. For example: "rraetsde"—meaningless. But rearrange the pieces into "arrested" and you get a meaning.

Some behavior patterns can be problems. It's an obstacle clerical workers run into when they're trying to be efficient at filing. The way most of us learned the alphabet, by singing that ABC song, is fine as long as you need to remember the alphabet according to it's pattern—from the beginning, and forward. But to require someone to quickly find a letter going backwards and not from the end of the alphabet interrupts that pattern of learning, and their efficiency takes a nosedive. They must learn a new pattern of recall other than that pattern of the tune. If you learned the alphabet using the song, take a minute and try to say the alphabet backwards as fast as you can say it forward.

Someone's behavior can be changed not by changing any particular behavior in question, but by changing the pattern of which the behavior is a part. Interrupting a pattern can be as simple as standing up and walking around for a minute, or as complex as rewriting an entire manual.

I was buying frozen yogurt one day; I had a receipt from another store of the same chain that needed to be transferred to this store as a discount coupon because I had forgotten my coupon the last time I went to another shop. There was even a note on the receipt to the effect that it needed to be transferred. I presented the receipt and the coupon to the woman behind the counter for transfer to the discount coupon, and she began to go into what looked like her "I'm not going to do this" mode. She stumbled around, stared at the coupon and the receipt, asked me where it was from (I didn't know if it was her store or another of the same chain in town) and started giving reasons and excuses for not being able to do it.

They weren't doing that anymore, she said; she couldn't be sure where the receipt was from; I'd have to take it back to the other store, etc. She mumbled about four or five reasons at me, and tried to hand the coupon back to me.

I had a variety of choices available and, hopefully, you can think of several options as well. In this case I chose an interruption of her pattern of behavior. I figured her refusal pattern was designed to handle most types of responses; including meshing, matching, or escalating, and she would still carry on her "I'm not going to do this" mode. I wanted to interrupt the pattern. I behaved in a way that didn't fit any pattern she was familiar with. Instead of complaining, arguing, or acquiescing, I simply stood absolutely still and absolutely silent, and stared at her.

There was no easy way for her to continue her usual pattern in response to this behavior. It was an interruption. I wasn't looking at her hatefully, just being quiet, looking at her straight on. After a moment or two, as I continued to be still, I dropped into a process comment, "So are you saying you're not going to do this for me?"

That was also an interruption of her pattern, as I switched from the conceptual language of reasons as to whether or not she "should" do it to sensory—language and whether or not she was "going" to do it. In response she made another excuse, going back into her pattern. This convinced me my original hypothesis had been correct; her pattern could adjust to just about any active behavior on my part. So I dropped back into my pattern-breaking behavior of being still and quiet.

After a few more moments of this, as you might imagine, the woman became quite uncomfortable and asked to see the receipt again. I picked it off the counter and handed it to her. A chagrined look came over her face and she began to apologize, saying she had been mistaken, that the receipt was actually from her store, and she would apply it to the discount coupon, no problem, and she was sorry. I continued to look at her blankly as she handed me back the coupon. Finally I thanked her, paid for the yogurt, and left.

Through all of this I had not been nasty, rude or insulting. If anything, I had been, to put it bluntly, strange. Her pattern of behavior was very effective because it invited a response of meshing, matching or escalating, and she would have stood by her refusal. But to get no response at all was strange, she had no ability to respond to it from her usual pattern of behavior. As a result it threw her off, and she had to search for other behavioral options. She couldn't come up with any behavior short of what I wanted her to do.

The incident apparently made a big impression on her because Pam went into the store a few times over the next couple of weeks. Each time the woman commented on how sorry she was that she had upset me. Pam and I had been in the store together a few times, but I didn't even know that she knew we were married!

Many of the other techniques listed in the book can be used as pattern interrupts. Process comments make great pattern interrupts. They change the subject, and suddenly illuminate people's behavior. I'll be talking with a couple about their marriage and they'll hit a hot subject and begin to argue, trying to convince me of their point of view. I'll play along for a while, and then say, "And is this typical of how you talk to each other? Is this what you're like at home?"

This comment is a jolt, an interruption in their pattern. There'll be a moment of confused silence, they'll usually blink a couple of times, "coming to" from their arguing pattern. Often it's enough of a shock that someone gets honest and immediately says yes, it's typical of them, but not as bad as they usually are. The argument almost always dies down at that point, because interrupting its pattern takes the steam out of it.

The basis for some conflicts between people is that one person defines a behavior as part of a pattern and the other person defines the behavior as an event. This happens with such simple things as being on time. One person sees they are running late for a meeting because they're delayed by an important phone call. They scurry to the meeting, apologetic about being late, but not feeling that it's particularly significant. Later, their manager reprimands them for their tardiness because she's responding to a pattern of being late. The person is upset about the confrontation because they've felt there is a "good reason" for being late, a reason that makes each time an independent event, not a meaningful pattern.

This happens to couples when one spouse says to the other "You never talk to me!" The other spouse replies, "I do too, I'm just busy right now."

One sees lack of talking as a repetitive pattern, and the other sees it as a problem of the present circumstance, as an event.

Being able to interrupt patterns is a very powerful tool. It means you don't necessarily have to directly deal with a behavior to alter it. You may affect it just by scrambling the patterns surrounding it. I'll talk more about specific applications of pattern interrupts in the chapter on changing people.

Part IV

Purposes

Chapter 11
Preventing Problems With People

In dealing with people, there will never be any way to prevent all problems. Some conflicts, upsets, or difficulties are going to occur no matter what you do. Some problems are unpredictable, and others seem to stubbornly defy all attempts at prevention or early intervention.

Nevertheless, the fact that some problems with people are not preventable in no way means all problems with people are unavoidable. It's quite possible most difficulties can be partially, if not fully, deflected. If I had to venture a guess based on my own observations, I'd say about half of all problems with people can be stopped, and a majority of the other half partially halted or minimized through early intervention.

Think of problems with people as being like problems with your car. You'd have to be from another planet to think any car, no matter how well built, is going to be totally free of defects. Something is going to come loose, wear out, or get damaged. You won't prevent some problems because there's no way to foresee them, and you'll just have to deal with them when they come up. There are other hassles, though, you can prevent, or at least minimize, if you perform proper preventive maintenance. Under normal circumstances you never have to run out of gas or oil. You never have to get caught with a dead battery because it's out of water, or have your car overheat because of a low radiator.

But let's face facts. Most of us are bad at car maintenance, so we don't even stop the preventable problems. We don't get our cars serviced when we should, we don't have regular checkups. And as bad as we are with our cars, we're worse when dealing with other people. At least we know that we should perform preventive maintenance with our cars. With each other we often don't even think about preventing problems. We either don't know how to do preventive work, we dismiss it because we think it's impossible, or we have just never given much thought to the idea at all.

This chapter is designed to examine the causes of preventable problems with people, and to discuss some effective ways of preventing and minimizing them.

Preventable Problems

There are two main causes of preventable problems in dealings with people. The first is flawed agreements. It's agreements, more than anything else, that structure our dealings with others, that actually control our relationships. Flaws in our agreements are like cracks in the foundation of a house; they may go unnoticed once the house is built, but over time they often begin to cause serious dilemmas. Learning to recognize how agreements work and how flaws appear in them can enable you to prevent a good deal of potential predicaments.

Because most of our agreements aren't formal or clearly defined but assumed, we're rarely aware of their existence. This creates a high risk for flaws which means we can unwittingly create ticking time-bombs.

The second common cause of preventable problems with people is the avoidance of facing issues that seem small or only "potential" problems. Because our survival wiring is designed to handle the most pressing, dangerous issues first, "small" problems or "potential" problems take a back seat to the critical issues. Unfortunately, in the world of people-handling, small things often don't go away by themselves. There are the occasional small or potential problems that, like the common cold, do clear up without conscious attention, but more often small issues manage to grow ever larger.

Agreements

Agreements are the most fundamental, primary, and important aspect of the structure of relating between human beings. They're the element that patterns the type of relationship that exists, the expectations, limits of the relationship, and meaning of the relationship. They create our understandings of and the meaning of the things that do happen.

Agreements are not just those things that are formally discussed and defined. Agreements are formed any time there's any kind of joint action or joint understanding, no matter how informal. At a cocktail party there's an unwritten agreement of civility according to cultural standards. If someone becomes insulting or abusive, they're violating an understood agreement of behavior. As a result, others at the party feel offended and betrayed. In contrast, at a gang fight there's no such agreement so there's no such expectation and no reaction of offense or betrayal.

Flawed Agreements

Because agreements create our expectations and our understandings regarding our dealings with people, if there are problems, flaws, or misunderstandings in those agreements, there's going to be trouble in the relationship. What typically happens is the flaw is unseen at the time the agreement is made. Both parties think they have a mutually understood consensus. However, the hidden problem creates a discrepancy in expectation that ultimately shows up when it's time for the expectations to be realized. At that point problems, conflicts, upsets, and difficulties occur. It's often difficult to see the problems were set up earlier because those agreements are in the past and their role in shaping expectations for the present are a cloudy memory.

Many times when we feel hurt, upset, or betrayed by someone, it's not because they suddenly did something "wrong." It's because our agreements were flawed from the start, which makes trouble a delayed, but inevitable, occurrence. This is the reason that marriage counselors often have to retrace a couple's relationship to the day they met.

I once consulted with a colleague who been looking for a job and who had interviewed with a particular company for a staff position. Her description of the interview was like listening to a nightmare. It wasn't that the interview process itself was particularly bad, it was just that every expectation and understanding she had about the nature of the interview was violated, from what was going to happen during the interview to how long it was going to take to complete the interview. She came away shell-shocked as well as bewildered by the whole process.

I told her immediately not to accept the position because if the interview itself involved flawed agreements, then the job would probably be even worse. She would find herself having agreed to a job involving one set of stipulations, but finding herself involved in a job much different. She took the job anyway. Just as predicted, in short order every agreement about what she was supposed to do, how she was supposed to do it, and what was supposed to happen was violated. Looking back, we could see the expectations were totally unrealistic from the start. Ironically, I ended up being brought in later in an attempt to salvage something of the situation. Alas, it had gone so far and was based on such seriously flawed agreements the best thing to do was stop everything and start over, which is what ultimately happened.

Let's take an example of an informal agreement, something people never think of as fitting into a category called "agreement." We'll examine how it works, and how a flaw sets up problems later on.

Two people have been dating for a while, and have begun to see each other fairly regularly. They are at the stage where they have some kind of "relationship," but it's that uncertain area where the exact nature of the relationship and the exact nature of any commitment is unclear.

Although they haven't talked about it, they're operating based on an unstated agreement. Here is how that agreement is understood: One partner's understanding of "relationship" is an explicit agreement of exclusivity and commitment is required for a relationship to be considered exclusive. In the absence of a formal agreement, they feel that partners are free to see other people if they want to and there are no particular strings attached. The other partner's understanding of relationships is that a formal agreement for exclusivity is unnecessary because it's a natural developmental progression. As a result, those elements are assumed to occur as partners see each other more frequently.

Because each partner sees his or her way of understanding relationships as natural and universal, they see no particular reason to talk about it. They assume their understanding is shared by the other person in the same way. But this is incorrect, the understanding isn't shared. The partners unknowingly possess different expectations for the relationship while assuming that they agree.

So what happens? The partner who feels the agreement for exclusivity doesn't exist unless it's stated goes out with someone else, or neglects to talk to the other partner in the expected rhythm, or in another way breaks the pattern that has been going on in their dating. When this happens the other partner, who is assuming an agreement for exclusivity and commitment, feels hurt, angry, and betrayed because they feel that the relationship has been violated. This reaction, in turn, makes the other partner feel upset as well.

The problem is there was a major flaw in their agreement about their relationship. Each partner had a different understanding regarding exclusivity and commitment, and didn't know it. There was no sign of trouble until the partners' behavior conflicted with the flawed aspect of their agreement. But the partners didn't realize the trouble was set up; instead, they felt, "Everything was just fine, until you . . . "

In order to understand agreements and to prevent flaws, you have to understand the different types of agreements and how they work. There are two categories. One is called "agreements of intention." The other is "agreements of methodology." The two types are different, incompatible, and require different methods of establishment to prevent trouble down the road.

Agreements of Intention

Agreements of intention are the basic, fundamental agreements we make with people to establish the general nature of our relationship with them. Agreements of intention are just what they sound like—an understanding that we share an intention. If we are marriage partners, our agreement of intention may be we intend to create a happy marriage; if business partners, that we intend to create a successful business. If you're a salesperson and I am a customer, our agreement of intention may be we are going to engage in a sales transaction.

Because intentions exist in the conceptual world, agreements of intention consist of conceptual entities, and use conceptual language in their formulation. Marriage vows are not sensory: "We agree to live together, eat meals together, and share soap." No, they're conceptual: "Love, honor, cherish."

Because of their conceptual nature, agreements of intention feel close to our hearts because the conceptual world is where our sense of self exists. We're deeply, personally invested in our contracts. Agreements of intention mean that because people share the same aims, they're on the same team. They're working together, they're partners. They define who we are and are not allied with. Republicans and Democrats, for example, are thought of as being opponents, but they're actually on the same team because they share an intention—to make and keep America a successful, viable country. This differs from Soviet Communists, who were not on the team that shared an intention of making America a successful and viable country.

Agreements of intention are the starting point in our dealings with people. If you don't have an agreement with someone you're going to have trouble because you're working at cross purposes with them. If you want to sell me something and I want to avoid buying it, we're going to have difficulties in our dealings from the outset because we have no agreement of intention to engage in a sales transaction. We're not playing the same game, so there will be a great likelihood of trouble and problems in our dealings with each other.

A good example of this kind of trouble is how the Middle East has functioned for many years. There has been no agreement of intention regarding the concept called, "Israel's right to exist." As a result, there has been no basis for Arabs and Israelis to work together toward solutions or plans of any sort. They don't consider themselves to be on the same team. This lack of agreement of intention has created ongoing, repetitive, escalated, problems. Only recently has there been any change in this situation.

This is also why, so often, making business deals is so difficult. The parties involved may have little or no common intention. One wants to get the most money for what they're selling, the other wants to pay the least money for what they're buying. Totally different intentions, totally crossed purposes. Any good salesperson or deal maker will tell you the only hope such deals ever have of being made is both parties share an intention to just make the deal.

As far as prevention of problems goes the issue is to know whether an agreement exists. Are you and the other person seeking the same thing? Forget if you can make the thing happen or how you're going to do it. Just attend to whether or not you're both aiming for it. If you're dating, are you and the other person looking for potential marriage partners, or is one of you looking to play the field? Either one is fine, but you both need to know what the intentions are so you know if you're on the same team.

If you want to take the first step in preventing problems, the best thing to do is to walk away from situations where you don't have any agreement of intention with someone. Where you and the other person have cross-purposes, the likelihood of problems is close to 100%. It's that simple.

Agreements of Methodology

All that being said about agreements of intention, 90% of problems that are preventable by making good agreements are not caused by misunderstandings with them. Instead, in most of our daily lives, the preventable problems almost always exist in methodological agreements. In addition, while there are relatively few agreements of intention in our lives, there are many, many methodological ones. We're constantly making new ones and living out old ones. These are what set us up for trouble if we aren't careful.

Methodological agreements are about how we're going to do things. They're our understandings about what we've agreed we're going to do, and what our expectations are about what's going to happen. The understanding determines how we evaluate actions and outcomes. As a result, it's the nature of them that largely determines whether we feel satisfied and happy or hurt and angry about results.

In contrast to agreements of intention, methodological agreements exist in the sensory world. That means in order to make successful methodological agreements, sensory language must be used. That's the problem most of the time because we're unaccustomed to using sensory language in making agreements, even informal ones. But if we use conceptual language to create methodological agreements we set ourselves up for trouble.

If you use conceptual language to create a methodological agreement, there's no guarantee the partners involved have the same understanding of what is expected to happen. There's no shared agreement about what is going to happen, but the people making the agreement don't realize it. When the time comes to fulfill the agreement and things go haywire, it seems as though our partner has just broken our relationship. In reality, it often means we just didn't know we didn't have the same understanding of what was going to happen.

The basic flaw in methodological agreements that are structured with conceptual language is the nature of conceptual language itself; the same term can be interpreted different ways by different people. If we make an agreement to be "reasonable" about something, we are assuming we have exactly the same definition of reasonable as does our partner. But because reasonable can be interpreted differently this assumption is highly suspect.

One of the ironies of conceptual language being used for agreements about how things are going to be done is that it actually becomes more of a problem the better you know someone. That's because the closer people are and the better they know each other, the more they're likely to assume they have the same interpretation of conceptual terms. There may be some truth to this, because sometimes they may have the same interpretations, but it's always going to be a crapshoot to a greater or lesser degree, because there's never going to be complete agreement. Different interpretations become apparent only after the upset or problem shows up. The use of sensory language is important even when people think they know what each other means.

I've been in many marriage counseling sessions where I've pushed couples to use sensory language in their agreements about how they're going to do things, and they've looked at me patronizingly and almost pityingly. Several have even said "We know what we mean." I push ahead nevertheless and sure enough, nine times out of ten they don't agree in their interpretations.

For example, say that a wife asks her husband to "spend more time with the kids." He agrees to do so. A month goes by, and an angry wife confronts the husband.

"You agreed to spend more time with the kids. It's been a month, and nothing's changed. Are you ever going to do what you said you'd do?"

He's shocked. "What are you talking about? I've spent more time with them! I've been doing what I said I'd do. I've been making a concentrated effort to spend more time with them! Remember, just last Saturday my boss asked me to come in to complete some work on the new account, and I told him I couldn't because I'd promised the kids to take them to the zoo? So what are you talking about?"

"That isn't spending more time with them," she replies. "One day at the zoo? You still don't get home most nights until after they're in bed. Where are you at homework time? At bath time? At dinner time? One Saturday of saying 'no' to that boss of yours isn't going to make a good relationship with your children."

"Good relationship with them? I have a good relationship with them! And I don't know why my spending time with them like I've been isn't good enough for you. Maybe nothing is good enough for you, because I've been doing exactly what we agreed I'd do!"

"Yeah," the wife replies sarcastically as she turns to leave the room. "Sure."

This whole argument was set up by the way their original agreement was stated. It sounded like sensory language, because the term "more time" seems obvious in its interpretation. It sounds like you'd have to be an idiot to misunderstand its meaning. But it's a conceptual term because its translation into action depends entirely on your own interpretation of the term "more." The wife and husband assumed they had the same interpretation. But they didn't, and that made trouble inevitable.

The whole problem could have been prevented by making the agreement in sensory terms. That is, the wife asks the husband to be there during certain times, or the husband asks about specific meanings of "more" time. Then they would have defined when the husband would be with the children, and both partners could evaluate whether this agreement met their expectations. They should have done this at the time they made the agreement, rather than a month later, when they were upset.

When making methodological agreements, which are so common you might as well consider it to be virtually all of the agreements you make, sensory language is absolutely required. You can only be sure you and the other person have the same expectations if you use sensory terms. The words used in determining your agreement have to be those that, as directly as possible, represent objects or actions that can be seen or heard. You don't have to be obsessively detailed, but the sensory words, which guarantee they mean the same thing to everyone involved, are the only ones that allow any certainty at all that everybody involved has the same understanding of what they're agreeing is going to happen.

"Move the car out of the garage" is an agreement, the outcome of which is clear to everyone—either the car did or didn't get moved out of the garage. The conditions for satisfaction are pretty much undeniable, not much interpretation is required. "Make some space in the garage," on the other hand, leaves the nature of the agreement up in the air. It can mean clearing off a foot of work space to one person, and moving the car out of the garage to another person. This is because "make some room" is conceptual.

I recall as a child having a similar situation happen with my father. We had been doing yard work and he handed me a push broom and said, "Go sweep up the clippings that fell over the edge of the lawn onto the driveway." I trotted off, saw the clippings, and swept them up—back onto the lawn where I figured they belonged. All seemed OK until some time later when I saw my father with the broom sweeping the same clippings out of the lawn and into a pile. Call me naive, but sweep them up didn't necessarily mean to sweep them into a pile to me.

Many times people are reluctant to move an agreement into sensory language because doing so can sound picky, and as though you don't trust the other person. The truth is, as far as agreements go, you may very well trust the person's intention, but the fact is conceptual language itself is untrustworthy. Even with the best of intentions the idiosyncratic interpretations of conceptual language make it unreliable making methodological agreements.

Reviewing the section on sensory language in the techniques chapter can help you refine the idea of translating conceptual language into sensory language. These are words that relate directly to things you can see and hear, that don't require interpretation. The use of this language is a big deal. It's one of the two factors that distinguish creating from preventing problems with people. Master that, and you have mastered half the preventive skills for heading off problems with people.

I was working with an executive committee running a mid-size business—about fifteen million dollars total annual revenue. Their industry was undergoing difficult changes, and the executives had developed an impressive visionary plan for their company. They hoped it would put them at the forefront of changes in their industry. They had worked long and hard on their plan, and I worked with them while they were planning their presentation to their potential financial backers. They needed several million dollars backing to put their plan into action.

In their initial meeting with the venture capitalists, the executives presented their plan and financial outline, including the backers' share in the company as return for the capital. The potential sponsors took the proposal under advisement and shortly thereafter presented a counter-offer. To no one's surprise, the counter-offer gave them a larger share of the company than suggested in the initial presentation, and altered the financial arrangements so the company was required to ensure more return for them. Pretty standard as far as such negotiations go.

But the counter-proposal gave away much more than the company executives had agreed, among themselves, to offer. I worked with them while they talked over what to do next. The meeting lasted about three hours. Throughout most of the meeting, four of the five executives were in agreement they would present a third financial arrangement. This third plan gave the backers some of what they wanted, but also protected the company from them more than did the original counter-offer.

One executive, however, didn't like one part of the third plan, and wanted it changed so that there was a "grace period" during the initial phase, where the backers would not get so high a return. This would give the company time to get their feet on the ground, which this executive strongly felt was going to be needed. After a certain length of time, the terms of the third plan would become fully in effect.

The other executives were concerned the backers wouldn't go for the grace period and would drop the whole deal. They argued against it, but the one executive stood firm, citing evidence and history to support his contention that this kind of special condition would be required at the start of their new venture.

The executives talked and talked, with me on the sidelines helping the process be clear and progress. I deglossed, translated from conceptual to sensory language, made process comments, and tried to keep them from getting snagged by their communication behaviors. After a while they were having trouble agreeing, but the conversation was winding down. Eventually one said he thought they actually were in agreement about a final plan, and he would read the plan that they agreed to submit to the financiers. He read the third proposal plan.

After reading he asked, "So, are we all in agreement that this is the final plan?" The rest of the executives, including the one who wanted the grace period included, nodded. The executive reading the proposal paused. It sounded like a done deal.

It wasn't. There was the most subtle hesitancy in the air, a certain feeling of something being incomplete, or missing. Something unspoken, covert, that had not been made overt. But I was the only one who noticed it enough to press the issue.

I decided that whatever was creating the discomfort needed to be addressed. I turned to the man who wanted the grace period. "John, when you just now nodded that you agreed to that plan, did you mean that it was OK with you to present that plan to the backers as it is?"

"Yes," he answered. "I think it's a good plan."

"Do you mean beginning now, without the grace period, just this plan from the first day forward?" I asked.

"Oh, no," he said. "Of course not. What he said was that we agreed that this was the final plan. That means it's the one that we end up with after the grace period."

At this, the others groaned, they shook their heads, saying it wasn't final due to the grace period, but final due to being the last one they were going to present to the backers.

There had been, in short, no agreement reached.

Now, had I not been present to identify the unidentified disagreement present in the executives' apparent agreement, there would have been big trouble down the road. You could almost predict the conversation that would have occurred in the break at the meeting where they were presenting the plan to the backers:

John: "Why didn't you tell them about the grace period? Are you saving that for after lunch?"

Other executive: "What are you talking about? We agreed that this was the plan, we didn't agree on any grace period."

John: "What in the world do you mean? We certainly did! We talked about it in that meeting!"

Other executive: "What planet were you on? We agreed to this plan!"

And no one, not John or any of the other executives, would have any idea that this trouble was all caused by one word during the last reading of the plan: final. Had this flaw not come to light during the meeting, not only would the executives have still been in conflict, but the backers could have become involved in it too. The whole thing could have unraveled before their eyes, turned into a nightmare, and their whole future could have been jeopardized.

When you're dealing with someone about virtually any joint action, plans, or expectations, make sure you use words that are sensory in nature. Make sure they're direct representations of actions, occurrences, or objects in the sensory world. If they aren't, you're setting yourself up for trouble.

Avoidance

If there's one mechanism universally characteristic of human survival wiring, it's avoidance. It's what keeps you from falling off cliffs, wandering into active war zones, and drinking harmful chemicals. It also tries to keep you out of upsetting or anxiety-producing situations.

Unfortunately, in order to be able to prevent problems with people, you have to talk about potential issues before they're major problems, and this can be somewhat uncomfortable or anxiety-producing. Bringing up potential problems or concerns over small matters produces the possibility of survival reactions on everyone's part, and people tend to avoid doing it. The issue may be troublesome unto itself, it may also have the potential to uncover larger, more threatening issues that are attached to the small one.

This makes it even more threatening to bring up. This means it's very difficult to contend with small problems or potential problems before they become big problems that demand attention.

Realize you may not even be aware you're avoiding dealing with an issue. Avoidance is not generally someone adopting the "see no evil" posture. It doesn't look like avoidance. It most often masquerades as something else. When I was in graduate school I lived in a sizable two-bedroom duplex, and one day I noticed the only time I could ever really get the place clean was when I was supposed to be writing a term paper for school. But it wasn't that I consciously decided to clean instead of write; I wasn't consciously aware I was avoiding anything.

The house really did need to be cleaned, and at those times I "happened" to feel like cleaning it. But what interesting timing! When I needed to write a paper, cleaning suddenly sounded like a pretty good idea. The rest of the time the place was messy. The real reason cleaning house sounded good to me was it was a justified way of avoiding writing that paper. If it weren't avoidance, I'd be cleaning the house when it wouldn't interfere with writing the paper.

This is what happens in our dealings with people, especially as regards the "little" issues we need to talk about in order to prevent bigger problems. We have some small thing we want to talk about, but the prospect of such a talk sets off our survival wiring and we feel afraid, stupid, or petty. We talk ourselves out of it by telling ourselves it's "such a small thing," or else we find ourselves doing something else. This can go on for a long time, until the issue grows and grows and finally blows up in our face. At that point we wonder how things got so bad without our noticing.

One of the comments made to me by an executive, that I took as a high compliment, was when I sat in on meetings with his people nothing got by me. That didn't mean I jumped all over everyone's case about every little thing. In fact, frequently, I was quiet for long periods of time. But it meant if something was out of whack or unclear, I caught it and required it be addressed or cleared up even though it was "little." It was often stuff nobody else would pick up, but had the potential to lead to bigger problems later on. Often I would point it out and insist it be addressed. It might take one or two sentences, or it might take a month. But it almost inevitably turned out to be important. I can't count the number of times the "little" things revealed big problems growing unchecked. By dealing with them when I saw them, big trouble was averted down the line.

Of course, not every little thing grows up to be a big problem, and no one wants to spend every waking hour addressing every little thing that has any possibility of being a problem. In fact, that prospect often puts people off about dealing with potential problems. How can you tell when a "little" thing is going to grow into a big problem and when it isn't? You can't.

There isn't any reliable way to know what is and what isn't going to eventually grow into a serious situation, just like there isn't any way to tell who is going to turn into an alcoholic when they have their first beer. The best thing to do is be willing to bring up anything, so that you have the most freedom to address problems in their early stages. It isn't that you have to talk about every little thing, only that you have to have the ability and the willingness to do so. It's the inability to talk about the little things that inhibits your ability to prevent problems with people. When you can't talk about little things the scene is set to have them fester and worsen.

The rule of thumb I use is when some issue nags at you and just won't go away, then it's important to address it even if it seems small or imaginary. If it nags at me three times I know I should address it. It's no absolute or foolproof principle, but it can serve as a reasonable guide.

As to the worry people have that if they talk about small or potential problems all they'll be doing is talking about problems, let me note that in my experience it doesn't work that way. Often, people have avoided talking about potential problems for so long they have a backlog of dozens of them. And if that's the case, you may be talking a lot, but it's not prevention. You're in problem mode already, and your work will be better described in the chapter on conflict.

Avoidance of addressing small issues happens frequently, even among people who should know better. I once had the opportunity to watch with growing horror as the head of a large organization avoided opportunity after opportunity to confront the multiple, small, misbehavior of a member. The actions were small at first, but they didn't stop because they weren't dealt with. The behaviors steadily worsened until the chief was forced to suspend the individual and a big mess resulted, filled with recriminations and difficulties. Most, if not all, of the mess could have been avoided if there had been earlier intervention into the behavior, intervention which might not have to have been much more than conversations addressing the small matters that kept appearing. I tell you, it's amazing what just "bringing something up" can accomplish.

One of the places where I learned much about the importance of confronting seemingly small things was running outpatient adolescent psychotherapy groups. In order to effectively do therapy with teenagers my cotherapist and I had to confront everything. For example, in the office suite where we met a radio played soft classical music in the reception room. One day one of our adolescent patients changed it to a rock and roll station. No big crime; neither myself nor my cotherapist had anything against rock music. But that wasn't the issue. The issue was that the teenager had changed the station without asking permission from the person who owned the office. That's what's called, in technical terms, a "boundary violation." To let that go without addressing it would be not to deal with the issue of the teenager acting like something was his that wasn't. By confronting his changing the station without permission, we were re-establishing his boundaries, the limits of his legitimate control. My cotherapist and I quickly learned that if we didn't confront such small things, teenagers' controlling behavior quickly spread and before long they were trying to run the therapy group.

The second technique for heading off problems, after making clear agreements, is really very simple: talk about things. Talk about issues such as concerns, worries, and other little things you notice or are concerned about. It's not being petty or nit-picky. It's preventive maintenance. There's a direct correlation between how possible it is to talk to someone about issues and how preventable problems with them are.

Much of the reason people let little things become big is they're afraid to talk about little things. They're afraid it won't work out well. That's where the "how" of talking about little things comes into play.

The basic point in discussing small or potential problems is you want to trigger as little survival wiring as possible when you bring them up. You want the conversation to be as focused on the content as possible. It's supposed to be a discussion, not an argument. In bringing up small or potential issues, the techniques most useful are those involving joining or diminishing survival reactions.

Sharing

Bringing up something that's small or only a potential problem can often be started effectively by sharing. Remember the core qualities of sharing: you reveal yourself without making the other person wrong. If you're feeling the issue you want to bring up can't be addressed without making them wrong, then you've uncovered a possibility you're in danger of triggering survival wiring. That's good, now you have the chance to rework it to stay content-focused. See if you can work it around so it's sharing. You can review the section on sharing to remind yourself about the specifics.

The power of sharing in dealing with small issues acknowledges the concern is yours. It can even help diminish upset to admit you feel picky, silly, or concerned the other person will be upset and you aren't wanting to cause trouble. And if the other person says, "Well, that's just your worry, it doesn't count," you know you've set off their survival wiring; they're in defense mode, and you can move to another survival-wiring-reduction technique. For example, you can counter with a statement of, "I know I may be being silly, but that isn't making it go away, and I need to talk with you about what to do about it."

Pam did this with me once, telling me something was bothering her but it was "so small that she felt silly being bothered by it." That piece of sharing put me immediately at ease, because it served to reassure me it was "small," not something awful, and it might even be she was over-reacting to something. Those implications took away the danger of my being wrong, and kept my survival wiring from stirring up.

It turned out that she was upset that I hadn't been fully rinsing out the sink after I did the dishes. She didn't use make-wrong words like "the sink is a mess" or "you're a slob" or even a subtle version of that kind of statement. Rather, the way she brought it up, talking about herself and her feelings made it easy for me to talk and for us to quickly and easily come to a solution. It unplugged my survival wiring before I could even start getting it charged up.

Our survival wiring doesn't like us to admit we're wrong, of course, but sharing admissions of the possibility we're wrong or that we're overreacting, can be very helpful in our ability to bring up small issues. It can make conversations about them easier. This is another place where Cognitive Diversity is important. Have you ever been absolutely, positive of something and then discovered later you were wrong? Of course. So even if you feel you're right in this instance, an acknowledgment that you might be wrong can be helpful. Even if someone agrees you're being picky, or overreacting, you still have the conversation started and can move into what to do about the issue, even possibly by using a problem-solving style as is discussed in a later chapter.

Positive Communication Behaviors

Positive communication behaviors are often essential to introduce potential or small issues. Remember survival wiring is often not set off by the content of the conversation, but by its style. Rather than simply attend to the content of what you want to talk about, you also need to attend to your communication behaviors as well. In fact, if I were to have to choose between handling the content well or handling communication behaviors well, I'd choose communication behaviors every time. You can vastly diminish the emotional reaction on the other person's part by using and sticking with positive communication behaviors. Remember it's not sugar-coating, or being indirect, it prevents implying extra things in the conversation. It takes the irritating noise out of the communication channel.

You can review the section on positive communication behaviors to remember how tones of voice, facial expressions, eye contact, and vocabulary all play into diminishing the probability that someone else's survival wiring will go off. And here is what may be the most important factor regarding using positive communication behaviors; you need to stick with them even if the person you're talking with doesn't. It's more difficult and takes more time to get a positive reciprocity going than a negative one, so don't bite if someone uses negative communication behaviors in response and tries to start a negative reciprocity. Stick with unloaded, positive or neutral nonverbal actions. To give yourself the very best chance of succeeding in staying content-focused don't get suckered into a negative reciprocity.

Sensory terminology

It's best if you can address the small issue in sensory terms. That keeps you out of the realm of a "personal" attack. Phrase your statement about the issue in terms that describe what you can see and hear.

Distinguishing intent from methodology

This is what sensory terms do. They allow you to stick to addressing methodology, to what happens, rather than whether someone's being malevolent. It helps to keep survival reactions low.

Just Listening and Empathic Responses

These are two more survival-reaction-diminishing techniques that can be helpful when opening a conversation on small or potential issues. Talking in order to prevent problems or to deal with small ones is supposed to be a discussion, to get stuff out on the table and sift through it. The conversation needs to be a give-and-take discussion, as any normal conversation would be. We are not talking about anything fancy here, in conversations to prevent and minimize problems. The other person is going to need a chance to talk so while the other person is talking the appropriate thing to do is to just listen. Empathic responses can be helpful if appropriate. The point is to get into the conversation and to start getting the issue talked about.

Reframing

You may need to frame your concern in a helpful, neutral, or concerned light. Look for reasons for the concern that don't reflect badly on someone else's motivations. Or if you believe there are bad motivations frame the whole point of the conversation as a desire to prevent them from getting worse. (That should be true, or you need to reexamine what you're doing altogether.) Remember, people's survival wiring goes off when they pick up any danger of being made wrong, and once they sense that threat, they begin to defend. A valid and helpful frame on the issue may be very important.

There are several common reframes people use in bringing up small issues so they're as nonthreatening as possible. One is to place the issue in the context of getting clarification. For example, if you're concerned someone will be late for a meeting because of their history of being late, you can say something like, "I want to be sure we're sure that the meeting time is 1 o'clock, is that right?"

Another frame is to remind the person you're wanting things to go well for everyone involved. "I want us to get the best outcome we can in this meeting, are you set to be there at 1 o'clock?" The point is to keep potential survival reactions to a minimum, so you have the best possible chance of being able to stay focused on the topic.

For several years the office where I saw patients didn't have a receptionist. Because of this, I always gave new patients explicit instructions how to handle coming into an empty reception room: come in, sit down, and wait for me. I told them I would know they were there, and I would be out as soon as I was finished with whatever I was doing. Despite my specific instructions, occasionally someone wouldn't sit down, but instead would come wandering down the hallway crying, "Hello?"

This disregard was a fairly small matter, but one I thought was important to address in order to head off possible problems later. I always dealt with wandering by framing it as an acknowledgment of the possibility of my not being clear with them. I would say "Did I neglect to tell you no one would be in the reception area and to just have a seat, wait for me, and I'd be out shortly?"

Now, I didn't think I had neglected to tell them, but it was certainly possible, and that frame allowed me to address the issue with them without being accusing. It also encouraged them to examine their own behavior because they weren't having to defend themselves against me. Over the years I got varying answers, from, "You did tell me, I just forgot," to "I don't remember," to totally blank stares. But I did notice one thing—whatever their responses, there were no survival reactions, and no one ever did it twice.

The bottom line is that it's helpful to frame the issue you want to talk about in a way that removes much of the implication the other person is wrong. This is harder to do when issues are larger or have built up a lot, but if the issue is truly small or potential, it shouldn't be that hard for you to do. It just takes some thought and the use of some techniques that moderate survival wiring.

Other People's Avoidance

Sometimes people have a concern it's not them having trouble talking about small or potential problems, but the people they want to talk with who are avoiding it. They feel the other person will simply not talk. These people aren't concerned someone will get upset so much as they'll shut down, withdraw, or refuse to discuss the issue.

If that's the case, what happens is the other person had a survival reaction and retreats in order to be safe. The person has been trained, somehow, by someone, that conversations about small things or potential problems are dangerous. Usually what has happened is they've learned during past conversations they end up being made wrong, and the "small" thing is bait to trap them into being wrong in some larger way. Sometimes parents unwittingly train kids this way by approaching conversations about big problems they're upset about with innocent-sounding questions and benign beginnings to conversations. Then, whenever the kid hears the parent start a conversation about something that sounds small, their survival wiring goes on full-alert.

Remember, if you want someone to talk, making them wrong is generally going to punish their talking behavior. If you want someone to talk, you're going to have to be able to tolerate hearing what they say, even if you think it's wrong. If you're dealing with someone who does withdraw or refuses to talk about small things, it's up to you to retrain them that such conversations (with you, at least) are safe. If you give in to their refusal to talk and throw your hands up in despair, you become party to allowing small things the ability to become large problems later on.

And if someone really, really won't talk about issues, and nothing you do to retrain them works, then your relationship with them is in big trouble already. You're beyond needing techniques for prevention, you need means for handling problems, such as conflict resolution, change, or motivational procedures.

If someone has trouble talking with you about small issues, several techniques can be helpful:

Shaping

Shaping can be a powerful retraining tool useful in teaching someone to have preventive conversations with you. You mold them to talk about small issues bit by bit, step by step, through the reinforcement of successive approximations. Start out by getting them to participate in conversations with you. Forget content, talk about anything. Talk about what they want to talk about. Just get "talking behavior" reinforced in them.

This is a technique I commonly use with adolescent patients. They're reluctant to talk to a "shrink," so I spend as much time as necessary talking with them about friends, music, clothes, video games, or whatever else they like so they simply learn to generate verbal behavior with me. And I'll talk about anything with them until they know it's safe to talk to me. Then, little by little I'll begin to introduce significant topics into the conversation.

During the shaping, be sure to use joining techniques to show their survival wiring it's safe to talk with you. Ask in-depth questions. Just listen. Use empathic responses. Use positive communications behaviors.

Reinforcement

Reinforce each of their steps. Do whatever makes their behavior repeat. Then, after talking has become more ingrained, gradually begin to talk about the areas that are of potential concern to you. Realize this process is not accomplished in one sitting, or even two or three. It can take weeks, even months. If someone shuts down their verbal behavior with you, you may be dealing with a very powerful force in someone's survival wiring, and it's going to change slowly. You'll have to stick with it, so make sure your dealings are of sufficient value for you to put in your time and effort.

Unfortunately, people all too often unwittingly punish verbal behavior in others. Managers do this with employees, they criticize their employees when they talk, and then wonder why they're the last to know when anything happens. Married couples do it, too. One spouse will complain that the other never talks, but every time the other one opens their mouth, the spouse makes them wrong.

If you want to talk with someone about potential problems, they have to feel able to talk with you. However they became the way they are, you have to retrain them that it's safe to keep a conversation going. It's a gradual process, so be patient. And if you're not willing to be patient, you might ask yourself what your position really is in your relationship with this person, and whether it's worth it to you to do what is required to maintain the relationship in good order.

The basic point is, being willing and able to talk about potential problem areas is of great importance in dealing with people. The more readily you can talk about things, and the more things you can talk about, the more chance you have to prevent and minimize problems with people.

Chapter 12

Getting People To Do Things

Whether you're trying to get a waiter to bring you water, a child to clean up their room, a boss to give you a raise, or a customer to buy something, many instances of people-handling have the purpose of getting someone to do something.

Getting other people to do things is so important and can be so difficult to accomplish that the human race has logged a long and shameful history of doing terrible things to each other in service of trying to accomplish it. On both the large scale and the small, human beings have turned to the twin demons of force and fraud to compel others. The methods range from lying, manipulating, and coercing, to unbelievable atrocities.

There's no doubt the techniques of fraud and force can be successful in getting people to do things. You have a pretty high probability of getting someone to give you their wallet by pointing a gun at their head. You can also get someone to give you money by developing a phony prospectus that portrays a rip-off as a terrific investment and you can lie to your spouse, boss, employees, and kids to gain your ends. It's no surprise these techniques are still around.

The problem with the coercive and deceptive methodologies are, they only produce short-term results. The price they exact is the destruction of long-term results. You can lie to make something happen, but you forfeit your credibility for the next ten years when you do it. The same is true with all techniques involving force and fraud. And not only do these methods set you up for practical trouble over the long term (people abandoning you, treating you badly, not believing you anymore), but they also set you up for trouble with yourself. You do severe damage to yourself in order to tolerate using the techniques. You have to distort situations so much in your conceptual world in order to justify the damage caused by using these techniques, your survival wiring gets shifted permanently into high gear. The result is, you, your life, happiness, and self-image take a nose dive. You end up carrying around such a terrible burden you have to do still more adaptations to cope with a continuing negative spiral.

It's not worth that kind of burden to get an action from someone. I've seen people try it over and over and over, and I've never seen it work over the long term. If you're trying to accomplish something by force or fraud, unless you're a police officer or an undercover agent, whatever it is isn't worth the price. Don't hock your future for a single, immediate goal.

Because of the cost to others and to oneself in the use of coercive and fraudulent methods of getting action from people, I don't teach them. I'm in favor of effectiveness and productivity and people taking action when needed, but I don't consider it helpful to adopt strategies that are almost certain to cause long-term problems. In fact, I would venture to guess that many of the problems you have in your life now may be because you have used these techniques in the past. I'm not willing to teach you how to continue that cycle.

I'm going to make one of the very few general, blanket statements in this book: Unless you're in law enforcement, or some other specific area where such methods are appropriate and socially sanctioned, getting people to do things by using methods involving force or fraud don't work, and you should not use them. Period. If what you want requires force or fraud, you need to reconsider what you want, because something is wrong.

In fact, in becoming effective in handling people, you have to stop using those kinds of methods. Many of us turn to them because we don't know what else to do and what we've been doing isn't working. That's the whole purpose of this book; to help you to find other effective ways to go about dealing with people.

Now, this isn't to say some methods of people-handling aren't going to cause some discomfort at times, or you're not going to institute consequences or even punishments, or your actions aren't going to cause some upsets sometimes. When I talk about force and fraud I'm referring to physical violence or threats of physical violence, and to intentional deceit on your part. But I'm not saying everything is going to feel wonderful to everyone, or there will always be agreement, or your communication behaviors will always be pleasant. I wish it could be done, but it isn't going to happen.

The methods I'm going to teach you for getting action from people are designed to attain short-term outcomes without sacrificing long-term results. They also happen to respect your own and the other person's humanity, and preserve your relationship with them, if at all possible. I expect you to use them in that spirit.

As we start, remember, no techniques, mine included, are guaranteed to work. Nothing, where people are concerned, always works. However, they're designed to give you your very best shot at getting someone to do something without doing things that are going to hurt you or them.

You know by now the most important factor in determining what someone does is survival wiring, and that it's complex and variable in its behavioral expression. Despite what some authors would have you believe, no other "entity" is consistently responsible for people's actions, so trying to alter one particular aspect of people isn't necessarily going to get action. Forget the idea that if you change beliefs you necessarily change behavior; lots of people do things that are inconsistent with their beliefs. Nearly everyone believes extramarital affairs are wrong, but estimates are about half of married persons engage in them. Only survival wiring moves people to action.

If an action is OK according to survival wiring, it's something a person will be able to do. If this is the case, it will be fairly easy to get someone to do what is already consistent with them. For example, it's fairly easy to get someone to talk if their survival system involves talking a lot. So it's easiest to get from people what they're already wired up to do. It's easy to get a butcher to cut things.

The easiest and most reliable way to get someone to do something is to pick a person who already "naturally" does the thing that you want done.

I think it's a bizarre quirk of human nature that we think all human beings should be able to do the same things. When the Constitution says, "All men are created equal" it means equal in value, not equal in talents and abilities. You don't deal with all physical objects or even animals in the same way, yet when you want someone to do something and they can't or won't do it, we make them wrong. Since we think they should be able to do it, when they don't or can't they're being bad, or oppositional. But we never get mad when a stone won't pour like water, or that water isn't solid like a stone. People have very strong and demanding survival wiring, survival wiring that commands their behavior and feelings much of the time. This wiring can differ in the behaviors it generates and inhibits every bit as much as a tiger's wiring produces different behavior from a cockroach's.

Appropriate selection of people is a primary issue if you have the option. Effectively choosing people is a whole other topic beyond the scope of this book, but if you do have the opportunity, use your ability to find someone who is already wired up to do the things you want done.

Because people come to you with their survival wiring already pretty much intact, you have to take some bad with the good. You might not even have known about aspects of their behavior before you got involved with them. You might also have to deal with people that you didn't get to choose. Because you don't have much control over their survival wiring, and if their wiring runs counter to the kinds of actions you need or simply doesn't make provision for the actions you're wanting, it's going to be more difficult to generate the particular actions you want. In that case, you'll have to be skilled at getting people to take action, and that's what the rest of this chapter is about.

Let's start out by being realistic. You aren't always going to get people to take the action you want. Survival wiring is strong. There are people whose head you could put a gun to and they would still defy you. And since coercive methodologies are out of the question anyway, if you want to be an effective people-handler, you have to understand that getting action is one of those areas where nothing always works. If you have a lot of trouble getting someone to do something, you've probably moved from the realm of getting action to the realm of trying to change someone, which is a different issue.

Sensory Language

A particular vocabulary is needed to produce action. It consists of sensory language. This is because all action is sensory; it happens "out there" where it can be seen and heard. It can have concepts applied to it, but it's completely sensory. If you use conceptual terms to get action, which most people do, you vastly increase the probability you will get no action, or the wrong action. You must ask for action using action words.

This is trickier than it sounds. As when discussing agreements, most of our normal talking is done in our shorthand language of conceptual terminology. So we're accustomed to using conceptual terms. We usually don't stop to change vocabularies when we're wanting to get action. In fact, we tend to get so accustomed to using conceptual language that to ask for action in sensory language can sound strange because it's not as colloquial. For example, it doesn't sound strange for a manager to tell an employee that they need to "get with the program," to "clean up their act" or to "improve their performance." And if the manager is being motivational, as we'll talk about in a later chapter, that kind of language may even be appropriate. But it's not a request for action, so you don't increase your chances of getting any specific actions you may want.

Principle #1: Asking for it

You've probably noticed that most talking doesn't produce action. Sometimes people use this fact to criticize talk itself, saying, "talk is cheap" or, "talking doesn't accomplish anything." That's untrue. Most talk isn't intended to produce action, and even talk that is isn't done in a way that makes action likely.

Just like anything else when dealing with people, you have to talk in the right ways to get action. I don't care how much you intend to start your car, if your methodology is to beat your head against the steering wheel to do it, you're going to end up feeling like it's an impossible task. And if you're trying to get action from someone, then you have to use the right methodology as well.

Getting action from people is one of those areas where the methodology initially sounds so obvious everyone thinks they already do it. But they don't. I've listened to tens of thousands of conversations, and rarely do I ever hear an effective conversation which gets action from someone.

The first step in getting action from someone is to ask for it. How many times have you heard "Ask and ye shall receive?" What may go through your head is "Is that all? Ask for it? I knew that. What good is it to tell me that? I already knew that, and it doesn't work. I ask for action all the time and I still don't get it."

The issue isn't just asking for action, but how you ask for it. There is a specific way of talking that's designed to produce action and that's different from other ways of talking. Just like you would use one vocabulary to talk to brain surgeons about their work and another to talk to fifth graders about their work, so there's a specific vocabulary for talking to someone about action. Just like you would get a weird response from the fifth graders and the brain surgeons if you switched the two vocabularies when talking with them, so you can get weird reactions—and usually not the action that you want—when you're working with someone to get action but you don't use the right kinds of talking.

The basic form of talking designed to produce action is to ask or tell someone to do a particular action or set of actions using sensory terms to define the action you want done. You don't have to be overly detailed about this, but you probably need to be more detailed than you think you need to be. "I want you to take care of this" is insufficient. "I want you to write him a letter about this matter" is better, and might be sufficient. "Give me a hand here" leaves it up to their imagination as to what you mean, even if it seems absolutely obvious to you. "Help me carry this" is better. Have you ever had someone carrying a heavy object say "Help me out here," but when you try to take on some of the weight they snap, "Not that, stupid,—open the door for me!" To them, it was obvious that "Helping them out" would be to open the door. But it wasn't so obvious to you, so the action they generated was different than the one they were requesting.

Asking for action comes down to the very simple, basic semantic form:

"Will you . . . (action word)"? Or: "Please . . . (action)," or simply: (Action words).

When I talk about these things as specifically as I'm doing now, it can seem like a word-game. But this isn't an issue of using the "right" words according to some arbitrary external psychological standard of "healthy talking" or "political correctness" or anything of that sort. We're talking about ways to talk so you increase the chance of producing the action you want, and that means using the kind of talking that's more likely to be effective.

While this type of talking isn't complicated, people often don't do it because in its raw form, a request for action is pretty blunt, sharp, or harsh. It isn't "soft" or "nice," and as a result can set off some people's survival wiring, which can cause resistance to performing the action you have requested. You want to consider ways of softening requests for action while still being sensory in your request. You don't have to be crude, blunt, or commanding.

When you ask for action, you'll probably want to limit the other person's survival reactions as much as possible. This may sound difficult if what you're asking them to do they don't particularly want to do, but the point is you don't want to make any survival reactions they have worse than they already are. Further, you don't want to inflame them in response to you when they're already responding to the tasks they already have.

I worked with a vice-president of a company who was forced to make a variety of changes to solve problems made by his predecessor. Not only were his supervisors upset by the changes, and had survival reactions to them, but he was very blunt and rude to them, which redirected their defensive reactions onto him. As a result, he lost all credibility and loyalty; nobody could work for him, and he eventually had to resign. It could all have been avoided if he had simply attended to how he asked them to do things differently.

One of the reasons conceptual language gets used in requests for action instead of more effective sensory language is because people want to soften their requests. A good example of this is in Anthony Burgess's novel, *A Clockwork Orange*. He develops a whole new vocabulary to refer to the violence of his characters. The use of unfamiliar terms and words with multiple syllables and rich sounds softens the violence as you read the book. It just doesn't feel or sound as violent as the content suggests it is.

Conceptual language is useful in softening requests or demands for action if it's used around the requests for action. There's no problem with that. The problem comes when conceptual language is substituted for sensory language in making the request for action.

Some examples of softening conceptual language techniques are:

1. *Sharing*. "I think it would be a good idea for you to . . "
This is sharing, it's not a request for action. It's soft because it states this action is "a good idea." Now, if you used this as the request for action, you'd be in trouble, because if someone agrees with what you're saying, what exactly are they agreeing to do? They're only agreeing an action is "a good idea." But there are lots of good ideas people never take action on, and even an agreement with this statement isn't an agreement for action. You can use sharing, but you have to follow it up with a request for specific action, like, "So will you do this?"

2. *Reframing*. "I think it would be reasonable to . . . " Again, this is a soft statement because the frame makes it "reasonable." But it's not a request for action because someone agreeing with you isn't agreeing to perform any particular action. There are lots of things people agree that are reasonable but have no intention of doing. If this phrasing is used, a direct, sensory request for action needs to follow it.

   "Would it be a problem for you to . . . " is another soft reframe that shows concern for the other person, but again, is not a request for action. If they say that something is "no problem" what are they agreeing to do? They're only agreeing it's not a problem, whatever that means. Once again, there are lots of things that would be no problem for us to do but we still don't do, and there are things that people are asking us to do even if they're a "problem." So this must be followed up with a request for action.

   "Would it be a problem for you to run these over to the post office today?"

   "No, that would be no problem."

   "Great, then will you do that for me today?"

   "Sure, I'll do it"

In the above example there was a conceptual statement about whether something would be a "problem," followed by a defined sensory request for action. Sometimes these kinds of conversations sound redundant because it sounds like you're repeating yourself—the post office has been discussed twice, once regarding whether it would be a problem for the person to go there, and another regarding whether the person will go there.

Some people, unaccustomed to how all this works, may be a bit puzzled, feeling they've already agreed to go there by saying it would be no problem. They may even be a bit annoyed, and feel that you're belaboring the point. You aren't. In the first sentence they only agreed it "would be no problem" to take the things to the post office, you haven't actually asked them to do it. It's only in the second statement that you have asked them to do it. Some people may actually get upset about your seeming to "repeat yourself" in asking if they "will" go after you ask if it will be a "problem" for them to go. They may get huffy, feeling that they have already agreed that they will go, and accusing you of "not trusting them." Well, here's a tip:

Beware of people who get upset that you phrase an action request in sensory language when you have softened the request with conceptual language or positive communication behaviors. They're often the very people who like to have loopholes so they get out of doing things, and their upset is probably that you have closed the loopholes, not that you're repeating yourself.

At the very least you want to minimize the triggering of people's survival reactions to you when you're asking for action. In addition to using conceptual language to surround your request, a very powerful way of lowering survival reactions is to use positive communication behaviors.

Positive communication behaviors are one of the most useful techniques presented, they can do much to avoid triggering or worsening a survival reaction. The person may still not like that you're asking them to do the particular action, but you're at least not making it worse by inflaming them with survival-triggering communication behaviors. Remember, "positive" or even "neutral" communication behaviors include such things as even tones of voice, use of words that aren't emotionally loaded, pleasant facial expressions, congruent verbal and nonverbal behavior, and nodding and otherwise acknowledging their responses.

Notice the Receipt of the Request

Getting action from someone is the result of the process of a conversation. The conversation can be as little as one sentence, or it can last years. In either case, there's obviously more to it than just making one request for action. The other person's response to your request can be very telling as to whether there's going to be a problem getting the action. As a result, it's very helpful to check out the effects the request is having on the person. Are you getting somewhere, are they being hesitant, resistive, looking for a way out, or are they going to do what you ask them to do?

What can be very helpful in this is to watch their communication behaviors. Look for signals that there's some glitch in their receipt and processing of your request. These can be such things as hesitations in their responses, facial expressions that communicate confusion, or lack of response. Noting these elements is an important element in preventing problems before they occur.

So it's important to look at the person when you're making your request for action. I know this is another point that seems obvious and simple, but just like so many other "obvious" things, it's something so taken for granted it gets overlooked. For example, the last time you ordered dinner at a restaurant, did you look at the waiter or waitress while you ordered? Lots of time you can pick up cues when they're getting your order wrong just by looking at them. You can sense they heard the first part of what you said, but were busy writing when you instructed them about substituting the sauces. That can be a clue that dinner is going to come with the wrong sauce. If you're looking at them you see behavioral indications that they were not responding, and you can do something about it right then.

So look for the common signals that indicate someone is paying attention. These are simple positive communication behaviors like head nods, "uh huh," eye contact, or thoughtfulness. Notice whether you're getting those in response to your request. Also, watch for negative communication behaviors, such as facial expressions that seem to indicate confusion, disagreement or displeasure. These are simple behaviors like frowns, furrowed brows, widened eyes, or even extreme stillness.

What is important regarding these signals is you not overlook them, but deal with them. Don't hope they don't mean anything, because they very well might. And don't just keep repeating your request over and over, to try to worm out of the person a sign they're agreeing to do what you're requesting. Some people can get you dancing in circles with your requests, leaving you frustrated and confused.

In fact, this happens a lot of times when people request action. They're looking for a sign of agreement by the other person, but they aren't aware that their behavior has begun to be run by the lack of signs of receipt of the request on the part of the other person. Instead, they start repeating their request or start talking about the reasons for the action. The point is simple—if they don't seem to be getting it, ask them if they're getting it!

Sometimes when I'm consulting with couples where one is trying to get the other to do something and they're not getting any signs the person is receiving the request, I'll let them repeat themselves over and over for a while. Then I'll stop the conversation and ask the person who is being talked to if they often feel "nagged" by the person asking for action. Usually they look surprised I can tell this, and will say yes, indeed, they do.

Then I ask them if they get tired of the person seeming to repeat requests for action over and over. Again, they'll look surprised I can tell this and they'll say yes, indeed they do. I tell them their communication behaviors are what is resulting in the nagging and repeating. At this they also look surprised, because they thought the other person was just a nag or had verbal diarrhea. They never realized their lack of response actually had control, that the other person was simply trying to elicit a sign they were receiving the request. Then I teach the person requesting how to stop and ask for feedback about the other person's receipt of their request.

It's generally no accident that people don't give signs of receiving a request for action. It usually is a reliable indicator there is, in fact, a problem with them getting it and agreeing to the action. In fact, I can hardly remember an incident where, when I commented on someone's apparent lack of response to my stated desires for some kind of action, there wasn't some sort of problem in their receipt of my message. It might have been an unwillingness to take action, confusion, or a misunderstanding, but it was something that had a high probability of interfering with the action I wanted to occur. So you need to actively look for the signals that someone is getting your request, that they're hearing you and understanding it while you're giving it. If they look blank, puzzled, confused, distant, or "glazed over," deal with it.

A powerful way to cope with such signals is by making a process comment. Talk about their behavior and your interpretation of it. Say something like "You're looking puzzled. Are you confused about what I want you to do?" Remember, your goal is to not inflame their survival wiring in response to you, so don't make their lack of response or their negative-appearing response wrong. Watch your communication behaviors, keep them positive. The important thing is to comment on that behavioral signal so it can be dealt with in the open and any blocks to the person taking the action addressed.

Here's what we've covered so far: The structure for getting action involves a request for action which is stated in sensory terms, and while giving the request you're watching for signs of receipt or problems with the request. In addition, conceptual language and positive communication behaviors can be used to soften the request and keep survival reactions low.

There's one other element in a request for action that's very important, but often gets taken for granted. It's often overlooked because it literally belongs to another dimension—time.

Locating the Action in Time

We tend to think of ourselves as living in a three-dimensional world (height, width, depth) because those are the three physical dimensions in which we have freedom of movement. But, we live in a four-dimensional world. While the fourth dimension is one which isn't physical and in which we don't have freedom of movement, time is still a dimension through which we move. We tend to forget that because we move through time just like we move through space, sensory things are located not only at points in space, but also at points in time. Time is a "place" just as physical spaces are. We call a time location a "when" instead of a "where."

When you're trying to get an action from someone, you must locate that action in time. If you don't, your request is incomplete, and you leave a gap though which your request can fall. Just as is the case with the other aspects of agreement for action, you also have to talk about time locations in sensory terms. Conceptual terms like "a reasonable period of time" aren't going to work, because the amount of time considered to be "reasonable" is going to vary from person to person. My definition of reasonable and yours are probably not the same but, we each feel our concept of reasonable is right.

There are three types of sensory time that can be used. First, there's "clock" time. This involves the actual numbers on a clock. A clock is a sensory entity that everyone can see in the same way, a shared aspect of time. Second, there's "calendar" time. Similar to the clock, a calendar is a sensory entity where everyone can see the same number and day of the week. Third, there's "event" time, locating one event in time by its relationship to another. For example, an event location is "at sunset" or "at high tide" or "when this television program ends."

I can't tell you how often there are upsets and problems about when something is supposed to be done simply because there was no clear statement of and agreement about the time-frame for the action. The problem is that someone can, in all good faith, agree to do something, not do it, but still not violate their agreement. Without a specific location in time, there's no identified point when the action was to be done.

This happens frequently in families, more so than in businesses, because businesses often have more clear and stated deadlines. A man and his teenage son were having a fight in my office one day over the son's cleaning out the garage in preparation for a family garage sale. The son wasn't resistive to the idea, given that he was going to get some of the money from the sale, but he still had not done the work and the father was mad about it.

"I've been telling you to get that garage cleaned out for the sale for a month now, and you've just sat on your behind and done nothing about it," the father groused.

"I'm gonna do it. I said I will, and I will," the son retorted. "Just get off my case about it. The sale isn't for another two weeks."

"But it's going to take you two weeks just to get through the stuff, much less to decide what we're going to sell," the father shot back.

"It's not. I can get it done. Just get off my case about it. You're always on me about something," the son huffed.

"Yeah, that's because you never do anything . . . "

The conversation degenerated from there.

That whole fight was set up by one factor that was never dealt with and which was still not being dealt with in the argument in my office: an agreement about when the kid would do the task. The father complained that the kid had not done the task, but he never asked for the kid to do the task at any particular "when." The father had one time frame in his head, and the son another. And by leaving it all unstated, it set them up to fight about it.

In working with this father and son I pointed out they had different ideas about when the task was to be done, but they had never decided what time frame to use. Ultimately they decided, and in a subsequent meeting I learned it had gone very well. In fact, the son had done the job in about three days. Again, the point isn't that making a specific location in time is magic and solves all problems, it's just that if there isn't a specific agreement about when an action is to happen there's an opening for trouble, and even for the action to not happen.

A woman consulted me whose boyfriend was experiencing some psychological symptoms which interfered with their relationship. She asked him to get help. He agreed to but didn't. She asked again. He agreed again and didn't. Finally, frustrated, she asked him "when," and he all he would say was "I don't know, but I will." Notice that in literal terms he would be keeping his agreement for action even if he waited to get help when he was eighty years old. Now, the spirit of the request was certainly that he do it sooner than when he was eighty, but a request for action doesn't live in the spiritual world. By closing this loophole in her request she knew that he wasn't going to get help anytime soon, and his saying that he would wasn't going to happen. So she knew the relationship was in very, very serious trouble, and she could plan accordingly.

Agreement to Perform the Action

The last element in getting action is to be sure that the response you get from the other person is an agreement to perform the action. This can be tricky because people find lots of ways to say no that sound like yes. Instead of directly saying no, they can respond in a manner that's positive, but allows them to not carry out the action without having broken their agreement.

Believe it or not, people would rather not be liars. They would much rather have semantic loopholes which provide their biology some squirming room when they don't follow through. Most of the time, people who are going to resist action will give clues to that effect in the way they "agree" to your request for action.

Many agreements to perform actions are what I call "non-agreement agreements." When one of these occurs you think someone has asserted to do something, and it even looks and sounds like they have, but in fact they either have not actually agreed or they have left a loophole that will allow them to not perform the action while not breaking their agreement. Non-agreement agreements are statements similar to the conceptual terms people mistakenly use to make requests for action. When agreeing to do something, these statements are phrases like; "I ought to do that," "It should be no problem," "I really should do that," "That's a good idea," "I need to do that," or "I'll get to it," or "Pretty soon," or "We'll see," or "I guess," or "I'll try."

A common non-agreement is the phrase "OK." It's one of English's major contribution to the world, because it's used in many other languages now. I've heard bilingual receptionists talk in flawless, rapid Spanish, and punctuate their speed with an occasional "OK." The problem with it is that while it's a positive response, it's nonspecific. That makes it a conceptual term, because it can mean different things to different people. Unless you know someone well and have experience with their particular meaning of "OK," you don't really know exactly what someone means by it. From one person it can mean "I'll do that" and from another person it can mean "Get off my back." So if you're going to accept it as an indication that someone has agreed to do something, the important thing is either know what they mean or get a more specific statement of agreement. If I'm uncertain of what someone means by it, I frequently say "Forgive my uncertainty, but lots of people mean lots of different things by OK and I want to be sure I know what you mean. Do you mean that you're going to . . . ?"

The problem with non-agreement agreements is that they're not an agreement to a sensory occurrence, but to a conceptual formation. For example, if someone says that doing what you're asking "Should be no problem," then what are they saying they're going to do if there's a problem? They have only agreed that there should be no problem with it.

Again, this isn't just semantics in the sense of picking apart irrelevant or unimportant elements of grammatical structure. The meaning of words is both literal and figurative, and to overlook either aspect is to invite trouble when dealing with people. Surprisingly, the most common aspect overlooked is the literal. You must cover the literal as well as the figurative.

Here's an example of a request for action and a response:

"Would it be a problem for you to run these over to the post office today?"

(Hesitant tone of voice) "No . . . I don't suppose so, at least as far as I know."

"Then you'll take them over there for me today?"

"I'll do my best."

Now, what does the person requesting the action have to show for this request? They have an agreement from that the person will "Do their best." What does that mean they have agreed to do? They have agreed to do whatever action happens to fit their definition of "their best." Does that include going to the post office? What might be legitimate, from their view, as a reason not to go? At the time of this conversation, who knows? This doesn't mean they can say, "I will go to the post office" and that nothing will prevent it or that you can count on it like you can count on the sun going down tonight. But it does mean that if you leave an agreement for action in the state of conceptual understanding and nonspecific statement, there's a high probability something else is already going on, something that can result in the action not happening. You're simply stacking the odds against you.

It's amazing how, once you're alert to the use of sensory versus conceptual words in getting people to take action, you can frequently spot potential trouble. There are almost always warning signs that an action isn't going to happen if there's something blocking it other than a genuine world-induced, unpreventable event. The problem shows up in the words or the style of the request, in the cues given off by the person of whom the action is being asked, or in the words or style of the agreement.

Now let's talk about the many different ways requests for action and agreements to perform action work in the real world. It would be great if all there was to it was to ask someone for action, get specific agreement, and they do what they agreed to do. Sometimes that does happen. But sometimes it doesn't happen.

When Someone Doesn't Agree to Perform the Action

In sales and in psychotherapy, lack of agreement is called "resistance." It occurs when you ask someone to do something and they refuse to agree to do it by either clearly say they won't do it, or by equivocating to the point it's clear to you that they aren't agreeing to do it. They may also present some block that prevents them from agreeing to perform the action, usually some reason such as, "they're too busy."

First, remember that it's good when you know up front that someone isn't agreeing to do something, better they let you know right then. You're ahead of the game because you have some ability to deal with the problem before time passes and you base future actions on the action you expect them to perform. If you walk away thinking there's an agreement and there really isn't, or that someone agrees and then doesn't do what they agreed to do, you're in a worse spot because you're likely to not know there's a problem until you discover the action hasn't been taken.

Nevertheless, someone's lack of agreement to take an action is likely to set off your survival wiring. You have some stake in the action being taken, or you wouldn't be trying to get them to take it in the first place. So by their not agreeing to do it, there's some threat or some cost to you. Whatever your usual pattern of survival reaction is, you'll probably have it occur at that time. If you do have any kind of escalated survival reaction, your job of dealing with the refusal is going to be made a little tougher. Survival reactions tend to narrow our choices of behaviors and get us to act in ways that set off others' survival reactions as well. Your first reaction may be something that makes things worse.

There are always reasons behind a refusal. Whether they're good reasons or bad, realistic or unrealistic, they are reasons. The first thing useful to do is to find out the reasons behind the unwillingness to agree to the action.

Now, there are circumstances where someone won't give you the reasons. Usually this will be accompanied by an upset on their part, either anger or tears, along with a refusal to give reasons or a claim of not knowing why they won't do the action, just that they "don't want to." If this happens, it often means the person has had a serious survival reaction to your request for action; the reaction is so strong their defenses are even protecting the reasons behind a wall of upset. You've most likely hit a nerve that has been rubbed raw by some historical experience in the person's life. It might be past experience with you, or with someone else. In any case, it's probable some greatly vulnerable area has been entered, and the strongest defenses available are being called to deal with you, the intruder.

This is, of course, likely to set off an even larger survival reaction in you (as you remember, large survival reactions beget large survival reactions). Which will inflame their reaction. At that point their defenses will inflame your reactions, and on the cycle will go. Some ways of working with it include:

1. Keep talking. They may be sending signals out to go away, but if you can keep engaged in conversation, a process may continue that may eventually get you someplace. Don't necessarily keep pushing for the action, just keep the words going back and forth between you. Just stay with it, keep talking with them. If you do you might be surprised by the changes that can happen.

2. Just listening. If you can get them to talk, so much the better. This can deplete their survival reaction. Don't even worry about the action so much, just keep the conversation going, and adopt a listening stance.

3. Empathic responding. This is one of the places where empathic responding can work wonders. What you're trying to do is to calm down the survival reaction that has flared up and gotten in the way of the action. By using empathic responding you can calm this down, reestablish a conversa-

tion, and even get back to the action. But don't worry about talking more about the action, just deal with the survival reaction.

In any case, if you get a response of no reason, especially with an escalation of upset, you're involved in a big survival reaction and you'll need to deal with that first.

But let's say they do tell you reasons. When you get the reasons, they'll fall into one of two categories: they will be practical or personal. Practical reasons have to do with events in the sensory world that may be in the way of the action. Personal reasons are survival wiring reactions. There are, as usual, different ways of handling each of these.

Practical Reasons

Remember that your purpose is to get action. It's not your purpose to straighten someone out, or change them, or get them to be different. It's easy to try to go too "deep" into the person and how they're or what their motivations are for refusing your request, especially if they're being unpleasant about it. But if the failure to get agreement to perform the action is based on practical reasons, then the best thing is to only go as deep as the practical issues. Just stick to dealing with those—actions and circumstances.

In response to practical reasons, figure out a way to circumvent the barriers so the action or the result you want can still be accomplished. Forget the refusal, look for a way to get accomplished what you want accomplished. You may want to figure out an alternate action that can still satisfy the goals you're requesting. This may be difficult because either there aren't many alternatives, or because allowing for another action is flexibility that your survival wiring doesn't particularly take to.

For example, sometimes people feel they are "letting someone get away with something" if they agree to an alternate action. If this is the case for you, then you aren't really wanting action from someone, you want to change them, or "teach them" something. You should refer to the chapter on changing people.

Coming up with an alternate action occurs completely in the sensory realm. It doesn't deal with reasons or feelings (except perhaps to take them into account in suggesting an action). There's an extensive discussion of this process in the chapter on conflict, so I'm just going to talk about it here in a summarized way.

First, you can simply request another action.

"Will you take this over to the post office this morning?" (Request for action.)

"I can't, because I must finish this report by noon." (Refusal to agree because of practical reason.)

"OK, will you take it this afternoon?" (Request of alternate action.)

"Sure, I'll do that." (Agreement.)

Or:

"Will you lend me your handkerchief for a minute?"

"Well, OK, but I've used it already."

"OK, then will you get me a Kleenex?"

You can see that in many small examples in life this is how we work intuitively and automatically. If you get an agreement for an alternate action that will accomplish what you need or want accomplished, then you're in good shape. If you don't, you can suggest another possible action, or you ask the other person to suggest one. For example:

"Will you take this over to the post office this morning?"

"I can't because I must finish this report by noon."

"Well, I need it to be at the post office before noon. I can't leave the office, so help me figure out how I can get it there."

Personal, Survival Wiring Reasons

Often the reason someone won't agree to do something isn't due to practical issues. It's because their survival reactions get in the way. They could perform the action, but they have difficulty, for internal reasons, agreeing to it. Now, no one says "I won't do that because it threatens my survival wiring in the conceptual world and so makes me uncomfortable, leading me to refuse." Instead, they find reasons that sound logical, but aren't really to the point.

This is a difficult spot for you because you have to determine how willing and able you are to confront someone's survival wiring. If you're not willing to confront the wiring and try to get the person to take the action, then you can withdraw the request or work on some other way of getting the result. This means going back to methodology to see if there's some way to "work the action around" so the person is willing to agree to do it.

If you decide you do want to confront the survival wiring there are several methods that can be useful. First, you can simply enforce the request and re-request the action, to see if they will agree if you're more persistent. This really doesn't need much explanation. Just ask again. Remember, sometimes people need a little nudging. They may be willing, they may just get scattered.

Second, you can work with the person to deal with the "block" that prevents them from agreeing to take the action. This block is whatever the reason they present, or whatever reason lurks beneath the supposed reason they give. So you might do some digging to find out if there's something else going on that's driving their resistance.

When inquiring about the block, you'll want to use joining techniques and positive communication behaviors. Don't make them wrong, because you want to get to the bottom of the resistance, and making them wrong is going to increase their survival reaction. There may be some valid reason you can't see why the person isn't performing the action. Empathic responding can be helpful to lower their survival reaction so you can get closer to the reason they aren't able to agree. By reflecting what someone is saying in an empathic manner, sometimes you can get to the bottom of things.

Sharing can also be useful. This might be a place where you can share your own experiences with this kind of situation, where you felt unwilling or incapable of doing something. The purpose of sharing is to take the emotional charge off of the block the person has, to remove their "on the spot" feeling, and calm them down. One of the important aspects of group therapy that reduces people's upset, is "universality." It means when you discover something you're struggling with isn't specific to you, you're more able to deal with it. It's less personal, and this reduces the threat on the conceptual level. Sharing that you have struggled with the same kind of issue (only if it's true, of course) can have the same effect.

Finally, you can escalate in either the sensory or the conceptual world. Escalating in the sensory world means you use increasingly negative communication behaviors in re-requesting the action. The first thing this is designed to do is to trip the person's survival wiring off just a bit so they're more alert to the issue. You might speak more loudly, or more abruptly. You might frown, or call their name a little more sharply. What you're trying to do by using these behaviors is make the issue more significant than whatever other survival wiring issue they're dealing with. You're also making yourself a survival threat as well. So be prepared for some possible upset feelings with you when you use this method. But you can get through some blocks this way.

I was in a grocery store one day and heard the front-end manager say to a sacker: "John, don't you walk by an order! Do you hear me? DON'T WALK BY AN ORDER!" It was clear from the manager's tone that not walking by an order (whatever that meant) was a pretty basic rule of sacking that John had just violated. She had escalated in the sensory realm by using a stern and harsh tone of voice. I also noticed she was looking at him, even though he was a distance away from her. This appeared to be a very good and effective escalation. It had enough energy to get through whatever else was going on in his head, and woke him up with some urgency.

I also had a store owner tell me one day about dealing with a customer who was being mean to one of his employees. The customer was confronting the employee very rudely in the middle of the store. The owner asked the man to wait a minute and he would help to deal with the issue, if they would step to the back. The man didn't wait a minute as requested, and continued to talk to the employee.

The owner looked at him and said, "I told you to shut up for a minute!" This stunned the man into silence. The owner then told his employee to go with them to the back of the store. The man started up talking again, and the owner looked at him and this time just said "I said shut up until we get to the back of the store! If you want to deal with this, come with me and we'll deal with it." Then he walked with the employee to the back of the store. This was also a nice little piece of sensory escalation.

You can also escalate in the conceptual realm. This is an escalation of the right and wrong aspect or "significance" of the action. You can be direct about it, or you can use reframing. I use a reframe with businesses I consult with if they're being chronically late. I note to them the percentage of time they were wasting by being late, and suggest they might be wasting that **percentage of** time and efficiency in all their work. This is expanding the frame to say, in effect, "Hey, this being late stuff is about more than meeting with me. It has a big impact on you. Think you have too much to do? That you're overworked? No wonder, if you waste this much time."

I performed a similar escalation with a psychotherapy patient who called to cancel and reschedule an appointment by going back and counting up his cancellations and reporting to him that he had cancelled or rescheduled 40% of his appointments with me. I suggested that this was how he lived his life, at 60% rather than 100%. I also told him I would from that point on charge him for late cancellations. This increased the value of being on time, and he mentioned the impact of this insight over and over again after the incident. He was also never late again.

Using conceptual terms that are more negative in implication can be used to escalate conceptually. You can talk about "having" to perform the action, it being "required" or "necessary."

Please note that if up until now you have been thinking I'm trying to propagate "positive" communication behaviors as the only legitimate way to communicate, and as the solution to all interpersonal issues, realize that it isn't true at all. The problem with negative communication behaviors isn't that they're wrong or useless, it's just that they're like dessert—real inviting and attractive, but easy to overdo and cause problems. And because they can be potent survival wiring triggers, they can impede your getting what you want with people if having others' survival wiring go off isn't consistent with what you want. They aren't bad, you just have to use them judiciously.

One final point about negative communication behaviors and escalations designed to get action. You need to be aware that escalations have limits. If your limit of escalation is below someone's threshold of survival wiring, it isn't going to be effective. They're essentially going to become deaf to you. This happens all the time with parents and children. Children become "parent deaf" because they've learned that the parents are all talk and no action. That's why it's usually best to use primarily direct, behavioral intervention methods with kids when you're having trouble getting action. Too many communication behavior escalations, with nothing else to back them up, will diminish your effectiveness as a parent and train your kids to ignore survival threats.

Finally, you can use direct behavioral intervention methods to confront someone who is unwilling to agree to take an action. The important thing to remember about behavioral methods is they aren't about talking. They aren't threats. Often we contaminate behavioral and talking methods with threats. Behavioral methods work because of their nature, not because they're talked about, understood, or threatened. They aren't coercion. You can explain what is going to happen, but it's not in the telling that the effectiveness comes, it's in the willingness to follow through, the occurrence of the consequences. Talking about it is only making clear what is going to happen, as a courtesy.

Rewards and punishments are probably the most useful of the direct intervention techniques. Remember, as I talked about in the chapter on behavioral techniques, these don't necessarily feel good or bad, but result in a behavior recurring or stopping. The very best rewards and punishments, and the ones I usually recommend to people, are what are called "consequences." They're a specific sub-set of rewards and punishments because consequences are naturally or logically related to the action or inaction in question. Not all rewards and punishments are. You tell a child that they can't go to a party on the weekend because they didn't mow the grass like they said they would. This is a punishment unrelated to the action, because mowing the lawn and going to the party aren't inherently related. Alternatively, you can require the child to pay someone out of their own money to get the lawn mowed because they aren't doing it. This is a consequence because losing the money to pay for what the child isn't doing is related to the lack of mowing the lawn.

Agreement to Perform the Action, but Failure to Do It

If you have requested action and someone has agreed to do it and they do it, fine. But what if you have requested the action, and you even have clear agreement about it, and the person still doesn't do it? This could be as small as the waiter not bringing your ketchup, or as large as a manager under you not handling a problem with a major account after he or she agreed to do so.

First, realize that when this happens two things have occurred, and each is a separate issue. One is you have not gotten the action you requested. This means whatever it was that needed to be done wasn't done. Second, you have a broken agreement on your hands.

There are two possibilities that could have resulted in the action not being taken. The first is there was some kind of realistic block. You assign a staff member to take the deposit to the bank, and they have a flat tire. Or the bank is closed. Or a meteor comes down and smashes them. We have only a limited amount of control over the world, and sometimes things just happen that preclude the ability to do something. If you aren't able to tolerate that being the case in the world, you'll have trouble. Sometimes the failure to perform the action was just unavoidable. If that's the case, you use the same approaches that we talked about when an action has been prevented by a realistic reason. You re-group and figure out how to get the action done.

But sometimes the reason isn't one that was a real, practical reason. Sometimes people didn't do what they were supposed to do for other reasons. Like they didn't want to, or they changed their mind, or they forgot.

Sometimes it can be difficult to decide if the reason was real and practical or if it was resistance. How do you tell? About the only way I've ever seen is to have a history of the person that you can compare. If someone does what they say ninety-nine percent of the time, and then they don't, the chances are good the reason was legitimate. On the other hand, if they repeatedly agree to do things and regularly don't do them even though their reasons seem legit there's probably something fishy going on. How many violations of agreements constitute a pattern? About three.

What do you do if the agreement to take the action has been violated for a reason you don't see as legitimate? You use the same procedures you used when there was a balking about performing the action. You can get a new agreement, work with the nature of the reasons, or escalate. You have to decide, based on the particular circumstances involved, which is most appropriate.

What is different, though, from dealing with someone refusing to agree to an action, is you have the second part, a broken agreement. You have to deal with that broken agreement with the person.

How do you do that? By acknowledging, out loud, that the agreement was broken. It doesn't have to be a formal statement in a public forum of some sort. There simply has to be some sort of open acknowledgment that the person agreed to do the action and they didn't. It has to be admitted by you, them, or both. Then there has to be some conclusion about what is to be done about it. Sometimes the acknowledgment is all that's required. Sometimes consequences are needed. It will depend on the circumstance. But the most important thing is for there to be an acknowledgment that the agreement was broken.

This is simple, but that doesn't mean it's easy. Remember humans hate to be wrong, and not keeping one's agreement is commonly considered to be wrong. So there's likely to be an emphasis on justification and rationalization to try to protect one's rightness. You may have to just accept that as a matter of course. It's still more important there be an open acknowledgment of the broken agreement. Trouble is created when such events occur "in the dark" without being talked about.

Chapter 13

Resolving Conflict

Dealing with conflict is an important area of people-handling, and a difficult area as well. Because conflict almost always involves heightened survival reactions, people become very self-righteous during conflicts. This, of course, makes them difficult to deal with. I was reminded of this yesterday, when I read that a person involved in a conflict was quoted as saying "We know right is on our side, and now we must make sure right prevails." How would you like to be dealing with that person in a conflict?

The first step in being able to deal effectively with conflict is to understand it. "Conflict" is a conceptual term, and, like all conceptual terms, its meaning depends entirely on whose interpretation you're referring to. If two people are talking about conflict they may not even be aware they are talking about two different things. We need to be clear what we're talking about.

There are two common misconceptions about conflict. The first is that conflict is the same thing as wanting someone to change. Trying to change them and having a conflict with someone are two completely different processes. Many times people complain of conflict when the real issue is that they don't like how that person is, they want that person to change. There's nothing unusual about wanting someone to change, and I devote a whole chapter to it later in the book, but it's different from conflict.

This confusion is often the result of people having an easier time talking about conflict than admitting they don't like how someone is and they want them to change. Conflict sounds more neutral and less blaming. This definition happens a lot in organizations in which people have an investment in looking good. It happens in churches. Saying you're having a conflict with a staff member (or better yet, a personality conflict) sounds more charitable than saying "I wish that jackass would stop shooting his mouth off." But calling this situation conflict is glossing over your dislike.

The second common misconception is that arguing or fighting is conflict. That may sound strange to you, because the term is often used synonymously with fighting. Conflict isn't the arguing and fighting itself, it's what the arguing and fighting are about.

Conflict creates the need for what I call a "resolution technology." Arguing and fighting are resolution technologies, attempts to resolve a conflict. The conflict is what makes a resolution technology necessary.

The Nature of Conflict

Conflict consists of two elements, disagreement and the need for joint action, and it's necessary to understand each of these elements.

Disagreement

In the chapter on preventing problems I talked about agreements being a fundamental element in all dealings with people. Because agreements define people as being on the same team, or expecting the same thing, disagreements make people feel they're on opposing teams and divide their expectations. Being in this position is a survival threat which creates conflict.

If you look around the world you'll see much of its trouble grows out of disagreement, and the world is structured to prevent disagreements from being a problem. The reason separate states exist, for example, is so laws can disagree with each other without causing havoc. States are designed to peacefully coexist side by side while having laws in opposition. On a more personal level, separate housing means neighbors can live side-by-side and disagree about taste in interior decorating.

However, disagreement by itself doesn't always lead to the need for a resolution technology. In fact, there are a few areas of life where disagreement is even helpful. Disagreement is the driving force behind scientific progress. When a scientist investigates a phenomenon, collects data, reaches conclusions, and publishes the work, other scientists get interested, investigate it and reach different conclusions. The original scientist returns to the laboratory, refines his investigation, and reaches still different conclusions. This process results in a thorough and intense scrutiny. Inaccurate conclusions are weeded out, a consensus is reached, and a piece of the world begins to be less mysterious.

Another example of the usefulness of disagreement is the way in which the federal government is structured. What demonstrates the brilliance of the founding fathers of this country was their awareness that they needed to establish a government designed to disagree with itself, to routinely experience internal conflict. With that element built into the government's structure, there's less chance the government can become a monolithic dictatorship, a big fear of the founding fathers. There are always going to be fractures, splits, and opposing positions, that will keep governmental activities in check and relatively inefficient.

The Need for Joint Action

The second fundamental element of conflict is the need for joint action. Because action occurs in the consensual sensory world, it cannot be self-contradictory, so disagreement is incompatible with it. Something can't be done and also not done. As a result, when there's disagreement and joint action is required, there's a problem because only one thing can be done.

If you and your spouse disagree about what your dream vacation would be—you love the mountains and he or she loves the seashore, it's a disagreement but not a conflict. It only becomes a conflict when you win the Dream Vacation package on a television game show and the host asks you where you're going. Then you're required to reach a resolution about what to do, and your disagreement becomes a problem for which a solution must be found.

If you deal with someone long enough, disagreement is unavoidable. We like to think this isn't inherently a problem, and we tend to give a lot of lip-service to the idea that every person is "unique." We say we respect everyone's uniqueness, and every person has value. "After all," we sigh with great gushing kindness, "every snowflake is different."

But that's not the way it really works. When we're confronted with a need for joint action and someone is in disagreement with us, the sweet snowflake talk flies out the window.

This is why upset usually goes with conflict. A conflict situation is a survival threat, and our psyches energize for defense by generating upset. The way we use language demonstrates how much of a potential survival threat disagreement is. What do we call something we find to be unpleasant? "Disagreeable," as in "That's a most disagreeable smell." The use of the word isn't an accident. Disagreement, to our biology, presents the potential of a survival threat, which is actualized when the disagreement is wed to the need for joint action.

Now, isn't it possible to have a conflict even when there's no direct need for action, like conflicts over beliefs, thoughts, or ideas? There are religious wars, after all, and people do get upset about what other people think about them, don't they? Certainly both of these are true. But let's look at why people get into conflicts about ideology and about what others think.

People regularly disagree with each other about what they think, and most of the time people don't even know it. Most of the time it doesn't matter and it's not a conflict. If I like bananas and you don't, there isn't going to be a problem if we never eat together. If I believe in God and you don't, we may still be able to have a pleasant conversation at a cocktail party. We may never even know we disagree.

The reason conflict can appear to be about what people think or believe is these can be reflective of what they do and how they do it. So people get into conflicts over what other people think because there's a potential for action based on those thoughts. Survival wiring looks for possible problems as well as actual problems, so the potential is a trigger to survival wiring. We react to what they think because our defenses are trying to launch a pre-emptive strike.

There is the possibility of some kind of disagreeable occurrence resulting from that disagreement in thinking. So despite what you might have thought, you're not crazy because you care what other people think, even though at this moment there's no practical problem with someone thinking differently from you. But your biology knows it might result in action, so it goes into high alert.

This is why dictatorships try to control what people think. Why should they care what people think? Because it can turn into what people do. The logic is that in order to prevent the doing, control the thinking. If you look at any religious war, you'll find that it's not simply over disagreement in theologies or ideologies. The war is over the way those ideologies result in things being done, and who gets to decide how things are done, who gets privileges and benefits. It's about control, power and behavior. It's about the actions the ideologies create that turns the disagreeing thoughts into "conflict."

Resolution Technology

When there's disagreement and joint action is required, there must be some mechanism for resolving the disagreement so that action can occur. If you're selling your home and I don't like your price, our disagreement isn't a conflict unless I decide I want to buy your home. Once it becomes a conflict, no action can be taken unless there's some method for resolving it. If there weren't some way of resolving a conflict over price, a house could never be sold or bought.

This mechanism is what I call a "resolution technology," a methodology for resolving the disagreement so action can occur. Resolution technologies are required whenever there's conflict, which is a disagreement and the need for joint action.

If two businesses merge, a resolution technology will be required to establish the ways things will be done in areas where the formerly separate companies did things differently. If two people are dating, many differences in preferences may be fine, because there's no need for joint action. They can each decorate their houses differently, have different tastes in food, and visit their families with different frequencies. But when they get married many of these areas of disagreement will need to be resolved because joint action will be required. They'll need some method of resolution, which they may never have needed before. This is what makes marriage difficult to maintain in a satisfying manner.

The important issue regarding dealing with conflict is that some kind of process or procedure is needed to enable joint action when there's a disagreement. The key to handling conflict with people is being able to choose and apply a resolution technology.

Resolution Technology #1: Fighting

Fighting (I'm including "arguing" in this term as well; although there are some distinctions between the two, they're irrelevant as far as the present discussion is concerned) is an attempt to resolve a conflict and produce conjoint action by threatening the other party's survival wiring until they agree to act in accordance with your position. In practical personal terms, fighting is the use of negative communication behaviors to change the position of someone who disagrees with you.

Let's say you and your spouse are having a conflict over going to a movie. First, you disagree on the movie. You've had your eye on a thriller, your spouse wants to see a comedy. Second, you need joint action, because you want to go to a movie together. So you need to be able to take joint action. Let's look at how fighting as a resolution technology might work in this case.

First you say to your spouse, "I'd really like to see this movie. I've been wanting to see it for a while. Let's go tonight, OK?"

Your spouse responds "No, I don't want to see that movie, I want to see this comedy. Let's go to it instead."

The disagreement and need for joint action is now stated, so the conflict is established. Resolution technology is required.

"But why don't you want to see the thriller?" you ask, using a slightly complaining tone of voice that implies, ever-so-slightly, that you're upset because your spouse is in disagreement with you. (Remember how sensitive human perception is to communication behaviors. You're already implying they're being wrong because you're suffering at their hands. If you think this is an overstatement of the way these things work, you've never watched people talk on videotape.)

Your spouse replies, "I don't want to go because I don't like thrillers, and that one looks really nerve wracking. If we're going to a movie I want to see something entertaining."

This is subtle, but that last phrase, "I want to see something entertaining" is a clever negative communication behavior. It makes the thriller wrong by defining it as not "entertaining," which is, of course, what a movie is supposed to be. A movie that's not entertaining is a bad movie. Although you don't consciously perceive this aspect of the conversation, it will not be lost on your survival wiring.

"But *it is* entertaining," you retort. (Like I said, you'd pick up on that.)

This statement is also the first noticeable escalation, as you're now directly making your spouse wrong in their definition of entertaining. You have openly said what they said isn't true. Notice how this is possible as a result of the conceptual term "entertaining" being defined differently by two different people.

"Well, maybe it's entertaining for someone like you, but it isn't for me," your spouse replies.

Another subtle escalation. There's a slightly harsh tone of voice used on the words "you" and "me," suggesting something negative about your difference. In addition, the phrase "someone like you" is also a negative communication behavior because it implies that you're someone who exists in a particular, negative way. This is also the first twinge of the conversation getting personal, so the escalations are just about to take off.

"But," you plead, "We always go see the movies you want to see. Just this once can't we go see one I want to see?"

Now you've escalated in the conceptual realm from a disagreement over choice of a movie to a general issue of power and dominance in your relationship. You've just implied that you're your spouse's victim, so by implication it would be wrong, and unfair, to refuse you this request. You've also escalated in the sensory realm by using a pleading tone of voice and emphasis on particular words (always, you) that imply your spouse is being unreasonable. Now it's really going to pick up steam.

"What do you mean we always go to movies I want to see?" your spouse replies indignantly.

Your spouse has now taken the bait of the being made wrong, and responded with a new negative communication behavior, an indignant tone of voice. This implies that you're out of line, the one being wrong.

Then your spouse makes a final comment, "Remember how many of those stupid concerts we go to because you want to?"

What's happening now is what generally happens with fight technology; the behaviors and the conversation begin to generalize, and personalize. In this case, topics are starting to be used not as topics, but as tools to threaten each other's survival wiring—to demonstrate the degree to which the other person is wrong. Your concerts have just been made wrong by being called stupid, and you're now being an inconsiderate jerk because your spouse has been graciously going with you when they really didn't want to. They were being nice by going, and here you're refusing to go to the movie they want to see.

"I don't make you go to those!" you yell.

Yelling is a negative communication behavior, of course, so the negative reciprocity continues to escalate. In addition, the content of your statement makes your spouse wrong because it implies that it's your partner's own fault if they do something they don't want to do, such as attend a concert. Now you're turning the tables by making them wrong for accusing you.

"No, you don't make me go, you just have a complete fit if I even hint that I don't want to go!"

The conversation has now gone from the topic of movies to examples of right and wrong and, a direct discussion of personal qualities or characteristics. The attacks are becoming increasingly personal.

"What are you talking about? I'm not the one being a jerk about going to some stupid movie."

Now the direct insults are starting. You just called your spouse a jerk. The conversion from topic of conflict to personal attack and defense is now complete.

"No, that's right, you're never the jerk, are you? I always am. I'm just one great big jerk."

This is said in a sarcastic tone of voice, which is a discrepant verbal and nonverbal communication behavior, and is also a biting way of saying the content isn't intended to be literal rather to demonstrate the stupidity of your statement.

"This is ridiculous!" you scream. "I never said that! You're being crazy. Why do you have to make a federal case out of everything? Why can't we just talk about it like normal people?"

You have just called your spouse an over-reacting, abnormal person.

"Fine. I'm wrong, I'm stupid. Fine. We'll do whatever you like. In fact, you do whatever you like, because I'm not doing anything with you. You can just go to hell."

Storming out of the room, your spouse ends the argument with a final escalation. This time it's physical. They slam the door.

The above shows the standard course of a fight:

1. *Conflict.* There's disagreement with the need for joint action. It doesn't really matter what the topic is, what matters is there's some topic on which there's disagreement.

2. *Survival threats.* Some form of threat is used in an attempt to change the other party's position. In the case of an argument, the threats are generally negative communication behaviors. In the case of nations, it might be the threat created by undertaking "military exercises" near the border of the opposing country.

3. *Responding survival threats.* Usually the return techniques are in the same ballpark as the survival threats being received. In the case of an argument, negative communication behaviors are sent out and negative communication behaviors are sent back. There are variations to this, as when someone who feels less competent than the other party in verbal warfare becomes physical in their response. In the case of fighting among nations, military "alert" status may be used in response to the military exercises of the country.

4. *Escalation of survival threats.* Each party escalates in an attempt to change the position of the other. In an argument, this usually means escalating negative communication behaviors.

5. *Personalization.* The topic goes from the original disagreement to the rightness or wrongness of the individuals involved. Remember during the Iraq-Kuwait conflict how personal the attacks became between Saddam Hussein and George Bush? It stops being about an issue and starts being about "you" and "me."

6. *Victory, defeat, or standoff.* One party ultimately escalates beyond where the other party is willing or able to match, producing victory and defeat, or there's a limit to the

willingness to escalate resulting in a standoff. The fight in the example produced a standoff. There was no resolution, so no joint action could occur. In personal relationships, a standoff is the most common result. Sometimes it only looks like victory because the party giving in stores the resentment away for later use.

You see this same pattern in virtually every argument or fight on the planet. You see it between co-workers, spouses, friends, kids, and nations. Fights can be very short and consist of just a couple of words, or they can be extensive and last years.

Once you're involved in a fight as a resolution technology, it's difficult to stop until the victory, defeat, or standoff occurs. This is because the survival stakes steadily rise as the fight continues, the longer it goes, the more danger to you. And the more danger, the less likely you are to stop defending yourself.

Fight technology isn't always bad technology even though with the couple it didn't produce resolution. As is the case with any people-handling method, the key is to choose the right technology for the right circumstance. In this example it was probably a bad choice. It didn't achieve the desired results of agreeable resolution and instead produced upset, which we can assume the couple didn't want. But that doesn't mean there aren't other situations where fight technology would be appropriate. Some examples are:

1. If your physical survival is at stake and it looks like fighting might be what saves you, it would be best to fight. After all, what have you got to lose? The side-effects of upset and discomfort generally caused by fight technology are going to be less of a price than your life.

2. If there's no need or desire to maintain any kind of relationship with the other party, fight technology may be an appropriate choice. The side-effects of upset and problems aren't particularly important to you. This can be seen in business, where competitors battle each other. Why do you think war analogies are commonly used in business competition? Because it's an appropriate place to use fight technology. You're on opposing sides, and you might not care about your relationship with your competitors.

You want to be a problem for someone. Sometimes this may be to accomplish a feelings-transfer, you want to give upset feelings to someone and throw a monkey wrench into the system. Sometimes this may be to find out if you make yourself enough of a problem you can get your way. Sometimes this may be to get people's attention (which I talk more about in the chapter on motivating).

I once picked a fight with a college where I was teaching part-time. I got a letter informing me I had to forward official transcripts for my undergraduate and graduate degrees by a particular date. Now, at that time I had been out of graduate school thirteen years and out of undergraduate school nineteen years. I had already been teaching without the transcripts, and I had been licensed to practice psychology for over ten years. Just being licensed meant that I had to have the degrees I said I had. In addition, I was in private practice where my time was limited and valuable, and I didn't feel like spending it writing for transcripts that were two decades old.

I called the registrar to ask if the letter was true. I had received one like it a couple of years prior, and was told not to worry about it. But this time she said it was true, that it was an order from "higher up." I stated I thought it was silly, and asked what would happen if I didn't do it. She was quiet for a minute and said she didn't know, but that I'd have to ask the Vice Chancellor for Academic Affairs. She then offered to call him for me, and I accepted.

This was a fight. I was being obstinate and resistive by calling their request silly. I was using negative communication behaviors and making them wrong. In this case I didn't mind being a problem, and I thought I might be able to get out of ordering the transcripts.

About twenty minutes later the phone rang. It was the Vice Chancellor himself. Now, you have to understand I was hardly important in their scheme of things. This was a good sized private university, and I taught one class that was given about every two years. I wasn't, shall we say, prominent. So for the Vice Chancellor to get on the phone to me made it clear I'd cause a stir. That was my intention, so my first technique was effective.

But that's where my effectiveness ended. He was better at making me wrong than I was at making him wrong. Throughout the conversation he exhorted me to order the transcripts right away, and gave me lots of reasons and justifications for their need for them, all of which were clearly quite valid.

I still asked if he didn't think the need for twenty year old transcripts was a bit excessive, and he stoutly denied it. He made it perfectly clear that it wasn't personal, but that "there was a lot of fraud in academics" and they were going to have a site visit from their accreditation agency, so he was going to require that I get the transcripts.

At that point I escalated directly to the final stage of a fight (getting personal) in order to transfer some feelings. I laughed, said that I would get the transcripts, and that I appreciated "his attention, if not his understanding." That worked. He suddenly fell all over himself saying that he understood, that he knew it was a hassle for me, etc. etc. I felt better, thanked him, and hung up. Then I ordered the transcripts.

Why did I do all that? First of all, I did it to find out if I could get away without ordering the transcripts. I wanted to see whether I could be a big enough problem to them to where it wouldn't be worth their while to force me to order the transcripts. I had a limit to how far I was willing to escalate because I still wanted to teach and I didn't feel it was justifiable to get too nasty, but I was willing to do some escalating and be somewhat unpleasant to try to get out of doing what they were asking. It didn't work, but I got my answer, and I did have the opportunity to transfer some feelings. That was enough for me.

4. You have some kind of power and have a good chance of producing a victory, and side-effects of upset will not be much of a problem. The example I used some chapters ago about yelling at the clerk at the rental car place is an example of this. My escalation essentially produced a fight, but because I was the customer, I had a certain degree of power.

I was very clear that this clerk was hired to do a job that he wasn't doing, so he was in a more precarious position than I. In addition, he had a boss who also had a boss, to whom I could appeal. And I didn't care about my relationship with that clerk.

Caveat

Whenever you use fight technology, you must be prepared for your survival wiring getting stirred up as well other people's. Fight technology is just not very nice, and to engage in it consciously you have to realize you're not being very nice. Most of the time people aren't willing to be conscious of their nastiness, and justify it with reasons and rationales about the other person's behavior. If you're going to be aware and conscious in your people-handling, though, you're going to have to see that if you're unpleasant, it's not justified by the other person; it's the way you're choosing to be. You have other options. So it's your fault you're being the way you're being.

I don't think unpleasant is always bad, but I think many times it's unnecessary or produces more problems than it's worth. The point is there's a price to pay, if you use fight technology. You have to tolerate that you were unpleasant, or made someone feel bad, or hurt someone's feelings. After the incident with the rental car clerk, for example, I felt upset for quite a while. My position about fight technology is that it's better to use something else when possible, have limits on the level to which you're willing to escalate, and abide by them.

So don't make excuses or try to defend, rationalize, or justify yourself. Admit to yourself when you're being a jerk. I acted like a jerk to the rental car clerk, and to the Vice Chancellor as well. I knew it, and it wasn't their fault. There's no particular justification to make it right, it was just the technology I decided to use. So you need to decide how much tolerance you have for behaving in that manner.

Do be aware that one of the drawbacks of the use of fight technology is that other people may write you off as a crazy, which may actually be a force against their agreeing with you or giving you what you want. It may be OK with you if people think you're crazy, but realize it can be self-defeating. I once had a run-in with a bank over a loan. It was clear the individual mishandling things had presented me as a lunatic to several levels of bosses. As a result, when I complained to them I got no action. They were patronizing and made me wrong in subtle ways. (They were, "sorry if I 'felt like' I had been mistreated . . . ") So my use of fight technology with the person making the errors backfired on me.

The problem with fighting as a conflict resolution technology isn't that it doesn't have its place, but rather that it's used where it doesn't produce the desired effects. It's frequently because people misuse fight technology and don't produce their result that they move on to the second conflict-resolution technology.

Resolution Technology #2: Avoiding the Issue

People learn over time that if they attempt to talk about a conflict with someone, no resolution gets produced. Instead, unproductive arguments or fights, with the associated upset and difficulties, are created. Because this makes things worse, their survival wiring learns to avoid the situation because it has become even more dangerous than the original conflict.

People avoid dealing with things for various reasons: to keep peace, to not cause trouble, to not rock the boat, to keep things smooth. And, again, avoidance isn't always wrong; it's usually only a problem when there's a pattern in a situation where it doesn't help the overall purpose. It doesn't produce happy children when parents avoid dealing with issues.

Avoidance is often a problem in ongoing relationships because the conflicts remain on an unspoken level. But remember, unspoken things can still be reacted to by survival wiring; what happens is a "tension" builds between people. It's their survival wiring being on alert. This makes for worse feelings in the relationship, which requires increased avoidance.

However, avoidance can, as any people-handling technique, be an appropriate method as well. It can be useful in several different situations:

1. Where potential risk is too high and potential benefit too small. If you're mad at your boss about something you disagree with, but your boss fires people easily and you need the job, you might want to consider other options.

2. If you don't care about your relationship with this person. If you don't care about it, or it's not an ongoing relationship, the benefit for going through the process of dealing with conflict may not be worthwhile. I'm certain that rental car clerk has ideas about me that I disagree with, but it's not worth my while to try to resolve any conflict about the kind of person I am.

3. If there are more immediate, pressing, urgent issues present. First things first.

So don't think avoidance is necessarily bad. Like everything else, it's only bad when misused.

Resolution Technology #3: Capitulation

Capitulation is giving in when you don't want to. It's swallowing your own feelings, going against what's OK with you to do the same things that avoidance is designed to do—keep the peace. But capitulation differs from avoidance in that you present yourself as being resolved about an issue when you really aren't.

A pattern of inappropriate use of capitulation is sometimes called "codependent" or "over adaptive" behavior. This occurs when someone is agreeable but secretly resentful. This pattern is a major problem for ongoing relationships and an inappropriate use of capitulation. There are appropriate uses for capitulation, though, such as:

1. Times when there's going to be immediate, serious damage if you don't capitulate. If the mugger has the gun to your head, give him your wallet. You can deal with the issues later. Remember the words of my flight attendant friend, who said their training to deal with hijackers was called: "Do what they tell you to do." It's stupid not to avoid making things worse in a life-and-death situation.

2. When you're clear your capitulation will achieve a more important purpose. This is called "losing the battle to win the war."

3. When the situation is structured to give you no power. For example, capitulation may be a good technology to use if you're a private and the general gives you an order to do

something you don't want to do. Unless you don't mind being court-martialed, capitulation is probably appropriate.

4. When you don't want to get bogged down in a conflict that isn't relevant to your purpose, or when dealing with it is not worth the time and effort involved. I had a couple of short long-distance calls that I didn't make show up on my office phone bill. I could have dealt with my office-mates to see whose client might have made the calls, but that would have required more time and energy than the couple of dollars the calls were worth. So I readily paid the bill, realizing full well I was giving in. If it became a pattern that cost me more than a couple of dollars it might have become worth my time to deal with it, but at the time it was more trouble than it was worth.

5. When you don't care about the relationship. It's interesting how avoidance and capitulation tend to create the same kinds of side-effects as does fighting. One of the easiest ways to mess up an ongoing relationship is to use capitulation as a repeated method of conflict resolution. The reason is because it looks like everything's just fine, while more and more debris builds up in the form of resentments. This creates distance between people and subtle upset feelings. It can be detrimental to a relationship that you want to maintain in good order.

    I capitulated on a magazine article I wrote which was substantially rewritten by the editor and then published without my permission or review. I was furious because I didn't like the way it was organized and it wasn't faithful to my original. I also thought it was handled in an underhanded manner, misleading me about why they wanted copies of the article on computer disk. But I decided to give in and not make a stink, because publishing is a small enough world that I didn't want to jeopardize my reputation in publishing circles or my future relationships with other editors. But my survival wiring reaction continues in the form of latent anger with that magazine, an unwillingness to ever write for it again, and a sense that they do things I consider to be wrong. It's OK with me to have this going on, because I think it's more important for me to maintain a good reputation in publishing circles than to deal with the magazine over this issue.

6. If you're using capitulation as a paradox. As I noted in the section on paradox, sometimes people hold their position in a conflict as a resistance to the other party's position. It usually doesn't look like that, though, and so it's not often possible to identify, but when it is, capitulation results in the other person giving up also. This happened in an example I used in a previous chapter where I was trying to get a client to see something about his behavior. He couldn't see it and I finally said I realized I was badgering him and we needed to talk about what he wanted to talk about. My client then started talking about the issue and admitted it was a problem.

The tricky part of using capitulation as a paradox is that you can't do it as just a technique designed to try to get the other person to give up their position. Paradox is the only technique that isn't a technique. If it's used in that manner, it's just a sneaky fighting method. If you're going to paradox, you really have to give up your position. You have to be OK with it if they don't give up theirs. In other words, you have to move to a new level of understanding where it's OK with you to lose.

Resolution Technology #4: Separation

The fourth resolution technology is the technology of separation. What I mean is separation on the issue involved, so joint action is no longer needed. I don't necessarily mean splitting the relationship itself in which the conflict is occurring. For example, the couple in the example in the fight technology section could use separation by going to dinner together, each going to a different movie, and then meeting afterward for coffee.

Separation works by removing the need for joint action, removing the conflict from the disagreement. Sometimes people get into trouble and conflict because they set things up so an unrealistic degree of joint action is required. If there is no room for people to be able to disagree and do things differently, then the situation is set up to create problems. Couples fall into this by thinking they have to agree on everything or do everything together. It's possible to separate some issues or decisions so joint action isn't required, thus lowering or resolving conflict.

Although there are sufficient drawbacks so it's unworkable in many instances in the present world, the old "man goes to work, woman stays home with the kids" separation served as an example of this. If it seems there was less family conflict back then, it's because it's true. The arenas of decision-making were more separate, making for fewer conflict situations. Of course it was restrictive as well, but you can see how expansion and overlapping of roles has created more conflict in the process. This is why increased conflict is so often an inherent part of growth, change, and progress. Because new things are combined that used to have differing realms of decision-making.

Pam and I have learned to use separation as a resolution technology when we go shopping together. We have very different styles of shopping, and they grate on each of us. I think she takes forever looking at something, and she thinks I race through places and want to spend too much time in bookstores. So we go to the mall together, decide on time and a meeting place, and go our separate ways. We meet back at the appointed time and share about our shopping and what we bought. If one of us wants to show the other something we found before we buy it, we take them back to look. (We used this method when we were picking out our "good" china before we got married, and were astounded to discover that out of the hundreds of patterns in several stores, we both, independently, picked the same one.)

A couple consulted me who had very different approaches toward finances, and I suggested they separate their finances, each paying a particular percentage of common expenses such as house and insurance, and control their own. For some couples this feels like a violation of their partnership, but to others it can be relationship-saving, as neither has to try to control the other's spending habits. Again, the point is to achieve separation in that particular area or instance, in order to remove the need for joint action, and thus the conflict.

Corporations often use separation by making different departments separate subsidiaries. What the packaged foods division decides would be best to do may be completely different from what the restaurant division decides is best. To try to make joint decisions would create all kinds of conflicts that may be extremely difficult to resolve, so different "companies" with different boards, management, and philosophies may work best. But they all may still be part of one larger, overall company.

Separation can be a touchy area for people because it has to do with people's definition of "relationship." Some people may not feel a marriage is really a marriage unless finances are joined. I knew a couple who lived together but who had such extremely different housekeeping styles they maintained separate bedrooms. They still slept together at night, but the separate rooms diminished conflict about their sharply discrepant housekeeping and cleanliness styles.

Ken Cooper, the man who coined the term aerobics, talks about this technique in one of his books. He notes how he and his wife are both committed exercisers, but they have conflicts when they exercise together; they complain about each other's pace of running. Their solution was to exercise, but not to run together.

Separation is also a technology parents use with teenagers. It may be more trouble than it's worth to get them to clean their rooms, so they separate their room, closing the door and leaving it to the teenager to manage. Or they get the teenager their own phone line so there are no more conflicts about the phone.

There are a variety of situations where separation can be used:

1. When joint action isn't absolutely required. It wouldn't be possible to use separation to move the television set if we both have to do it because one of us can't do it alone. Then we both have to do it. But in any area where joint action isn't absolutely required, it can be done separately.

2. When the area separated doesn't violate the basic definition of the relationship. As I noted previously, some people might find separate bedrooms or separate finances a violation of marriage. Others might find it a relief to not worry about conflicts over that stuff. There are many areas in relationships where separation can be successfully used. Both partners don't have to go to bed at the same time, eat at the same time or eat the same thing, go to the same movies, or use the same bathroom to get ready in the mornings.

Separation doesn't need to mean "not being together," either. For example, Pam likes to record a favorite TV show and watch it at night, at the very time when my creative juices are flowing about writing. But we still like to be together, so I have my desk in the room where she watches TV. She wears earphones while watching her show as I pound away at my word processor. During commercials we can talk about what we're doing and share with each other. This gives us togetherness without doing exactly the same thing.

Resolution Technology #5: Negotiation

The fifth technology for conflict resolution is negotiation. We often think of it as a term that only applies to things like hostages, wars, and buying cars and houses, but those are just the most obvious and formal forms. In truth, we spend a great deal of our lives in informal negotiations that we don't label as that, but they are negotiations nevertheless.

Negotiation is a middle path between the technologies of fighting and avoidance or capitulation. It has some important differences from both. First, it doesn't operate from survival reactions. In fact, the process and the behaviors required in negotiations often run counter to those that survival wiring tries to generate.

Because of this, negotiation technology is often more difficult for people because it often feels less natural than either fighting or avoiding. Many of our families trained us well in fighting or avoiding, but few if any taught us how to negotiate. So it's not a technology that we often consider in our daily lives. Nevertheless, it holds an important place. Because it does tend to be a less familiar method than the other three, I'm going to discuss it in somewhat more detail than the others.

There are two key aspects of negotiation as a conflict resolution technology:

1. Any conflict to be negotiated must be translated from conceptual terms into sensory terms. You can't negotiate concepts. They must involve tangible, sensory entities.

    This is one reason why people don't think to use negotiations in their private lives. They haven't translated the issues they have with people they're close to into sensory issues. They may even have the sense that it can't be done. How do you translate attitudes or feelings that are in conflict into sensory entities?

The truth is you can. Nearly every conflict can be translated into sensory language. There's twenty years of solid, consistent, psychological research that suggests negotiations be used successfully and reliably in many relationships. It doesn't turn the relationship into some formalized, distant entity. To the contrary, it can prove to be a powerful force for intimacy and closeness. Nevertheless, one of the big stumbling blocks for people is learning to translate their conflicts into sensory terms. I will talk more about this, but for now let me just say that nearly every issue between two people, every disagreement, can be stated in sensory terms so that negotiations technology can be applied to it.

2. Conversations that are part of negotiations must stay on the topic of the disagreement and not mutate. The methodology of negotiation isn't to threaten survival wiring, as in fighting, nor is it to avoid survival wiring reactions, as it is in avoiding or capitulating. Instead, negotiation works by creating new possibilities, that haven't been seen before or taken seriously. Things that change the conversation onto other paths, such as "getting personal" due to negative communication behaviors, have to be eliminated from negotiation conversations.

These two factors make negotiations much more difficult and demanding than fighting or avoiding. Negotiations require creativity (thinking up new things) and staying on topic (editing out survival threats). However, negotiation technology is the only one which can reliably produce particular outcomes.

There are several situations where negotiation is useful as a resolution technology:

1. When you want to maintain a good relationship with the person with whom you're having the conflict. That's why negotiation, even though it's often called other things, is the basis of many forms of marital counseling, team-building, and interpersonal relations training. Even if you only want to maintain the relationship in the short term negotiation technology can be useful. If you're buying a house, you may only be concerned that the relationship stay in good shape

until the deal closes, but you're aware that you could blow it by messing up the relationship.

I was once negotiating with a building owner to rent office space, and there were a lot of things that needed to be worked out for the deal to close. Apparently the owner didn't want to mess with those details. Instead of negotiations, she seemed to prefer fight technology. As we talked, she began to define me as unreasonable, made me late for sessions by demanding that we talk about an issue during a particular phone conversation, and told me of her "fiduciary responsibility" to the other building partners, as if that should be the driving force in my decision. She upset me so much I didn't care if it was the most perfect office space in the whole world, I wouldn't have rented it from her. Her mistake was that she didn't attend to the effect the resolution technology she was using would have. It seemed kind of stupid to me because I'm a psychologist. Did she think I wouldn't notice her subtle threats and implications that I was wrong? Did she think I wouldn't know what her actions were designed to do? Did she think I would overlook it, when I know that people generally behave in the future as they behave now? It was a classic example of someone using the wrong resolution technology for the situation.

2. When you're in an ongoing relationship with another person. Because most people have not been taught to negotiate, they often don't think it will work. They think the other person is never going to go along, and won't cooperate with the negotiating process. We tend to see the people with whom we deal as unreasonable. However, this perception is the result of a history of applying the wrong resolution technology, and mistakenly thinking the difficulty is in the other person's character.

In some of my training sessions I videotape participants while they're talking about disagreements, and they get to see that a large part of the reason others react the way they do is because of the trainee's own behavior. It's often small behaviors, they aren't even aware of, that are the problem. They give off subtle negative communications that put other people off and sideline the conversation. Most of the time when we show people themselves they can hardly believe it. They don't even know they're doing what they're doing. It can be upsetting, and we keep a box of tissues ready when we do this. But it helps explain why they feel that something goes badly for them, and why negotiations don't work for them.

3. When the other person has easily activated survival wiring, and you don't want to stir up their defensive reactions. The language and behaviors required in negotiating tend to keep survival reactions limited, so it's a good way to handle "touchy" people when there's a conflict. Touchy people often get us into fights by using behaviors that get our survival reactions going, so if we're approaching them with the understanding that we're applying negotiations technology, we have a better chance of staying out of trouble.

    This is why formal negotiations are carried out in sensitive situations, such as hostage situations and war. It's also why outsiders are usually called in. It's designed to make use of the possibility that negotiations can diminish survival wiring reactions and create new possibilities for action.

4. When it looks like nothing can be done to solve the issue. Creating new possibilities is the core of negotiating, so applying it as a technology even when things look hopeless, can be very powerful. I've worked with married couples who have been struggling with particular conflicts during their whole marriage who were able to come to satisfactory resolution after I taught them a particular form of marital negotiation.

I also used this form of negotiation with a group of managers regarding several problems some of them were struggling with. They felt they had hit a brick wall. In their practicing a form of business negotiation (which was actually called something else), they generated no less than 160 new possible solutions, several of which were quite workable and which solved the problems. They could hardly believe it.

The Process of Negotiation

I'm going to give a fairly detailed explanation of the basics of the technology of negotiation resolution. While it's meant to be fairly generic, it's going to be directed toward personal relationships such as marriage, because that's the place where people have the hardest time imagining the application of negotiation technology, even though it's one of the places where it works best. So do realize that the procedures for negotiations do vary depending on the circumstances in which they're being used. But because most books about negotiations are almost strictly about people on opposite sides of business deals, I'm going to lean the other way just a bit, to the personal side.

Step one: State the issue. You don't have to do this formally, in writing, but you do have to do it in sensory terms, that describe things that can be seen or heard. This is often the most difficult part of the entire process for many people. Below I list some "translations" from the conceptual to the sensory pertaining to the types of conflicts found in personal relationships. This statement of the issue in sensory terms is a statement of the problem at hand, or the conflict that's a problem.

Conceptual problem: "You're sloppy."

Translation into sensory: "You leave your clothes on the bedroom floor at night."

Conceptual problem: "We don't get along."

Translation into sensory: "When we talk we use harsh tones, scowls, and insulting words."

Conceptual problem: "You're irresponsible."

Translation into sensory: "You're late for meetings, you miss deadlines on your report, and you don't produce the volume of work required."

Step two: Generate a list of as many possible alternative solutions as possible. When I meet with couples, the first time I go through this process I insist they come up with twelve possible alternative solutions. Most look at me like I'm crazy because they haven't been able to come up with more than the standard three: "Your way, my way, or some way we'll both hate." But that's just because they haven't stayed with the process. Instead, they have reacted to their fear of never finding a solution they can both live with and switched to fight technology.

Reality is what determines the number and nature of possible solutions to conflicts. None of us is smart enough to know all possible solutions. As a result, we tend to limit our perception of what's possible. We get, as Scott Peck would say, "lazy in our outlook." Then we mistake our narrowed outlook for reality, and since we can't see any solutions we say there aren't any.

It's hard work to look for new possibilities, which is part of what negotiations are designed to do. The other resolution technologies are often a lot easier and more "natural" feeling. But there are plenty of solutions waiting out there; we just have to use a process that can help us find them. That's what negotiations are designed to do.

Step three: Generate the list without regard for whether or not you "like" any particular one. This is a way to shut down the evaluating, assessing thinking that runs most of us. You must shut this down in order to be creative. If you don't, you start getting discouraged and begin thinking in a critical, diminishing style rather than a creative one. "Assessment" thinking has its place, but it's incompatible with creativity.

Step four: Review the list and throw out any solutions that any of the parties don't like. In negotiations, persuasion or pleading isn't allowed. Those are survival-wiring techniques. In negotiations, you talk about how things can be done to accommodate the desires of each person. Those desires often moderate during the process of negotiations, but the moderating is done through the process, not through survival-threat techniques. (This may vary in some extreme situations, like hostage situations. But this discussion is intended for everyday life.)

Step five: Review the remaining list and fashion a plan from one or more of the remaining solutions. Realize you're now "safe" because the only solutions left on the list are ones that all parties are OK with. They may not be the most perfect solutions in an ideal world, but they're ones that are genuinely OK with them. That keeps survival wiring to a minimum, because no one feels they're in danger of having an undesirable solution shoved down their throat.

What if you don't have any solutions left when you review the list? Then it's back to Step Two, to create more possible solutions.

Preventing Survival Reactions

During negotiation conversations, survival reactions need to be kept to a minimum. This means that positive and neutral communication behaviors and vocabulary are important to use. Remember, fighting isn't the result of a topic, it's the result of communication behaviors.

Have you read the newspaper articles that say things like, "The four leading causes of divorce are money, sex, in-laws and parenting?" That's completely inaccurate. The topic isn't the issue. It doesn't matter what the topic is, it's how the topic is handled. Good, successful marriages have as many issues and conflicts as do failed ones. The difference is that the good marriages apply resolution technologies that produce good results. So the newspaper articles would be accurate if they said "The cause of divorce is failure to deal effectively with conflicts regarding money, sex, in-laws and parenting."

Much of what allows for a resolution technology other than fighting to be used is control over communication behaviors during the conversations. When you're negotiating it's best to use the behaviors listed in the positive communication behavior section of the first techniques chapter. Negative communication behaviors will set up a cycle of negative reciprocity, and will degenerate into a fight, capitulation, or avoidance. That's OK, if those technologies are appropriate, but they often aren't—they're just easier. And remember, you probably will have strong urges to get negative in your communication behaviors when dealing with conflicts, since they are survival threats. Biology can scream at us to be nasty, withhold, transfer our upset to the other person. And of course it's OK to do that, if you're OK with the results it will produce. It just won't produce the results called "negotiating," and it may damage the relationship.

The process of negotiations has also been called "collaborative problem-solving." Obviously, there's some variation in it depending on the circumstances involved. It's easier if you're working with someone who is on the same team as you, such as a colleague or partner. It gets a bit more tricky and involved if you're on different teams, such as buyer and seller, or if the sides involved are so antagonistic they need an intermediary to hold the negotiations. Nevertheless, the process is similar with variations such as presenting possible alternatives one at a time, and evaluating each after its presentation. That's an OK way to do it, but I think the way of generating a list first is more powerful because it gets people on a roll of being creative. It's often surprising what they come up with. I can't count the number of times I've heard people say, "Why didn't we think of that before? That'll work!"

This is a powerful technology. It's also demanding, and most people need training to do it. It just isn't natural for most of us. Our tendency is to use our automatic defensive reactions. But, as is the case with all people-handling methods, the question to ask yourself is: "Is what I'm doing now working?" If it isn't, a different method needs to be used.

Chapter 14
Motivating People

People are often called on to motivate people. However, motivation, like many of the terms involved in dealing with people, is conceptual and means different things to different people.

While all human action is motivated by something, not every type of action fits what we usually mean by the term in the sense of motivating someone. For example, we don't use the term when someone does something because they have to, lest there be bad external consequences. We don't say that people are motivated to pay their taxes, or refer to blackmail victims as being motivated to pay a blackmailer.

We also don't call people "motivated" when they're doing something that's obviously and inherently pleasurable. It sounds stupid to say something like "I was feeling motivated to have sex last night," or, "I admire his motivation in eating that hot fudge sundae." When we talk about motivating someone we're usually referring to something different from that, something more specific than just doing something for an obvious reason. We usually mean someone does something they don't have to do and that's not inherently or obviously pleasurable. In short, something they don't have to do and don't want to do that they do for no apparent external reason.

We call this motivation because human beings aren't very good at doing things they don't want or don't have to do. When we say someone is motivated we're implying there's something special inside that person which pushes them to do the non-demand, non-pleasurable thing they're doing. We say they're "committed," a "self-starter," or, simply, "motivated." Whatever terms we use, we're talking about something that exists in their conceptual world which turns into action when there's no particular sensory reason for it to do so.

The question, then, is what exists in the conceptual world that leads to action, to self-starting? What is it that makes some people seem to be motivated and others not? And why are some people easier to motivate than others?

Here's the problem: nobody knows what it is. It's internal and conceptual so it's a very difficult thing to identify, measure, or replicate. For all our work and all our knowledge, it remains a mystery. There are, however, some good potential candidates for the position. Experience has shown there are several qualities in the conceptual world which seem to enhance the generation of action in the sensory world, so these are probably the best we have as far as identifying a "motivating" factor in people.

One factor is excitement. It's not an accident that, in physics, particles that move around a lot and are active are called "excited." Excitement in a human being is a state of heightened energy and arousal, which makes behavior easier to generate and increases available energy. So a good target for motivation is to increase excitement. Another possibility is caring, or commitment. Individuals who give time to good causes without getting paid talk about caring and commitment, how those lead them to do the things they do. Another possibility is belief. While there's a lot of excess power ascribed to believing in the self-help literature, it nevertheless seems to have some potential candidacy as an entity that enhances motivation.

Let's sum it up: motivation comes from some kind of internal state that increases energy and the frequency of directed action therefore making spontaneous action increasingly likely. So when we're talking about motivating people we're talking about helping them to have, or develop, the conceptual entities likely to lead to this state. There are various names for this, such as getting someone excited about something, or invested in a particular goal, or interested in a cause, or "owning" something. Whatever you call it, it means helping people attain whatever it is that gets human beings taking action.

It's important to remember we're talking about dealing with an entity in the conceptual world. While action may be the measure of someone's motivation, we're not talking just about getting someone to take action, as was discussed earlier. You can get your kids to clean up their rooms with the methods we talked about in that chapter, but that won't make them fit the definition of being motivated to clean up their rooms. It just means you get them to do it.

Motivating is installing the conceptual entity that energizes someone enough for them to be self-generating in action. It means you don't always need conversations designed to get them to take action when something needs to be done. It means the force for action is installed inside them, and can operate without you being the one to trigger action.

We already know that altering things in the conceptual world of a human being is extremely difficult; conceptual entities are anchored to survival wiring, and are well defended against changing. So getting and keeping people motivated isn't an easy task and you're once again up against that formidable opponent of survival wiring.

Over the past decade or so, business and industry has learned a lot about the difficulties involved in motivating people. In the heyday of "motivational speakers," companies would hire the equivalent of a secular revivalist preacher, whose job involved standing in front of the employees, usually the sales staff, and getting them stirred up, and energized. He or she would lead the equivalent of a pep rally, increasing the energy in the room, encouraging the staff to whoop and holler and increase their expressiveness level. There isn't a thing in the world wrong with this. In fact, it gets people charged up and it feels good, too. People would come out of those sessions excited, full of energy, with goals to achieve and new worlds to conquer. If we were talking about molecular particles, they came out of those meetings "charged."

Interesting, then, that those rallies aren't done much anymore. Why is that? Because while they successfully produced the desired effects, the effects lasted only a very short time. So despite the charging they received in the rally, it wouldn't be long before it was back to business as usual, and there would be few, if any, effects to see as a result of the rally. But you can't have a sales rally every other day, so the results of the rally weren't enough to be worth putting them together for the businesses that put them on.

The problem with this kind of motivational exercise is the effects just don't last very long. Why do you think schools have pep rallies on the day of the big game? Why do you think they don't just have one big pep rally at a convenient time, say, the start of the school year, and get it out of the way? The energy and excitement generated by them only stays in existence for so long, and then it's back to business as usual.

Motivating people, really motivating them, is not as simple or easy as having a pep rally. You have to understand that people tend to automatically live at a generally unexcited, unmotivated level. They do what they have to do and want to do, and not much else. It isn't that they're lazy, uncaring, or stupid, it's that survival wiring tends to support the status-quo because it sees things are working so why mess with it? In addition, conserving energy, just like conserving anything else of limited supply and high value, is often important to survival wiring. Why squander that important commodity? Excited people not only rock the boat and do risky things, they use up more energy as well.

So it's not necessarily to survival wiring's advantage to be motivated in the sense we're talking about. Or, to put it another way, aliveness, or motivation, is low on survival wiring's priority list. True, some people are more energetic and naturally excited than others, but if your goal is to motivate someone, to increase their energy, excitement, or commitment, you're probably going to be fighting some natural tendencies. In its extreme form it can be depression, and in it's usual form it's a form of "resignation" about life. That's what you're up against.

Motivational Technique #1: Creating a Conceptual Threat

Given what we've covered previously about how human beings are wired, what most commonly and most readily increases someone's energy? Their survival wiring going off. Want to get someone energized? Create a threat to their survival; drive that bus toward them at sixty miles an hour. That's as motivating as it gets.

But because motivation as we mean it here operates in the conceptual world, you wouldn't get what we're calling motivation. If you did drive it at them, after you pass by, the person's level of motivation is going to diminish pretty rapidly. Their heart rate is going to return to normal, their breathing will slow down, and their overall level of motivation is going to return to normal. Their heightened state of motivation is going to last only as long as you're chasing them around with that bus. And that's not what we're talking about, because that's just getting action from them.

So the threat you create for someone has to be something conceptual, something that doesn't rely on your being there waving a literal survival threat in their face. The threat, the enemy, must exist in their conceptual world. It must be an idea, principle, value, or a goal. Only that can endure beyond the immediate and sensory.

The most common way a conceptual survival threat is created is by creating an enemy the person perceives as needing to defeat, or conquer. If that enemy has an effective representation in the person's conceptual survival wiring, then they'll develop a survival reaction to it, much like an allergic person develops an immune reaction to dust. Then they will walk around with their survival wiring going off in response to this internal representation and you get—motivation.

There are several places where it's easy to see this process at work: sports, business, war, politics, and religion. Sports, despite their being played in the sensory world, aren't driven by sensory factors. Sports are all about enemies, rivals, and competitors. Sports are all about not being losers, about being the best, about being champions. The concept of "being a loser" is real and present for athletes, and it can keep them motivated.

Business is similar. There are competitors and rivals to be defeated. The concept of being a loser, or of being a winner, motivates lots of people in business. In fact, you can see that the best athletes and business people aren't nearly as motivated by money as you'd think they were. Even after they've made enough money to last forever, they're still at it, seeking success and fighting to be a winner. It's an internal process.

The military and war are other obvious examples. They contain a real, tangible sense of an enemy that needs to be defeated. And it's perceived as life and death. This is why war analogies are used so frequently in other areas of life. They're used even in humanitarian causes like anti-disease campaigns. They're campaigns inviting people to "beat" the disease, "conquer" it, or "eradicate" it.

But perhaps the real masters of this motivational technique are the religious leaders and the politicians. They have clearly defined foes, largely conceptual in nature, and are very direct and up-front about the "right versus wrong" nature of this conflict. Politicians have opposing political parties and conflicting ideologies as forces of evil to defeat. Religions have the devil, infidels, or competing theologies to battle. From such are born political campaigns, holy wars, and crusades.

Have you ever noticed the similarity in style between politics and religion? People in both always fight for the "right" against the forces of "wrong" (or "evil"). Both use conceptual terms in their talk, and both are basically designed to motivate people (in one case to vote and give money, in the other to attend church and give money). Self-help books are a close cousin of religion and political techniques in this area. They also conceptualize an enemy—be it "being ordinary" or "being a loser." This kind of stuff gets people stirred up, and if the enemy sticks with someone, they're "motivated."

There's one potential pitfall in this technique. When you stir up someone's survival wiring, you can't be very exact in predicting exactly what the resulting behaviors are going to be. Remember, motivation is a state of heightened energy, arousal, and activity. You may very well get someone motivated about the enemy, but the behaviors generated and the target of those behaviors will only be what you want it to be if their wiring agrees with yours about the nature of the threat and the appropriate means of battling against it. There's never any absolute guarantee that it will. A political candidate who stirs up a crowd is likely at the same time they energize their followers, to also energize their critics, who put increased energy into assailing them. That's why, after a particularly notable and stirring speech by some political candidate you'll not only see positive "stirred up" reactions, also critical "stirred up" reactions. The nature of the behaviors from any particular individual's survival reactions is just not all that predictable. Even people motivated to side with the person doing the motivating may decide to pursue the results in a manner that's unworkable or makes trouble.

This problem often bedevils parents dealing with kids. For example, a mother consulted me who saw herself as the necessary agent to "teach her kids responsibility." She wanted them motivated to be responsible in their lives, reasonable sounding as far as it goes. If the kids didn't seem to be upset about something she thought was important (such as grades, finances, dating practices, or curfews) she would throw a screaming, horrendous, hissy fit designed to upset them. Her methodology was to instill in them the issue (such as grades) and to pair it with the upset she created through her fit. She thought if she didn't go crazy and instill upset, she was "letting them get by with something" and indirectly sanctioning their misbehavior, which wouldn't motivate them to do better.

Unfortunately, while her reaction was designed to create the enemy she saw (ruining their lives, doing something wrong, getting bad grades, etc.), the kids never created internal representations of those enemies. They didn't take on grades and the finances and all that as the enemy. Instead, they took on her. They didn't buy that they were ruining their lives at all, so they weren't motivated to do anything about it.

But their survival wiring was stirred up and directed toward an enemy all right—the one called mom. They definitely created an internal concept, called "mom," and usually "bitch mom." After all, it was mom who made them miserable, made them wrong, and made them feel bad. She was much more unpleasant for them than their schoolwork. And they definitely became motivated by this enemy, and acted in opposition to it. Instead of learning grades are important and something to be upset over if you don't make good ones, they learned that defending against mom was the most important thing. As a result, their excitement, energy, and motivation increased alright—in order to fight against her.

In one way the mother had been successful. The kids became motivated, energetic, aggressive, and purposeful. But in another way she failed. All that motivation was directed toward dealing with her, not the issues she was trying to point out. So take this as a warning, there's a lot of unpredictability in the behavior that stirred-up survival wiring produces, especially if you're doing the stirring. Unless you create the "enemy" effectively in someone, you may be the target of it.

If you're going to use this technique, you have to do a very good job of creating the enemy, making it real, making it something the other person can clearly perceive. Notice how revivalist preachers will go on and on and on ad-nauseam about the Devil, and the Devil's ways, and the Devil's powers. That's to make the Devil "real" for people. I once watched a religious network show that was a mock courtroom in which they were trying and convicting Secular Humanists. In doing so they had to tell the viewers all about those Secular Humanists so that they would know in great detail why they should be motivated against them. Remember how Joe McCarthy went on and on and on about the communists? He wanted to motivate people to be against them. Notice how political parties go on and on and on about how terrible the opposing ideology is, about how terrible the Liberals or Conservatives are. All of these people aren't fools. They're sincere in their efforts, and aware of the technology required. The reason all of these groups go on and on, detailing the atrocities of their enemies, is they know they have to be effective in creating a conceptual representation of the enemy in someone else.

A relative newcomer on the scene of turning on survival wiring in order to create motivation are the television news shows. News used to be reporting, but that was before there was cable, competition, and the need to attract audiences, before there was a need to motivate people to watch their news. So news shows have started creating their own conceptual enemies in the way they present their stories. I read a quote that said news is now in the "outrage" business. If you find yourself getting more "riled up" about the news these days than you used to, it's not just that the news is actually worse than it used to be, there have always been good things and bad things happening. It's that the news shows have gotten more sophisticated in their techniques of stirring people up to motivate people to watch their shows.

Motivational Technique #2: Becoming Special

The second way to stir up survival wiring is by going to the opposite end of the survival spectrum from survival threat, to pleasure-seeking. In the conceptual world, this can be thought of as "becoming special," sometimes it's also called "goals," but those terms are insufficient to capture the essence of what brings power to it. Anyone can make a wish-list of what they'd like to get in life, and most people do it regularly in the back of their minds. The issue here isn't the presence of that list, it's getting someone into a position where they're willing to generate behavior that will go after their goals.

Some of the premier motivators using this end of the motivational spectrum are the personal sales and multi-level marketing organizations such as Mary Kay, Amway, Herbalife, and others you've probably heard of. They're masters at dangling carrots in front of people that people feel they must have. They showcase people who have become "special," who have reached their wildest dreams through selling the company's products and following their principles. Then they invite you to see yourself having what others have, and what your life would be like if you met your dreams like these people have met theirs.

I had a young woman in therapy who was turned on by one of these companies. Although she was flunking school, had never had a date, had no job prospects, could hardly keep a friend, and was barely functional, she became convinced she could be wildly successful through this particular company. Unfortunately, as I discussed previously, specific behaviors are unpredictable in response to survival wiring being stirred up. What got stirred up in her wasn't sales behavior, it was, for lack of a better word, fantasizing behavior.

She spent a great deal of time driving around the most expensive parts of town looking at mansions because, according to the company, "she was supposed to dream." Unfortunately, that was all she ended up doing, and at the end of a year with the company she was actually in the hole a few dollars. And her story isn't particularly unique, although other people can certainly use these companies to be successful.

In whatever way you do it, stirring someone up is designed to turn on their survival wiring. You're presenting either a threat to be conquered or a pleasure to be gained. So if you're selling sailboats you might want to stir up feelings and sensations about the wonders, excitement, romance of the ocean. If you're selling burglar alarms you might want to stir up fear about the dangers of crime. In both cases it has to do with the conceptual world and survival.

I was once the chairman of a community leadership board that was helping a local community college in its work to better serve students with disabilities. The board had no authority and was primarily designed to get community agencies, school officials, and programs working together. But everyone invited to serve was very busy and in demand, and I could readily see this was going to be one of those "Oh no, I've that damn board meeting today" kind of deal. The kind where people cancel for "good reason." We needed some way to get people motivated, not only to attend the meetings, but to participate with each other to form new partnerships and new possibilities for serving those with disabilities.

I realized the threat end of the spectrum was being handled by the various laws and task forces that had real authority inside the college systems. That offered the push from behind. So what I got the board to do was to instigate a pull from the front by establishing an award for excellence in serving the disabled that would be presented, with great fanfare, to a local organization, company, or school that had an innovative and quality approach to serving those with handicaps. The publicity, honor, and notoriety that went with receiving (and presenting) such an award would be motivational for everyone involved.

Now let's talk about the specific techniques that go into "motivating" people:

1. *Conceptual language.* Motivating is done in the conceptual world. As a result, you don't use much sensory language. Instead, you talk in the realm of concepts, meanings, and possibilities. When I was presenting the idea of an award for excellence to the leadership board, I talked about the award's power in creating possibilities, partnerships, excellence, participation, and stature. I didn't talk about the specific menu items for the awards dinner. You use the terms of enemies or specialness. And the more, the better.

2. *Reframing.* The frame of the issue may be the most important thing because it controls the meaning, and the meaning is what creating an enemy or a desirable thing is all about.

Something has to be framed as being greatly desirable or greatly dangerous.

News organizations are masters of reframing. One method they use is to contract the frame. In this method they start out saying that something is enjoyed by many people, but not by everyone. Then they go on to present "one person's story." They present the story in such full, heart-wrenching detail, you forget the general good this particular thing is, and get completely involved in the frame of this one instance. By the time the story is over, you're ready to call your congressional representative to pass a law forbidding this horrible thing.

Another method is to expand the frame. You know, those headlines that "such and such has been shown to increase your cancer risk by 40%?" Do you think it's an accident that sentence bears a remarkable similarity to "such and such has been shown to increase your cancer risk to 40%?" But here's how it really works. If this particular cancer has a "normal" rate of 1%, then one person out of every hundred, on average, will get it. Now, if the such and such increases the rate by 40%, that means that now 1.4 people out of every hundred will get it. And while nobody wants increased cancer rates at all, it's a lot less alarming to hear that the risk of cancer goes from one out of a hundred to 1.4 out of a hundred than it does to hear that it increases by 40%. And it would sell a lot less newspapers and advertising spots on your local news shows.

Shifting the frame is also a powerful motivational tool because it tells people who the "real" enemy is. Oliver North did a masterful job of this during his testimony to congress. He presented such a powerful frame-shift away from "did he or did he not do something wrong" to "patriotism and service" that he became somewhat of a national folk hero. Lawyers do this in court, too, shifting the focus of the crime to something other than the defendant.

If a reframe doesn't work, the ability to motivate falls flat. I had a friend who attended an introduction to a multi-level marketing organization, where the presenter asked each person to imagine what they would do with a million dollars. Unfortunately for the presenter, my friend was a "newly reborn Christian" who had no particular interest in money, and the frame of a million dollars didn't move him at all. When he told me about attending the meeting he was laughing. It wasn't a frame that produced desire or danger for him at all.

So the framing of the issue is something that matters tremendously. The most powerful motivators in the world are great reframers. The frame has to create meanings and concepts that matter to the person to whom you're talking. Even if sensory entities are used as motivators, such as money, the issue is still the concept the money brings. It may be an "easy life." Or it may be "security." Or it may be "the good life." But whatever it is, it's a concept. Also you have to frame the benefits as consistent with what that person sees as being valuable or horrible. How do you tell? There's no special way, just be aware of who they are and what they do and how they're reacting to you.

3. *Escalation.* The conceptual entity you're installing has to be perceived as important to the person. Because motivating is done primarily in the conceptual world, escalation is typically increasing the conceptual survival value of the issue, which is making it more right. This is why motivators tell people they "deserve the best." That's a lot more powerful than, "It would be really nice for someone like you to have the best." It's not righteous enough. You have to raise the stakes. It has to be terrifically right, terrifically important.

4. *Sharing.* This is often a very powerful technique. Why do you think revivalist preachers have people "witness" at their revivals? Because by sharing their world of right and wrong, good and bad ("salvation and damnation"), people resonate to it. The sharing provides more of an opportunity for people to experience what they're saying. It's about the best way possible, short of a brain-transplant, to transfer experience in the conceptual world. This gets people to experience the danger or the desire on an emotional level. It generates the excitement that's helpful to motivation.

5. *Performing feelings transfers.* This is the core essence of sharing, but it can be done in other ways, too. The point is to

get the other person to feel as you do, to resonate to your feelings. That's why it almost doesn't matter what someone who is "witnessing" says. It's more how they say it, that their style gets other people to feel, that makes them effective. This is the reason ads in magazines asking for donations for children's relief funds show pathetic-looking but cute children.

Feelings transfers are also why it's easier to sell something you believe in. People can sell things they don't really care about, but it's a lot easier if they do because then just their presence, just their sharing, can effect a feelings transfer and have a powerful motivating effect on others. You can certainly sell things you don't believe in, but it's not so easy to transfer feelings in an effective way.

6. *Representational Matching.* Because, in motivating someone through conceptual survival wiring, you're wanting to instill in them a conceptual representation of an enemy that they can carry with them, you want to be as effective as possible in getting your message coded into their minds. As a result, matching their preferred representational system can be very helpful.

    I did this with a boy whose family I had in therapy, and who was extremely argumentative. He was also very physical, not skilled with either words (auditory representation) or images (visual representation). As a result, the parents had a hard time motivating him through the usual channels of talking. When I had them in session, I elicited an argument from him. At that point I reframed his arguing as being "like a puppet" that he had no control. After that, every time he argued during the session I cried out "Argue!" and thrust my left arm into the air, as if it were being pulled by a string.

    A few weeks later one of the parents told me how the boy had been arguing with his brother and suddenly said, "Argue!" and thrust his left hand into the air, which stopped the argument. It was that motion, a bodily representation, which could stick with him and hook the issue of arguing in his mind. It helped motivate him to quit.

7. *Metaphors.* It's best to "speak their language." You want the people you're motivating to receive your message as directly and as easily as possible. Use metaphors they can relate to.

I won't go into a lot of detail here about how to do it since it is discussed earlier in the book. Refer to that section.

8. *Separate intent from methodology, and focus on intent.* Leave methodology out. Remember, intent lives in the conceptual world, and motivation is about intention. It's a conceptual process. Motivation has to do with possibility much more than actuality, and you want to go for the possibility, the conceptual entities. So talk about the meaning, the purpose, the opportunity, the possibility, the "goodness" of the issue or whatever it is you're wanting to motivate people about. Talk about "commitment" and "intention."

9. *Gloss.* Motivation time isn't a time for sensory specifics. The point is to create the conceptual entities, get people riled up over the enemies and goals, and get them to keep these conceptual entities alive in themselves. It's not a time to flesh out what is required to achieve what you're talking about. That comes after the motivation, when they're sure you're right and begging to do what's required.

10. *Use both positive and negative communication behaviors.* I threw this one in because it's one of the rare times in people-handling when you don't have to pay much attention to whether you're using positive or negative communication behaviors. Use them both. All they have to do is to be consistent with your frame. When you're talking about possibility and positive goals, use positive behaviors. Use excited tones of voice, smiles, nods, laughs. When you're talking about the enemy use negative communication behaviors. Yell, frown, scowl, shake your head.

    Again, fundamentalist preachers and politicians are masters of this methodology. Look beyond their content at their communication behaviors. Watch them on TV, with the sound off. Then turn on the sound and listen to the category of words they use (conceptual). Notice their escalation of behaviors. They use all kinds of communication behaviors, but they're always consistent with the content of their talk.

11. *Paradox.* Something that often prevents people from being motivated is external pressure. Nearly twenty years ago I was involved in research that studied kids who liked to draw. By

taking kids who inherently liked to draw and paying them for drawing, they actually were less motivated to draw. The upshot of that research is that increased external incentive may, in some way, actually decrease internal motivation. This may occur because people attribute their behavior to external reinforcement, so they consider themselves less interested in the task, or their interest shifts from the task to the reinforcement. I'm not sure there's any final conclusion. But the existence of the phenomenon is undeniable.

As a result, something that often helps people get motivated is to use paradox. Tell them the difficulties required of them. Tell them how hard it's going to be. Tell them they should search their souls to make sure they're up to the task. Tell them they might not be. Try to talk them out of being motivated. Tell them all the reasons "not to." In essence this communicates the specialness of being willing to, which is motivational.

The very best example I've ever seen of paradox being used in this manner was presented in the movie *The War of the Roses*. The movie is about a couple divorcing and how they declare a war on each other which results in self-destruction. But the point of the movie was the paradoxical method a high-powered divorce attorney was using to test a potential client's motivation for divorce. By showing the horrible, destructive possibilities in divorce, he could tell whether the client was motivated to do what was required in seeking one.

I sometimes do this with people who consult me regarding therapy. I'm very selective about who I will take on as a therapy patient, and I explain to potential patients that therapy is often very difficult, slow, and frustrating, and that it can turn their worlds upside down. I tell them to expect it to be a big deal in their lives. This not only prepares them for what is to come, it's motivating in the sense that if they decide to enter therapy they're geared up for work. In addition, every word of what I say is absolutely true.

This kind of paradox is also the basis for the Marines' advertising slogan that they're "looking for a few good men." This implies they're being very selective, and you might just not be good enough, so you had better think twice about applying. That "you might not be good enough" implication is never stated, but it lives on a deeper logical level, and can stir up survival wiring.

So you want to get people motivated? Send them away, and tell them to return only if they feel like they're up to the task. Tell them you only want the best and the brightest, and that they should disqualify themselves if they're not prepared to call forth the best in themselves. Tell them what you're asking is extraordinary. Tell them it may be too much. You'll lose some people, of course, but you'll turn on the wiring of other people. The people you'll get will be motivated.

And, as always, remember that paradox is only useful when what you're saying is true. Paradox works because it's a reflection of a truth in the world, not because it's some kind of trick.

12. *Joining techniques.* One problem you can get into when motivating people is that, as I talked about in my earlier example of the woman who was trying to "motivate" her children, you can become the target instead of the entity you're trying to make the target. As a result, it's often good to use joining behaviors, such as just listening and empathic responses, in order to ally with the person you're trying to motivate.

And, finally, remember that motivating isn't easy, it's not necessarily quick, and you must practice to do it well. Just remember it's an activity that occurs in the conceptual realm, and taps into survival wiring. Then try out these techniques or other ones that seem to apply and keep at it.

Chapter 15

Handling People's Upset

Because upset feelings are a frequent occurrence in human life, you can't be effective in dealing with people unless you can cope with their upsets. Whether people are upset with you or upset with someone or something else, they are going to cross your path regularly.

Upsets are often difficult to deal with because they can set off your own survival reactions. If you were having lunch with a friend and they suddenly became very upset, you would likely experience some sort of upset feelings in response. You might feel frightened, irritated, sad, guilty, embarrassed, or any number of other upset feelings. Because this is part of a survival reaction on your part, and survival reactions are designed to protect us, they take your focus off the other person.

There's nothing inherently wrong with responding out of your own upset, of course. But if your purpose is to deal with another person's upset, the automatic behaviors generated by your survival reaction aren't likely to be particularly efficient or effective. In fact, because one person's survival reaction tend to trigger—or worsen—another person's survival reaction, your behavior may inadvertently intensify the other person's reaction and actually make things worse.

Early on in our relationship Pam and I learned a lesson about this regarding minor upsets over things like stubbing a toe or smashing a finger in a cabinet door. When I'm in the throes of that kind of pain, I do a kind of momentary emotional retreat, giving myself the room to fully experience the pain in order to get through it as quickly as possible. I like to have anyone around me just stand

283

by for a while, allowing me to get over the worst of the pain without distraction. Then I'm open to them approaching me to help deal with my hurt and upset. But if someone tries to hug me, talk to me, or nurture me during that initial acute phase, I feel intruded upon, distracted, and irritated. Pam, on the other hand, reacts in almost exactly the opposite way. She feels emotionally vulnerable during the intense phase and wants someone to be with her, touching her, talking to her, and reassuring her. If she is left alone she feels abandoned, unloved, and irritated.

You can see how this would result in some confusion. The first few times Pam hurt herself, what do you suppose I did? I did what my survival wiring said was appropriate, I stood by, of course, waiting for her to get over the worst of the pain, undistracted. After all, that's what helps me. And what reaction do you think I got? More upset, of course. The first few times I hurt myself, what do you suppose Pam did? She did what her survival wiring said was appropriate, and rushed right over, put her arms around me, and started hugging me. And what reaction do you think she got? More upset, of course.

Fortunately, it took only a couple of incidents for us to realize we were reacting to each other out of reaction to our own upset over the situation rather than the other person's. Our own instinctive responses were projections of how to handle our own upset; we did what we would want done for us. So we learned to alter our responses to do what helps the other person. When I'm hurt Pam still experiences the urge to rush over and throw her arms around me, but she knows to wait and watch a minute until my face stops scrunching up before she approaches.

When Pam's hurt, my initial impulse is still to give her space for a minute, but I know to go to her immediately and put my arm around her. These behaviors may never feel as "natural" or "automatic" for either one of us as are our instinctual ones, but because we have no question that our purpose is to help each other, it's not difficult to divert from our instinctual behaviors and do what we know will help.

When I refer to "dealing with" upset feelings in this chapter, I'm talking about how to shorten, limit, and diminish others' upset. I'm talking about helping them feel better, or feel less upset. There are times, when you're motivating or confronting, or working on changing someone, that you may not be interested in diminishing upset. You may be unconcerned with the upset, or you may even be doing things that increase upset. These are times when trying to take away someone's upset may be counter-productive. But there are many occasions in life when you're going to want to help them feel better. You may want to calm an angry customer, soothe a grieving spouse, calm a fearful child, or assist an employee who has experienced hurt feelings. So in order to be an effective people-handler you need to have the ability to identify, define, and generate behaviors that have a good chance of helping someone else's upset, whether or not they're the behaviors that make sense to you about yours.

There may even be times when you'll have to diminish someone's upset before using some of the methods listed in the other chapters. When an issue has a great deal of emotional upset connected to it, there's a strong, immediate survival reaction going on about it. That kind of upset can short-circuit people's ability to think effectively, and diminish their ability to engage with the other techniques for resolving conflict. You may even find yourself needing to shift back and forth between dealing with upset and using the other techniques when you're in the process of dealing with someone. As I've said repeatedly, handling people isn't clean and neat, doesn't involve "doing just one thing."

About Upset

Upset feelings are the emotional component of a survival reaction and the conceptual world's method of energizing itself for defensive maneuvers. As a result, even if what has gone wrong is something physical or sensory, the upset itself is usually generated in response to some kind of meaning. People can have a certain emotional pain from physical upset, but the upset actually caused by the physical pain usually doesn't last any longer than the pain sensations. As a result, the upset we're almost always dealing with in other people is generated in the conceptual world.

Some years ago my ear, nose, and throat physician gave a shot up my nose. He used a very long needle, and yes, it was as awful as it sounds. As he was pushing the needle into the back of my nostril, big tears rolled down my cheeks. I wasn't crying as if I were sad, but there was some type of bodily response to the pain, some type of upset. When he was done he asked me if I was OK. I was fine. That's not the kind of upset I'm talking about in this chapter. I'm talking about upset that's emotion, anger, sadness, embarrassment, guilt, irritation, frustration, or anxiety. These emotions come from meaning. They're elements of the conceptual world.

Because upsets exist primarily in the conceptual world, they're more complex than simple physical pain. There are several elements that make them trickier to deal with.

First, the upset emotions themselves are very difficult to distinguish from the thoughts and meanings that cause them or accompany them. They're all wound together like a ball of yarn, and people often cannot distinguish one element from another. You can tell this is the case because when you ask someone who is upset what they're feeling, you're likely to get an answer like, "I'm feeling like she was really insensitive to have said that to me." Now, that's not a feeling, it's a thought—She was insensitive, and a meaning—What she did was bad. A feeling would have been something like hurt, or sad, or angry. But the emotion is all wrapped up inside the meaning, thought, and concepts. As a result, in dealing with someone's upset you're dealing with a multifaceted issue.

Second, an internal struggle is frequently triggered when upset feelings occur. Sometimes this is called an emotional reaction to an emotional reaction, or a "secondary" upset. While upsets are part of survival reactions, the upset itself triggers more survival reaction, triggering a defense against the original upset. Many times people hate being upset, don't think they should be, don't want to be, try not to be, feel guilty, and try to push it away. Not only are thoughts, meanings, and emotions all wound up together inside an upset, in addition there may be other meanings, thoughts and feelings that conflict with the upset and make the whole situation even more complicated.

When you're dealing with someone's upset, you're dealing with a complex system of interrelated elements that affect each other and that tend to feed each other. As a result, you're going to need to have at your disposal a variety of techniques for addressing upset, and an understanding of its mechanisms. The interlocking system of elements that controls upset renders it one of the most paradoxical and ironic of all human functions. So the methods that are intuitively logical and sensible often don't work, and can even make things worse. However, other things, that may not make a lot of sense initially, may be very helpful.

Principle #1: First, Do No Harm

This is an old medical saying. "First, do no harm." Any time you intervene in anything, there's always the potential for making things worse as well as better. People who go into the hospital for treatment can pick up an extra infection which then becomes the problem. These are called "nosocomial" or "iatrogenic" problems. So we want to talk first about those things that often seem helpful but often aren't. Remember again that in people-handling there are almost no absolutes as regards what to do and when. When I talk about these things generally being unhelpful, I mean just that— generally. There may be times when you can gently try one of them to see if they work, but just be aware that the seeming obvious logic of these methods of helping with upset can be misleading. They often don't work.

Saying "Don't Be Upset"

Often the first reaction is to try to stop someone from being upset. Unfortunately, what this tends to do is to make the person wrong for their upset. Obviously, because upset is part of a survival reaction in the conceptual world, it's already a reaction to some kind of "being wrong." So making the person wrong for being upset is clearly not going to help. But it can seem like it would help sometimes, especially if you're upset with their upset.

A supervisor of mine some years ago used to tell a story about a case he had early in his career that taught him this lesson. A woman came to him upset about something in her life, and he listened to her for a while. Then he proceeded to list for her the things she had going for in her life and pointed out she had plenty to be grateful for, and that indicated she really shouldn't be so upset about what she was upset about. He said she looked at him in irritation and mumbled, "Geez, sometimes all people want is a little sympathy."

Sometimes making someone wrong for their upset is done directly, as in "You're overreacting" or "You're being crazy about this." It can also be done indirectly. This is often done by pointing out how they caused the problem themselves, with the implication being that because they brought it on themselves, they have no right to be upset. The point here isn't that neither of these things is necessarily untrue; they very well may have lots of things going for them in their lives, and they very well might have brought their trouble on themselves, but the issue is that neither of these will likely help to diminish their upset. It's like stepping on someone's toe when the toe is already sore.

A teenage girl who was a patient of mine was feeling depressed and bemoaning her inability to get others to listen. "My mother," she said, "is a schoolteacher. So whenever I'm having a hard time, or have a problem or am upset about something it's like she turns it into a 'lesson' for me. She tells me about how I could change it, or that it happened because of my own behavior, or that I must have something to do with it. Basically she's telling me it's all my own fault. I just want her to listen, to hear me out. It's like she can't do that. It's so frustrating."

This parent was, quite understandably, using her teaching skills with her daughter. She was reframing her daughter's upsets as opportunities to learn. There's absolutely nothing wrong with that, and is a very powerful reframe to allow teaching. But it rarely works well in dealing with upset. Unfortunately, her daughter heard the reframe as blaming and accusing, not as caring or helping.

This doesn't mean people should not be encouraged to take responsibility for their behavior, to be able to own up to and accept their own actions and their consequences. To the contrary, that's the only way people learn to have effective lives. What I'm saying is if your purpose is to diminish upset, then it's probably not going to help to point out the person's culpability, even if it's true. That may have to come later, when the person isn't so enmeshed in a survival reaction, and they can address the topic more clearly and openly.

And remember, it doesn't matter if you think someone, like my teenaged patient, "should" have heard what someone else said to help—they often don't. If something you say makes an upset person wrong, you aren't going to help diminish the upset. Even if you don't think what you're saying should make them feel wrong. It only matters if it does make them feel wrong.

People often make others wrong because the way the upset person is behaving irritates them. In that case people often use negative communication behaviors and fight technology to try to get them to change. Upset people's behavior is often designed to effect a feelings transfer. If they're feeling angry, they're likely to behave in ways that make you angry. If they're feeling hopeless, you may start to feel the same. It can be easy to make them wrong for their behavior while thinking you're trying to help with their upset. Actually you may be taking on their feelings, being irritated at how you're feeling dealing with them.

If you just want to stop their behavior because you don't like it or it's causing a problem, that's fine. The techniques discussed in changing someone or getting action may be useful. But your goal isn't to deal with the upset, it's to deal with the behavior. If your child is whining and driving you crazy, go ahead and use the change techniques to handle the behavior. Just realize that it may inflame or at the least leave the upset in place. That may be OK with you. Just be aware that it's a different purpose than what I'm talking about here.

Failing to Separate Content and Upset

It's important to realize the content of what someone says can be distinct from their upset. Often, content is simply a mechanism designed to express upset. I had a patient whose son became upset with him for some reason and angrily blurted out "I hope you and mom get divorced real soon!" In fact, the parents' marriage was having trouble, and as you can imagine, this comment upset the father. But the content of the statement, wasn't the point, simply the method used by the son to express anger and to transfer the upset to the father.

Often, getting caught up in a discussion about a particular comment can be beside the point and unhelpful. What's required is to deal with the upset, the survival reaction, rather than the content itself. Unfortunately, we're often tempted to deal with these kinds of remarks in terms of their content. We may feel offended by what the person says, by the rudeness or the gall of such comments, so we get into dealing with the content of what they say, and off the issue of the upset. That's OK, and sometimes may be appropriate to do, but realize that it's probably different than the goal of trying to diminish the upset. You'll need to decide which is the more important of the two—to continue diminishing the upset, or get into dealing with a comment or another issue. Remember, if you feel that you need to deal with that kind of statement, you can always do so when the upset is lessened. In fact, people are usually able to listen better to statements of, "That was rude, please don't say that to me again" when they're not in the midst of a survival reaction. I'm not saying a child's rude behavior shouldn't be dealt with. I'm just saying it probably can't be dealt with at the same time as the upset. It's very difficult to both "straighten someone out" and diminish their upset at the same time.

Premature Problem-Solving

While there's often an urge to jump in and try to resolve the issue when someone is upset, it's a problem if that attempt is undertaken too soon. Upsets are about problems, but upsets are also distinct, they often have lives of their own. And while it can seem like solving the problem will eliminate the upset, the upset may need to be dealt with as a separate entity. Here's a sample dialogue:

"I'm so upset about that car having trouble again I could spit nails."

"Why don't I take it to the shop and get that part replaced.

"I just don't understand how it can keep breaking down! What a lemon!"

"Maybe we should talk to the service manager. He might be able to tell us how to keep it from breaking again."

"I wish we'd never bought it!"

Can you see how the two people are having different conversations? One is talking about their upset, the other is talking about fixing the practical problem that started it. It's certainly OK to work with the person on fixing the problem, but having two different conversations is probably not going to be helpful. Upset is a conversation in the conceptual world, problems are generally in the sensory world. Solutions are in the sensory world, and involve sensory entities. Solving the problem may ultimately be required for a total resolution, but the upset is the conceptual version of a racing heart from a scare. It isn't going to go away immediately just because the practical issue goes away.

Don't necessarily rush in and immediately fix the problem on which an upset is based. People can feel more upset because their psyche is demanding attention to their experience, rather than the practical problem itself. People often need to have their upset attended to, much as we kiss a child's wound even though that has nothing to do with physically healing it.

Of course, the speed with which you may move from attending to upset to solving the problem is going to vary depending on the circumstance. If you're in customer service, after you attend to the upset, you may need to get to correcting a problem right away. In that case dealing with the upset may just be a couple of sentences. Or it may be more involved. If you're dealing with a child's upset, fixing the problem may come a long time later and may not even be all that important. But all in all, the point is still the same: usually people need to feel that their upset is being received in some form, that the other person "gets it." That's often what is most important at the outset, no matter what the content or nature of the upset happens to be.

A member of one of my therapy groups used to trigger the other members' "fix-it" mode when she complained of upset about her life. She felt worse when these suggestions were given, because she not only felt people weren't understanding her experience, she felt that they thought she was stupid for not being able to come up with solutions herself. This reaction may or may not have been reasonable, but the fact remained that the other members were trying to be helpful, and were failing. Ultimately, she trained them in how to deal with her upset. She just wanted them to use empathic responses, and to leave solutions alone until later. What she needed first was understanding. So she even coached them in what to say to her.

Trying to "Cheer Them Up"

Trying to cheer someone up when they're upset often seems like the logical thing to do. But remember, an upset person is in the midst of a survival reaction, and they usually can't just "cheer up," anymore than they can just slow their heart rate after they've nearly been hit by a bus. The truth is they probably don't want to be upset any more than you want them to be, and if they could "cheer up" on command they would. But they can't. It just doesn't work that way. Upset feelings serve a purpose in the psyche, and it has to be reckoned with in order to deal with them. In fact, there's a good deal of psychological research that demonstrates telling someone to cheer up when they're feeling bad not only doesn't help but usually makes them feel worse.

Now let's talk about specific techniques that can be useful in dealing with people's upset.

Techniques for Diminishing Upset

When there's upset, there's a lot of defensive, psychic energy being put into some issue in the psyche. A primary method for diminishing upset is to deplete some of the energy.

1. *Talking.* While this may sound obvious, it's often avoided by people because it can be uncomfortable. The listener may have survival reactions in response. But if you want to help diminish an upset, the first step may be to get the person to talk about it. It doesn't matter what they say so much as they simply begin and continue a conversation expressing the upset. Putting things into words, especially those in the conceptual world, is powerful in giving us the ability to deal with them. If it isn't spoken, it can't be dealt with.

2. *Positive communication behaviors.* Using positive communication behaviors with someone experiencing upset does two things. First, they invite the other person to talk. They diminish the chance you'll shut the other person down by causing a survival reaction. Second, they reduce your own survival reactions by diminishing the chance you'll get into negative reciprocity with them. You can't control their behavior, but you can keep your own communication behaviors "clean." This will help your reactions stay moderate, and to keep you out of the fray while they're giving form to their upset.

   Keep your voice even, be direct in eye contact, don't get into negative reciprocities. If they're angry with you and you're feeling the urge to get back at them for what they're saying, remember that taking on the feelings, getting angry in return, often gives the anger exactly what it wants—the ability to get you acting like a jerk, "proving" that you're worth being upset at. If you don't bite, it thwarts the survival reaction, it blocks the feelings transfer.

I was once upset with a company that was overseeing some insurance on a clinical patient of mine. I finally got a supervising psychiatrist on the phone, shared my upset, and escalated my behaviors about how my client and I had been treated. He stated that he understood. During the entire conversation his tone was respectful, sincere and kind, and I never felt any danger of being made wrong. I was angry and upset, he used non-inflammatory words and let me talk. By the end of what turned out to be a very short conversation, I was virtually over my upset, felt much better, and thanked him for his time. He was very good at handling upset, and it left me feeling OK about the whole thing.

In contrast, I already mentioned my upset with a Vice Chancellor at a university where I was teaching part-time because I felt that he had made what I considered to be an unreasonable request. When I spoke with him on the phone, he used urgent tones of voice, no empathic comments, didn't listen to my upset, and instead exhorted me to cooperate with his request, justifying it over and over. He couldn't understand my behavior was expressing upset, and it was my upset that needed addressing, not the issue itself.

All he had to do was to say that he understood that it was a hassle, and that he was sorry he had to insist on my doing it! But he was reacting to my upset with aggressive tones, making me wrong, and not letting me talk at all. I think this was from his own fear that I would not comply with his request, and that it would cause problems for him. So remember something he forgot—no matter what someone says, you don't know what they're going to do until the upset is diminished some. People say all kinds of things in the center of a survival reaction, and you don't know which are credible and which aren't until the upset is diminished. So diminish the upset before taking what they say as gospel and reacting to it. Cut a little slack in the midst of an upset.

3. *Just Listening.* This is obviously going to be important if you're going to get them to talk. You can't do it if you won't stop talking. Have you ever had someone do that to you? Ask you about something you're upset about and then almost immediately take the conversation off on some other topic, maybe about something that happened to them that was similar? It doesn't help at all. It's really true that sometimes people need to "blow off steam." It may just take enough talking to diminish the energy on the upset. So get them to talk. In a reversal of the classic instruction, "Don't just do something, sit there!" Just be their audience, confidant, and companion during their episode. Make their issue and upset the most important thing in the conversation.

When I have an upset consulting client or clinical patient, often I'll do little besides just listen, possibly for an hour or two at a time, if that's required. They almost always talk about how much better they feel after the conversation, but I haven't done anything fancy. I've just made the conversation focus on their upset, left myself out of it, and just listened. But people have such a hard time doing this with others that my willingness to do it is a precious commodity. I may have made it clear that I would listen to them for as long as it takes, to midnight and beyond, if we have the time, and if we don't I'll listen some more as soon as we do have time.

Do you know how little most of us have the opportunity to have something like that in our lives? So it may sound obvious or like "not doing anything," but in fact it may be something that an upset person has nowhere else in their lives. They may have no one who really listens. So what you're doing may be very, very powerful.

Another factor that adds to the importance of just listening is that it's often not easy for people to talk about their upset. Survival reactions can close us up, wall us off. You may even have to push someone a little bit to get them to talk about upset, because their reaction may be to withhold.

Pam and I've learned to push each other when we need it. If Pam senses I'm upset she'll look at me and say, "OK, start talking." I may grumble a little, not wanting to let go of the upset, and she'll say again, "I said start talking."

In the same way, when I sense that she has not fully discussed an upset she's experiencing, I'll say to her, "Don't stop, keep going." It doesn't matter so much what is said as that the talking is happening, energy is being used for verbal behavior on the topic. This, by itself, helps diminish the energy not the upset present in it.

4. *Empathic Responses.* The use of empathic responses lets the person know you're receiving what they're saying, not over there daydreaming, planning lunch, wishing you were somewhere else, or plotting rebuttals and make-wrongs. Say what they're saying back to them. Tell them the understanding you're getting of what they're saying. Take yourself out of the conversation by using comments designed to reflect back the content of what they're saying. Upset is often generated by feeling unimportant, or being slighted, so just the obvious attention you're giving them and their upset can be soothing and upset-reducing. That was all I wanted from the academic dean I had the phone conversation with; just an empathic statement of "I realize this is a pain for you." Then I would have pleasantly (rather than angrily) complied with the request. Just let the person be important!

5. *Give it some time.* Because upsets, being part of survival reactions, don't just go away at the snap of your fingers, time may be an important part of diminishing an upset. Time by itself often reduces it. By talking about it you're simply accelerating the process, reducing the amount of time required for the upset to diminish. So understand that one conversation won't necessarily take it all away. There may need to be several perhaps spaced out over hours, days, or even months.

There are even circumstances where talking about an upset is either impossible due to the situation or because the upset is just too strong and has the person totally haywire for a while. This may result in the need for some time to pass before there's even conversation about it. Whether or not this is the case is one of those factors that varies with the circumstances and issues involved, and for which there's no particular hard and fast rule. Time and space without conversation may be needed and may help also. A cooling off period can be useful.

6. *Reframing*. Because reframing is one of the primary methods for dealing with meaning, it can be a powerful technique for dealing with upset.

First, remember making someone wrong is a type of reframe, as in the example of a mother making her daughter's upsets into "teaching opportunities." The type of reframing that we're talking about softens the meaning causing the upset.

While I was in graduate school there was a lot of upset between faculty and students, with anxiety and anger getting to high levels at times. One day some fellow classmates and I were sharing our upset about the way certain things were being handled, and how upset we were with what we perceived as the faculty's uncaringness and insensitivity. One amiable professor who was listening commented that he certainly understood our upset, because some things were being handled badly. He also told us he had learned that institutions are given a lot more credit than they were due as regards being organized and cohesive. Most of the time, he said, chaos was present, and there was a lot less order than it seemed like there should be. He told us he felt we were feeling the effects of that disorder, which was always troublesome, but it wasn't a plot designed to slight us. In fact, he said, there was so much going on for the faculty that there wasn't even the ability to launch a plot if they wanted to! It was just a sign of the inefficiency of institutions that such bad things happened.

This comment reframed our upset in a larger picture, called "How Organizations Work." It didn't take away the problems, of course, nor did it make us any happier about the practical issues facing us, but what he did was to offer a reframe that took away the personal feeling from the upset. This reduced our upset from a kind of paranoid and overly intense "Why are they doing this to us?" to a more benign and less intense "Isn't it amazing how crazy organizations get?" This diminished the intensity of our upset.

Expanding the frame means bringing in more factors, outside issues, against which the meaning of what causes the upset changes. Another example I witnessed was an administrator who had an upset supervisor because someone in their division had apparently stolen about a hundred dollars out of someone's desk. The administrator listened to the story and said what upset her was that someone in the department apparently needed money and didn't feel free enough to come to others to ask for it, but had to take it. (This wasn't an unrealistic interpretation, because the organization wasn't of the type where people stole for stealing sake.) What this reframe did was bring in the motivation for the apparent theft. When viewed as an act of desperation rather than maliciousness, the upset about it was moderated.

But don't get caught up in the reframe example, some actions do indeed have malicious motivations. Rather, get the point that expanding the frame by bringing in a broader perspective of some sort can help.

I use an expanded reframe commonly with consulting clients when there's something going on in their work or their business that they're upset about. Frequently what we do is go back to their overall purpose, their goal, and look at the problem in relation to it rather than to the day-to-day activities that usually frame our upsets. What they usually see is the upset is small in comparison to their overall vision and goal. It doesn't take the problem away, or eliminate the upset, but by putting it in this perspective it takes on a smaller role in their psyche.

This type of expanded frame can be very powerful for other people as well. When someone becomes upset the survival reaction moves it to the front of their lives. By putting it back into their overall goals and purposes in life, it can diminish in intensity. For example, the question "What is this (the subject of the upset) going to mean to what you're trying to accomplish?" can be very helpful, especially if the upset will ultimately mean very little. What is the person trying to do—to raise happy and responsible children, create a happy marriage, be successful in their work, or whatever. Remembering there are upsets all along the way, and that they're part of the process and don't necessarily mean the process derails can be very helpful.

My associate, Susan, and I began a research project in about 1990 that we intended to complete in about six months. We were experimentally examining a hypothesis that had never been tested before. We were excited about it, and we thought it was important, so we started the project. And almost immediately we started having upsets. We had trouble with everything, much of it was an immense hassle, and we nearly gave up a variety of times.

But with each upset, we had an understanding that what we were doing was of value, had not been done before, and could still be done despite the problem. I even had a colleague who was invested in the research and who would urge us on by reminding us of the value of studying this particular area. As a result, the upsets were manageable because we kept a large enough frame. As it turned out, it took us nearly two years to complete the project, and had we lost our large frame, we probably never would have completed it.

This, in fact, is one of the important functions of "vision" and why I think most people should have a vision for their lives. It provides a ready expanded frame in which to place upsets. For example, I've said to the parents, "I think your child will continue to make a crummy kid, but will make a great adult." This still leaves the issue in place and needing to be dealt with, but softens the upset of "If this kid continues what they're doing they're going to be the next Charlie Manson." It helps diminish the upset.

The second type of reframing is contracting the frame. A contracted frame can be given to people in the form of attending to their upset as a wound or hurt that needs attention. In this way the frame is contracted off the issue completely and to just them, themselves, as people. I often say to people who have been or are being very upset that they need to treat themselves like they have been in a physical trauma—have broken a leg, heart attack, or a major surgery. They need to allow for recuperation, and to take care of themselves. This contracts the frame to them, and can also diminish upset.

The third type of reframing is to shift the frame. This is reinterpreting the issue against a whole new background, sheds a new light on the issue and brings about a new meaning or transformation. Religious groups are expert at this kind of reframing, because they've been dealing with upset and suffering for centuries. What they're able to do is to provide a new frame for the upset. A common one is the upset is designed by God to produce something. This is also an expanded frame, but it serves to alter the meaning. They also present frames such as "offering up" suffering or upset in service to others, or to find meaning in it. Bible stories about Job and Jesus's suffering can also instill a sense of nobility or personal integrity to upset and suffering.

However, it doesn't take religious terminology or beliefs to provide a shifted frame. This was the frame that people coming to my office during the street repair used when they would say "Won't it be nice when it's all done." It's also the method used in sayings such as "Nothing ventured, nothing gained." So if someone is upset about what is going on in a new project at work, a shifted reframe could be a comment about how big endeavors always produce problems to be dealt with. In fact, the more important the endeavor, the bigger the problems there are.

This type of reframing is also called "giving something meaning." Victor Frankl, who I cited in an earlier chapter, said suffering isn't so bad when someone can find meaning in it, when it has value. So a frame that gives the upset meaning can be of great value.

In general, no matter what type of reframing you might do, it's always important the reframe not be done in the manner of, "You're looking at this all wrong," because that makes people wrong. Rather, it's done from the angle of "I understand, and here's something I see about this." A frame is additional information, another valid option of how to view things.

The addition of another option not only softens the upset because it's a more benign way in which to view the issue, but by simply providing an additional frame, removes some of the power of the upset because the issue is no longer "just this one way and that's it."

7. *Separate intent and methodology.* Upsets often involve the concept called motivation, or "why did they do that?" When we're upset, our psychic worlds tend to write the story of the outside world consistent with the upset. If we're angry, they become big, bad people who "meant to do it." If we feel guilty we become the big baddies who "should have been able to not do it" and so on. If we see the intent of the occurrence as being malicious or personal, we tend to be more upset than if it were accidental. But when they're upset, human beings have a tremendous ability to villainize, that's, ascribe more motivation and more malicious motivation, to actions than they warrant.

But it often isn't true. As my professor said of university faculties, so I say about human beings in general—they're just too chaotic and taken over by survival wiring to be that skilled at conspiracy. Sure they do lousy things, I'm not denying that. And there's the occasional conscious conspiracy. But it's also easy to overplay that aspect in everyday life when one is upset.

Of course, sometimes there's a malicious, personal, or uncaring motivation beneath the situation that caused the upset. In that case, this method is probably inapplicable. But those cases are probably the exception, and it's probably more common that the upset is the result of perceived personal offense rather than actual personal offense. Conspiracies take a lot more coordination and purposefulness than human beings are generally capable of. Most of the time actions about which we're upset are caused by oversight, error, misunderstanding, or other nonspecific motivations. But we can still be upset because it feels personal. In this case, separating intent from methodology can be extremely helpful.

The tricky part, though, is you can't use a frame of intent as being strictly benign in an attempt to get rid of the upset. It's a version of making someone wrong by saying "Oh, come on, they didn't mean it." You make the person feel bad about feeling bad, which isn't going to achieve your goal if your goal is to diminish their upset. So if you do separate intent from methodology, you need to comment on both aspects. This gives importance and validity to the upset, avoids making them wrong, and softens the upset by reframing the intent as more benign (if in fact that reframing is valid).

A woman came to see me who was very upset over a comment a coworker had made. It was a general, offhanded comment, but it had upset her a great deal. We talked about it and how much it had upset her, and how understandable that upset was. Then we talked about her coworker and the kind of person they were. There had been some history between the two, always cordial and pleasant, and this particular behavior had seemed out of context to the casual and cordial nature of their relationship. So the evidence didn't support the comment as a coordinated or motivated personal attack. It did support it as a thoughtless comment, made without realizing its potential impact on this woman. If anything, it was simply stupid.

As a result, she had received an inadvertent, thoughtless comment, not designed to wound, but hurtful nevertheless, perhaps equivalent to someone accidentally knocking into her with a piece of furniture they were moving. Should they have been more careful? Probably. But did their doing it mean they were bad or they were out to get the other person? No. But was her upset valid and understandable in the circumstance? Of course. It hurts just as much to be elbowed in the face if it's accidental as if it's on purpose.

With this assurance, my patient could experience her upset without the extra edge that it might have been personal, that it might have "meant something more." This didn't take the upset away immediately, but it accelerated the process of finishing and diminishing.

I can't emphasize enough the importance of both acknowledging the validity of the upset while commenting on the (if true) benign nature of the intent. Don't discount the appropriateness of the upset even if there was no malicious intent.

8. *Paradox.* Remember that paradox works by accessing more than one logical level at a time, with each level addressing a different frame of the situation. You end up saying things that sound the opposite of trying to calm someone down, but on a more profound level allow for depletion of their survival reaction or acceleration of its loss of energy. Because this is a tricky area, it shouldn't be used unless you know what you're doing, are very skilled with paradox, and the situation is safe enough so if it backfires you won't make things worse.

Paradox can be useful in several different instances. First, when someone is resisting their own upset, making themselves wrong thus prolonging their upset, paradox can be used to break down their resistance. For example, if someone is minimizing their upset it's often the case that they aren't even as upset as they ought to be or as you would be under the same circumstances. You may have even said to someone "I think you should be more upset than you are. I'm surprised you're not completely undone. You're being awfully restrained in your reaction." The paradox in the technique is that it encourages them to be open to more upset, while your purpose is to reduce it. But what you're dealing with on another level is their resistance, which is actually making it worse by making them wrong for how they feel.

Second, paradox, like reframing, can be helpful in changing the meaning of an event upsetting to someone. For example, I had a woman client complain to me that she felt really upset she was "relationship hopping." To this I replied, "Good!" She looked at me, puzzled, not expecting to hear that at all.

"I don't mean 'good' that you're upset," I clarified. "I mean 'good' that you're relationship hopping. You had better get it out of your system before you settle down! You'd better take as long as you need. Some people need a long time. So you'd better keep it up until you're done with it, or you'll be courting trouble"

What I was doing was complimenting her on the very thing she was upset about. It was paradoxical because it appeared to validate her upset. But the frame I was giving the paradox made her actions OK. This transformed the meaning of what she was doing, and softened the upset.

Again, let me remind you, as I always do when using reframing and paradox, that you can only do successful paradox if what you're saying is true. If I didn't believe what I was saying when I was talking to this woman, I would never have used that paradox. It would have been manipulation.

I've also used paradox in dealing with couples, telling them they're not only right that their relationship is a mess, but that it's a tribute to their courage and commitment that they're still together. I remind them that to keep working at a relationship in that kind of mess is a Herculean job and a tribute to both of them. It looks like I'm actually telling them they're worse off than they think, which should be upsetting. But I'm flipping that around, using it as a contrast to show their strength and other positive traits. So this isn't only a paradox, it's also a shifting of the frame from "You're a couple of jerks beating each other up" to "You're a couple of powerful, committed people to struggle along as well as you have given the problems in your relationship." And every word of it is absolutely true, or I don't say it.

9. *Fight technology.* OK, here comes one of those times when people-handling technology stops being logical, neat, and nice, when people start to shake their heads and wonder how they'll ever know what to do. To this point I've been talking about methods that directly diminish upset or soften or shift meaning so it doesn't generate so much upset. I've repeatedly said not to make someone wrong, as that increases their survival reaction and makes things worse. The techniques so far are designed to bleed the energy off of upsets or otherwise provide for softening. But now I'm introducing the technique of fighting, which is counter to all of them.

The plain fact of the matter is sometimes the best way to discharge the energy in an upset is to have an argument. To escalate, vent that energy directly, yell and scream, or at least escalate the energy. Sometimes that's best. The problem is people think arguing is a good method for reaching solutions, that the argument will improve the problem. It won't.

Negotiations do that much, much better, but they're impossible during times of high upset. So while arguing isn't a decision-making process, it does require an increased expenditure of energy. And like puncturing a balloon, it can help to discharge energy.

It certainly isn't wrong to argue or fight, as long as it isn't physical, there are no chemicals involved, and no one makes low blows that wound and become a new problem. But if you and someone else are upset with each other, it's not wrong to argue some. It may be helpful in discharging the energy. Just don't kid yourself that the argument itself is the solution to the disagreement that produced the upset. It's simply a way of blowing out the energy.

This is a risky technique because of the possibilities for creating new problems, so I don't suggest you use it commonly, and if your dealings with the person show over time that it creates new problems, don't use it. But don't dismiss it out of hand or make it wrong automatically. Think about its possible usefulness in diminishing upset by more quickly discharging the energy. Sometimes a solid, "You're being crazy about this," with an ensuing argument can blow the lid off the pressure cooker. Just be real careful, and when in doubt, don't use it.

Chapter 16

Achieving Intimacy and Closeness

At its base, human existence is an individual one. Survival wiring is designed, fundamentally, to protect the stuff inside of our own skin, to keep the right things oozing around in the right directions in the right amounts so we can continue successfully as an individual organism. It's designed to provide us with the concepts and meanings that give us the motivation to keep doing what is required to maintain our lives. We begin, end, and live life as individuals, we're fundamentally alone in our experience, and we inhabit only our own bodies. So while there's much talk in the popular press and among social scientists and philosophers about the social nature of human beings, it's still individual experience that's at the base of being human.

It's our status as individuals that assists biology in effectively maintaining the state called life; if one dies, the others can keep going, continuing life's presence. But as regards our experience of living, it's this same individuality that brings on anxiety and the struggle for survival with all of its difficulties and sufferings. If our existence weren't individual, death would hold no fear for us; if we were part of one large experience of consciousness, we would not be losing "us," we would just be losing a part of ourselves, like an eyelash, a fingernail, or a hair. It wouldn't be stuff that would drive us like survival wiring does.

Many religions state life really is this large mass, and our individuality is an illusion. Whether or not this is so, it's not how most of us experience life, so for most of us it's not experienced as real. We exist as individuals.

As a result, for life's purposes our existence as individuals is helpful, but for us, individual existence is precarious and often lonely, and makes living inherently uncomfortable and often frightening. "Life is inherently unsatisfactory," the Buddha wrote as his First Noble Truth. The impermanence of existence is for individuals; life itself has no such impermanence. It's never going to go away. So this is a place where life and us as individuals are at cross-purposes. We experience the anxiety of existence and non-existence from which we seek some kind of refuge, but life itself could care less. It has wired us up for its purposes, not ours.

So a major question for us as individual human beings is how to handle that existential anxiety we feel between the time we got here and the time we cease to exist here. What's to be done about it? How are we to cope with this most uncomfortable of existences? We're like Salieri in *Amadeus*, who could recognize genius but couldn't have it. We can see eternity, we can see "Oneness" but we can't have it. We're impermanent, transient beings in this existence. How does one live with that?

Humans have come up with a variety of methods for coping with it. One answer is to just ignore the whole thing. We can lose ourselves in activities or involvements that literally take our minds off of the whole issue. Another answer is to numb ourselves. By using chemicals or other mind-numbing aids, you don't have to think about or feel about it very much. Of course, you don't get to think about much of anything else, either. And you pay a stiff price in the loss of your functioning. Still another method is to look beyond the problem of impermanence and individualness by building something—or someone—which will outlast us. That way, we leave a piece of us behind. We can leave children, endowments, memories, legacies, good works, or "differences" we've made.

All of these solutions have their place, and all work to a greater or lesser degree. But for all of their applicability, there's still a piece missing for most people. They're still left with a craving for a more pronounced bridging of our sense of separateness, for a joining that overcomes, to some extent at least, the individuality of human existence, even with its anxiety. As a result, there's only one thing that seems, for humans, to truly offer relief, closeness and intimacy with other people. These have become commonly associated with sex, which makes sense since that's intimacy on a physical level. But when I'm referring to them I'm talking about more than that. I'm talking about emotional intimacy and closeness, the kind that makes us feel connected to and a "part of" another person. This kind of pairing with another person or with other people seems to be the strongest drive people have in overcoming the separateness of human existence.

Ernest Becker, in his award winning book *The Denial of Death*, refers to this as the "romantic" solution to the dilemma of impermanence. As he does with nearly all methods of trying to cope with death, he cites its inadequacy, its ultimate failure to adequately relieve or resolve the issue of individuality, existential anxiety, and death. But its inadequacy is only a tribute to the impossibility of humans being able to completely and adequately embrace their own fate, not to the irrelevance or uselessness of being close to another person. The only problem occurs when people really expect their closeness to allow an escape from the condition of being human once and for all. The fact remains that joining with others emotionally seems to be a craving present in the human species that doesn't seem to go away. Even though we divorce often, we still get married at a rapid pace. Even people with a history of painful, traumatic, troubled relationships still yearn for a relationship, still feel frustrated without one. Being close seems to be one of the few things that achieves any true muting of the loneliness of human existence. And, as a result, despite the inadequacies pointed out by Becker, it continues to be an important and powerful factor in human life.

Because intimacy and closeness are so valuable in ameliorating the aloneness in human life, it's surprising there isn't more of it in the world. In addition, it's interesting that what closeness there is, isn't only difficult to get, but even more difficult to maintain. Have you ever wondered why this is? Why marriages are so difficult to maintain, why love affairs don't tend to last, why friendships are hard, why closeness with anyone seems to be fragile and transient? It seems if people need this salve of connectedness to ease the loneliness of existence, then they should be able to do a lot better job of being close. So what gives with it being so difficult?

What gives is what I talked about earlier regarding the cross-purposes of life and individual experience. Intimacy and closeness, while valuable for easing life's existential anxiety, are also two of the most dangerous and threatening states possible for human beings. They run counter to survival wiring. In fact, much human misbehavior is not only not directed toward obtaining intimacy and closeness, much of it's motivated by an attempt to prevent getting there. For all their apparent desirability, they're terribly risky.

As I've discussed frequently in this book, human biology is wired up to protect and prolong life. That means ensuring one is safe from possible threats and dangers. The problem is being close to someone requires letting them in, letting them beyond your defenses. It's the same issue I discussed when presenting the technique of sharing; being close means unlocking the door and inviting someone in past the barbed wire, the alarms, and through the steel doors held tight by the defenses of our psyches. Once they're inside, we're vulnerable, endangered. The defenses that keep us safe are all on the perimeter, and letting someone into our physical or psychological house means we have relinquished nearly all protection against the hurt, pain, damage, and destruction that could occur if they cause trouble. As a result, we're constantly on the lookout for ways to push people out. That's how we experience the single most common reason for failed relationships: to yearn for intimacy, and have our behavior ensure we don't get it.

When I was studying the martial arts I had an instructor who had a whole array of black belts. He was experienced in judo, karate, and ju-jitsu. The first black belt he received was in judo. He used to tell us the story of his first karate tournament, which he entered just after he started studying karate but after he was already a black belt in judo. He won the tournament. When the match started, he rushed his opponent, got right up next to him, and grabbed him. The opponent couldn't hit him because he was too close. Then he did a judo throw, putting them on the mat, and threw a winning punch. Nobody was prepared for that kind of tactic, so he easily won the tournament over all of the karate black belts that entered.

The whole key to his technique was their vulnerability when he got close to them. Their defenses were based on maintaining the distance required to punch and block, so his getting close neutralized their defenses. After telling us the story, he also used to laugh, it was not only the first karate tournament he ever won, but also the last. After that everyone was onto his method and wouldn't let him get close to them.

This is how it works for us, too. If someone gets close to us, we're vulnerable, and our survival wiring doesn't like it. It sees it as dangerous, so no matter the discomfort of being alone, the other danger is worse. So it works against it. That's why people seem to sabotage their very most intimate relationships, why we treat our intimates worse than we treat strangers.

In addition, not only are we vulnerable to being hurt by someone when they get close to us, but being close or connected to someone means that whatever is hanging on them, also gets on us. To put it in physical terms, if someone stinks and gets close to us, we smell the odor. If we rub up against them, we start to stink, too. Not only are we in danger from them, we're in danger from whatever toxic physical or conceptual entities they may drag along with them. It could be like letting a possessed person into your house.

The dangers to us occur both in the sensory and the conceptual world. Obviously, if you let someone close to you physically you have the potential to be hurt by them. If you start dating someone and they turn out to be a dangerous psychopath, they know where you live, they were invited into your house, you are vulnerable to them.

But the conceptual world is no less risky. If you tell someone secrets about you or truths about how you feel or what you think, those entities can be injured if the other person mishandles them. You could be belittled, rejected, scorned, exposed, or abused. There can be all kinds of pain and damage to your self in the conceptual realm just like there can be all kinds of pain and damage to your body in the sensory realm.

Closeness and intimacy are risky. Trusts are betrayed, people are hurtful, things go wrong. What this means is humans are caught in the dilemma of craving a closeness and intimacy that can only be attained by being the very things they're wired up to avoid— vulnerability. Humans have a love-hate, approach-avoidance relationship with intimacy. We want it, but we have trouble tolerating it, so after we get it we screw it up. We get close and then do things that distance ourselves, push others away. We aren't satisfied without it, but we're uncomfortable with the riskiness of it.

This is an inherent state for human beings, so this chapter presents no illusions. It's focused on attaining and maintaining intimacy with the understanding that you are going to be gaining and losing it all the time. But there are ways to make the losing and regaining less painful than it tends to be for people.

There are really two different aspects of emotional closeness and intimacy, and they're different enough to require separate discussions. The first is getting close to someone, attaining intimacy. The second is staying close to someone, maintaining or regaining the intimacy. Each aspect has its own process and requires its own set of techniques.

Achieving Intimacy

Intimacy is something that can never be achieved by demanding it. In fact, "shoulds" kill the opportunity for intimacy. Pressure does, too. Intimacy can, at best, be invited, not forcefully induced.

Many of the people-handling methods we've discussed so far, such as escalations, behavioral techniques, and reframing, are practically useless in achieving intimacy because it isn't created by trying to alter things, as many of these techniques are designed to do. Intimacy leaves most meanings and behaviors alone, It's a goal and purpose all to itself, and differs from other goals with people in profound ways. There are three basic components involved in achieving intimacy with someone:

1. *Sharing.* This is, perhaps, the most important method for attaining intimacy with someone. Sharing is, by definition, revealing yourself. It's telling yourself as you are, telling yourself in a way that allows the other person to grasp it, to "have some of you." Sharing is never defensive, it makes no one wrong. It's not designed to keep you safe or to justify or make you right. It's simply handing some of you over to someone else. It isn't a story told for an audience, or an image or tale told from a distance but a revealing of you. It lets people past your defenses.

The greater the sharing with someone, the greater the intimacy. The more important, the more close, the more sensitive and personal the sharing, the more intimacy that will occur. And, of course, along with that, the more vulnerable you become. So you never want to take an intimate-level of sharing lightly. It leaves you exposed to someone else. You become an open book to a greater or lesser degree. It's difficult to do completely, and emotionally threatening as well.

2. *Just Listening*. This is the counterpart to sharing, and the other half required to produce intimacy and closeness. While one person is sharing, the other needs to be receiving the message. This is, as I noted in the section on Just Listening, easier said than done, because it requires you to suspend all judgment thinking, which is usually a pretty significant part of our thinking. It's not a complicated point: you have to receive, if you're going to attain a two-way intimacy.

3. *Empathic Comments*. As I've noted before, Empathic Comments don't need to be fancy, and aren't a magic potion for doing something to someone. They aren't psychobabble. They're whatever comments allow the other person to know you're receiving their share, you're understanding them and their experience.

That's it. But don't be put off by how simple it sounds. It's simple, but not easy. In fact, its whole problem is that it's way too simple. There are so many other things humans do with each other, so much else that can go on, or can get in the way, that just doing those three things with someone is often a monumentally difficult task.

Most of the time the person who experiences the greatest intimacy is the one who does the sharing. Often this is a two-way street, and made safe by reciprocity from the other person; if you want someone to be intimate with you, being vulnerable to them is one of the best invitations. It demonstrates you're throwing down your weapons first, you're not going to present a threat.

However, there are times when relationships are designed as one-way intimacy. Psychotherapy patients feel emotionally intimate with their therapists, while their therapists don't experience the same degree of emotional intimacy with their clients. Clients pour their hearts out by sharing deep emotional parts of themselves, and while therapists can and do use sharing (often called "self-disclosure") in their work, it's not the same as what their client is doing. It can't be. Their sharing is always a part of helping the client get what they want in life and change the ways they want to change. The therapist's sharing is going to be done with the intention of using it to help rather than feel vulnerable. So while some level of emotional intimacy may be produced, it's a by-product of the work, not the purpose.

As I noted before, the difficulty presented by intimacy is, from the perspective of the one doing the intimate sharing, becoming vulnerable. The difficulty presented by intimacy from the perspective of the receiver is whatever is put out on the table can't be messed with or fled from if intimacy is to be generated. You can't try to fix, adjust, judge, change, improve, or criticize it. You cannot turn from it, change the subject, walk off, or block it out. You have to let it be as it is. It's not your task to mess with it, or being given to you to work on. Intimacy is actually most produced by sharing on the edge of discomfort. It's talking about those embarrassing, difficult things, uncertainties, mistakes, problems, worries, and self-doubts.

Certain elements breed the ability to share and put people into positions where intimacy often occurs.

1. *Working with a common purpose.* People who feel united in a common goal, purpose, or commitment, tend to become close. This is because they tend to identify with and trust each other because they feel they're similar, on the same team, and have a similar investment in supporting, not hurting, each other. The closeness may not generalize beyond the particular project, but during the work they may experience a good deal of emotional intimacy.

2. *Sharing an adversity.* Shared adversity breeds a great deal of intimacy. People who have been through terrible ordeals together, combat, prison camp, or natural disasters, tend to be able to share and be more intimate. They've been through something that tests each one, makes each vulnerable through no decision of their own, and have that vulnerability in common. In fact, such adversity itself can short-circuit survival wiring because people can have nothing left to lose.

When I worked at a psychiatric hospital before I went to graduate school, I was part of a staff who did very stressful and sometimes dangerous work. Several times I was injured, and once nearly killed. The staff developed among itself a closeness and intimacy that resembles that experienced by soldiers in battle. There just wasn't any way to hide our fears, flaws, upsets, or difficulties from each other; we faced them and experienced them every day. As a result we were very close and intimate with each other.

3. *Having a common need.* A common neediness is also a breeding ground for sharing and intimacy. It's another thing that leads to two people being identified with each other, and so feeling more readily safe regarding sharing and closeness. A great deal of intimacy is created, for example, among people who find themselves without sufficient food, shelter, or clothes. Refugees experience this kind of intimacy, as do concentration camp prisoners and unemployed people.

4. *That certain "chemistry."* Remember, people-handling isn't an exact science by any means. There are just so many things that we can see, but can't understand or control. One of those things goes by the colloquial name of "chemistry."

This is a quality people can sense in others. They seem to immediately feel a kinship or bonding with someone else. They find that person easy to talk to, easy to get close to. This "feeling" continues to defy scientific definition, even though there are theories about it. Maybe the person reminds you of a parental figure, or some smell or other element triggers off powerful brain chemicals for you. Nobody knows. Eventually we'll find out what it is, but until then all we can do is to acknowledge it and to appreciate its importance. Some people just "fit" together better than others. This can be what is called falling in love but it can just as easily be the beginning of a friendship. There are people you trust implicitly, that you just seem to already "know" somehow, and with whom you feel freer to share yourself than with other people.

Maintaining Intimacy

Attaining intimacy is tricky and uncertain, but it's easy compared to maintaining intimacy. After all, before you're close to someone, they aren't much of a threat. It's only after some intimacy has been achieved that survival wiring really gets worried. So that's when the games begin.

The reality of any relationship is you can't be intimate or close all the time. First, it takes a lot of time, effort and energy to become and to stay close. Second, intimacy is just too threatening to the survival wiring, and nobody can tolerate for too long being as vulnerable as intimacy requires. So you will, inherently and normally, experience fluctuations in closeness and intimacy in any relationship you have, no matter how committed, compatible, and close it is. You and the other person will go through cycles where you back off and then get close, back off and then get close again. In fact, there's a certain rhythm to good relationships regarding their level of intimacy. It rises and falls like waves on the ocean. The cycles aren't really predictable or regular, but there's a natural rhythm to it.

As a relationship continues, becomes more a part of your life, your survival wiring not only considers that person a threat, but also considers threats to the relationship to be a threat. As a result, you become less and less willing to risk the relationship. This makes it more difficult to share uncomfortable things that might threaten the relationship. When there's something at stake to you regarding whether the relationship works out, the ability to be intimate begins to deteriorate. That's when we start hiding, manipulating, trying to be safe, to maneuver away from danger. We even sacrifice intimacy in service of maintaining the relationship.

There's also an additional aspect of close relationships which makes intimacy more difficult. At the start many irritations are tolerable because you don't have an unpleasant history with them yet. But after time spent in the relationship, some of "those things" can begin to grate on you. If someone is in enough pain, and the pain keeps pouring out in some manner that's unpleasant, it may be difficult for you to stay close to them. You may start to back off, or try to change them, make them wrong, or make yourself wrong. All of these have a chilling effect on the intimacy in the relationship.

Maintaining intimacy, or maintaining a relationship where intimacy can occur, requires two elements:

1. Continued sharing, just listening, and empathic responding. In everyday life, amid the demands, stresses and strains we have to respond to, the sharing and listening that create intimacy are often the first things to be discarded. Again, they aren't essential for survival, so life considers them to be luxuries at best and dangerous at worst. In addition, some of them are going to be threats to the relationship. You may have to share with someone you want to be close to something that has happened or that you are doing or that you are feeling that's a problem for the relationship. You may have to risk the relationship, and that isn't easy to do.

    In addition, there are many other, practical, demands on you that take precedence because they have so much more urgency. Getting the baby to the doctor may be essential, while sharing about what a tough day you had may look superfluous. When there are things that need to be done, concerns that need to be coped with, and upsets that need to have the lid kept on, intimacy goes way down in priority. After all, survival wiring knows you'll survive even if you're not bridging that gap of individualism, so the sharing and listening required are easy to overlook and easy to lose track of over time.

    Often a rediscovery of the ability to share suddenly makes people feel alive. This is what generates affairs. People find they're able to share again, to have someone just listen, and even make empathic comments with them. There isn't so much to lose because an affair isn't a marriage or exclusive relationship, so people find themselves freer to share themselves. When this ability has been lost, its rediscovery is enlivening.

    Unfortunately, unless you go from one to another, all relationships stop being new at some point, and change from attaining intimacy to maintaining intimacy. Extramarital affairs, while sometimes bringing back those feelings of aliveness for a while, are ultimately an invitation to disaster. As far as maintaining intimacy in a relationship, the issue of sharing keeps rearing its head, demanding it be done to keep the partners close. But it takes work because the odds are against you in several ways. Survival wiring won't want you to do it. There will be a million and one demands on your time that look more important. You won't want to share things that might rock the boat when you have a lot invested in keeping the boat afloat. You also will have an investment in looking good to the other person. So you'll find your survival wiring pushing you to withhold or start fights to distance. The issue of sharing never goes away, and in fact, becomes more of an issue, more of a concern, as relationships continue.

It's this decay in the ability to be intimate that often produces symptoms in a relationship. A reduction of the ability to be intimate ultimately produces compensatory behaviors—symptoms—to make up for the loss of the previously soothing intimacy. These symptoms can be any of the behaviors people use to numb their pain or distract them from it. Some of these are compulsions, including the use of chemicals, affairs (sexual addictions), overeating, television, and over-involvement with work. Others can be chronic mood alterations such as anger, irritation, depression, and moodiness.

One of the most deadly elements of a relationship, as far as the ability to share and be intimate is concerned, is unresolved or mishandled disagreements. These conflicts begin to backlog, form a pile of upset between people which pushes them farther and farther apart. This brings us to the second essential ingredient in being able to maintain intimacy.

2. A mechanism for dealing with and resolving conflicts and disagreements. The more overlapped your life is with someone, the more opportunity there will be to experience conflict. And this will set off survival wiring and distance the partners in a relationship. This means that the partners need to have some way to diminish their survival reactions to each

other. In short, it means that they need to be able to resolve disagreements.

You can think of this as being the need for an ability to repair the relationship during breakdowns. Anything that can't be repaired is eventually going to become irreparably damaged and unworkable. Relationships are no exception. What do you think it would be like if you owned a car that could never be repaired when something went wrong? It wouldn't be long before you were driving a wreck. That's like having a relationship where you and your partner can't resolve conflicts. How do you think that would affect your closeness? It would steadily erode it.

Some relationships, of course, are more prone to conflicts, survival reactions, and their resulting debris than are others. There are two factors that determine the potential for such debris, and the need for a method to clean it up fairly regularly. The first is the compatibility between the partners. There really is a valid and valuable concept of compatibility between partners in a relationship. It's a general term that means how well the partners fit together in outlook and behavior. It doesn't necessarily mean the partners are exactly the same in outlook or behavior, rather that they come to the relationship with similar ways of conceptualizing and behaving in the world. High compatibility means they tend to automatically work together fairly naturally or smoothly.

The second element that tends to determine the degree of risk a relationship runs for developing intimacy-diminishing debris is the number of joint decisions required by the relationship. The more these are required, the more chance there are going to be disagreements that require the application of some kind of resolution technology.

The irony of this is relationships that are most important to us are the ones that are the most overlapping. As a result, the very relationships that are most important to us are the ones most prone to develop the most serious problems with intimacy. Perhaps the best example is marriage. Others with a great deal of overlap include parents and kids, friends, and business partners. All possess the potential for a great deal of conflict, and as a result present the need to have an effective method for resolving disagreements.

The method for cleaning up the debris that develops in a relationship has to effectively resolve problems while avoiding the creation of new ones. That's why fight technology is often so unworkable in intimate relationships. Fights can produce resolution at times, but can have side-effects that harm the relationship in the long run, creating its own new set of problems.

There has been a lot of study of this issue over the past twenty years, and results show that probably the best method to deal with disagreements and conflicts in relationships where intimacy occurs is a form of negotiation specifically designed for ongoing relationships. I'm going to give some details regarding this procedure, because it's so well-documented in its applicability to this part of maintaining relationships.

This technique, often called "problem solving" in the psychology research literature, is very similar to the negotiations procedures discussed earlier. However, it has a fairly specific structure for partners in an ongoing, intimate relationship, where the goal is to reach resolutions so they aren't in the way of the partners getting close and staying close.

Problem-Solving

First, problem solving is done in short conversations spread over time. Many couples set aside a problem solving time in their day. It's essential it be at a time when there are no distractions, when the couple isn't in the middle of an upset, and when they aren't exhausted. I usually forbid couples from problem solving after ten at night. I worked with one couple who just couldn't seem to make problem solving work, and I was baffled by their failure until they finally let it slip that they were doing their problem solving sessions at midnight, in bed. It needs to be done when the partners are alert, and sitting up.

During problem solving sessions, there's one purpose and one purpose alone—to work on solving one problem. The entire solution process may not occur during any one sitting, but there's a reliable and structured process they go through. Partners can stop and start with no trouble. This can also be aided by using a paper and pencil to write down the problem statements and solutions.

During problem solving sessions only positive communication behaviors are used. This is what prevents fights from occurring because fights are the result of negative communication behaviors, not the topic of disagreements. This is often difficult for couples to accomplish when they're unaccustomed to it, so I often teach them to monitor their communication behaviors, and note the negative communication behaviors that occur so they can learn to stop them.

A fascinating part of this process is that there's an extremely powerful and reliable way to predict arguments and fights, and stop them. During problem solving sessions the only way an argument or fight can occur is through the increasing use of negative communication behaviors with a resulting escalating negative reciprocity that then turns into upset and arguments. When I'm working with couples I give them a safety valve regarding negative communication behaviors. If they note a total of three negative communication behaviors—three total, from one or a combination of both partners—they stop the session at that point. By the time they have noticed three negative communication behaviors, certainly others have occurred that they haven't noticed. If they don't stop talking, they'll be well on their way to a fight. But by consistently stopping before a fight starts, they train their psyches to stop using negative communication behaviors. Their psyches get trained that problem solving sessions are a kind of time out from fighting. This is essential, because the partners must feel safe with each other to resolve disagreements.

At first, couples may only last about five minutes in problem solving before they reach the safety valve cut-off. That's fine. It's a process of relearning, of extinction actually, and so stopping before an argument is more important than getting lots done in any particular session. And even if they're able to complete an entire session I still limit them to ten minutes for the first several weeks—because problem solving is very hard work, they get tired, and their ability to edit out negative communication behaviors diminishes.

The setup is regular, short sessions during which the goal is to solve problems or disagreements in the relationship, with only positive communication behaviors being used. What this sets up is a circumstance where negative communication behaviors cannot be used as a way of changing the other person. This keeps the conversation from turning off the topic of the disagreement and onto each other, as happens in fights.

What this also means, though, is that there's the need for an alternate technology to be able to resolve the problem. That's where the format of their talking comes into play.

The first thing the couple does is choose a problem in their relationship to work on. It's amazing how many couples don't even know what a "problem" is. A problem in a relationship where intimacy is desired is anything that either partner doesn't like. Partners are famous for saying things like, "Well, that may be a problem for you, but it's not a problem for me, so it's not a problem in the relationship." Wrong. Every problem for either partner is a problem for a relationship where emotional closeness is the point.

Anything that causes upset in one partner automatically alters their behavior toward the other partner. They go into some form of fight or flight, back off, or get combative. This affects the other partner, who responds with some kind of survival reaction. This begins a ping-pong of survival reactions, with closeness and intimacy being the casualty. It is to both partners' benefit to work to resolve every single disagreement or conflict, even if it only upsets the other person, because it'll remove the partner's survival reaction and make them more available for closeness.

The reason most partners don't do this automatically is they have the idea there are only three possible solutions to disagreements and conflicts—their way, the other partner's way, or some way they'll both hate. So they want to avoid having to solve upsets that the other partner has, lest they have to give in to something they don't want. A cardinal rule in problem solving is no one is ever to agree to a solution they can't live with.

The couple begins the problem solving session by choosing a problem they both agree to work on, even if only one of the partners is upset about the problem. The first major step is to state the problem in sensory terms that can be seen or heard. No statements about attitudes or feelings, or concepts like messes. Statements like, "I don't like that you leave your clothes on the bathroom floor," or "I don't like that the backyard is muddy when it rains," or "I don't like that you're late getting ready in the mornings," are desired. Also, the statement must be a statement of what's wrong, rather than a desire for what's right. No statements like, "I don't like that you aren't ready to go on time in the morning." The problem with this is it limits you to one possible solution, the one mentioned in the problem statement. It's an assumption this is the only possible solution, so you need to find a way to make it happen. I've been working with couples for over fifteen years, and I've seen repeatedly how often they find new solutions that they never thought of before, that solve problems. It's important not to limit them to one.

The next step is to brainstorm a list of possible solutions, stating them in sensory terms. The list must be a minimum of a dozen or so solutions. If the couple has fewer, they're not thinking creatively. Because there's a rule that neither partner is allowed to accept a final solution with which they're unable to live, couples are safe to state lots of different solutions, even ones they don't like. The point is to be creative, not judgmental, so more and more possible solutions occur to you.

After the list is generated, the partners review the list, throw out solutions that (and this is absolutely essential) either one of them doesn't like. Only the ones both partners are OK with are retained. That way, no one is being forced to accept something they can't live with because that wouldn't be a resolution to the problem anyway. It would simply send the disagreement underground, and that won't help.

In the final step the couples fashion a solution from the remaining solutions, and institute a plan based on it which they will then try out. If they end up with no solutions that are OK with both of them, it's back to the drawing board for more brainstorming.

Not only is this process a well-studied and effective method for dealing with issues that diminish intimacy, it's also a very effective compatibility test for couples. If a couple repeatedly and routinely can't ever generate lists of possible solutions that they can both live with, they're in great danger of never being able to make their relationship work out. They may very well be incompatible. Of course, a reliable determination of this requires their working with a skilled therapist, but you may be able to see the logic of this. If a couple can never agree on anything, even given the optimal situation of problem solving sessions, then they're in trouble trying to maintain a relationship where intimacy is going to be possible.

Now, as you can tell, this procedure is highly structured, quite demanding, and exacting. That's because it was developed working with couples who were in distress. If you're in a relationship that isn't suffering, but you want to ensure that intimacy and closeness can be maintained to the greatest extent possible, you might not need to do this kind of procedure in such a formal, structured way. In fact, even when working with relationships that are in trouble, the goal is for the problem solving to eventually not have to be so formal and rigid, and instead to do problem solving informally, casually, almost automatically. You'll just instinctively talk about issues in sensory terms using positive communication behaviors, toss out various possible solutions in search of one you both can live with. By then you'll know that it's possible to accomplish that goal, that a failure to find solutions you can both live with is a failure in your process, not a failure of the relationship. So you'll feel less reliant on fighting as a resolution technology because you'll come to trust your process of solving problems collaboratively.

Pam and I use an informal version of this process all the time. I already mentioned how we used it to solve our disagreement over what time we go to sleep. We put my desk into an alcove in our bedroom, and I bought a notebook computer that I can use there. Then I'm close to her, because we're in the same room, but she can sleep and I can work. I can even sit up in bed beside her and work if I want to. That solution may not be OK with every couple, but it's OK for us, and that's the beauty of this kind of problem-solving. The solutions that may be OK with one couple might never work for another, but it doesn't matter. As long as they're both OK with it, it's fine.

You can see how problem solving isn't, itself, an emotional process. To the contrary, emotion is intentionally kept out of it. It's strictly logical and intellectual. But its purpose is to solve issues that are problems emotionally, to produce solutions that make partners feel better. This is, itself, a separation of intention and methodology. The problems are emotional, but they're solved with non-emotional methods. Sharing is the emotional part of the relationship.

In fact, arguments are a contamination of problem-solving and sharing. It isn't that partners can't get upset with each other and express that—they do and should. The problem is couples try to solve the problem along with the expression of upset, which doesn't work. It's called a fight. Sharing feelings, even upset, angry feelings, is one process, and solving problems is a whole different process.

I'm well aware there are many reasons why using this kind of collaborative problem-solving can be difficult for partners. People are unaccustomed to it, and many are so accustomed to using some kind of fight technology this kind of process seems strange and foreign to them. So if you don't come away with anything else from this chapter, come away with three points:

1. Sharing is the key to attaining intimacy with other people.
2. Successfully resolving problems, conflicts, and disagreements is the key to maintaining intimacy with other people.
3. The methodology used for resolving problems needs to solve more problems than it creates.

If you're able to address these points in your relationships, then you'll acquire and maintain the most intimacy possible to human beings in their relationships with others. You'll experience the normal rising and falling of intimacy, of losing it and rediscovering it.

Chapter 17

Changing People

The topic of changing people is one of the most misunderstood and distorted in all psychology and in all of the popular understanding of psychology. The sense about it is usually summarized by the statement, "You can't change anyone but yourself." This statement is popular and you can run into it almost anywhere. In fact, as I write this I recall I heard it just this week when a therapist to whom I'm a consultant told me he had said it to a client.

"You can't change anyone but yourself." It sounds so logical and rational. So profound. So right. Therapists, self-help books, parents, friends, nearly everyone says it. There's only one problem: it isn't true. The truth is not only is it possible to change other people, but it happens all the time. You do it all the time. Much of human behavior is designed to do it. We just don't notice or do it in a way that achieves the changes we desire.

"You can't change anyone but yourself" isn't only untrue, it carries with it a supreme irony; the main proponents of the statement are therapists, and therapists are the very people who are paid to change other people! In fact, when therapists say it to their clients, they're saying it to the very people hiring them to change someone else—the client! If it's true nobody can change anyone but themselves, then what does the therapist think they're being paid to do? A therapist's whole job is to help change people! If I had a therapist say that to me, I'd say, "Then what am I paying you for?"

Therapists are a sophisticated bunch, though, and they have all sorts of comebacks to this criticism. They say things like "The therapist is there with the client, but the client has to do the changing." Or "Therapists only help if the client wants to change," or "The therapist is only a facilitator for change." But all those responses beg the issue. Is the therapist a change agent or not? If they are, no matter how it works, then they're being paid to change people in some fashion and through some method. If they really believe "You can't change anyone but yourself," then why don't they say to their clients: "Don't come to see me. You have to change yourself anyway, I'm no good to you. Save your money." They know they're important in producing the changes in the client's life. They know they do change people.

So why do therapists say that statement if they know it isn't true? Because the clients they say it to are stuck, struggling and suffering in their lives because they're trying unsuccessfully to change someone else. The client is failing and hasn't stopped the failing behavior even though it's producing negative effects in their life. By saying "You can't change anyone but yourself," the therapist is trying to get them to stop their repetitive, frustrating, symptom-producing, unsuccessful attempts to change someone else. The statement is simply a change technique—paradox."

Do you understand what an ironic joke this is? It means that the statement "You can't change anyone but yourself" is itself a technique designed to change someone!

The only trouble with the statement is people take it out of context, and instead of seeing it as a therapeutic technique, they start to take it as truth. But it's not intended as dogma but as a method of changing someone.

So the issue is not that it's impossible to change them, only the extent to which it is possible to change them and whether or not it's desirable. Nothing is always possible when it comes to dealing with human beings, changing included. And from the information we've covered so far you know changing someone isn't likely to be one of the easier tasks in dealing with other people, either. If it were easy to change people, every salesperson would close every sale, there would be no crime or juvenile delinquency, no antisocial behavior, and everyone would get along just fine. Obviously things don't work like that. When you set out to change someone you're going up against one of the most powerful opponents on the planet—survival wiring. So while it may not be a rule that it's always impossible, it's a decidedly formidable task. There are limits to the extent to which it can be done, and you need to be honest with yourself about what you're getting into if you try to do it. Survival wiring runs deep, and you want to be sure you're willing to do what is required to successfully mess around with something of that magnitude.

Because there's so much mistaken information about how we can change other people or even how people change, I'm first going to present several general principles regarding change both for human beings in general and individuals as well.

General Functional Principles of Change and Changing People

Changing Someone is Different from Resisting Someone

Most of what people experience as their attempts to change other people aren't attempts at all. They're protests, or resistances, against them. They're behaviors that make a public statement about your unhappiness with the other person. Protests are essentially designed to be feelings transfers. They bring attention to your unhappiness and upset about the people you're protesting against. That's why protesters carry picket signs that say insulting things. On a personal level, sulking is a good example of a protest behavior, as is slamming doors, the silent treatment and dirty looks.

There's absolutely nothing inherently wrong with declaring one's displeasure at someone else's activities. Social protest is a prized and protected right in America, and on a personal basis we often call it "expressing our feelings." The problem is that people confuse protesting with trying to change someone. Protests rarely, if ever, change people. Have you ever seen a pro-life or a pro-choice individual change their mind as the result of a protest held by the other side? Have you ever seen a Republican or a Democrat change parties because of protests? In fact, they tend to actually work against the other side changing. They're often treated as escalations, with the other side feeling they have to escalate as well, and as a result serving to harden one's already established position.

But protests do have one thing going for them. Because they involve so much self-righteousness, they're satisfying. The self-righteousness available is as sweet as any chocolate cake ever baked anywhere. It's warm, fulfilling, and inviting. It feels good, or at least noble. Actually working to change people, on the other hand, is often none of those things. It often requires surrender of self-righteousness, and it's not fun or noble. It's work. That's why people protest instead of getting down to work to change someone. It's more fun.

The problem, if you want to try to change someone, is protest often gets in the way of methods to change someone. If you're using protest behaviors and decide you actually want to try to change them, you'll probably have to give up your protest behaviors. You'll have to relinquish some of your self-righteousness and victim-anger. They trap you into one set of responses and aren't designed to produce change; upset, yes, but change, no. To get someone to unlock the front door and let you in where you can get your hands on what you want to change, you're probably going to have to knock off your protests. This can be difficult to do because a protest is a public statement of opposition, and giving it up can feel like sanctioning the very thing you want changed. It also means giving up those good feelings.

If you're currently sulking, being nasty, giving someone the silent treatment, or being resistive with them in order to register your unhappiness, you'll need to decide whether you want to continue to do so or take on the task of trying to change what you don't like, because in all likelihood you can't do both.

Change Requires Unhooking Something from Survival Wiring

Changing what someone is doing or how they are means severing the connection of that function to survival wiring. Obviously, this is a big deal. Messing around with survival wiring in any form is a tall order. This is the reason why even positive changes in someone's life can be such a big deal and can create upset and anxiety in the early stages.

A psychotherapy patient I had been seeing for some time was feeling less guilt than she had before. In fact, for the first time in her life she was relatively guilt-free. But as soon as that happened she experienced a new feeling—anxiety about her lack of guilt. She said, "I sure am glad I'm coming here, so I know what's going on, because if I weren't I would think I was getting worse, not better, and I'd probably go back to the old way before I got out of this stage and into the next one."

This woman's guiltiness was connected to survival wiring. In order to maintain her feeling of being right—her conceptual survival—she learned at a very young age to feel guilty. She didn't enjoy feeling guilty, but enjoyment has nothing to do it. Her guilt had hung on because without it she felt like she was bad. So to unhook that guilt stirred things up for a while and brought new issues to deal with.

You already know how true it is that even positive changes can be problematic if you've ever tried to stop a bad habit. If you've ever tried to stop smoking, biting your fingernails, cracking your knuckles, you know a behavior or function doesn't have to necessarily be pleasant to be hooked into survival wiring. It won't want to let go even if you don't like it and it's bad for you. So all attempts to change people, even to make small changes, are a big deal.

Change is Always Replacement, not Elimination

Nature hates a vacuum, and no behavior or function can be eliminated without being replaced with another. Even if what you want is someone to just stop doing something, like talking so much, that behavior has to be replaced with some other. The behavior may be looking straight ahead without talking, but some kind must still take its place. The rule of thumb is the replacement behavior has to have equal or greater survival value than did the original. This is a place where people fail in their attempts. They try to diminish one function or behavior without allowing an alternate that's amenable according to the other person's survival wiring.

For example, I've worked with a lot of single people whose problem in finding a suitable mate is they get stuck in relationships that are inappropriate for them. They spend a year or so in those dead-end associations fully aware this particular partner isn't who they want to marry. When they finally get out they've lost a year of searching time. When this happens several times in a row, it can be pretty frustrating.

It doesn't work to say to these people, "Don't get caught up in inappropriate relationships" because that behavior is wired into survival for them. It won't just diminish by itself. Their internal mechanism locks on to dating partners and before they know it, they're in an exclusive relationship with someone resembling Dracula. I get them to not concentrate on avoiding getting involved, but rather to make sure they're dating more than one person at all times even if they're getting involved with someone. Instead of simply eliminating attachment behavior, this helps replace it with another, alternative behavior, dating several people. It's much easier for people to do this than give up their attachment behavior.

Only Three Processes Produce Change in Human Beings

Much is written about how people change and how you can change yourself. Most of it sounds good, logical, and sounds as though it makes sense. But if you've ever tried to apply any of it, you already know that despite its realistic appearance almost none of it works. That's because there are only a few things that really produce change in people, and most of the principles presented in those writings aren't consistent with them.

These few processes usually occur accidentally, which is why people change without trying to at times. They can also, of course, be applied intentionally. I'm going to explain these processes in some detail, because all change methods must fit into at least one of the processes or it won't have the slightest chance of working.

The Three Change Processes

When the Pain of the Problem
Exceeds the Pain of the Solution

We want to change things because we experience pain with the way things are. But any solution, any new way of doing something, is going to carry pain with it as well. It carries the pain of the unfamiliar, disloyalty to the familiar, and its own special difficulties as well. Nothing's perfect. We don't change or don't adopt solutions as long as our survival wiring perceives the pain of the solution could be more than the pain of our problem. And despite people saying they know the pain of their problem is worse than the pain of the potential solution, don't you believe it for a minute. If that were really the case, they would change automatically, it wouldn't be an issue. When the pain of the problem exceeds the pain of the solution, people change. Period.

It's easy to see this process when you look at an extreme situation. Giving away your money to someone you don't want to give your money to is painful. But if someone held a gun to your head and said, "Give me your money or I'll kill you," you'd most likely be willing to give your money to them.

Your psyche has little trouble weighing these options and choosing the one with the least potential for pain. The reason this is hard to see on a smaller scale, when you have a problem you can't seem to solve, is that you're focused on the pain of the problem, but your psyche is focused on survival, and the cost of changing and adopting a new way of doing things. So you're doing one thing (wanting to change) while your survival wiring is doing another (hanging onto the problem because the alternative looks worse).

Remember, everything we do is felt by our wiring to serve some kind of survival function, and just because we call something a problem doesn't necessarily make it any less valuable to our survival wiring. Survival wiring doesn't care whether you like it or feel happy. Survival wiring is designed to override you and your emotions and to do what it looks like will work. And because you've made it this long doing things this way, survival wiring takes that as a very good recommendation for the status-quo.

The good thing about this particular change process, though, is that it can happen naturally, without outside intervention. It often happens if you give something enough time, as when people get "fed up" with something or "get tired" of something going on. In fact, this process is the one that underlies a lot of change in human beings, and is a reliable process; it works well when it works.

The bad thing about this process is it's unpredictable. There's no way to tell if it's ever going to happen by itself or not. If it does, great, but if it doesn't, then change doesn't happen. Many people have a high tolerance for pain, and it can take an ungodly amount of pain to exceed the cost of changing. This is especially true for people who grew up in painful, dysfunctional families. They're so immune they can tolerate a tremendous amount before their survival wiring says "ouch" loud enough to make the pain of changing worth its while. So for them, waiting for this process to kick in can take a lifetime. That can be a problem.

A "Transformational" Experience

A transformational experience is one so strong, deep, and contrary to one's current functioning it produces changes in how the person functions. The essential characteristic of transformational experiences is they're severe survival threats that are out of the person's control. They're experiences that challenge the very tenets of what someone bases their life on. Because the person experiences a threat to their survival and has no control over it, the connection between survival wiring and their "usual" responses is severed. Given this new experience, those old responses no longer work. They no longer are experienced by biology as effective survival methods. Because of this, the psyche says, "Gosh, those responses are failures, forget them" and opens the door to new ones.

Perhaps the most dramatic example of a transformational experience written about in recent years is called a near-death experience (NDE). Literally hundreds of reports have demonstrated that when someone has an NDE and experiences the now-familiar elements of the tunnel, light, and beings of light talking to them, they're "different" when they return. Several authors have documented the validity of this change in people, even in children. While there's continuing debate over the nature of these episodes, whether they're spiritual or biological, there's no argument about the transforming quality.

Another example of transformational experience is "conversion." I went to college in the time of the "Jesus freaks" and there was no doubt that people who suddenly "got Jesus," as a roommate of mine did, were suddenly transformed. Whether the changes in the people were good or bad was often a matter of opinion, but the fact they changed dramatically wasn't. For better or worse, no one would argue this conversion experience wasn't transformational.

People who are victims of crimes are often transformed by the experience. Their survival is in danger during the crime, and they come away from the event different than they were before. Maybe the difference isn't so good, maybe they feel that they can never trust anyone again, but they're nevertheless transformed. They're changed. Similarly, Vietnam was a transformational experience for many people. It also didn't generally produce positive changes, but it did produce changes. Other events that can be transformational are natural disasters, the death of a loved one, the breakup of a marriage or relationship, or the birth of a child. All threaten survival wiring, all make previous survival reactions powerless to control the experience and all disconnect reactions from survival wiring.

The good part about transformational events is they can produce change nearly instantaneously. People get sudden insights, and experience a newness in very short order. There isn't necessarily a lot of work or effort on the part of the person changing.

The bad part about transformational events is they are, by their very nature, threatening and dangerous. They're experiences which directly confront, and directly threaten, survival wiring. When they threaten physical survival, such as in a crime or disaster, people can get hurt or die. When they threaten conceptual survival, such as in a broken marriage or the death of a loved one, they can damage someone's identity and result in serious depression or other psychological symptoms. In addition, the nature of the transformation isn't always predictable or necessarily what you might consider to be "good." So they're tricky things to mess around with.

This is why most transformational events occur by accident. They aren't things easily "set up" for people. There are a few ways to set them up on purpose, but it's risky. I've seen some assaultive and threatening seminars (such as the "Scared Straight" seminars put on by the lifers in prison for young offenders), ropes courses where participants jump around on the top of tall telephone poles, and wilderness survival courses where members must survive without the use of familiar methods used as transformational events. Zen masters are said to be able to set up transformational events for monks. All of these can be valuable, I think, but there has to be caution applied as well, because you have to be willing to have your basic identity confronted. That can be extremely unsettling.

Targeted, Ongoing, Outside Intervention

There's a serious glitch in the philosophy that underlies many self-help books. Helping yourself through a book relies on the conceptual assumption there's more than one of you inside. One of the "you's" is having trouble and doing things that don't work, believing things that aren't helpful; the other "you" is clear and can read a book and apply the principles to the one having trouble. If that weren't the case, then it would be the troubled one reading the book, and trying to apply it. Clearly, that wouldn't work, because in that case the troubled one would have the trouble get in the way of applying the book.

The concept that there are two of us inside is supported by our ability to talk about and think about "ourselves" as if we are two people. We can observe ourselves, even shake our heads at ourselves, so it sure seems there are two of us.

But there's bad news about this. It's an illusion. There's really only one of you in there, and the idea there's a "you" that can act as an independent agent on "yourself," independent of the contaminating influence of the "you" that's troubled, is all an illusion created with concepts. The truth is you're connected inside by a large, overriding monolithic entity called survival wiring, and that it affects the rational one in you just like it affects the troubled one.

When you read a self-help book, the very part of you causing the problem or difficulty in your life is the same part that reads the book. There's no uncontaminated part of you that can read the book and use the data in it independent of the forces causing the problem in your life. Instead, your survival wiring, which is the basis for the problem in the first place, reads the book and applies it. And you know what that means—it interprets the book consistent with what you're already doing. An aggressive person reads a book on assertiveness and says, "See, I'm doing the right thing." A shy, guilty person reads the same book and says, "Gee, I feel guilty that I'm not like that." Each usually comes away with what they already had, just more of it.

The only thing that can really confront survival wiring is something outside of itself, something functional according to different principles than your own survival wiring, and can confront your survival wiring. This is called another person.

This is the final nail in the coffin of the "You can't change anybody but yourself" philosophy. The truth is it's very, very unlikely you can change yourself. Other people are almost always required in changing. It's easier for someone else to help change you, because that person isn't debilitated where you are, and can operate independently of your survival wiring and get you to do things you can't already do. That's also why therapists don't have to be perfect to be able to help you. All they need is to not have glitches in the same area as you.

There are many examples of people who are outside interveners. Therapists and consultants are the most obvious examples: both are outsiders; a therapist is essentially a stranger to you, and a consultant isn't a staff member. When I come into an organization as a consultant, my power is that I've no axe to grind, no political connections to preserve, no job to save, no ulterior motive beyond doing my job. As a result, I'm a more credible entity than an insider who is concerned for the safety of their position. I can tell the boss things the employees have been saying for a year, and I can get listened to when they haven't.

Similarly, I can tell a spouse something that their mate has been saying to them for years that they have been able to discard or write-off. But they have no such ability to write me off, because I'm not biased. I'm an outsider who has only known them a few hours. So if my observations happen to validate their spouse's observations, it's pretty powerful feedback.

But therapists and consultants are only a couple of the more obvious change agents. There are many others. Coaches are another good example. Have you ever wondered why athletes who are the best in the world at what they do, who are more skilled than anyone else, have coaches? If they're the best, why do they need someone else to tell them what to do? Of what earthly value to them is someone who isn't as talented? The coach is an outsider, who looks at them with an eye not altered by their own survival wiring. A coach doesn't care that the change they're telling the athletes to make is one that feels "wrong." They can see it's needed, and this kind of "seeing" can only come from outside. Coaches can also push athletes harder than they can push themselves. The athletes' survival wiring may say, "This is as far as I can push," but the coach can get them to push farther still. Teachers and trainers are other examples of outsiders whose job is to change someone else.

The good thing about this particular process of change is that it can be set up to happen on purpose. It can occur without waiting for someone to get fed up or for the accidental transformational experience to occur. It can also be more readily tailored to someone's tolerance and needs.

The bad thing about outside intervention is that it usually is a more gradual process than a transforming event or the experience of being fed up. It can take time, sometimes a lot of time. In addition, finding someone who is skilled as an outside intervention-ist can be tricky as well. There are lots and lots of people who call themselves therapists, consultants, coaches and teachers, and while some of them are good, others of them are doing what they're doing in order to avoid their own problems. Some are even outright crazy. It can be difficult to tell the good from the bad. So finding someone who knows what they're doing is a tough part of this process. The other bad part is when you do find them, they're likely to be expensive.

In addition to the three change processes, there are other principles to keep in mind as well:

Change Methodology Is Often Counter-Intuitive

Changing people isn't like changing your clothes, where the steps you take and the behaviors you perform proceed logically, rationally, in order. The interior of the human landscape isn't run by logic and rationality. It's often filled with irony and paradox. It's like the difference between Newtonian physics and Einstein's physics, when you try to change someone, the shortest point between what they're doing now and what you want them to do may not be a straight line. You may have to do things that seem illogical and may even seem to prevent from changing, sanctioning what they're already doing. You may have to find positive things to praise in the functioning you don't like, and reasons why they shouldn't change or shouldn't do what you want them to do. Stuff that's going to sound crazy to you on the surface, if you just look at logic.

If changing other people worked according to simple logic, the world would work very differently from how it does now. First, changing people would be easy. Second, no one would do unpleasant things for long. But the world doesn't work like that because when you deal with people you're not dealing with passive physical objects, rather with active human beings with an internal, self-correcting, tenacious process called survival wiring.

Psychotherapy is a good example of the counter-intuitive nature of a change process. It's a tool for change, and yet I've often thought how stupid it is when it's described in literal terms. A person comes to the office of a virtual stranger for an hour conversation once a week, and then goes and lives their life. That's what produces changes in someone's life? Why in the world should that work? It seems nonsensical, stupid, and yet, in a surprising number of cases, it does work. It does help.

So the actual methods and procedures that may need to be used in changing someone may be entirely counter-intuitive. You may have to suspend judgment to learn to be creative and to appreciate the illogical and the paradoxical.

Resistance to Change Is Variable and Unpredictable

How difficult or easy it is to change varies not only from person to person but also from function to function within people. It all depends on how deeply rooted into survival wiring any particular function is, and how escalated the issues of survival are in any particular person. Some functions, what I call character functions, are so basic and fundamental to survival wiring they contain identity and one's sense of existence. As a result, trying to change characterological attributes requires a tremendous, almost superhuman amount of effort, force, and time. Character is awesomely resistive to change, and isn't something we're very good at yet. Addressing character touches someone's very existence, so their psyche will fight you to the metaphorical, and sometimes literal, death. If you take on an attempt to change character, you're taking on a task much larger than sending a space ship to Mars. I would advise against it. If you don't like "who someone is," there's not much you'll be able to do about it.

The reason for this is character is the way someone "is" as opposed to what they "do". What someone is and what they do are certainly connected, but there's a sense of someone being some way that's distinct from any one specific set of behaviors. It's unlikely that you're going to have the power to be able to change character, or the fundamental way someone "is." It's rare, for example, that a strongly introverted person is going to be changed into a strongly extroverted person. They may demonstrate more extroverted behaviors, but their natural inclination is likely to remain introversion. They'll be an introvert behaving in an extroverted manner. Similarly, aggressive people or passive people, laid-back people, or hyper people, are probably always going to have that quality of "being" in the background of their behavior no matter what happens to them. Character changes are simply unrealistic most times.

However, character changes aren't necessarily required in order for you to accomplish desirable changes. Other functions and behaviors aren't so deeply rooted in survival wiring and are more amenable to change. They may be more attached to the pleasure end of the survival spectrum, or less fundamental to identity, or more controlled by social factors. So they may be subservient to other functions that survival wiring considers to be more necessary, and can be replaced with other functions more easily. Specific behaviors and more narrowly defined interpersonal patterns, for example, can often be affected by change techniques.

Changing Someone Is Almost Always a Messy Process

Because change upsets the apple cart of survival wiring, it always produces some kind of chaos, some kind of side-effect. These can be upset, confusion, irritation, distance, or any number of other things. Even rats can behave strangely for a while when experimenters alter their behavior. They can start to urinate a lot (a sign of anxiety), get agitated and run around, sleep more, or do other such strange things when change techniques are applied.

Changing someone also can have one particular side-effect that I want to focus on specifically. For a while, at least, after the change techniques are started, behavior can actually get worse instead of better. Change doesn't occur in a straight line.

I talked about this phenomenon in the section on extinction. Remember how the rat who stops getting food for pressing a bar first increases the times he presses the bar. This phenomenon is a common reason for failure in attempts to change other people, because it looks like what you're doing isn't working, that it's going backwards, making things worse. So people often abandon their attempts at this point. Unfortunately, the increase in the undesired behavior can indicate that the change techniques are actually being successful and you're having an effect. But it's difficult to tell when this is the case or when you're really doing something that's making things worse.

Changing someone also has dangers that go beyond just being messy. Trying to change someone can produce serious damage to one's relationship with the person you're trying to change. Sometimes it can produce permanent damage. Some distance is often required to apply change techniques, and if you're in an intimate relationship with that person, the distance required may cause trouble all by itself. Second, there can be an angry backlash against the person trying to produce the change. This is the reason that change agents are usually outsiders. And, finally, what you want changed in the other person may or may not be in their best interest, and if it's not you've no business trying to change them.

A woman I was seeing as a client decided to start changing her husband to get him to handle some tasks she had been doing but she wanted him to do. She decided to start with laundry, specifically his shirts. She stated she wanted him to take them to the laundry himself, instead of her washing and ironing them. Of course, her doing his shirts had great conceptual survival value to him, even though it was, physically, a relatively small matter. He eventually took the shirts to the laundry himself, but he also had a series of world-class temper tantrums that were awesome to behold. His wife had to be prepared to handle these, understand where they came from, and watch their course. It was very difficult for her.

In addition, there's danger because changing someone else is difficult and can take a long time and a lot of energy. You can get tired out and bogged down in it. The danger is that it can become a quagmire for you, costing much more than it's worth, and sinking you into a pit.

In any case, there's always some cost to the one who is the agent of change. Remember how I've said therapists have shortened life spans and high rates of suicide and divorce? If you decide to try to change someone, be prepared for the costs to you. If you're involved with the person, part of their everyday life, not only can there be a backlash, but to produce the changes you may first have to produce changes in you. These will be the behaviors in you that produce the changes in them. In this circumstance you're likely to have to face your own unwitting participation in the very thing you want changed, and confront your perhaps unwitting resistance to the change yourself. Remember, it goes for you, too, the pain of the solution has to be less than the pain of the problem for you to change, even if your change is going to produce change in someone else.

If you're not regularly involved in a relationship with someone you're trying to change, you still pay a price because you're going to have limited power. There may be no reason why the person should change in response to you because you're not wired into their survival wiring. Therapists and consultants, for example, have no "real" power to make anyone change. If I tell someone to do something different, they can say, "Go to hell" and I can't really do a thing about it. As a result, therapists and consultants rely almost exclusively on the power of social status and their credibility as an outsider to have an effect on people. People take therapists seriously for the same reason they took witch doctors seriously in primitive society; they have socially sanctioned credibility, and no particular reason to lie. That's why I can say exactly the same thing to someone that their spouse has been saying for years, and even though I've no real authority, I can get changes where they can't.

But the downside is if the person thumbs their nose at me, the evidence of no real power becomes evident. So I'm always at risk of being dismissed, of being made wrong. And you know how much human beings like that. That's one of the risks of a change agent.

Trying to change someone also goes directly against what produces intimacy and closeness. The change may be part of trying to resolve a conflict or problem in the way of closeness, but the actual methods of change can trigger survival wiring rather than calm it down, as the techniques for intimacy are designed to do.

And, finally, in trying to change someone there's always the very real danger of failure. In some ways it's a lot easier and safer to protest and resist someone than it is to really try to change what they're doing. By protesting and resisting, you don't have the danger of failure. Instead, you get the sweet benefit of being a self-righteous victim and just tell the world how you're being mistreated. That sounds nasty when stated bluntly, but it doesn't feel nasty when it's being done. It feels inviting, safe, and secure.

But if you give this up to change someone, what happens if you find out you can't do it? What happens is you're stuck, face-to-face with reality, and the realization that it can't be done. It can be a troublesome spot to find oneself in, and the danger of realizing that change isn't going to occur is why many people shy away from really trying.

There Are No Guarantees

I know I keep repeating this, but it can't be overstated; when it comes to dealing with people there are no certainties, no guarantees. With as much as we know about how and why people function the way they do, there are still so many variables, and possibilities, so much unknown brain wiring, that consistent and accurate predictions are impossible. Sometimes I can predict what someone is going to do or say with such accuracy and specificity people think I'm clairvoyant. Other times I'm so wrong and off the mark I feel totally stupid. And there isn't even a reliable way to discriminate between the times when I'm likely to be right and when I'm likely to be off-base.

Nowhere is this uncertainty greater than when it comes to trying to change someone. You may do one little thing, maybe even a paradoxical intervention of giving up trying to change them, and you get the change you want. Other times you may try everything you know to do, and you still can't produce the change you're looking for. You may get all these strange side effects and make a big mess. You may get nothing at all, no effect in any way. And it's virtually impossible to tell which of these is going to happen.

Because of this it's very important that if you decide to take on the task of changing someone you carefully weigh the potential risks and benefits to both you and the person you're trying to change. Don't take the task lightly. Ask yourself what the outcome will be if you fail. Will your relationship survive? Will you want it to? Are you willing to face failure or find out the whole thing is unworkable? Be careful. You don't want to harm or disable yourself or someone else. So if you're thinking of trying to change someone, consider the possibility of approaching the issue as a conflict between you and that person using a conflict resolution technology. Or think of it as an action you want to get to happen, and try the techniques for getting action. Think through your options carefully before you set out to try to change someone.

Practical Principles of Changing People

Try Everything Else Before Trying to Change Someone

I talked about this at the end of the previous list of principles. Changing someone is so difficult it's worth your while to see if you can use another people-handling technology to deal with the issue before you go into an attempt to change someone. Maybe you can define the problem as a disagreement and seek to resolve it using resolution technologies. Maybe you can use the techniques for getting action with the person. Or perhaps there's a way for you to maintain your relationship with the person but to be able to separate from the part that's a problem for you. Possibly you can let go of your desire that the person be different, accept them as they are. In any case, explore your options first, so if you do decide to undertake trying to change someone you're certain it's your best option.

If Possible, Get Their Agreement to Change

It's possible to do things that change what people do without their conscious involvement, but it's best if you and the other person can work together on the changes. If you do talk to them about this, don't be hypocritical or try to sugar-coat your intention. People who say, "We both need to make some changes," without being able to define true changes they need to make, are just trying to soften their statement of wanting the other person to change and are as transparent as glass. It tends to set off other people's survival reactions. Certainly using positive communication behaviors, and non-inflammatory sensory terminology is helpful to not stir up survival wiring when you talk to someone about changing, but don't say things that aren't true. Don't say, "I want us to not have such miscommunications" when you're really wanting them to stop yelling at you. Similarly, "I want you to stop acting like such an ass" probably won't be helpful, either. "I want you to stop yelling at me" might be more along the lines of what you're looking for.

If the person is agreeable to work on changing, maybe you can work together on a plan of action to produce and maintain the change. That would be the best of the options. You might even use the negotiations technologies described in the chapters on conflict and intimacy to work on this. Even with an agreement for change there will still be resistance in the other person's survival wiring, of course, but you'll have more power with two of you working on it together. And, perhaps most importantly, there may be fewer side-effects and dangers to you and your relationship if there's agreement.

Of course, sometimes such agreement isn't possible. Maybe your relationship with the person isn't close enough to make such a conversation appropriate. I mentioned earlier how I once altered the behavior of a colleague of mine regarding how he talked with me. Our relationship was such that trying to get them to agree to change would have been way overstepping my boundaries. But he drove me crazy at lunch, and I wanted to change that behavior. At times people may have survival reactions to such a conversation, so agreement won't be possible. Because relationships and situations vary greatly, you'll have to determine this for yourself in the circumstances you find yourself. But make no mistake, if it's possible, it's best to have them work with you on the changes.

Admit to Yourself that You're Out to Change Someone

I'm always amazed when I point out that someone is trying to change someone else they almost always shoot back, "No I'm not!" as if they feel it's wrong. It's not. If you're trying to change someone, admit this is what you're up to. Don't lie to yourself about it. Instead, take it on consciously and intentionally as a task. Changing someone is hard enough to do even when you're very good and very intentional about it, and it's virtually impossible if you do it haphazardly, without admitting to yourself that it's what you're doing.

If you don't feel good about intentionally, consciously trying to change something in someone, then it may be better you not do it at all. Or if you don't think you can do it without causing damage or hurting yourself or someone else, don't do it. If this is the case, your survival wiring will sabotage you. Don't set yourself up for regret over causing worse problems. But if you do decide to do it, do it on purpose. Plan it, carry it out, and evaluate the results.

Define Your Limits

Trying to change someone is going to have some side-effects. There's going to be some kind of chaos, upset, or trouble caused by the attempt, or what you're trying to change may even worsen temporarily. It's also going to take time, energy, and effort on your part. So you need to decide, before you start the project, how many of these difficulties and demands you're willing to tolerate and you think appropriate. Your decision is going to depend on the severity and cost of the problem, your own and the other person's safety, health, well-being, and emotional condition. If they get mad at you during the change attempt, how long are you willing to tolerate their anger? How much anger are you willing to tolerate? If they might leave you over your attempts, are you willing to face that possibility? Don't do anything that's going to harm or damage anyone—them or you.

There's no possible way I can define or identify every possible pitfall, problem and demand that could crop up in your attempt, so know that you're going to have to think about it and decide for yourself. You may face things that I haven't thought of here, and only you can decide specifically and realistically what your limits are and should be. So don't ignore this issue. Think carefully about it. Be responsible about it. If in doubt, consult a professional to get some advice before you do anything.

Be Specific About What You're Trying to Change

Changing someone's character or changing someone's mind aren't specific enough goals. In general, the more specific and precise you are about what it is you're trying to change in someone, the better your odds of being able to pull it off. Wanting someone to just be different is unlikely to produce much ability on your part to apply change techniques and evaluate their success. The more specific you are, the better, and this usually means stating the change in sensory terms. This means identifying things you can see and hear as the things you want to change. Forget about "attitude" or "mind" and concentrate on behavior. It's easier to change things you can see and hear than things you conceptualize. You may still be changing an attitude, but the only way you can probably do that is to work on the behaviors the person uses to express the attitude.

You also need to specify whether you're trying to change what they're doing right now, or are you wanting to produce an ongoing, enduring change? I'm talking in this chapter as if you're trying to change a pattern, but sometimes you might just want to produce a change in what they're doing now, in this situation, like if someone is acting badly at a party.

I also previously mentioned the time I was at a tennis match where the man in front of me was occasionally yelling out obnoxious things, and agitating a lot of people. I decided I wanted to change his behavior right then, I didn't care if he was a jerk when he got home. If I lived with him, I might have wanted to produce an ongoing change in his behavior, more of a change in pattern.

Choose Your Change Technology Consciously

If you don't choose your techniques with conscious awareness, your survival wiring will choose them for you, and that means you may become part of the system that maintains the status quo rather than producing change. If you're involved in an ongoing relationship with the person you're trying to change, your survival wiring has probably already been choosing how you're dealing with them, which means your use of knee-jerk, automatic behaviors will continue to produce what you're already getting. So be conscious and aware of the techniques you're using.

Remember, too, because your current behavior may be run by survival wiring, it's likely to feel natural, while adopting effective change-inducing behaviors will likely feel unnatural. In fact, change behaviors may be strongly counter-intuitive and thus feel very strange to you. If that's not OK with you, or you can't do it with integrity, then you might need to stop trying to change the person and look for another way to achieve your goal.

Set a Time Limit

This is very important. Remember how I talked about therapists using the "You can't change anyone but yourself" line to get people to give up their nonproductive, symptom-producing attempts to change people? Most of the time these clients had been trying to change someone (although, in truth, it was usually protesting against them) for years, making themselves miserable in the process. They were playing a losing game, and didn't know when to stop. Their lives became a losing game. Know how long you're willing to give your attempt.

There needs to be a reasonable period of time for you to see if you can produce the changes you want, and if it looks like you can't produce them, you need to stop, rethink, and regroup. This will keep you out of quagmires. It will also keep you out of offices where therapists are saying you can't change anyone but yourself.

Be Prepared for the Ups and Downs

Remember the road to change of any sort isn't straight. It moves in various fits and starts, progressing and regressing. As I've noted before, there may even be temporary worsening of what you're wanting to change. Be ready for this stuff, determine ahead of time that the side-effects will be manageable and not damaging, or don't start the attempt.

Be Prepared to Admit Success or Failure

I have a relative who some years ago got a car stereo with a digital tuning dial on it. He said he loved the digital readout, because of the clarity it offered. "When you tune in a station," he said, "it's either there or it isn't." The digital readout left no uncertainty about the matter so there was no time lost in confusion over what was going on. If there was a station there, fine. If there wasn't, then the answer was clear and it was time to move on to another station.

Many times people are so afraid of failure they set things up so they don't know if they've succeeded or failed. Don't do that. Instead, examine your results, look at your progress in producing the change. Both success and failure move you forward. The only real failure isn't, as the saying goes, "stopping trying." There are losing games that you should stop trying to win. The only real failure is uncertainty whether you've succeeded or failed. It's this uncertainty that gets you stuck. It puts you into an unwinnable spot. Any good scientist will tell you all experiments are a "success" that give clear results, whatever the results are. The only failed experiments are those that don't give a clear answer. So set it up to get yourself a clear answer, even if it isn't the one you want.

Techniques for Changing People

Unlike previous chapters, where for a particular purpose some people-handling techniques were usually appropriate and some not in trying to change someone, virtually all of the people-handling techniques are potentially useful. In changing people you need all of the tools you can get. With intimacy, for example, escalations are generally not useful. But escalations might very well be useful in trying to change someone. For fight technology, positive communication behaviors are generally not useful. But for changing people, they may be quite useful.

In my work as a change agent, I use all kinds of different behaviors and techniques. If you were to observe me during an average week you would find that I behaved quite differently depending on who I was with and the changes that were trying to be produced. So any of the people-handling techniques we've discussed are fair game. However, I'm not going to present all of the people-handling techniques in terms of changing people. That would produce several books all by itself. Instead, I'm going to talk about the most useful techniques, and hopefully not only will that be useful for you, but it will also trigger your own thinking so you can see where other people-handling techniques could be useful as well.

Jennifer

In order to apply the techniques to changing people in some sort of understandable, organized fashion, I'm going to take the example of Jennifer, a woman dealing with her middle-aged mother. I will then present the way in which different people -handling techniques can be applied according to the three change processes I presented previously.

Jennifer and Her Mother

Jennifer is a woman in her early thirties, single, with a mother in her early sixties. Her father died some years ago. Jennifer's mother lives alone. Jennifer is the only offspring living in the same town with her mother.

Jennifer's mother has a disease that has impaired her vision. She can still see to read and to get around, using very thick glasses, but she is unable to drive. In addition, she has several other medical conditions, which require her to see physicians fairly frequently.

Jennifer reports her mother "drives her crazy" and that she gets mad and snaps at her, then feels guilty for doing this. As a result, she goes though lots of private emotional upset in dealing with her mother. She experiences the contradictory feelings of not wanting to hurt her mother, and wanting to strangle her (metaphorically speaking) at the same time.

Jennifer has tried everything she can think of to give up her upset, all to no avail. She has decided she would like to change her mother so she doesn't drive her crazy so much. She has tried talking to her mother about some of the things that bother her, but her mother either denies she is doing what Jennifer says, or she retreats into angry, hurt silence, with Jennifer feeling guilty and angry.

When pressed to get specific on what she would like to change, Jennifer says that while there are "tons of things" that are difficult for her, one thing that "really gets to her" is that her mother complains and whines that Jennifer doesn't do enough for her, even though Jennifer is the only offspring available to help her. As a result she feels she does a lot to help her. She routinely takes her to the doctor several times a month, and helps out in a variety of other ways as well. Often her mother's whining and complaining takes place during their car trips to the doctor and, to make it worse, Jennifer's mother criticizes Jennifer's driving during these trips as well.

Jennifer doesn't feel her mother is feeble and so would be harmed by Jennifer trying to change her. To the contrary, Jennifer's mother seems quite strong-willed and resilient. Jennifer is "at her wits' end" in figuring out what to do, and she has been using the protest behavior of angry silence during the car rides. But this makes her feel bad, too, so she feels OK giving this up. She has tried to grin and bear it, but still finds herself angry and acting in hostile ways. Jennifer feels she has built up such a feeling of aversion to the whole issue she considers it unlikely that a worsening of the relationship through making change attempts is going to be a problem for her or her mother. As it is she can barely stand to be civil to her mother.

Her first target is the whining, complaining, and criticizing her mother does during the car trips to the physicians. The first principle guiding her approach will be the pain of the problem exceeding the pain of the solution.

The first change process Jennifer could use involves increasing the level of discomfort present in the functions she wants to change, while decreasing the level of discomfort connected with new functions that are OK with her. If Jennifer decided to use this method of change, there are several techniques that can help to accomplish this:

First, she would need to do things that increased the discomfort her mother felt when she complained or criticized her driving.

1. *Negative communication behaviors.* These are commonly used between people, but they rarely result in changes in the other person. This isn't because they're necessarily an inappropriate technique, but because they end up as part of negative reciprocity rather than a focused technique designed to change someone's behavior. When used on purpose, with awareness, and as part of an overall change plan, they can be an effective technique.

   If Jennifer were to use negative communication behaviors regarding criticizing her driving and whining about how Jennifer doesn't do enough for her, the first thing she could do is to interrupt her mother every time she started whining or criticizing. Interrupting is a negative communication behavior. She could talk right over her mother, changing the subject or talking about something irrelevant. It doesn't matter what she talked about, because interruption itself is the negative communication behavior. This is also a form of pattern interruption. Jennifer could interrupt in a cheerful or "distracted" manner, so it doesn't seem hostile or angry. The important thing is that it interrupt her mother's whining behavior.

   Jennifer could use a harsh tone of voice, even raise her voice a little, when talking to her mother during her mother's whining and complaining jags. She could also glare or refuse to look at her at all. She could also be quiet for a few seconds before answering, using the "long latency of responding" talked about in the section on negative communication behaviors. Finally, the use of nonverbal negative communication behaviors, rolling her eyes, sighing heavily, or looking at her mother with a shocked expression of confusion and disbelief are possible.

Understand that these behaviors are done specifically, as a way of increasing discomfort during the whining and complaining. They are done differently than if they were done in protest or to display displeasure. Jennifer doesn't need to care whether her mother knows she is doing these things in response to her whining and complaining, it's not a communication of information. They're designed to make those periods uncomfortable, so are done only during the mother's complaining or criticizing. If her mother switches to another topic after one sentence, Jennifer switches her behavior, too. She doesn't continue to "punish" her mother after she has stopped generating the complaining behavior.

Jennifer would need to do these behaviors every time her mother started to criticize or whine, so she would begin to consistently feel uncomfortable during her whining and complaining.

As part of the negative communication behaviors Jennifer might want to use conceptual language, because it has the good/bad, right/wrong quality imbedded in it. Using that, she could increase discomfort by using words with a negative emotional loading on them. She could be direct in responding to her mother, saying, "Mother, you're talking crazy," or "You're driving me crazy," or "Stop back-seat driving me." Or, she could talk about something else, but use negatively loaded words that are uncomfortable to listen to. She could suddenly launch into a tirade about other drivers, calling them "Asses, lunatics, idiots" and other highly negatively charged terms. The point is it doesn't matter exactly what she says, or what the topic of conversation is, it's just that the words have a negative loading and are unpleasant to listen to. And, just like with the negative communication behaviors, these words would need to be used every time her mother starts criticizing or whining, and then be stopped at any time she isn't being whining or critical.

2. *Escalation.* If the level of negative communication behavior and conceptual make-wrong isn't working, Jennifer can escalate. In the sensory world she increases the intensity of her negative communication behaviors. She could yell, pound her hand on the steering wheel, and use more angry, harsh tones of voice. She could also get steely in her silence. She can escalate the intensity of her demands that her mother stop criticizing, again, only during her mother's whining and criticizing.

   Jennifer can also escalate in the conceptual world by using words that have an even greater wrong/bad loading. She could tell her mother that she is "acting horrible" or that she is being "abusive" to her only helpful daughter, or that Jennifer is "appalled," "outraged" that her mother would "be so ungrateful, hostile, and mean."

3. *Reframing.* Putting a new label on the behavior gives it a new meaning. This altered meaning can result in the person actively trying to change the behavior because the new meaning makes the behavior less OK with them. If Jennifer wanted to reframe her mother's criticizing and whining, she could expand the frame and conceptualize it as a potentially serious medical problem. "Mother, you know how I've told you to stop whining and criticizing my driving and you say you don't do that? Well, you're doing it again, and I'm aware that people doing things over and over that they don't know they're doing can be the result of a serious psychiatric problem" (this is true, by the way) "and I wonder if you're starting to develop some kind of psychiatric disturbance. I don't think you can tell that you're doing what I asked you to stop doing. I know you love me and wouldn't want to hurt me, and you're hurting me. I'm thinking I need to make an appointment for you with a psychiatrist to get you checked out."

   Jennifer has now reframed her mother's behavior so it takes on the meaning of being "sick" rather than whatever her mother might think it means.

Jennifer could also contract the frame by saying "I know you don't think you whine and criticize with me, but you're doing it again. I've been thinking about it, and maybe what's happening is you don't want me to take you to the doctor. Maybe you feel guilty about my doing so much for you. Maybe you're trying to upset me and make me feel bad is your way of keeping from being appreciative because you feel so bad about how much I put myself out for you. I think maybe you're upset because you can't pay me back for all I do for you, so you try to make it seem less than it is."

This reframes the behavior as an avoidance of being appreciative and appropriately grateful. Then Jennifer has license to respond to her mother's criticism with something completely different, like "It's OK, mother, I know you appreciate what I do for you. You don't have to feel guilty." That might throw the mother's motivation to criticize and whine into a tailspin.

This frame, by the way, offers a perfect opening for hammering home a change instruction, because her mother might very well say "Why, I'm not trying to make you feel bad, Jennifer!" To this, Jennifer can say "Great! I'm glad. So let me tell you how to not make me feel bad. Don't complain that I don't do enough for you, and don't criticize my driving. Then you won't make me feel bad." This puts her mother in a double bind—she has to do what Jennifer tells her to do to support her own interpretation of her behavior. Otherwise, she's being inconsistent with herself.

While I present these reframes as examples, remember you have to use a frame that you see as valid and offers you increased ability to effect change in the meaning of the behavior. If you see the ones I've presented as invalid and as manipulative, remember I'm presenting them with the assumption that Jennifer has some Cognitive Diversity and can see them as valid.

Remember, reframing is best done with positive communication behaviors. You have to really mean it, and it has to be done graciously and kindly. It must not be a disguised way for you to make them wrong. In this example, it's designed to increase the discomfort of the behaviors Jennifer is trying to change, but the discomfort is increased through meaning, not communication behaviors. In this way, any wrongness that produces discomfort must come from the tension between the behavior and its meaning for her mother, not from her. It's the internal conflict which produces the discomfort that's part of the change process. If you just make their behavior mean they're wrong because you think it's wrong, you're escalating in the conceptual world, not reframing.

This is why a spouse can get so angry when their partner tells them they're being just like their mother (or father), even if it's true. They respond in an angry way, rather than by changing because you tell them in a way that makes them directly wrong. You can't tell them they're wrong in reframing, the frame has to mean to them that they're wrong. You have to be neutral, allowing the meaning to do the work of increasing their discomfort.

4. *Metaphors*. Jennifer could use metaphors to get through to her mother. Let's say her mother had been a nurse by training. Jennifer could use medical analogies. She could say, "Mother, I don't want to treat you like a child, but I have to give you another dose of reality here. You're making me sick with your whining and criticism of me. You're going to have to get cured of this, and quick, like right now, STAT. Follow my orders and discontinue it now."

    She could also use representational matching, using visual, auditory, or tactile words, depending on her mother's preferred way of representing the world. Because her mother has a vision problem we could guess she probably should use auditory or tactile, but we don't really know from the information in this example. In any case, she can say "Mother, do you hear what I'm saying," or "Mother, can you see what I mean?"

5. *Pattern Interrupts*. This is a powerful one, but it requires Jennifer be willing to be dramatic and even perhaps a bit bizarre because she'll need to generate behaviors that are completely contrary to the conversation and the manner in which it's occurring. By using a pattern interrupt, Jennifer would do something, anything, that interrupts her mother's

pattern of whining and complaining any time she starts doing it. Remember my stillness and silence in the yogurt shop?

When her mother starts to complain, Jennifer could suddenly start to cough or choke, sing, or suddenly start talking about something completely irrelevant, maybe gruesome or unpleasant. It could just as easily be something pleasant, but completely irrelevant. Whatever she does, it must interrupt the pattern of her mother's complaining, it must interrupt every time her mother begins whining or criticizing. I would recommend the use of a variety of pattern interrupts.

I've actually recommended a dramatic pattern interrupt when people are driving. I've recommended people immediately pull over to the side of the road, or into a parking lot, slowly put the car in park, and turn off the motor. Then they get out of the car, go around to the passenger's side, open the door, and start a short, reasonably pleasant conversation about the need for the person to change their behavior. I've even recommended on occasion that the person start a conversation about some irrelevant matter, but this is very bizarre, and you have to be willing to allow that person to think you're crazy. But it can be very effective.

The point of all of this isn't to be ugly or threatening, but to be strange, to suddenly exhibit behavior that's out-of-place so the pattern of conversation is completely disrupted. Remember, other's behaviors can use your behavior as part of the pattern in order to continue, so your behavior has to be something that isn't in any of the scripts for their behavior. This creates a major stir in the other person's survival wiring.

I've recommended similar things regarding problems while talking on the phone: coughing, sneezing loudly, holding down one of the touch-tone keys for a few seconds so a tone is produced, dropping the phone, or starting to gag. They can suddenly ask if the other person has heard a particular song on the radio lately. They could suddenly scream, "What was that!" and say they'll be right back. Then they can return and apologize, noting that everything was OK.

Pattern interrupts have to be surprising, nonsensical, and not done as an escalation of negative communication behaviors. Like reframing, if done as negative communication behaviors, they're an escalation, not a pattern interrupt, and they don't work the same as a pattern interrupt. Because pattern interrupts have to be a little strange or unexpected to the other person, they can actually be kind of fun. Jennifer could even learn to play with her mother, breaking into song when her mother started whining or criticizing, and exhorting her mother to join in. She could scream, "Get down!" and then, like James Brown, start to act like a rock and roll singer.

But remember, pattern interrupts, like most any change technique, have to be done over and over several times to break up the pattern of the other person's behavior. They really work. You can see people starting their old behavior and then getting "derailed" after a couple of seconds once you've interrupted the pattern often enough.

6. *Feelings transfers.* Jennifer could perform whatever behaviors would make her mother feel bad while her mother was criticizing or complaining. She could tear up, or get silent and sulky. She could also transfer positive feelings when her mother wasn't whining and complaining.

7. *Making the covert overt.* Jennifer could just say, bluntly, what her mother is implying through her whining and complaining. "You think I'm a lousy driver. You think I don't do enough for you." "You feel like I'm an inadequate daughter." Again, these are best when done with positive communication behaviors, because then it's the bluntness of the message that makes someone feel bad, not your behavior. But this can be difficult, so even if negative communication behaviors are used, making the covert overt can be a useful technique.

The second aspect of this process is to decrease the discomfort of alternate behaviors available to her mother. Often people are unsuccessful in changing other people's behavior because they don't do this step along with the first step. If you just increase the pain of what you want to change, without presenting a more attractive alternative, you'll likely only escalate their survival reaction and their defense of what they're already doing because they don't have another option. You may make them uncomfortable, but you back them into a corner by not letting them have a comfortable way out. So they may feel they have to either escalate in return, or stonewall. You have to provide an alternative that's better for them, than the function you're trying to change.

Most of the methods for making other responses attractive to someone involve conceptual techniques. Those are the ones that alter meaning.

1. *Reframing*. Jennifer could reframe an alternate behavior for her mother intimating the behavior will accomplish what she is trying to accomplish. For example, she could say, "I'm glad you're willing to share your feelings about those things with me because when people are just silent and don't actually say their complaints out loud, it can really make someone uncomfortable." In this way, if Jennifer's mother really is trying to make her uncomfortable, by framing the behavior Jennifer actually wants her mother to generate as the one that will accomplish her goal, she encourages that behavior. She could also tell her how important honesty is between a mother and a daughter, and how that's more significant than any bad things said, that it cancels them out, makes them irrelevant. She's glad for the honesty because that makes bad things that are said meaningless. That frames the mother's criticisms and complaints as useless. The bind this produces is that if she says the complaints, they're not heard as complaints, so she shouldn't say them. Of course, then they're not heard, either, so her ability to complain and criticize is seriously short-circuited either way.

2. *Paradox*. These techniques are extremely counter-intuitive, and address the underlying force of many behaviors as being resistances or desires to upset.

   Jennifer could encourage her mother to say more of her whining and criticizing, thereby taking control of her mother's behavior. This lack of resistance and loss of control will probably make stopping the behavior look mighty attractive. Jennifer could say "You know, mother, I think my getting upset with you for what I'm calling criticizing and whining is stupid. I think you need to express your feelings to me, and I want you to stop holding back. I think you aren't telling me everything. Tell me more." Every time her mother tries to stop whining or criticizing she can say "No, I know there's more, tell me more, there's more, I know there is. I want you to be honest with me."

She could do this over and over, accusing her mother of withholding from her, virtually demanding that her mother criticize, complain, and whine. "Mother, I want this relationship to be honest, now I know you're upset with me, tell me! I know you're feeling bad, so get it off your chest. Don't you trust me with your feelings?" She could start to get mad about her mother's resistance and stubbornness, and demand that she be honest. She could do this until her mother actually starts resisting her own complaining and whining.

This stops Jennifer from being the one trying to control her mother, thus giving her mother the ability to be resistive. Her mother ends up desperately trying to keep from having to whine or criticize. If Jennifer began this routine every time her mother started to complain and criticize, pretty soon her mother very well might start refusing to do so. In fact, Jennifer could actually initiate the conversation every time they got into the car. Then Jennifer could hammer a few extra nails into the coffin of the old behavior by occasionally and spontaneously demanding that her mother tell her criticisms or complaints, that she doesn't want her mother "building up upset inside that's going to be a problem."

If you're out there thinking, "That would never work with the person I'm dealing with, they'd go on forever. I've seen them do it" you're not getting the point. You're probably still resisting them, which is continuing to feed their behavior. In this kind of paradox, you have to not only go along with them, but actually take over control of the behavior, start making them do it. That way, the resistance that may be driving the behavior in the first place starts to demand they stop the behavior. You've turned the world on its head, they're virtually begging to stop doing what you want them to stop doing.

Jennifer could also use paradox by not only agreeing with her mother but by complaining more about herself than her mother does. This has to be done non-sarcastically, for real, and, of course, only if Jennifer can do it through understanding the validity of the complaints from her mother's point of view. She can relate story after story of how awful she feels about how badly she drives. The key is to emphasize how badly she feels about these things she is acknowledging of herself. This takes away the mother's power to upset Jennifer, or even to have her complaints or criticisms matter. Jennifer is already acknowledging them, and far beyond what the mother criticizes. Often this results in the other person emitting empathic, supportive and reassuring responses. It also reveals the deeper truth behind the behavior—Jennifer's mother really was wanting to upset Jennifer, because she can emit kind behaviors when Jennifer demonstrates self-inflicted upset. She can do it so much her mother is never again willing to inflict upset because she's so sensitized to Jennifer's upset.

Jennifer could even act this out some. When her mother criticizes her driving, she could take a wrong turn shortly thereafter. If her mother comments on it, she could get very upset, maybe even to the point of stopping the car she's so upset. She can talk about how awful she feels about how bad a driver she is, etc. etc.

In fact, an unconscious paradox is what is at the basis of many cases of low self-esteem. Growing up someone learned to handle someone by thinking and feeling bad about themselves. Their survival wiring seized on that as a good technique to handle that person; it just went on as a pattern even though that person wasn't in the picture anymore.

Paradoxes are sometimes powerful in their ability to break up patterns as well in addressing and countering the deeper level of motivation generating behaviors in others we don't like. I did this with a woman whose husband called her Stupid during arguments. She wanted him to stop. In a session with both of them present I told her to drool each time her husband called her Stupid. I even gave her a Kleenex and had her practice drooling, and I told her, "Stupid people drool," so she should do that every time.

When they returned for a follow up session, the couple told me how she had not been able to use the method, because he had never even been able to call her Stupid. In fact, he started to a couple of times, and before he could finish the word they both started laughing so hard they couldn't even continue the argument!

You can see many times people use paradoxical technique, but they do it from a negative-communication behavior approach that destroys its paradoxical nature. Paradox must be done sincerely and non angrily. It must not make the other person wrong. Parents who say to their whiny children who don't want to go to school "Fine! Then you can just stay home and rot!" aren't practicing paradox, they're escalating.

Paradox is perhaps the most effective of all change techniques, but it's also perhaps the most difficult, because it's completely counter-intuitive to the apparent level of cause and effect on which the current behaviors are functioning. In order to use paradox, you have to see the deeper truth in the situation; the one that turns the surface logic on its head. If you can't do this, don't use paradox, it won't work. You'll either be using escalated negative communication behaviors (which is OK if that's what you're intending to do) or you're saying things you don't see as having validity, and that's manipulation.

3. *Positive communication behaviors.* While I noted that most of making potential behaviors attractive involves dealing with meaning, it's also possible the person does exhibit the behaviors you want at times. You can increase their attractiveness by using positive communication behaviors when the person does them. When Jennifer's mother happens to talk in a way that's pleasing to Jennifer, Jennifer can use positive communication behaviors in response to reinforce that behavior.

The second change process Jennifer could use would be to instigate a transformational experience for her mother. I don't recommend you try to induce a sensory-world transformational experience. Those involve an actual threat to someone's physical survival, as happens in crimes, natural disasters, or survival courses.

The transformational experience that might be useful, is a conceptual transformation; the transformation of meaning in a deep and profound way. This type involves the use of the techniques having to do with meaning (reframing and paradox) to not only alter the meaning of a behavior in context, but what the behavior means about the person themselves, their identity or their quality.

I've talked about and given examples of these techniques in the previous section, but I'm going to discuss them again here, because this is an extension and a deepening of the technique. In this use you take the meaning further, all the way to it having meaning about the person themselves.

1. *Reframing*. For Jennifer to use reframing transformationally with her mother she has to provide a new meaning about the core nature of her mother, based on the meaning of the behavior Jennifer wants to change. For example, Jennifer could say, "Mother, you know, when I hear you criticize and whine, I feel bad that you're such an unhappy person. I wonder about the pain you've experienced in your life, and how you find the courage to go on. I'm sorry you're so unhappy, and that nothing I can do will help. I wish your life had been different for you."

Essentially, she has said her mother is a miserable person, not just feeling miserable about the thing she's whining about, but more general than that—a miserable person. If her mother rejects that framing of her nature, then she is stuck with a conflict between complaining and criticizing, which show her up to be a miserable person, or giving up her criticizing and complaining so she isn't coming off that way.

Jennifer could also use a reframe by saying, "I guess when you get old everything starts to bother you." This reframes her complaints as the result of being old rather than because there's truth in them. Again, Jennifer's mother has to resist being labeled old by stopping her whining and criticizing, or the subject of the conversation will change. Either way, Jennifer has achieved her goal by transforming the meaning of the behavior as it relates to her mother's self, life, or identity.

2. *Paradox.* In using a paradox, Jennifer could say, "I'm glad you can express your misery to me. I know you're a very unhappy person, and I care about you. So I want to know about your unhappiness." If her mother replies "Oh, no, I'm not unhappy, it's just you.

   Jennifer can easily retort, "Oh, no, mother, I know it's deeper than that, because we both know how much I do for you, and that you really appreciate it. This wouldn't be such a source of misery for you without other factors being involved. So tell me about your terrible pain, your unhappiness. I know you don't have anyone else to talk to."

   Jennifer could also use paradox by not only empathizing with her mother's upset, but stating that she's surprised that her mother is able to tolerate her level of pain at all. She could say, "I understand how awful that must be for you. How in the world do you cope with it? If I felt that bad I'd just want to lay down and die, but you go on, fighting for all you're worth. How do you do it? Tell me your secret."

   In this way Jennifer is again taking control over the behavior, and pushing her mother regarding another now-defined aspect of her self—her strength in carrying on in the face of such horrible, wrenching pain.

   Paradox can be useful in that it gives access to the ability to make things personal by the other person's own definitions, thus increasing someone's resistance to their own behavior in a very deep and profound way. But to accomplish this kind of deep transformation in meaning there's a high price for you. You have to give up your own resistance, look at a very deep, fundamental level on which human functioning occurs, then align yourself with that level of functioning. The result is like a judo throw, take the other person's momentum and redirect it so it works against, rather than for, their behavior.

3. *High-level sensory escalation.* There's one way to transform using sensory behaviors, but it doesn't involve threatening physical survival, instead, it directly threatens the survival of your relationship.

Have you noticed that in none of the examples have I used threats? I've never had Jennifer say "And if you don't, I'll . . . " Threats were intentionally left out because they don't work. Ninety-nine percent of the time when people use threats they're counter-productive. The only time a threat works is when you're going for broke, putting it all on the line, and stating what you're willing to do for real. As the old saying goes, "That's not a threat, it's a promise."

The only kind of threat to use is one that really makes a difference, to end something, in this case your relationship with the person. But you had better mean it. If you don't, not only will you not produce the results you're trying to produce, but you're lying and will lose your power in the relationship. There are times when that loss of power is permanent. So as is the case with any transformational event, this is the big time—Armageddon. So use it only if appropriate, and understand the level to which you're escalating.

For example, if Jennifer had genuinely "had it" with her mother, and felt her relationship was so destructive or unsalvageable without the changes she wanted, she could tell her mother something to that effect. She could tell her if she criticized her driving or whined about how little she was doing one more time, she would never take her to the doctor again. And then Jennifer would have to follow through.

This kind of conversation must be undertaken during a time when there's no immediate upset. It cannot be done during a time of acute anger. It's a different thing from the threats people throw out during arguments. This isn't arguing. It's "serving notice." And that's much of its power—it's done cold-bloodedly, not in the heat of the moment. Jennifer would need to tell her mother she wanted to talk with her, sit down in her living room, and tell her she felt her mother's behavior was too severe for her to deal with. Then she would announce she had come to the decision that if it didn't change, she would no longer be willing to take her to the doctor.

I did this type of thing with a patient who was absolutely refusing to deal with his life. Nothing I did worked, and he carried on the sessions with seeming glibness and casualness while still complaining his life didn't work. He wasn't taking anything seriously. So I finally laid down the ultimatum that he either get down to work (which I carefully defined for him) in the next two sessions, or his therapy with me was finished. The next session he didn't work. He carried on a conversation as if we were having an afternoon in the park. I reminded him that he had one more session. The next session he came in and started talking about my shoes! At the end of the session I told him his treatment was terminated and I would be glad to refer him if he liked.

I'm talking here about delivering an ultimatum, which is what a transformational event does. Remember ultimatums back people into corners. It turns on all of their survival wiring. So you only use them when the stakes are such that it's worth the risk, and you're willing to lose the relationship. Also realize that sometimes people may have to resist your ultimatum because of their survival wiring, so you had best understand there's at least an even chance you're going to have to make good on your ultimatum.

I've helped people plan for this in dangerous relationships or relationships with untreated addicts. I've helped spouses make extra car and house keys to bury in the garden to help them leave if things escalated, or take clothes to a friend's house, even make back-up plane reservations for leaving town. High-level threats are played for keeps, and they can be dangerous. But, nevertheless, they do have their place. However, don't do this with anyone who is physically dangerous unless you're working with a professional to help you with it. Don't put your physical well-being into jeopardy in any case. I'm talking here about danger in the relationship and having to make changes, not physical danger. Don't get into that. Get help instead.

In fact, I strongly recommend that if you feel you need to escalate to this degree, to ultimatums with someone, that you see a therapist to work with you on it. You're in very, very complicated territory.

The other change process Jennifer can use is targeted, ongoing, outside intervention. Because in this chapter we're assuming you're someone on the outside trying to change someone else, in reality everything we're talking about is of outside intervention. I want to take the opportunity in this section to talk about behavioral techniques, and how those are applicable to changing someone. They're very powerful change techniques, maybe even the most powerful, especially if verbal methods aren't working.

1. *Reinforcement.* This is the use of whatever responses, actions or elements increase the frequency of occurrence of behavior you want. Jennifer could either reinforce a new behavior or function or reinforce a behavior which competed with the whining and complaining.

   For example, using reinforcement with her mother could involve finding something that would increase a behavior other than her mother's whining and criticizing. She could play a cassette in her car stereo of music her mother likes, to see if this reinforces listening behavior, or even singing behavior or she could bring something for her mother to read, if it's reinforcing, point out things on the road, or ask her mother's advice on what she feels OK receiving advice from her mother about.

   Reinforcement provides a clear example of the difference between protesting against someone and changing behavior. Do you see how there's no revenge satisfaction in finding reinforcements for alternate behaviors? If your goal is to vent anger, to make someone feel bad so your protest is felt, then the techniques for changing someone, including reinforcement, are likely to feel unsatisfying. Be clear about your goal. If you want to make trouble because you're mad, OK, people do that all the time, but it's different than setting out to change someone. Just don't confuse the two.

2. *Punishment.* Remember, punishment isn't the same as doing what makes someone feel bad. It's not the same as increasing the pain of the problem, even though sometimes it may do that as well. Punishment is simply what diminishes the frequency of occurrence of a behavior. There are even people whose behavior you can punish by complimenting them on what they're doing. I have one couple where compliments from the husband punish the wife's positive communication

behaviors. Every time he compliments her, she starts to get argumentative. It's become kind of a standing joke during the sessions.

If Jennifer wanted to use punishment with her mother, she would need to find something that diminished her mother's whining and criticizing behaviors. Many of the techniques we've already discussed could technically be punishing to the behaviors, as many are designed to decrease their frequency. Jennifer must go through a trial-and-error search for what diminished them. She could use virtually any of the people-handling techniques. Maybe, if she did a lot of sharing, her mother's undesirable behaviors would diminish. Or use of empathic negative communication behaviors, pattern interrupts, or alterations in meaning through reframing and paradox would do it. Whatever diminishes the behavior is punishing to it.

Also remember punishment frequently brings side-effects with it. They're typically more pronounced than with reinforcement, because survival wiring hates to give up behaviors more than it hates to do new things. So watch out for those, and be careful.

3. *Extinction.* This means removing the reinforcement which keeps a behavior going. Again, this can be a search for what is reinforcing the behavior. In Jennifer's case, she would look for what supports her mother's whining and criticizing behavior. It might be Jennifer's attention, or Jennifer responding—even if the response is negative or upset. Remember, people's behavior can be reinforced by upset and negative responding every bit as much as positive response. Jennifer might try extinguishing her mother's behavior by allowing complaints and criticisms, but not responding to them at all, even with silent anger. Instead, she might immediately change the subject, acting like the complaints and criticisms didn't exist. This ultimately might begin to extinguish her mother's behavior. Perhaps it's Jennifer's upset that reinforces her mother's behavior, because her mother is trying to effect a feelings transfer. If Jennifer doesn't display upset, and instead is pleasant and empathic, that might

remove the reinforcement and extinguish her mother's behavior.

You may find the function you're trying to get rid of can increase for a while. For example, if Jennifer acts like her mother's obnoxious behavior doesn't exist, like the rat pushing the bar that used to give food, her mother might increase her rate of complaining. In this case, it would be a good sign, because Jennifer's lack of response has altered her mother's behavior, controlling it. Jennifer would need to keep doing her extinction to see if the behavior then begins to diminish, as it probably will. The worst outcome for extinction isn't that the behavior increases, but that it doesn't change at all. That means you're not affecting it, so you probably aren't altering the factor reinforcing the behavior. You had better try another factor.

4. *Shaping.* This means to reinforce gradual approximations of the change you want. For Jennifer this might mean giving her mother lots of attention, every time she doesn't complain or criticize, even if it's only for a moment. These alternate behaviors can be increased, gradually edging out her complaining and criticizing behaviors. Shaping is also called "successive approximations" because the goal is to reinforce behavior that's more and more what you want. So Jennifer would want to be alert to any moments when her mother wasn't engaged in her obnoxious behaviors, and reinforce her during these moments.

CONCLUSION

As I mentioned at the beginning of the chapter, I've not referred to every people-handling technique in this chapter, even though every one of them probably has some place in changing people. The important thing to remember is what works may not be what seems like it will work. Jennifer might, for example, find that just listening and using empathic responses changes her mother's behavior, because it was reinforced by Jennifer's resistance and upset. Or maybe she just wanted a little sympathy, and by giving her that she'll feel better and stop griping. But listening to the very things she wants stopped probably sounds completely illogical to Jennifer, and is something she doesn't want to do.

If you're going to undertake the task of trying to change someone, be ready for a project and plan it well. Then adjust what you're doing according to the results you're getting. Set your limits, and even try to have a good time at it. Remember, your purpose here isn't to "get" someone or be destructive. Rather it's to make things work better by changing what isn't working. You aren't out to be a problem; you're trying to improve things, so go at it with that spirit.

And if you try everything you can think of, and you can't change what you're trying to change, then you may not be able to do it. People change in strange and unpredictable ways, and some change and others don't. So be prepared for that possibility.

Remember: First, do no harm. Make sure what you do won't cause damage, even if there's some short-term upset involved. Don't do anything out of hate or destructiveness. If you feel like attacking someone, see a therapist to get those feelings handled prior to your change attempt.

Part V

Special Cases

Chapter 18

Exceptional People

This is the only chapter that's going to categorize people. In a general sense, categorization as a basis for handling people doesn't work. But there's one type that can be important.

Most people are "difficult" because their survival wiring goes off. During that time they can act badly and require handling of various sorts that we've talked about. People can also be difficult for us because they understand the world differently than we do, which sets off our survival wiring. But there are some people who are difficult to deal with as the result of far more serious and profound reasons than normal human survival wiring. They have some kind of underlying behavioral problem which renders them difficult beyond what we generally talk about. For example, Charles Manson fits the definition of "difficult," but his difficultness is obviously a whole different quality from that which we generally refer to.

People who fit the new category of difficult I'm discussing are suffering from what is commonly called a "personality disorder," which is different from a psychiatric illness such as schizophrenia or manic-depression. People with personality disorders aren't psychiatrically ill in the common use of the term. Many people with psychiatric disabilities aren't difficult, are successfully treated, and are as productive and appropriate as you and I.

These are people who show significant behavior that's extremely problematic for themselves and for others, but despite the severity of their troublesome behavior, they don't ever see they're being destructive. They don't complain about themselves causing their difficulties as someone with a neurosis might. Instead, they seem to be constantly mystified why bad things happen to them, except that it's someone else's fault. The degree of their lack of awareness of the root of their difficulty is so profound, so amazing, that it's nearly a loss of contact with reality. Despite tremendous evidence to the contrary, as far as these people are concerned, they're fine. If things go wrong, which they often do, it has to be for some reason other than their own behavior.

This description may sound like a person in the midst of a survival reaction—it is. Survival reactions of people with personality disorders are perpetual, severe, and rigid. These people seem to defend themselves as being right nearly all the time. They're destructive but unable to manage, or often even see, their own destructiveness. This is the definition of an escalated survival reaction, and for people with personality disorders, these aren't just occurrences, they're a way of life.

People like this don't just see themselves as being right, they see themselves as always right. They'll escalate immediately and excessively in support of their rightness. It's as if their survival reactions got stuck on high when they were very young, and now they are nothing but one big escalated survival reaction. This removes their flexibility in responding to others, or relating in a normal fashion. These people are virtually never self-identified as being wrong. Their survival wiring is energized at such a high pitch they can seriously damage, emotionally or physically, anyone who triggers their survival reactions.

For these people, this style is a deeply ingrained, resilient pattern which operates the same way in different circumstances and with different people. You might say these people are the very opposite extreme from Behavioral Diversity and Cognitive Diversity. They can only react the same dysfunctional way, over and over, and only think about things the same way, over and over. Their specific behaviors may vary but not much. It's as if they're defensive to the core.

Personality disorders are, by far, the most difficult of all human behavioral dysfunctions to deal with. Many times they're the cause of much of the truly bad trouble in the world. When there are headlines, heinous crimes, and atrocities, not far from the action will be someone with a serious personality disorder. They tend to wreak havoc in their own lives and in the lives of others around them. And they don't see anything wrong with what they're doing.

I'm going to talk about three types of personality disorder that I've seen make lots of trouble for the other people, and which I think are the most commonly troublesome. There are some, such as the sociopath (also called a psychopath), that may be more physically dangerous than the ones I'm going to discuss, but I see fewer of them commonly existing in people's everyday lives.

Andrew Tobias, the financial writer, notes that over 80% of people who play the commodities market get burned. The odds are almost completely stacked against them. It's the same with people suffering from serious personality disorders. Often the very best thing you can do with people suffering from these disturbances is avoid them. This is because the self-destructive, dysfunctional behavior, the distortions of interpretation and survival reactions, are so severe and so deeply ingrained, that to deal with them can be to experience a loss of reality in yourself.

To try to handle a personality disorder in an ongoing relationship is often to experience helplessness, rage, and a high level of survival threat. You may not have a choice, of course, and if that's the case, the methods presented previously are still your best tools. But I include these descriptions in order to acknowledge that there are special cases it's important to be aware of.

Remember how I said earlier that you needed to remember this book could be being read by someone about you, so you need to read with compassion? Well, I want you to know there are undoubtedly going to be people reading this book who are suffering from a personality disorder. Perhaps even the personality disorders I'm going to discuss. Understand this isn't intended to be critical. To the contrary, it's intended to be helpful in allowing for increased awareness of the possibility of fundamental kinds of difficulties for people.

In addition, if you're concerned about yourself or someone else, consult a professional for evaluation. It's not possible to diagnose accurately from this chapter, and it's not the purpose to give you the tools to diagnose people with personality disorders, so don't try. I want to raise your awareness so that you can be as effective as possible with people.

Borderline Personality Disorder (BPD)

In the 1930s, a man named Adolph Stern noticed a consistent cluster of self-destructive behavior some people exhibited but didn't seem to fit any known psychiatric category. These people were neither psychotic nor neurotic, but were so fragmented and scattered in their behavioral responses they puzzled psychiatric investigators. Finally, in 1938, he coined the term "Borderline" to describe these individuals, because they seemed to exist on the edge of being psychotic. They were terribly dysfunctional, but they never seemed to tip over the edge into an actual psychotic break. They seemed to ride consistently and constantly on the borderline between sanity and insanity.

For a long time investigators could never quite get a good, overall picture of the disorder or get a clear handle on it. Like blind people feeling the elephant, they could identify certain features, but never get an overall concept to fit because of the tremendous unpredictability of the behaviors involved. Finally, in 1953, Robert Knight was able to attach an overall term to the syndrome. He borrowed Stern's term, and dubbed the condition "Borderline States." This title reflected the issue as a "state of being" of the person that seemed to characterize the individual.

Further work on the condition followed, with Otto Kernberg in the 1960s beginning to write of it as a "Borderline Personality Organization." Subsequently, James Masterson in the '70s and '80s began to more clearly and specifically define the syndrome that has ultimately become known as Borderline Personality Disorder, or BPD.

There's a great deal more known now about Borderline Personality Disorder than has ever been known before. Of all the people in the world who are difficult, people exhibiting BPD may be the most troublesome to those around them. People with BPD can destroy families, wreak havoc in businesses, and corrupt organizations. It is a state of being that generates a tremendous amount of destructiveness. Handling someone suffering from a borderline state is difficult, frightening, and can be dangerous. Someone who has a borderline personality disorder can be trouble waiting to happen.

374

A difficulty, though, is that people with BPD aren't immediately distinguishable from people who don't have it. They don't always exhibit one particular set of behaviors, so they may be seen as though they have some degree of Behavioral Diversity. But upon closer examination, it becomes clear what they have isn't Behavioral Diversity, but rather behavioral fragmentation. Their varying behavior isn't the result of goals and purpose; it's the result of impulsiveness, over-reaction, dysfunction, and psychic pain. The behaviors are poorly organized and used in ways that don't work.

It's often said the hallmark of someone with borderline personality disorder is emotional inconsistency. People with BPD ride an emotional roller-coaster that careens from one emotional extreme to another, often with only the most minimal trigger. Small emotional slights, upsets, or miscommunication can result in huge, even life-threatening reactions, and often vicious personal attacks. Because of this style of intense and shifting reactions, people with BPD are all over the map in their behavior. The unifying feature is that it's all highly escalated, overly intense. Where most people would get irritated, they get enraged. Where others would get sad, they get dramatically and suicidally anguished.

Internally, people suffering from borderline states battle a terrible, chronic emptiness which they'll do nearly anything to avoid. I think of them as "emotional chronic pain patients." They're in ongoing distress, and nothing they do seems to alleviate it for long. For this reason their reactions tend to have a desperate quality to them. They seem to be desperate to find something, anything, that can help them escape their terrible pain. As a result, they do anything, including trying to bludgeon the world, to take away their internal discomfort. They're already in terrible pain, so they experience any aroused feeling, especially a painful one, as a terrible event, and they can react to it with vicious counter-attacks designed to destroy the villain causing them such terrible distress.

Many people with BPD have a terrible fear of both intimacy and abandonment. This means they're upset by people being close, and by people pulling away. This results in a kind of self-contradictory relating style, hanging on for dear life to people with one hand, while beating them up with the other.

Essentially, a person with a borderline personality disorder lacks a cohesive identity. They don't have an intact sense of self. It's as if their conceptual body is in disconnected pieces, and they can only feel one bit at a time. Whatever they feel is all that exists, it's the whole world. There's no proportion. Every feeling is a bottomless pit which causes a full-blown survival reaction. As a result, their behavior is scattered, contradictory, and extreme, because it's based on their current reactions and nothing else. One minute they'll be raging, vengeful, accusing you of every malfeasance in the world and hurling terrible, personal insults at you, and the next will act like nothing happened. If you threaten to leave them they'll attack and treat you as if you were evil, then dissolve into horrified shrieks over the possibility that you'd really abandon them.

A prominent feature of BPD is what is called "splitting." Splitting means the person sees sections of the world, and especially people, as either all-good or all-bad. Everyone is either a hero or a villain. There's no ability to tolerate a mixing of the two in one person, to integrate the goods and bad that run through all people. Instead, person A is an angel and person B is a devil. Person A can do nothing wrong, and person B can do nothing right.

But this isn't stable by any means. It can all change due to the slightest thing, especially a perceived snub or slight. Then, overnight, person A can change from being an angel to a devil, and person C might become the new angel. Only one thing is for sure: sooner or later, whoever is the angel is going to become the devil. In addition, their reaction to each is exaggerated. The people who are all good receive excessive and overly intense adulation, and the people who are all bad receive excessive and overly intense damnation.

The way I have come to think of borderline states is that they're a condition where an individual has a huge survival reaction, usually some kind of terrible temper tantrum, any time they have any emotion aroused. They're almost completely intolerant of the experience of nearly any emotion. If someone tries to get close to them, they fear suffocation and back off. If someone backs off, they're terrified of abandonment and either cling hysterically or become raging and destructive in response. No feeling feels OK, and no lack of feeling feels OK either. It's like a state of intractable pain.

At work, if a job is well-structured and the tasks clearly defined, people with BPD can sometimes manage, and their reactions can be muted or controlled. However, any change, shift, or break in the pattern can bring down the whole emotional house of cards, with terrible outbursts, scenes, and problems.

The reason people with BPD are so very difficult, even dangerous, to try to handle, is that they set others up in no-win situations over and over. Because they're looking for something to make them feel whole, to feel OK, and nothing can ever do that, ultimately nothing you do will be OK with them. They'll finally hate you for turning left, right, or going straight. In fact, they may be hateful just because you're there, you become a target. If you try to leave they'll hate you, too, and try to get you to stay. So you can't win. I had a patient who described his clearly borderline mother as saying to him one day, out of the blue, with venom dripping from every word, "Why don't you find something worthwhile to do, you sniveling idiot. You're no better than your father!"

People with BPD set up alliances, conflicts, and fights, always siding with whoever they consider to be the good guys, fighting against whoever they perceive to be the bad guys. They set up fights all around themselves. I consulted with a professional's office in which a person with BPD had been hired as office manager. Within six months the previously good friends in the office were at each other's throats, and there was talk of disbanding the practice.

People with BPD demand things but make it impossible to deliver. I had one patient with BPD say to me "I'm getting worse and there's nothing anyone can do to help me." This put me in the bind of trying to do something to help, but with her stating that it was no use, it was impossible. But if I didn't try, she would rage against me all the same.

People with BPD are often abusive and invite abuse. They lack true empathy. They may have an excessive ability for feelings transfers, but it's unreliable, as their reaction can just as easily and instantly turn assaultive.

If I were to tell you to look for any one thing that most typified people with BPD that was the most reliable, single warning sign that someone may have it, I would say this: Beware the Perennial

Victim. Although certainly not everyone who adopts a strong victim stance in life suffers from BPD, people with BPD are typically the persistent, angry victim through life. Anything that opens up their inner emptiness, which nearly everything does sooner or later, results in an almost paranoiac reaction, a personalizing of the problem, a "they're out to get me" reaction. When confronted about their reaction, they respond with increased aggression, rage, and escalated accusations of victimization. In fact, they can even present themselves as victims of themselves, wailing about their own behavior and its consequences as if they were talking about someone else—enraged at this "self" that's so abusive to them.

Now, there are real incidents of being a victim that people, including those with BPD, experience. People are hit by cars, abused by others, and wrongfully treated. But being a victim is distinct from approaching the world from the psychological position of being a victim. I recall seeing a women on a talk show. She was asked a question by an audience member and she reacted with an angry victim response that the person had, "Caused her unbelievable pain in asking that question." She was on a talk show. What questions did she think people were going to ask? So she wasn't truly a victim, she was approaching the world from a victim stance toward life.

Beware the perennial victim.

There are several specific characteristics that are generally taken to indicate that someone may be suffering from BPD. Not all of them are relevant from a people-handling standpoint, so let me just list a few that often are:

1. Unstable and overly intense relationships

   People with BPD often make unrealistic, unreasonable, self-centered demands on others around them, with a sense of entitlement to gratification and outrage when their desires aren't satisfied. Never mind that the gratification may be inappropriate or even impossible. If their needs aren't met, they can react with tremendous rage. Their relationships with others are generally overintense and stormy. One minute it's passionate sex, the next they're wailing at how horrible the whole relationship is.

2. Impulsive behavior

People with BPD can show sudden, dramatic shifts in behavior based on whim and impulse. Because they lack a cohesive and consistent conceptual body, sense of self, they can react in disjointed, inconsistent ways, much like having seizures, where you lose control of your arm which began to swing wildly out of control at everyone around you, sort of like Dr. Strangelove. Then, just as suddenly as it began, it would stop, and another part of your body would do the same thing. Someone with BPD can be acting warm, loving, and engaging and in an instant become a screaming, threatening, enraged beast. Then they act like nothing happened. People with BPD can also be significantly self-destructive. Not only do they alienate other people, but they also can be overtly self-destructive, hurting themselves intentionally or indirectly. They can even use this self-destructiveness as a weapon against other people.

3. Rapid, intense mood shifts

People with BPD have mood shifts that last generally only a few hours. They may fly into an intense rage where they're extremely vicious in their attacks on other people, and then a few hours later act as if nothing happened. In addition, their "normal" mood is rarely placid or pleasant, but is more likely to be altered—depressed, haughty, cynical, or anxious.

4. Rage attacks

A key element of people's behavior with BPD is they have sudden, unpredictable attacks of rage. These can be violent and frightening. Typically they're a reaction to a feared abandonment or the threat of intimacy. Because of this, the rage is generally aimed at whoever is most important to them, or whoever is closest to them.

5. Attention-getting behavior

Borderline individuals can be extremely dramatic, and can draw attention to themselves by being overly and inappropriately sexual, rageful, dramatic, or self-damaging. Some of the behaviors can be designed to get help or get others to take responsibility for them because people with BPD don't feel capable of taking responsibility for themselves.

The causes of BPD are still hotly debated. I think there's good evidence the disorder is at least partially genetic, biochemical, and/or neurological. Certainly there's also, in the history of many people with BPD, a history of early childhood trauma, so this may play a role as well. In addition, BPD seems to have some relationship to eating and addictive disorders, and there are some studies that rate the prevalence of BPD among such individuals as high as 50%. Whether the BPD, the eating disorder, or the addiction is the primary cause of the other is also a hotly debated subject.

My observation is that the best thing to do is avoid becoming involved with people who have BPD if possible. There's a school of thought that the disorder is untreatable in our present state of knowledge. Other people treat the condition and feel they can be reasonably successful with it. But even they admit it's a long, difficult process. People with BPD will quit treatment impulsively because they're "just fine" and then go out and do something self-destructive. Or they'll sabotage treatment by missing appointments, assaulting the therapist, or being unmanageable in their behavior. In any case, the dangers involved in dealing with someone who has BPD are often quite large, emotionally, if not physically, and avoidance is often the best course of action.

However, if avoidance isn't possible or desirable for you, and you're involved with someone who suffers from BPD, there are some additional steps in handling them that can be helpful.

You are always dealing with someone touchy, and extremely reactive. They can't tolerate closeness or abandonment. As a result, there's a technique for talking with them recommended by people who are familiar with dealing with them. This involves the consistent use of both conceptual language and sensory language in the same conversation. First, you use conceptual language in an empathic response, to acknowledge your understanding of the person's distress. This is designed to avoid the danger of the person with BPD perceiving a breakdown in empathy (abandonment) with a resulting rage attack. However, they can't tolerate much intimacy, either, so they'll get reactive if you leave it at that. After the empathic response, a sensory one is made, naming what they did or are doing. If it's a correction being made, then a statement of unwillingness to tolerate the behavior is made. This technique could sound like, "I understand you were upset by my asking you to stay late today because that's difficult for you (empathic response). But I will not tolerate your calling me an "ass" in front of other people in the office. Don't do that again" (sensory behavioral confrontation).

In dealing with someone who has BPD it's often essential you confront misbehaviors. Start with conceptual language and empathic responses, but then use sensory language to talk to them about their misbehavior. This is setting limits and it's essential.

Finally, if you do decide to be or stay involved with a person who has BPD, you'll need to adjust yourself to several things:

1. You'll regularly be in "damned if you do, damned if you don't" positions. This may be in the conceptual or the sensory world, but you might just as well get used to it. For someone with BPD, nothing is ultimately ever good enough, because nothing relieves the deep pain they feel. So something can be OK for a while, even you or what you do, but ultimately it will go from being all-good to being all-bad.

2. Their view of you will be exaggerated, you'll either be a hero or a goat. Most likely, after a while, you'll nearly always be wrong. Because people with BPD have their survival wiring in hyper gear, they'll regularly make you wrong. In fact, they can provoke you into misbehaving in order to make you wrong and then rage at you. Metaphorically speaking, they can push you in front of a bus and then scream at you for being so stupid as to get hurt.

3. You'll probably be put into a position of being responsible for them. People with BPD feel precious little ability to take responsibility for themselves and their lives, so they set it up for you to take over for them. Then, of course, they'll resist you and make you wrong for it as well. And if you try to quit, that's abandonment and they'll escalate. This can happen in marriages. A spouse stays with a mate who has BPD over the fear that if they leave the partner will kill themselves.

4. You'll never quite know what to expect from them. Remember, a hallmark characteristic of BPD is unpredictability. This, in fact, is what draws people to them sometimes— they're exciting and seem "free." But that's a misperception

that will rapidly disappear. They may idealize you, love everything you do, and tell you how wonderful you are one minute, and step all over your feelings the next. There's simply no way to predict it.

People can get involved because initially it feels wonderful. At first, the person is idealized, aggrandized. They feel they've found their soul mate and have become one in spirit. The sex can be great, the intensity of the relationship can be unbelievable. What the other person isn't ready for is the switch, waiting, inevitably, around the corner. At some point they're going to disappoint, upset, or otherwise have a conflict with the person (that's normal in every relationship, of course), but the reaction they get will be anything but normal. It's going to be so monstrously out of proportion they're going to be terrified and horribly confused about what hit them.

One of the best portrayals of borderline personality disorders is the character of Alex in the movie "Fatal Attraction" with Michael Douglas and Glen Close. Alex has a torrid affair with Michael Douglas's character, but when it comes time to stop, she pulls dramatic twists to prevent abandonment. At the same time she is expressing undying love to him, she is raging at him and trying to destroy him. In many ways it's a very effective portrait of BPD.

A danger with people suffering from BPD is that it can be very tempting to believe if you "just give them what they want" someone with BPD will calm down and be OK. It doesn't work like that, which is what makes it a disorder as opposed to regular human functioning. Nothing is ever enough, the demands will increase until they're fully impossible, then the rage will come from the dashed hopes of getting their emotional void filled. That's why confrontation of misbehaviors, and effective behavioral limits are so important, as opposed to letting things go.

An important task for you if you're involved with someone who has BPD is to keep consistent in your own responses. You'll probably not use a lot of different people-handling techniques, or rely on much diversity in your behavior. As you can tell in dealing with people I think consistency is over-rated, and you should try to do things that work rather than be consistent. With someone who has BPD, though, this is different. Nothing "works" for long with a BPD, because they'll be willing to out-escalate you, out-rage you, out-maneuver you, and out-manipulate you. So one of the best things you can do is to stay consistent in your responses. Empathy and limits. Over and over.

The value of consistency isn't even so much that it helps to handle the person with BPD, because they'll probably do the same things to you that they would if you were inconsistent, but it helps you to survive because it aids in maintaining your own cohesive sense of self. And because their attacks to your sense of self can be so frequent and vicious, you need to retain all of the sense of self that you can muster.

Narcissistic Personality Disorder (NPD)

In contrast to the fairly recent conceptualization of BPD, Freud himself began the identification of the category that has come to be called Narcissistic Personality Disorder. Freud noted in some of his patients an excessive self-involvement, an attachment to their image that was so prominent and all-encompassing, it pushed out their other functioning. While Freud related this phenomenon to various psychological processes at work in neurosis and psychosis, it was ultimately grouped with the personality disorders and is now called Narcissistic Personality Disorder.

Narcissistic personality disorder has probably had more attention in the popular press than has borderline personality disorder, so it's likely a more familiar syndrome to most people. However, in addition to its being better known, there are more misconceptions about it as well. The core of narcissistic personality disorder is an interest in and attachment to one's image to the exclusion of one's self. People with NPD don't experience much emotion, or experience empathy, and show the contradictory elements of being haughty and demeaning of others, while desperately demanding attention and adulation from those people. They look down on people, but they also require an admiring audience. And they demand that the audience applaud. A standing ovation would be even better. Someone with NPD will behave in just about any way necessary in order to be able to get others to provide for them the adulation they require.

The mistake people make when casually calling someone narcissistic is thinking narcissism is excessive self-love. It's not. It's excessive image-love. Remember how in the myth Narcissus fell in love not with himself, but his reflection. A reflection is only an image, it has no substance. That's why we think of narcissistic individuals as shallow. They can't respond to anything below the level of appearance. It's all that matters to them. Because their involvement is with their image and not their "self," people with NPD have little or no ability to return the appreciation they demand from others. There's nowhere inside of them for it to come from. They can act like they're appreciative, but that apparent appreciation is only designed to make them look good.

Metaphorically speaking, for someone with NPD it's as if they have come to mistake their clothes for their body.

A major characteristic of someone with NPD is called "grandiosity." This means that they elevate their needs, wants, and desires, to the level of absolute right and wrong. To them, right and wrong are defined by how well their needs are met. Because of this they're justified in doing anything that meets their needs, no matter what its effects on others.

Related to this, a characteristic NPD shares with BPD is a tendency toward rages. It makes sense—if one is entitled to things, and it's right for them to have them, then rage is the appropriate response to being denied it. If the narcissist feels his or her audience isn't being sufficiently adoring or gratifying, they can express rage at them. These people are "bad" and deserve punishment in their eyes.

Like someone with BPD, the person with NPD has no solid sense of self. It has been sacrificed to the needs of the image. But while the individual with BPD has a fragmented sense of self that leads them this way and that way, for the person with NPD, the self is numb. It's not experienced as existing at all. All they "feel" is the veneer, the appearance, which is mistaken for the self.

Talk to someone with NPD about feelings of self beyond the level of image, and they'll look at you blankly and wonder what you're talking about. But, in reality, most narcissists wouldn't dare admit confusion and risk looking bad, so they'd either look at you with pity for your silliness for talking about feelings or they would agree with you that you're absolutely, positively right, and think that you're so smart. This is an attempt to be gratifying to you so that you'll think well of them.

Individuals with NPD demand that others reflect their positive image back to them. As a result, they're sensitive to even the smallest slight or snub, and can react to it as if it were a heinous crime. That's where their rage can be seen. How dare someone not reflect back to them, by nature of their response, how OK they are? They want that positive reflection.

Often it's difficult to recognize NPD initially, because many are intelligent and talented and can "deliver" on what they say, bringing well-deserved and appropriately earned praise. But after a while, the person who is talented differs because NPD prevents someone from giving anything back unless it's to look good. They also lack compassion and perspective. They can't empathize. They only want to be loved, adored, and looked up to. In their attitude toward others they're haughty, demeaning, and devaluing.

The paradox of NPD is that people seem to actually love themselves. The element that distinguishes this from true self-love, though, is their incessant, desperate need to have others communicate to them how wonderful they are. They're endlessly demanding of admiration and adulation, and they can be rageful if they don't get it. An image is never satisfying, its only purpose is outward, to affect others. The person behind the image is left empty. If they really had abundant self-love, they wouldn't require such gratification from others and would not be so angry if they didn't get it.

A person with NPD lives in the delusion they're not a normal human, with failings and flaws along with strengths. They feel they're "special." They may even give some lip service to having flaws (because that makes them look good to other people when they say so), but if you listen, you'll note their talk lacks genuineness, and is designed to make them look good by being "open" enough to "admit" fault. But it's not genuine. Everything is for show.

There are several characteristics mental health professionals look at in formally evaluating whether someone is suffering from NPD. Here are some of them:

1. When criticized, the person reacts with rage, shame or humiliation. These may not be expressed directly, but however they're expressed, they're experienced way out of proportion to the situation.

2. They're manipulative and exploitative. These are people who really do use people for their own ends. They'll mislead and misrepresent in order to achieve their ends.

3. Without justifiable evidence, they feel they're special. They have an inflated sense of self-importance, and expect to be treated so by others.

4. They can't empathize. They demand others cater to their feelings, but can't return it.

5. They feel a great deal of envy. They'll always be in competition because they're fighting for the attention of others.

As is the case with people with BPD, my observation is it's often best to avoid involvement with such people. Where the BPD results in a fragmented, scattered personality, the NPD is rigid and inflexible. All the different behaviors they show are superficial and manipulative in order to get the positive reactions they feel are rightly theirs. So to relate to someone with NPD means either you have to feed them and get little or nothing, emotionally, in return, or put yourself in the position of possibly being raged at. Probably the toughest part of relating to someone with NPD is you constantly feel one-down and invalidated. They can't empathize, so you don't get your needs met and can experience yourself as overly demanding and crazy for what you need.

If for some reason you're involved with someone who has NPD, here are some methods for handling them and some you'll need to be aware of in your dealings with them:

1. You're likely to feel crazy because what you feel will not match what you see. You can feel lousy when relating to them, and have urges to get out of the relationship. But these urges are likely to seem crazy because the relationship looks perfect, so you can't figure out why you're feeling bad. That's the whole issue: the image doesn't match with the reality. But the person with NPD will be glad to reassure that things *are* just fine, and your upset feelings are the result of your own glitches—you're just a little loony. So if you're involved with someone with NPD it can be helpful to remember the reason they don't feel what you feel is they can't feel on that level.

2. You'll always be wrong if there's a conflict, or if you don't agree with them. Get ready for that definition of you and your position if it doesn't agree with them.

3. They'll seek to have the power in the relationship, and be very sensitive to you having power. People with NPD trade on power. It's their substitute for love. Watch out for them not supporting your goals, purposes, and personal effectiveness or independence.

4. People with NPD fear rejection nearly as much as do people with BPD, and they can become enraged when they feel slighted or threatened with abandonment. If you decide to leave a relationship with someone who has NPD be prepared for major escalation, because the withdrawal of their adoring audience can be devastating for them.

5. You're going to need to have outside sources of support and positive feedback for you, make sure you have good friends handy.

There isn't one particular response style to use with someone with NPD as there is with someone with BPD. Instead, the core element of dealing with them is to never violate your own integrity, and not expect they're going to be able to see your point of view when you disagree with them. They are, ultimately and unfortunately, highly manipulable themselves, as paradox and reframing which puts them in a positive light can sometimes get them to do about anything you want. You may have to restrain your desires to toy with them once you see how possible it is to manipulate them. But the problems go beyond their manipulative behavior and into who they are, so even though paradox and reframing can sometimes alter their behavior, if you want to relate you're likely going to be frustrated.

Perhaps the best portrayal of narcissistic personality disorder in literature is the main character in *The Picture of Dorian Gray*. He changes places with a painting (image) of himself and retains his youthful appearance. As a result, his image is all that matters, and his shallowness begins to destroy those around him. It's a trap from which he's unable to escape, as his image maintains and his life decays.

Untreated, Unrecovered Addiction

It's a common misconception that alcoholism is about drinking, drug addiction about drugs, sexual compulsiveness about sex, and compulsive overeating about food. An addiction is much more than compulsive behaviors. It's a complex and extensive internal process, some even say a "disease" process. Whether or not it's a disease, an addiction is a whole cluster of internal mechanisms, processes, and symptoms. The excessive and compulsive use of alcohol, drugs, sex or food is just one manifestation of its existence. It's not the addiction itself.

While addictions have always been around, only recently have we begun to appreciate their depth in any complete or adequate manner. We now know addiction is a disorder unto itself, and requires specific treatment. It involves quitting the compulsive behavior, but also much more.

I've found the best way to think about addictions, the way that seems to be most accurate to how they work, is to use the metaphor of being "possessed" by a foreign entity. This allows us to talk about the addiction in an anthropomorphized way, and helps make its processes clear. Please understand, this is a metaphor only, I'm not suggesting that there's in fact an actual physical entity that's an "addiction."

An addiction has a goal. Its goal, like that of any living thing, is to survive, progress, and grow. This is why addictions are said to be progressive, that is, they get worse and worse over time. And, like all living things, addictions defend themselves. The only problem is since an addiction isn't a real, live, biological being, it has no defenses of its own. Instead, it commandeers the defenses of the person it inhabits and turns them from protecting the conceptual and sensory world to protecting the life of the addiction. Thus, you find people's survival wiring working to protect their drinking, sexual escapades or secret eating instead of their identity or body.

This is exactly the same way a virus works. A virus can't replicate, it needs a factory for that. So it invades a cell and commandeers the cell's machinery of replication. The cell can't tell, but it begins to churn out copies of the virus rather than copies of itself. A virus is very short-sighted in its survival goal, because ultimately it kills the cell it inhabits and the host as well, as it bursts out of the cell to travel to other cells.

The exact same thing is true about an addiction. It grows inside of its host, takes over the machinery of survival, and ultimately kills the host if it's not stopped.

To relate to someone who is in the active grip of an untreated addiction, you are relating to the addiction which has taken over much of their mental machinery. They stop being themselves, especially when actively under the influence of whatever their addictive substance is. Their reactions will come largely from the addictive process, not from their sense of self. People in the grip of an addiction will lie, manipulate, deny, rationalize, justify, blame, and externalize in the name of defending their addiction, and lie about doing those things.

There are a couple of things to keep in mind if you do need to deal with people who are in the grip of an addiction:

1. They're not trustworthy. This isn't because they're bad. It's because addictions seek to stay alive, and so demand the person serve them without their even knowing what's driving their behavior. The addicted person will do whatever is required to keep the addiction active and alive. When confronted about the breaking of agreements, they'll go into survival reactions rather than address it, less the addiction be exposed and confronted.

2. Trying to change them is a quagmire. Addictions themselves turn the world of a human being upside down. They're paradoxical in themselves. This complexity combined with the fact so much of their behavior is controlled by the addiction, changing someone addicted can make you feel crazy and actually make things worse. Trying to change an addict's behavior can run you into direct confrontation with all the defenses and mechanisms guarding that addiction. To try to use change techniques with them is inadvisable, with the possible exception of a paradox. The paradox is to stop trying to change them, and instead focus on your own part in the system.

3. Addictions draw people into their patterns. Again, think of the metaphor of an entity that tries to get other beings under

their influence. If you're relating to someone with an active addiction, you'll need help to save your own sanity. There are lots of groups for people with addicts in their lives, the most prominent of which is Al Anon, and there are therapists who understand the addictive process as well. If you have an addict in your life, go to one of these groups or to a knowledgeable therapist. You may have to hunt around to find one you like, but these are the people who understand the ways of addictions and who can help you learn to handle an addicted person. In fact, this kind of outside intervention is nearly a requirement to handle someone with an active addiction.

Addictions are wily creatures, and have lots of defenses to fight off your attempts to deal with them. So you need outside help with them, and it's possible that most of the stuff in this book won't work very well with them. It's like they're possessed.

There has been a lot written and portrayed in the media regarding addictions these days, since so many high profile people have owned up to theirs. Nevertheless, I think the best portrayal of addictions is still the classic movie *Days Of Wine and Roses* with Jack Lemon. It's a wrenching, blunt look into the world of alcoholism, and I think it paints a more direct, stark picture of the workings of addictions than most of the more recent portrayals.

Conclusion

Let me again remind you the purpose of this chapter isn't to provide technically accurate psychiatric information, so don't go out and try to diagnose people. The purpose is to share some insights regarding certain personality issues. I'm trying to increase your awareness of these things, so you can be more sensitive about such issues. This is also designed to help you become more realistic, especially when it comes to changing people. If someone's behavior is based in a disorder of personality, you're not going to be able to change them. In any case, it's important to realize there are some people who have personalities that are problematic for them and for others on an ongoing basis.

Part VI

Conclusion

Chapter 19

The Final Analysis

This book has covered a lot of ground about dealing with people. It has talked about how people function and why they do what they do, and it has presented many different methods for dealing with people, and strategies for accomplishing various purposes with them. It has talked about the self-defeating nature of manipulating and misleading people. There are three final topics to discuss that underlie all the information in the book and tie it all together. These concepts are responsibility, possibility and resignation.

Responsibility

Responsibility means that something belongs to you, you're accountable for it. It means you're the one to accept the results as being your doing. Successful people-handling is based in responsibility. This means no matter how other people are behaving or how they're being, it's your responsibility to find ways to deal effectively with them. If you don't take responsibility for trying to make things work, you'll end up making them wrong for how they are. This leads to your justifying inappropriate behavior on your own part. Then, instead of being part of the solution, you become part of the problem.

No matter what other people do, it's always your responsibility to be aware, intentional, unmanipulative, nonfraudulent, and loyal to your purpose when dealing with people. There is, in the final analysis, no excuse for your not taking responsibility for how things work between yourself and others. If you aren't getting good results with someone, it's your responsibility to do something about it. This may not seem fair, but it's not really an issue of fairness—simply a fact.

You experience the consequences of your dealings with people, so it's up to you to take responsibility for making things work as well as they can. If you find that you can't make your dealings work, then it's your responsibility to deal with it. Not every relationship is workable and should continue. But what you must not do is to hang around and cause trouble.

It's accepting one's responsibility for dealing with people no matter what the other person is doing that separates the "good guys" from the "bad guys" in the world of people dealing with each other. The good guys know no matter what the other person does, it's their responsibility to deal appropriately with them. The police have rules they're supposed to follow, even in dealing with heinous criminals who are behaving outrageously. That's what makes them the good guys. It's the terrorists of the world who say, "We only did what we did because of what they're doing." If that's what you're doing with people, you're a terrorist. When it comes to dealing with people, you're always "on the hook." It's always in your court.

Possibility

People often justify their own misbehavior by saying there's no way to make something work with someone, so they're "forced" to misbehave. This book has provided many, many possibilities for you in your dealings with people, and there are many more that can grow out of the ones presented here. If your dealings with people aren't working well at the moment, even if you can't see how they can work, there's still the possibility they can. There are many, many possible ways to adjust what you're doing and how you're doing it to work on making things better with the people in your life. There are more possibilities than you have even started to tap.

Resignation

When you give up looking for possibilities and abdicate responsibility for your dealings with people you're being "resigned" about them. You're "resigning" from your responsibility. This is also called cynicism. Once you become resigned about dealing with people, you no longer see your behavior as yours. It disappears, and is replaced by theirs. Their behavior becomes the excuse for whatever trouble your behavior causes. Resignation allows you to act like a helpless victim who can't be held accountable.

I'm not denying there are situations where people are being virtually impossible to deal with. My point is even then it's your responsibility to be appropriate in your response, to continue to search for possible ways to make the situation work out well, even if it means your leaving the situation. You either need to be able to accept how the other person is and keep your behavior appropriate to the situation problem, or get away from them and give up that purpose.

My message to you is people's behavior with others often is much more troublesome than they realize. People give up on each other and on the possibility something good can happen. They become resigned, and begin to behave badly, making things worse. If you want your life to work well, to have Power with People, you need to stop relinquishing your responsibility, to stop blaming others for your own bad behavior.

No one else's behavior is justification for yours. There are lots and lots of different ways to go about dealing with people, and if you cause trouble instead of looking for ways to make it work, it's not their fault, it's yours. There's just no way around it. It's your responsibility. You'll be pleased at the results. And because I wish you the very best, I want you to take responsibility for your dealings with other people. That will make available to you the best that life has to offer.

BIBLIOGRAPHY

Bandler, Richard and John Grinder, *Reframing*. Real People Press, Moab, Utah, 1982.

Some discussion of reframing useful in handling people, although much of the book is devoted to a unique and complex type of reframing useful primarily in therapy.

Berne, Eric, *Games People Play*. Grove Press, New York, 1964.

Probably the first popularized text about interpersonal behaviors, goals, and outcomes. Many of Berne's writings are valuable for people who deal with people.

Bolton, Robert, *People Skills*. Simon and Schuster, New York, 1979.

A reasonably good basic text on dealing with people, although a bit less thorough in some ways than some might find useful.

Capaldi, Nicholas, *The Art of Deception*. Prometheus Books, Buffalo, N.Y., 1987.

An interesting book that explores the semantic, linguistic, and conceptual nature of arguments and communications. Covers a variety of topics, most centered on various forms of persuasion.

Carnegie, Dale, *The Quick and Easy Way to Effective Speaking*. Pocket Books, New York, 1962.

A good primer on the processes of considering one's purpose in dealing with people.

Cooney, Timothy J., *The Difference Between Truth and Opinion*. Prometheus Books, Buffalo, N.Y., 1991.

An interesting book exploring language and its relationship to the world. Also presents some helpful aspects of what are basically techniques of alliance with others.

Elgin, Suzette Haden, *The Gentle Art of Verbal Self-Defense*. Barnes and Noble, New York, 1980.
Elgin presents an effective breakdown and analysis of the semantics of talking to people, and defines various sensory modes of communication. Useful information and engaging reading.

Gottman, John, Cliff Norarius, Jonni Gonxo, and Howard Markman, *A Couple's Guide to Communication*. Research Press, Champaign, Ill., 1976.
A clear and concise text that includes practical information on listening, negotiating, and empathic skills. It is written for couples, but it could be a valuable text for anyone dealing with people.

Grinder, John and Richard Bandler, *The Structure of Magic II*. Science and Behavior Books, Palo Alto, Calif., 1976.
One of the first systematic presentations of representational systems in language and human behavior. A bit forced in its attempt to make the whole thing scientific and formulaic, but some powerful definitions are made as well.

Haley, Jay, *Uncommon Therapy*. WW Norton & Co., Inc., New York, 1986.
A book about the man who brought paradox and reframing to practical use with people, Dr. Milton Erikson. While this is a set of case studies of therapy, the exploration of Erikson's thought processes and skillful use of reframing and paradox are intriguing and often brilliant.

Iuppa, Nicholas V., *Management By Guilt*. Fawcett Crest, New York, 1985.
A humorous collection of different "techniques" of handling people. There is more truth in this book than one would like, and it is useful in that it keeps things from getting too serious or self-righteous.

Kirschenbaum, Howard and Valerie Land Henderson, *The Carl Rogers Reader*. Houghton Mifflin, New York, 1989.

What Milton Erikson did for reframing and paradox, Carl Rogers did for listening and empathic responding. Perhaps the first person to realize the power of alliance techniques in building intimacy, Rogers was the master. Useful reading for those who think listening and empathic responding are simple or superficial.

Kreisman, Jerold, and Hal Straus, *I Hate You, Don't Leave Me*. Avon Books, New York, 1989.

One of very few books in the popular press about Borderline Personality Disorder. Quite detailed and readable, with an approach to dealing with BPD that is similar, although not exactly the same, as mine. A worthwhile book if you are involved with someone with BPD.

Krumboltz, John, and Helen Krumboltz, *Changing Children's Behavior*. Prentice-Hall, Englewood Cliffs, New Jersey, 1972.

Perhaps the classic of all books that apply behavioral techniques to practical situations. The book focuses on children, but its descriptions of techniques such as extinction and shaping are so effective that virtually anyone would find them useful. A terrific text even after twenty years.

Lazarus, Arnold, and Allen Fay, *I Can If I Want To*. Warner Books, New York, 1975.

A useful description of some behavioral techniques. A bit too "self-help" for my tastes, but useful in learning some behavioral methods.

Lowen, Alexander, *Narcissism*. Macmillan, New York, 1983.

Still the best text I have found on Narcissistic Personality Disorder. Less filled with jargon than most texts, Lowen has a unique perspective on NPD, and one that is enlightening and useful.

Madanes, Cloe, *Strategic Family Therapy*. Jossey-Bass, San Francisco, 1981.

Strategic family therapy bases its approach on applying different approaches to different problems in families. They use many paradox, reframing, and behavioral techniques. They can sometimes become what I consider "manipulative," so I have some limitations in my approval of their methods, but they are useful people to learn from nevertheless.

Peck, M. Scott, *People of the Lie*. Simon and Schuster, New York, 1983.

An interesting approach to narcissism. A bit long on "evil" and even exorcism, but fascinating examples of NPD that are helpful in getting the "feel" of dealing with someone who has NPD.

Roberts, Wess, *Leadership Secrets of Attila the Hun*. Warner Books, New York, 1987.

Certainly a great title, but the book effectively portrays the approach of thinking about what you want to accomplish with people. Useful.

Saks, Oliver, *The Man Who Mistook His Wife For A Hat*. Summit Books, New York, 1970.

If you have difficulty accepting that all human functioning is biological, see what you think after reading this intriguing, funny, and poignant book. Soul or no soul, we function with biological machinery.

Satir, Virginia, *The New Peoplemaking*. Science and Behavioral Books, Mountain View, Calif., 1988.

Considered a pioneer in dealing with people, Satir is widely credited with being the first to effectively use representational matching and other sophisticated people-handling techniques. She has her own particular categorization of people-handling styles, but she was a master with people and it's worth becoming familiar with her thoughts.

Saunders, Tom M., *Go Ahead-Kill Yourself, Save Your Family the Trouble*. Distinctive Publishing Corp., Plantation, Fla., 1990.

A clever presentation of the uses of paradox. Interesting reading.

Skinner, B.F., *About Behaviorism*. Vintage Books, New York, 1974.
The man who made behavioral methods a force in human relationships, Skinner got a lot of criticism; some deserved, much not. But to really understand behavior and behavioral interventions, there is no substitute for going to the horse's mouth. An articulate and sophisticated thinker.

Shaw, Marvin C., *The Paradox of Intention*. Scholars Press, Atlanta, Ga., 1988.
The best text I have ever seen on paradox not only as a people-handling method, but on deeper levels as well. Required reading if you are to be effective with paradox.

Watzlawick, Paul, Janet Beavin Bavelas, and Don D. Jackson, *Pragmatics of Human Communications*. WW Norton & Co., Inc., New York, 1967.
One of the original texts about strategically dealing with people, and the semantics and methods involved. These are more writings from the strategic family therapy people, so I have the same reservations I mentioned earlier.

Wegner, Daniel M., *White Bears and Other Unwanted Thoughts*. Penguin Books, New York, 1989.
An interesting exploration of the workings of conceptual survival wiring. He also answers some interesting questions, such as how unwanted thoughts cause their difficulty. A bit like a textbook, but worthwhile.

INDEX

One upmanship 52
Operant conditioning 177
Outsiders 65, 261, 335, 339

P

Paradox 164
  human psyche filled with
    164
  must believe it 167
  paradoxical statement 84
  several elements to 166
Parent deaf 235
Parenting 16, 82, 264
Past experience 9, 55, 78, 81,
  230
Pattern interrupts 181
Penfield 97
People business 3
People-handling
  basic principles 69
  common mistake about 70
  conscious and intentional
    69
  determining your purpose
    70
  difficult to judge skills 11
  don't persist at failure 87
  handling vs. manipulation
    13
  has a price 88
  importance of 4
  intentional or unconscious
    13
  judged by results 73
  method different from
    purpose 79
  mixed motives 72
  no option 69
  nothing always works 80

poor skills, examples of 5
probabilities not
  certainties 82
purpose drives all 70
responsible for success
  and failure 3
skills self-assessment 12
try something else 82
try sufficiently 85
unhealthy aspects of 71
Personal life 5, 84
Personality
  disorder 371
  traits 45, 50
  types 23
Pleasure principle 28-29
Political correctness 219
Political positions 162-63
Possibility 394
Potential problems 190
Preventable problems 24,
  189-90
Prison
  code of morality 44
  rigid system of rules 60
Probability of success 82,
  105
Problems, preventing 189-
  211
Process comments 143-44
Professional football player
  153
Projection 43, 44
Psychological theories 25, 80
Punishment 173

R

Randolph 62, 63
Rationalization 42

X

Xerox 4

Give This Provocative and Enlightening Book to Your Friends and Loved Ones

ORDER FORM

YES, I want ___ copies of *Power With People* at $29.95 each, plus $3 shipping per book. (Texas residents please include 6¼% state sales tax.) Canadian orders must be accompanied by a postal money order in U.S. funds. Allow 30 days for delivery.

Name_____ Phone _____

Address _____

City/State/Zip _____

Card #_____ Expires _____

Signature_____

My check or money order for $_____ is enclosed.

Check your leading bookstore or fax your order to:

281-895-8668

Please make your check payable and return to:
Bookworks Distributing
15110 Benfer Road
Houston, TX 77069